PERSONALITY AT THE CROSSROADS:
Current Issues in
Interactional Psychology

List of Contributors

Henry A. Alker, *Cornell University, Ithaca, New York*

Michael Argyle, *Department of Experimental Psychology, Oxford, England*

Leonard Berkowitz, *University of Wisconsin, Madison, Wisconsin*

Jack Block, *University of California, Berkeley, California*

Kenneth S. Bowers, *University of Waterloo, Ontario, Canada*

Monique de Bonis, *University Rene Descartes, Paris, France*

Norman S. Endler, *York University, Downsview, Ontario, Canada*

Seymour Epstein, *University of Massachusetts, Amherst, Massachusetts*

Fred E. Fiedler, *University of Washington, Seattle, Washington*

Donald W. Fiske, *University of Chicago, Chicago, Illinois*

Stephen L. Golding, *University of California, Los Angeles, California*

Edgar Krau, *Cluj, Rumania*

Clarry Lay, *York University, Downsview, Ontario, Canada*

David Magnusson, *University of Stockholm, Sweden*

Martin Mellstrom, Jr., *London, England*

Walter Mischel, *Stanford University, Stanford, California*

Edward A. Nelsen, *Arizona State University, Tempe, Arizona*

Richard E. Nisbett, *University of Michigan, Ann Arbor, Michigan*

Joseph R. Nuttin, *University of Louvain, Louvain, Belgium*

Dan Olweus, *University of Bergen, Norway*

Lawrence Pervin, *Rutgers University, New Brunswick, New Jersey*

Donald R. Peterson, *Rutgers University, New Brunswick, New Jersey*

Harold L. Raush, *University of Massachusetts, Amherst, Massachusetts*

David W. Reid, *York University, Downsview, Ontario, Canada*

Irwin G. Sarason, *University of Washington, Seattle, Washington*

Daisy Schalling, *Karolinska Hospital, Stockholm, Sweden*

Charles D. Spielberger, *University of South Florida, Tampa, Florida*

Martti Takala, *University of Jyvaskyla, Finland*

Paul L. Wachtel, *City University of New York, New York, New York*

Michel Zlotowicz, deceased

Marvin Zuckerman, *University of Delaware, Newark, Delaware*

PERSONALITY AT THE CROSSROADS:

Current Issues in Interactional Psychology

Edited by

DAVID MAGNUSSON
University of Stockholm

NORMAN S. ENDLER
York University

 LAWRENCE ERLBAUM ASSOCIATES, PUBLISHERS

1977   Hillsdale, New Jersey

DISTRIBUTED BY THE HALSTED PRESS DIVISION OF

JOHN WILEY & SONS

New York   Toronto   London   Sydney

Lawrence Erlbaum Associates, Inc., Publishers
62 Maria Drive
Hillsdale, New Jersey 07642

Distributed solely by Halsted Press Division
John Wiley & Sons, Inc., New York

Library of Congress Cataloging in Publication Data

Main entry under title:

Personality at the crossroads.

    Papers originally presented at a symposium held in Stockholm, Sweden, June 22-27, 1975.
    Bibliography: p.
    Includes indexes.
    1. Personality—Congresses.   2. Psychology, Experimental—Congresses.   3. Personality and situation—Congresses.   I. Magnusson, David.   II. Endler, Norman Solomon, 1931—
BF698.P3694   155.2   77-4190
ISBN 0-470-99135-6

Printed in the United States of America

Contents

Preface

It is not surprising that there should be an international symposium on person by situation interaction. What is puzzling is that the first symposium on this issue did not take place until 1975.

The notion that the sources of behavior were not to be sought only within the individual, but in his interaction with his environment was formulated by theorists in psychology as early as the 1920's and the 1930's. These early theories, however, did not lead to two expected consequences, namely, empirical research on the person by situation issue, and the formulation of an integrated theory for the person by situation interaction process, until the 1960's and 1970's. During the last fifteen years there has been a proliferation of empirical studies that have developed almost independently of the earlier theoretical formulations. (See for example the recently edited book by Endler and Magnusson *Interactional Psychology and Personality*). The results of these studies have initiated a theoretical debate that has raised new issues. At present many investigators are involved in both empirical research and theoretical discussions regarding the person by situation interaction issue. For these reasons, we felt that a symposium at which active researchers would discuss the crucial problems of personality models and effective research strategies would be fruitful. Such a symposium, on Interactional Psychology, was organized (by David Magnusson and Norman S. Endler) and took place in Stockholm, Sweden, June 22–27, 1975.

All 28 papers presented at the symposium are included in this book. In addition, the introductory chapter (Chapter 1), which constitutes Part I, was written especially for this book by the editors. The 28 symposium papers (Chapters 2–29), which were revised following the symposium, are organized into four parts (Parts II–V).

The main aims of the introductory chapter are (1) to discuss certain conceptual distinctions that we think are essential for future research and theory, and (2) to present suggestions for future research on the person by situation interaction issue. This chapter does not attempt to summarize the major points of the papers presented at the symposium. However, in writing the introductory chapter, we have profited greatly from these papers and have attempted to refer to them in the appropriate places.

The book is organized into five parts. Part I, Issues, is the introductory chapter written by the editors. Parts II–V each contains an introduction and commentary, written by the editors, followed by revised papers from the symposium. The organization of the chapters in Part II–V is not necessarily self-evident. Many of the papers discuss problems and issues that are appropriate to all parts of this book, and several ways of categorizing the papers would have been possible. The organization (or grouping) of papers that we finally achieved is relevant to the following main themes:

Part II.   Consistency–Coherence (Traits)
Part III. Personality by Treatment Experimental Designs
Part IV. Methodological Critiques
Part V.   Strategies for Studying Person by Situation Interactions

Because many of the authors have used similar sources, we have placed all the references at the end of the book, for easy referral.

We would like to express our gratitude to the participants of the symposium. Their scientific attitudes and knowledge led to fruitful, stimulating, and exciting discussions during the symposium.

We are thankful for the valuable comments and suggestions, regarding Chapter 1, that we received from Jean Edwards, Donald W. Fiske, Marilyn Okada, Donald R. Peterson, David Reid, Daisy Schalling, Irwin G. Sarason, and Håkan Stattin. However, we bear full responsibility for the final version of Chapter 1.

The symposium was made possible by a grant from the Swedish Council for Social Science Research. It was also supported financially by the Department of Psychology, University of Stockholm.

We wish to thank Barbro Svensson for her assistance in preparing the symposium and the manuscript of the book, Anette Wåhlin, Beverly Brady, and Marla Endler for their secretarial assistance and Håkan Stattin for participating in the organizational work of the symposium and assisting with preparing the manuscript of this book for publication. Finally we wish to thank our families for their tolerance and patience while we were organizing the symposium and preparing this book.

David Magnusson
University of Stockholm, Stockholm

Norman S. Endler
York University, Toronto

Part I

ISSUES

1

Interactional Psychology: Present Status and Future Prospects

David Magnusson
University of Stockholm

Norman S. Endler
York University

AN INTERACTION MODEL OF BEHAVIOR

Within traditional personality psychology, it is possible to distinguish among three conceptions of molar individual behavior: the *trait model,* the *psychodynamic model,* and the *situationism model* (see Endler & Magnusson, 1974, 1976, for a review). The trait model and the psychodynamic model clearly differ with respect to their measurement models and the kinds of data on which they focus, and therefore also with respect to the kinds of methods used for data collection and data treatment (see Magnusson, 1974a). They have in common, however, their stress on *person factors* as the main determinants of behavior. Research within these trait and psychodynamic models has focused on studies of fundamental personality variables, their interrelationships, and how these variables function in relation to factors in the environment, including the immediate situation. Situationism, in contrast, examines the *environment* to find the important factors that determine the behaviors of individuals. Research within this model has aimed at finding general laws for behavioral reactions as functions of the kind and intensity of external stimulation.

The three different orientations have different consequences not only for the kinds of factors that are regarded as most important in determining behavior, but also for how ontogenetic development is explained, for various aspects of research strategy (e.g., which units of analysis are used), and which types of laws are sought. These consequences have been discussed in detail by Endler and Magnusson (1974, 1976).

However, on the basis of empirical research during the 1960s and the 1970s, which focused on testing the basic hypotheses in traditional personality research, a fourth model, called an *interactionistic model,* has been formulated. A basic element in this model is the focus on the ongoing, multidirectional interaction between an individual and his or her environment, especially the situations in which behavior occurs. Persons and situations are regarded as indispensably linked to one another during the process of interaction. Neither the person factors nor the situation factors per se determine behavior in isolation; it is determined by inseparable person by situation interactions. This view has the consequence that research has to focus simultaneously on person factors, situation factors, and the interaction between these two systems. The basic elements of the person by situation interaction model can be summarized as follows (see Endler & Magnusson, 1974, 1976):

1. Actual behavior is a function of a continuous process of multidirectional interaction or feedback between the individual and the situations he or she encounters.

2. The individual is an intentional, active agent in this interaction process.

3. On the person side of the interaction, cognitive and motivational factors are essential determinants of behavior.

4. On the situation side, the psychological meaning of situations for the individual is the important determining factor.

Endler (1976) has defined interactional psychology as the scientific investigation of a complex interplay of situations and persons in determining behavior.

The interactional view and the implications this has for personality research and theorizing are discussed later in this chapter.

CONCEPTUAL DISTINCTIONS

The effective development of the field of interactional psychology has been hampered by a lack of conceptual clarity (cf. Magnusson, 1974a; Bowers, Chapter 3, Nelsen, Chapter 5; and Raush, Chapter 22, in this volume). In order to either reduce or prevent confusion, it is important that attempts be made to outline some theoretical perspectives of interactional psychology. Therefore, let us turn our attention to a discussion of some basic conceptual distinctions.

Mediating Systems versus Behavior Systems

One area of confusion in discussions about the consequences of empirical studies for personality theory and research results from the failure to distinguish clearly between *mediating variables* (intervening variables, hypothetical constructs) and *behavioral* or *reaction variables* (see, e.g., Magnusson, 1974a). Bowers (Chapter 3) has pointed to this distinction in his discussion of the confusion between a phenomenon and its explanation.

Mediating variables (e.g., intervening variables and hypothetical constructs of various kinds) are inferred from observations of behavior and from our own inner experiences. They enable us to understand, explain, and predict the processes by which both situational and stored information is selected, interpreted, and transformed into reactions. These mediating variables can be classified in terms of (a) *structural variables* — characteristic properties of the mediating system (e.g., intelligence, cognitive complexity); (b) *content variables* — situationally determined or stored information (e.g., content of anxiety arousing situations), and (c) *motivational variables* — the arousing, directing, and maintaining forces of the processes, indicating *why* the individual selects and treats information and reacts as he or she does (e.g., values, drives, needs, motives) (see Magnusson, 1975, 1976a). (These are discussed in more detail in a later section of this chapter.)

Reaction variables, in contrast, can be classified in terms of (a) *overt behavior,* (b) *covert reactions* (feelings, etc.), (c) *physiological reactions,* and (d) *"artificial" behavior* ("test" behavior, role playing, and other reactions to artificial situations constructed to elicit individual differences in behavior for a specified variable).

Methods and Kinds of Data

It is essential to distinguish between the reaction variables actually being studied and the methods used to collect the data that are presumably an expression of

TABLE 1.1
Classification of Method of Data Collection and Type of Reaction Variable

Reaction variable	Method of data collection			
	Ratings (R data)	Self-report (S data)	Standardized test methods (T data)	Objective measures (O data)
Overt behavior	X	X		X
Covert reactions		X		
Physiological reactions	X	X		X
Artificial behavior	X		X	X

these variables. There is frequently a confounding between the reaction variables and the methods used for data collection. Cattell (1957) in his classification of various kinds of data relates molar behavior to rating methods for data collection (L data), covert reaction to questionnaires (Q data), and test behavior to standardized methods (T data). Obviously there is no one to one relationship between the kind of reaction being studied and the kind of method used for collecting data. We shall distinguish among four kinds of methods for data collection: (a) ratings, which provide R data; (b) self reports, which provide S data; (c) standardized psychological tests, which provide T data; and (d) objective methods, such as instruments for measuring time, frequency, GSR, EEG, EKG, adrenalin excretion, which yield what we shall call O data.

These distinctions among kinds of data and the previous distinctions among reaction variables can be integrated in a twofold classification. The most frequent combinations of reaction variables and methods for data collection are indicated in Table 1.1.

Personality Consistency

One of the key problems in the debate on the person by situation interaction issue is concerned with *consistency* (see Endler & Magnusson, 1974, 1976; Magnusson, 1974a, 1976a, b; Endler, 1976, for a discussion of the consistency versus specificity issue). As Raush (Chapter 22) indicates, the controversy is to some extent a problem of level of analysis. One important distinction is between consistency in terms of reaction variables and consistency in terms of mediating variables (Magnusson, 1976a, b). One cannot assume that there is a one to one relationship between consistency at the *mediating* level and consistency at the *reaction* level. For example, anxiety at the *mediating* level may lead to excessive talking (a *reaction* variable) or to minimal talking and withdrawal (reaction variables) in different situations, or excessive talking (reaction variable) may be caused by anxiety or hostility (mediating variables), (cf. Endler, 1976). Inconsistency of reactions (behavior) may be quite compatible with consistency at the mediating level in terms of how information is selected, interpreted, and treated by the mediating system (Magnusson, 1974a, 1976a). One consequence of this is that we cannot use consistency or inconsistency at the reaction level as a basis for conclusions about consistency (or inconsistency) at the level of the mediating system (see also Bowers, Chapter 3). This need not imply that there are genotypic consistencies underlying phenotypic diversities. The pattern of lawful regularity across levels (if it exists) needs to be determined empirically and conceptually (see e.g., Lazarus, 1971). The main points we wish to make are that there is not always a one to one relationship between mediating variables and reaction variables and that findings of consistency or inconsistency at one level may have little to say about consistency or inconsistency at another level, unless lawfully specified.

Consistency of Reaction Variables

The term "consistency" has been used for reaction variables in a number of different ways (see, e.g., Lay, Chapter 8, and Block, Chapter 2). Three possible meanings of behavioral (reactions) consistency have been distinguished (Magnusson, 1974a, 1976a, b):

1. An individual displays a certain type of behavior to the same extent across situations. This may be called *absolute consistency*. Its counterpart is individual variability, as discussed by Lay (Chapter 8) in this volume. Absolute consistency can be studied directly for one individual at a time. The degree of absolute consistency for a specified reaction variable (e.g., anxiety reactions) is expressed for an individual by a distribution of ipsative data for that variable, collected across situations. An indirect indication of high absolute consistency is obtained by low between-situation variance *and* high intercorrelations between measures of the same variable for a sample of individuals across different situations, simultaneously.

2. The rank order of a set of individuals with respect to a specified behavior is stable across situations. This meaning of consistency may be called *relative consistency*. It can be studied only by studying groups of individuals across situations. This is the kind of consistency that has been examined in most of the empirical studies relevant to the person by situation interaction issue. In order for the relative consistency hypothesis about stable rank orders to be valid, the correlations between measures for different situations should approach 1.0, except for errors of measurement.

3. *Coherence.* There is a third and more fundamental meaning of consistency. It refers to behavior that is inherently lawful and hence predictable without necessarily being stable in either absolute or relative terms as discussed above. We are referring to patterns of behavior that may vary across situations of various kinds but in which the behavior is coherent and lawful all the same. It is more appropriate to use the term *coherence* instead of "consistency" to characterize this kind of regularity. *Coherence* means that the individual's pattern of stable and changing behavior across situations of different kinds is characteristic for him or her and may be interpreted in a meaningful way within the interactional model (see Magnusson, 1971, 1974a, b, 1976a, b; Endler & Magnusson, 1974, 1976; Endler, 1976; Block, Chapter 2; Epstein, Chapter 4; Pervin, Chapter 27, this volume). For example, individual A behaves differently in various situations but the rank order of his or her behavior across a number of different situations may still be predictable. Individual B may rank order his or her behavior in a different way from individual A but would still behave in a predictable and coherent manner.

Research on Behavioral Consistency

In discussing research regarding the different conceptualizations of consistency and the consequences of these conceptualizations for models of behavior it is

TABLE 1.2
Absolute and Relative Consistency across Similar and Dissimilar
Situations

Degree of consistency	Situations	
	Similar	Dissimilar
Relative consistency	A Stable rank orders	B Stable rank orders
Absolute consistency	C Similar behavior	D Similar behavior

important to distinguish between consistency across situations that are *similar* and consistency across situations that are *dissimilar* for the individual. In traditional personality research the focus of interest has been absolute and relative consistency (Points 1 and 2 in the list above). Both can be studied with respect to similar and dissimilar situations (see Table 1.2).

Behavioral (reaction) consistency can also be classified and studied in terms of temporal (longitudinal) versus spatial (cross-sectional) variables (see Lay, Chapter 8; Spielberger, Chapter 11, for a discussion). However, because temporal and spatial factors are not independent of one another, and because no one can be in two situations at the same time, it may be more useful to distinguish between similar and dissimilar situations. The spatial–longitudinal distinction can be conceived of as a continuum, instead of a dichotomy, with studies differing in the amount of time between one assessment and the next one. Typically, *longitudinal* studies have been concerned with relative consistency of people across *similar* situations, ontogenetically over time (see Cell A in Table 1.2). The longitudinal studies have focused on personality variables, in terms of mediating variables, in that they have studied the correlation of data (degree of relationship), that is, relative consistency, for a particular mediating variable (e.g., dominance) over two or more time periods (e.g., childhood versus adolescence), without paying attention to specific situational variables. Block (Chapter 2) in this volume, and Magnusson, Dunér, and Zetterblom (1975) present support for consistency of this type. *Cross-sectional* studies have been concerned with consistency of people across *dissimilar* situations (within a relatively short time period) (see Cell B in Table 1.2). The cross-sectional studies have focused on situation variables in that they have studied the correlation (degree of relationship) for a particular personality variable (e.g., dominance) in two situations (e.g., at work versus at home), occurring over a very short time period (e.g., a few hours or a few days). The evidence for this type of consistency (e.g., W.

Mischel, 1968, 1971; Endler, 1973, 1975b; Magnusson, 1974a) is *not* very impressive.

Most studies of *absolute consistency* have been concerned with "test behavior" and have focused on consistency across similar situations (see Cell C in Table 1.2). Fiske and co-workers, in a number of studies (Fiske, 1961), have investigated intraindividual variability for "test behavior." Intraindividual variability has been suggested as an important *person* variable in personality research and in applied psychology. For physiological measures (adrenalin and noradrenalin) low variance between situations and moderate to high correlations for rank orders across similar situations indicate a rather high cross-situational consistency for these kinds of reactions (Magnusson, 1976b).

Relative consistency across *similar situations* (Cell A, Table 1.2) has been one of the main interests in personality measurement. It has been investigated in the numerous studies on test—retest reliability that belong to that tradition. In studying test—retest reliability we try to measure behavior in situations that differ in time but that are as similar as possible with respect to situational conditions (standardized situations). For example, the relative consistency of *ratings* (R data) of *overt behavior* in two similar situations was studied by Magnusson, Gerzén, and Nyman (1968). For ratings of cooperative ability, self-confidence and leadership in two similar situations, Magnusson, Gerzén, and Nyman obtained correlations of .76, .73, and .69, indicating a high relative consistency. For the objectively measured behavioral variable, *talking time* (O data), a correlation of .64 was obtained when it was measured in similar situations. Test—retest measures of physiological variables across similar situations also indicate a high level of consistency (see, for example, coefficients presented by Patkai, 1970, for adrenalin and noradrenalin). The same conclusions are valid for test—retest measures of *covert reactions,* and for measures of *"test behavior"* (see, e.g., Magnusson, Dunér, & Zetterblom, 1975).

Relative *consistency* across *dissimilar* situations (see Cell B, Table 1.2) has been investigated less frequently than relative consistency across similar situations in traditional personality research. However, many of the empirical studies on person by situation interaction issues conducted during the 1960s and 1970s were performed with the purpose of evaluating relative consistency across dissimilar situations (see Endler & Magnusson, 1974, 1975; Magnusson, 1974a; Endler, 1976). Magnusson, Gerzén, and Nyman (1968) studied the relative consistency of *ratings of overt behavior* across dissimilar situations by observing conscripts in two situations (see also Magnusson, Heffler, & Nyman, 1968; Magnusson & Heffler, 1969). The situations differed with respect to group composition and task. The correlation coefficients for the stability of rank orders from the two situations were distributed around zero (none exceeding ±.10) when the ratings concerned cooperative ability, self-confidence, and leadership. The same result was obtained by Magnusson, Gerzén, and Nyman (1968) for ratings of overt behavior, when the subjects were 7-year-old children.

ctively measured behavioral variable, *talking time,* Magnusson, Nyman obtained a coefficient of .41 when the situations varied with respect to both group composition and group task and the subjects were conscripts. Studies on *covert behavior* (feelings, etc.) indicate low relative consistency across dissimilar situations. For *pulse rate* Endler and Magnusson (1975) obtained a correlation of .54 for data from a stressful and a nonstressful situation. Data for *adrenalin* and *noradrenalin* secretion in stressful and nonstressful situations also indicate a moderate to high relative consistency for these kinds of reactions (Magnusson, 1976b). Relative consistency in "test behavior" has rarely been studied for dissimilar situations.

Although the empirical studies referred to above represent only a sample of those performed, they are presented to illustrate the point that different results are obtained for different kinds of reaction variables, as are different results for similar and dissimilar situations. However, we need much more research, investigating absolute and relative consistency across similar and dissimilar situations, both within a cross-situational and in a longitudinal research strategy, in order to arrive at a better understanding of the person by situation interaction issue. Reid (Chapter 12) suggests that our basic hypothesis for future research on this problem should be that behavior does *not* show relative consistency.

However, as noted above, behavior can be consistent in the sense of being coherent, that is, lawful and inherently predictable, without being stable in either of the forms discussed above. Some implications of this proposition are illustrated in Figure 1.1. The state anxiety profiles for four individuals (A, B, C, and D) across six situations are presented. Situations 1 and 4 are assumed to be neutral with regard to anxiety, Situations 2 and 3 are assumed to evoke physical danger threat, and Situations 5 and 6 are assumed to evoke ego threat (see Endler & Okada, 1975). The four profiles can be assumed to be characteristic for the four individual's ways of reacting to these different types of situations.

Figure 1.1 illustrates two important points; namely (a) that individuals can *differ* with regard to *mean* level of state anxiety reactions across situations of different kinds (compare profiles for A and D), indicating a stable difference in anxiety reaction disposition (trait), and (b) that individuals with the *same mean* level of state anxiety across situations *differ* in a systematic predictable way in their pattern of state anxiety reaction across *different* kinds of *situations* (compare profiles for C and D) (see Zuckerman, Chapter 13). (It should be observed that this implies an expected systematic positive correlation between trait and state anxiety measures.)

According to this view, therefore, behavior is consistent in the sense of coherence because an individual behaves in a way that can be predicted for each situation under the conditions that (a) the interpretation and meaning of the situation to the individual is known, (b) the individual's disposition to react in that kind of situation is known, and (c) there is a psychological theory providing the links between factors (a) and (b) (Magnusson, 1976a). Individual behavior

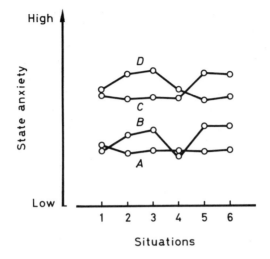

FIGURE 1.1. The state anxiety profiles for four individuals across six different situations.

across different situations provides a consistent, idiographically predictable pattern. This is one of the basic derivations of the interactionistic model of behavior.

The coherence of behavior, in the sense described above, has rarely been empirically explored. Several authors in this volume, however, are developing paradigms and planning strategies that may lead to knowledge about these most important regularities (see Block, Chapter 2; Bowers, Chapter 3; Pervin, Chapter 27, among others). The work of Fiske (Chapter 21) and Pervin (Chapter 27), particularly, and of Peterson (Chapter 23), Raush (Chapter 22), and Wachtel (Chapter 24) for those person by situation interactions where the most important aspect of a situation is another person, provide clear examples of proposed research along these lines.

Consistency of Mediating Variables

Consistency of the mediating system means that the person selects, interprets, and treats situational information in the frame of reference provided by previously stored information (experience and knowledge) in a consistent manner. That this is the case is a fundamental assumption of personality theories with respect to the functioning of the mediating system. However, the mediating systems themselves are complex. At least three discriminable sets of variables, namely structural, content, and motivational variables, appear to be involved (see page 5).

The importance of *structural variables* (intelligence, competence, cognitive complexity, etc.) in an interactionistic model of behavior has been stressed by Mischel (1973a, b; Chapter 25) and Reid (Chapter 12) in this volume. Even if we lack research evidence on the effects of systematic variation of situational conditions, it is reasonable to assume that the structural variables are little influenced by situational factors within a normal range of situational conditions. There are, however, examples of extreme situations, e.g., extremely anxiety-provoking situations or extremely tiring situations, when this assumption is not completely valid. Mischel (1968, 1969) has presented support for the consistency of structural variables.

The *content* process of the mediating system in a specific situation is determined by the situational cues that are selected by the individual or forced on him or her by the situation *and* by the stored information that is brought into action by the situational information. The content of the mediating process is therefore necessarily highly dependent on situational conditions.

The importance and role of *motivational* factors in the person by situation interaction model has been stressed by Fiedler (Chapter 9; see also Nuttin, Chapter 14, among others). Different contents, both situational and stored, evoke different motivational factors, i.e., needs, values, motives, interests, attitudes. The active motivational factors, like the content factors, will therefore also vary with the situational conditions.

The assumptions made above lead to the conclusion that in terms of information processing the mediating system is consistent and coherent in the *manner* in which it *selects* and *processes* various content and motivational variables, but the actual manifestation of the content and motivational factors differs from situation to situation (Magnusson, 1975, 1976a, b). The individual's specific, consistent way of *processing* both content and motivational forces is assumed to be the result of a social learning process. This is the basis for the coherence of his or her actual behavior across situations, in the sense that we have discussed coherence in the previous section.

Personality Models and Their Measurement Models

Magnusson (1974a, 1976a) has pointed to the important distinction between personality theories and their measurement models. A psychological theory is a consistent set of interrelated, hypothetical, intervening variables (mediating variables) that are used to describe, explain, and predict actual behavior. Different personality theories stress different kinds of intervening or hypothetical variables as the important ones in the mediating process. These mediating variables are assumed to underlie and determine actual behavior. (Compare, for example, a psychodynamic theory and a cognitive theory.) The different theories may use different mediating variables (hypothetical constructs) to explain the same actual reactions, and different reactions may be explained by similar hypothetical constructs (see the discussion on consistency, above).

A measurement model refers to the assumed relationship between the responses (reaction indicators), which are usually expressed by the data that we collect, and the mediating variables or constructs of the personality theory. The measurement model operationalizes, by actual measurement, the variables under investigation and describes in explicit terms the relationship between mediating variables and reactions. This enables us to (a) make predictions, under assumed conditions regarding the behavioral (reactions) outcome of the mediating process, and (b) interpret the empirical results in terms of mediating variables.

Trait psychology, which has probably been the most influential personality model in terms of empirical research, clearly illustrates the need to distinguish between a personality *theory* and its *measurement* model.

With reference to the trait concept in the trait personality theory, two basic assumptions are made in the *trait measurement model:* (a) There is a *true score* for each individual on a quantifiable dimension, for each of a number of personality traits, and (b) there is a *monotonic, linear relationship* between individuals' latent positions on each personality dimension and their positions on a reaction scale, which serve as an indicator of the same trait (see Magnusson, 1974a).

These two assumptions, taken together, lead to the prediction that there are stable rank orders of individuals across situations with respect to particular behaviors (e.g., anxious behavior, dependent behavior). The cross-situational stability of rank orders of individuals is a central issue for empirical personality research within the trait measurement model. (See the discussion of relative consistency earlier in this chapter.)

In those cases where the trait *measurement* model has been used as the prime basis for operationalizing empirical personality research, the interpretations and conclusions about personality trait theory have been necessarily limited and unsatisfactory to the trait personality theorists. Some of the misunderstanding in the debate about trait personality theory may be a result of the opponents of trait theory having discussed traits in terms of the trait measurement model, whereas the defenders have discussed traits in terms of theoretical formulations, without regard to the restrictions imposed by the trait measurement model (see Magnusson, 1974a; Schalling, Chapter 7).

Regarding the relationship between theory and measurement, the difference between the measurement models for the trait personality theory and for the psychodynamic personality theories are instructive (see Magnusson, 1974a). One basic difference between the psychodynamic measurement model and the trait measurement model is that the psychodynamic measurement model does *not* assume a monotonic, linear relationship between an individual's manifest behaviors and the underlying intrapsychic processes. Actual behavior as a function of latent dispositions (traits) is assumed to vary across individuals and across variables. Figure 1.2 illustrates the difference between the two measurement models (trait and psychodynamic) with respect to the relationship between aggressiveness (mediating variable) and aggressive behavior (reaction variable). For the trait measurement model (Figure 1.2A) aggressive behavior is supposed

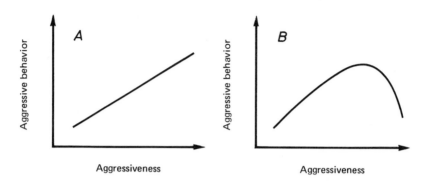

FIGURE 1.2.   The hypothesized relationship between a mediating variable (aggressiveness) and a reaction variable (aggressive behavior) according to (A) the trait measurement model and (B) the psychodynamic measurement model (Adapted from Magnusson, 1974a.)

to be a linear (monotonic) function of latent aggressiveness. The higher the individual's position is on the trait dimension (mediating variable) of aggressiveness, the more aggressive behavior he or she will exhibit. The curvilinear, nonmonotonic function for the psychodynamic measurement model (Figure 1.2B) is based on the assumption of psychodynamic personality theory that up to a certain level aggressive behavior increases with increasing latent aggressiveness (mediating variable), but after this level of aggressiveness, the defense mechanisms inhibit the actual expression of aggressive behavior.

With respect to data collection, in empirical research, the trait measurement model is the basis for the construction and use of homogeneous personality tests and questionnaires. With respect to data treatment, the trait measurement model is the basis for the use of linear regression models, such as correlation analyses and factor analyses. These methods of data treatment are obviously appropriate for the trait measurement model but may not always be appropriate for data generated by the psychodynamic measurement model. The failure to obtain substantial empirical support for psychodynamic personality theories in personality research (e.g., see summaries in W. Mischel, 1968, 1971) may be due to the use of data treatment methods that are not appropriate for the psychodynamic measurement model (see Magnusson, 1974a, 1976a).

The trait measurement model does not deny the effects of situations on behavior. However, these effects are supposed to be general and to influence the level of behavior or the strength of reactions but do not affect the rank orders of individuals with respect to the behavior being investigated. Thus, according to this model, there is no interaction (in the statistical sense) in data for a group of individuals across different situations with respect to a particular kind of behavioral reaction (e.g., anxious behavior).

Most of the empirical studies on the person by situation interaction issue during the 1960s aimed at testing the relative consistency hypothesis within the context of the trait measurement model. Two main approaches were used: the *correlational approach,* in which the relative consistency hypothesis was tested directly by correlations of an individual's behaviors across situations in a search for stable rank orders, and the *variance components approach,* in which the relative proportion of variances caused by individuals, situations, responses, and their interactions within a Person X Reaction X Situation data matrix were examined (see Endler & Magnusson, 1974, 1976; Magnusson, 1974a; Endler, 1976). (The limitations of the variance approach for this purpose have been discussed by Magnusson, 1974a; 1976a; Cartwright, 1975, and in this volume by Epstein, Chapter 4; Olweus, Chapter 17.) The results of the empirical studies clearly indicated that the relative consistency hypothesis with respect to stable rank orders of behavior across situations was not generally valid. One implication was that, contrary to the expectations of the trait measurement model, situations might and did affect stable rank orders with respect to the expression of traits, and this model was therefore inadequate and limited as a *general* model for personality research.

The above conclusions do not mean that relative consistency does not exist. As has been discussed earlier in this chapter, it seems reasonable to assume relative consistency for structural variables, and empirical results support such a conclusion. One of the important tasks for empirical personality research, within an interactional model of psychology, is the investigation of the kind of mediating variables and the kind of reaction variables for which the relative consistency hypothesis may be valid and the type of data for which it is not valid.

Two Aspects of Situations

The terms "situation" and "situational factors" have been used in a number of different ways and this has led to some confusion. One important distinction is between (a) the *situation as a whole,* and (b) the various elements or *situational cues within a situation* (see Magnusson, 1975, 1976a). When we are interested in *situations as wholes* (total situations) we can compare the effects *between* different situations and examine how each situation is experienced and interpreted as a whole. *Within* each situation, the various situational cues are continuously interacting with one another and changing in the process. That is, a situation can be regarded as a dynamic process wherein an individual affects certain elements or events and is in turn affected by certain elements or events. The two different aspects of situations are involved in two different levels of analysis of person by situation interactions.

Situations as Wholes

The situation as a whole forms a contextual framework for the individual. Examples of total situations would include church services, job situations, baseball games, club meetings, etc. Each situation has certain implicit rules (see

Argyle, Chapter 26), and the individual's interpretation of the rules determines his or her behavioral strategy. In some situations the options are very few, because the situational rules have a very strong effect on the person's behavior. For example, behavior at a church service is different from behavior at a baseball game, and in both cases the behavior is rather clearly constrained. In other situations, such as a cocktail party, there are more degrees of freedom.

A specific individual may interpret the same type of situation differently over different occasions, and different individuals may interpret the same specific occasion differently (see, e.g., Pervin, Chapter 27). For example, Individual A may interpret a party as a friendly event at one time (Saturday night party), and a hostile event at another time (Wednesday night party), depending on the people who participate. Similarly, Person A might interpret the same party differently from Person B.

For some purposes it is fruitful to distinguish between a general class of *situations* and a particular instance of this situation, which can be called an *event* (see Brunswick, 1956; Pervin, Chapter 27). For example "in the classroom" and "at a party" can be classified as situations, and "I have just received the results from my last exam" and "I am going to a dinner party with Jill" can be classified as events. By studying individuals' perceptions of particular events one may arrive at a general classification of situations. The distinction between "situation" and "event" is not always easy to make, as we shall see later on when we discuss units of analysis (see also, e.g., Golding, Chapter 29).

Situational Cues Within a Situation

After an individual has interpreted a total situation (and a specific event), this interpretation serves as a frame of reference, or context, within which the person "chooses" one of a number of possible strategies. He or she will subsequently be involved in a process in which other elements of the total situation (especially the specific event), primarily the behavior of other persons, will serve as important cues for his or her behavior. The behavior of other persons affects his or her behavior, but in turn his or her behavior affects the situation both for her- or himself and for the other persons involved. His or her own reactions, for example blushing, form important situational information, not only for the others but also for him- or herself. This continuous feedback and interaction between the individual and the situational cues is part of an ongoing "dynamic interaction," in which the traditional distinction between dependent and independent variables becomes less useful. The individual her- or himself is an active intentional agent within this interaction process.

The Trait Concept

In personality theory and research the trait concept has been used in different ways. In this volume it has been discussed by Alker (Chapter 19), Argyle

(Chapter 26), Block (Chapter 2), Epstein (Chapter 4), Raush (Chapter 22), Schalling (Chapter 7), and Wachtel (Chapter 24). Most researcher seem to agree that the trait concept refers to the functioning of the mediating system and that traits are inferred on the basis of generalized response characteristics. Three main uses of the concept may be distinguished:

1. The trait concept can be used as it is defined in the trait personality theory. In that theory a trait is *a latent disposition* to act in a certain way, and individuals manifest, by their reactions, a rank order with regard to this disposition. In terms of the assumption of the trait measurement model described earlier this rank order is assumed to be stable across situations. In the tradition using this definition of a trait, empirical research has been devoted to finding basic variables for which the transsituation stability hypothesis is valid. Relative inconsistency across *dissimilar* situations is interpreted as an invalidation of a trait defined in this way.

2. A trait is a certain aspect of the mediating system's way of selecting, interpreting, and treating information as a basis for coherent behavior across situations (see page 12). The basis for identification of a trait would be the coherent patterns of behavior across situations of different kinds that characterized individuals and groups of individuals, according to the interactional model of behavior (see page 10). This use of the trait concept is therefore in accordance with the interactional view.

3. A trait is a summary of consistent reactions (with respect to a variable) across a number of situations. This meaning was initiated by Cattell (1965) in his definition of surface traits, " . . . a bunch of behavior elements cluster together . . . " (p. 67). No inferences are made about latent dispositions.

Units of Analysis

What are the most productive units of analysis for a science of personality? There are two related issues within this question: (a) the type or *kind* of unit, and (b) the *size* of the unit. As to kinds of units, the most frequently used units in traditional personality research have been traits. This is primarily a reflection of the fact that trait conceptions have dominated personality theory for the past 50 years (see Endler & Magnusson, 1974, 1976). Traits are inferred from response—response consistencies. Personality dynamics or underlying motives, defenses and instincts have been used as the units of analysis by psychoanalytic theorists. For Zlotowicz (Chapter 28) the appropriate unit of analysis is situations. Perceptions of situations as wholes have actually been used as units of analysis (see e.g., Magnusson, 1971, 1974b; Magnusson & Ekehammar, 1973). One problem is that it is sometimes difficult to determine when a situation begins and when it ends. Do we focus on a specific event or on a family of situations? Do we focus on a total situation or on elements within the situation?

Another type of unit that could be used is the person—situation interaction unit (see Endler & Magnusson, 1974, 1976). Alker (Chapter 19), Nuttin (Chapter 14), and Pervin (Chapter 27) indicate that it may not be possible to separate the person from the situation in the interaction process and that therefore one should focus on the person—situation sequence as the basic unit of analysis. Argyle (Chapter 26) argues that we have to deal with discrete entities of behavior, situations, and perhaps persons, analogous to the discrete structural units in genetics or chemistry, and Fiske (Chapter 21) stresses the need of limiting our research to small units of behavior. The questions as to the *type* of unit and the *size* of unit that are most appropriate for personality research are important ones (especially within an interactional context) and require further, careful analyses.

The Concept of Interaction in Interactional Psychology

The concept of interaction is a central one for interactional psychology. It has had a number of different meanings. (See Olweus, Chapter 17, for an analysis and discussion of interaction in semantic and statistical terms.) Here we shall focus on the meaning, relevance, and use of interaction for interactional psychology.

In interactional psychology, the term "interaction" has been used in two different ways: (a) in the statistical sense of the word, reflecting interactions of main factors, such as situations (often as wholes), persons, and modes of responses (types of reactions), within a data matrix; and (b) in a model of behavior, integrating person mediating variables, person reaction variables, and situational variables to describe and explain the process by which individual behavior develops and maintains itself. The first of these meanings of interaction is called *"mechanistic"* interaction and the second is called *"dynamic"* (organismic) interaction, in terms of the two models of man discussed by Overton and Reese (1973; see also Endler, 1975b). The mechanistic meaning of interaction is connected with a mechanistic measurement model for interactional behavior. The mechanistic model implies a distinction between dependent and independent variables and the assumption of an additive, linear relation between situational and person factors. The dynamic model stresses an interaction *process* in which persons and situations form an inextricably interwoven structure.

The Mechanistic Meaning of Interaction

Four different subcategories of mechanistic interaction, referring to reaction variables, can be investigated:

1. The rank orders of individuals may differ for various kinds of reactions within a specific situation. In statistical terms there will be a significant interaction between *individuals* and *modes of responses* (kinds of reactions).

2. The rank orders of individuals may differ across situations for a specific mode of reasponse. In statistical terms there will be a significant interaction between *individuals* and *situations*.

3. The rank orders of situations may differ across various kinds of reactions for a specific individual (or group of individuals). In statistical terms there will be an interaction between *situations* and *modes of response*.

4. In a three-way matrix of data for *individuals, reactions* (modes of response), and *situations* there may be a significant three-way interaction.

The merit of the variance approach for the person by situation interaction issue in personality research has been that it has shown the existence of strong interactions for different kinds of variables, thereby indicating the direction for formulating a more adequate measurement model for personality research than the trait measurement model, and a more effective model of behavior than the traditional trait personality model. The variance components approach and the analysis of variance approach will still be very useful for some purposes in future personality research (see, e.g., Endler, 1976; Takala, Chapter 6). However, this approach reflects a mechanistic model of man and is not appropriate for studies of the dynamic interaction process within the interactional model of behavior.

Dynamic Interaction

"Dynamic interaction" refers to a model of behavior in which person mediating variables, person reaction variables, and situations (environments) are integrated in order to describe and explain the *process* whereby individual behavior develops and maintains itself. With reference to the two different kinds of situational influences on behavior that have been described earlier, two different kinds of dynamic interaction can be discussed: namely *within-situation interaction,* and *between- (across-) situations* interaction (Magnusson, 1976a).

Within-situation interaction Within the frame of reference provided by a particular situation, for example a committee meeting, having dinner, or a conversation during work, the situational cues affect the behavior of an individual. However, the situational cues continuously change, partly as function of the behavior of the individual her- or himself. At any moment the individual selects, interprets, and treats the situational information and transforms it into behavior, which in the next stage of the process becomes an important part of the situational information for the individual. Simultaneously this affects the behavior of others and thereby contributes to producing changes in the situation. In the process of within-situation interaction, therefore, the situation influences an individual's behavior in terms of situational cues, but an act of the individual is at the same time a cue for others and may form an important situational cue for the person her- or himself. The studies of dyadic transactions, as in the work of Raush (Chapter 22), Peterson (Chapter 23), and Golding

(Chapter 29), represent clear instances of dynamic interaction in the within-situation context (see also Fiske, Chapter 21). This dynamic model of behavior implies that the traditional distinction between dependent and independent variables may not be very useful (see Raush, Chapter 22).

Between-situations or temporal interaction. Dynamic interaction between individuals and situations also includes the kind of interaction process that occurs when an individual appears in a number of different situations. This kind of interaction is here denoted as temporal or between- (across-)situations inter-action. In the mechanistic measurement model the variance components ap-proach has studied interactions between different situations (as wholes) and persons in affecting behavior.

The situations that an individual encounters are not a random selection of all possible situations. Many of the situations in which we participate are chosen by ourselves (*selected situations*), but some seem to be imposed on us (*required situations*). We may choose to go to a movie or a party *or* be required to write an examination in an important course. By choosing a specific life career or occupation we restrict the kinds of situations that we encounter. Among the possible situations in our total life style, some are forced on us (required situations); however, even in these cases this may be a function of previous choices that we have made in terms of our own needs and motives (see, e.g., Pervin, 1968; Bowers, 1973; Endler & Magnusson, 1974, 1976; Stagner, 1976; Mischel, Chapter 25; Wachtel, Chapter 24), and in accordance with physiological states (see Schalling, Chapter 7). By choosing to go to a university, for example, one realizes that certain situations, such as examinations, are going to be required. By choosing to become a pianist one realizes that one may have to practice long hours. The result of this process of selection of situations that one encounters is that each individual appears in a restricted set of situations and these types of situations are a function of and have relevance for the person concerned. Mischel (1973a) has discussed this fact as one explanation for the general impression that individuals' behaviors are stable across situations (see also Spielberger, Chapter 11).

Individuals contribute to the situations they encounter. By their actions they can modify the situation as a whole or certain elements of the situation. This is often done in a manner that satisfies the person's own motivational dispositions. "Each person seemed, in cyclical fashion, to create conditions of life that fed back to confirm his characteristic feeling" (Wachtel, Chapter 24). The behavior of an individual is also affected by situations, not only in the general nomothetic way, as assumed by the trait measurement model, but often also idiographically, as confirmed by the variance component results of the empirical studies investi-gating mechanistic interaction. The idiographic patterns of behavior do not deny the existence of coherence, that is, the contention that behavior is lawful and predictable without always manifesting relative consistency. One of the tasks of a dynamic interactional psychology is to explore (and explain) *coherence* within the context of a continuous person by situation interaction process.

THE PERSON, THE SITUATION, AND BEHAVIOR: A CAUSE AND EFFECT RELATIONSHIP?

Part of the discussion on the person by situation issue during the early 1960s and the beginning of the 1970s concerned the relative importance of persons and situations as determinants of behavior. Some of the first empirical studies on this issue tested the relative consistency hypothesis about stable rank orders across situations and attempted to draw conclusions about the relative importance of person factors in the determination of behavior (see Magnusson, Gerzén, & Nyman, 1968). Other studies used the variance components technique (Endler, 1966) to estimate the relative proportion of variance coming from individuals and situations in a Person X Situations X Modes of response (reaction) data matrix (see Endler & Hunt, 1966, 1968, 1969; Endler, Hunt, & Rosenstein, 1962). These studies examined behavior as a function of persons and situations and the interactions of these two sources. The studies using the variance approach do not speak directly to the issue of relative consistency and have certain limitations with respect to their consequences for different behavioral models (see Cartwright, 1975; Endler, 1976; Epstein, Chapter 4; Magnusson, 1974a, 1976a; Olweus, Chapter 17). Lay (Chapter 8) questions the whole idea that the existence of relative consistency implies that person factors should be more important than situation factors as determinants of behavior. He suggests that it may be possible that the more stable the rank orders of individuals are across situations, the stronger are the situational effects. Endler (1973), in a reply to Alker (1972), concluded that the question "Is behavior determined by persons or by situations?" is a meaningless one. A more appropriate question is *how* persons and situations interact in a dynamic process in effecting behavior. From the preceding discussion about interaction in the interactional model of behavior, it should be clear that we regard a person and the situation in which behavior can be observed as inextricably interwoven in a continuously ongoing process. This process cannot be meaningfully discussed as a cause and effect relationship with persons and situations as the causal factors and behavior as the effect. The same view is expressed by several authors in this volume. Zlotowicz (Chapter 28) concludes that neither persons nor situations determine a specific behavior. He believes that behavior is a way of describing and classifying situations. Behavior is an inseparable aspect of the situation. Nuttin (Chapter 14) regards personality as a stable pattern of person—environment relations. Raush (Chapter 22) states that it is not possible to generalize about individuals without reference to the situations for which generalizations are valid. Neither is it possible to generalize about situations without reference to the individuals for whom the generalizations are valid. This implies the problems of defining significant "situational domains" (see Endler & Magnusson, 1974, 1976; Magnusson, 1971), "behavioral domains" (Goldfried & Kent, 1972), and groups of individuals (see also Sarason, Chapter 20).

In stressing the person by situation interaction process as indispensably and simultaneously dependent on both interaction components, the person and the situation, it is also important to emphasize that the individual is the active, intentional agent in this interactive process (see Endler & Magnusson, 1974, 1976). This means, among other things, that the person and his specific mediating processes play an important role in creating behavior and situational contexts within the interaction process. The subject *acts* in the situation (see Nuttin, Chapter 14) on the basis of his own reasons, expectations, needs, and motives.

The discussion above regarding persons and situations as codeterminants of behavior refer to dynamic interaction, the continuously ongoing process in which behavior develops and is maintained. This does not imply that there are no main person factors that can be studied and taken into account, either as moderator variables or as independent main factors in personality research. As stressed by de Bonis (Chapter 15), sex of subjects is such a variable that may have an important effect on behavior in the context of person–situation interactions. Other main person factors that should be considered in studies of certain problems are socioeconomic background and educational level (for examples, see Raush, Chapter 22). Such factors can be used as main factors in the analysis of variance approach that is favored by Nisbett (Chapter 18).

IMPLICATIONS FOR FUTURE RESEARCH

The important theme in interactional psychology, regarding the person and the situation as being inextricably interwoven as part of the process within which behavior develops and is maintained, is not new. However, as Magnusson (1974a) indicates, the formulations by earlier psychological theorists (see, e.g., Allport, 1966; Cattell, 1965; Lewin, 1935; Murray, 1938; Tolman, 1932) about the importance of incorporating the situation in models of behavior, have not until recently had much impact on (a) empirical research, investigating the person by situation interaction process, and (b) a model of behavior, integrating mediating variables, reaction variables, and situational vairables. Such an integrating model is essential in order to describe and explain the *process* of what we have called dynamic interaction. During the 1960s and the beginning of the 1970s we have seen some empirical studies on the person by situation interaction issue focusing on some of the possible combinations of variables and relevant kinds of data within a mechanistic measurement model. However, both empirically and with respect to theory we are still at the very first stages of a development that we hope will provide better knowledge about human behavior and more effective models for future personality theory and research.

In the chapters of this volume, the authors have presented a number of suggestions regarding directions for future research, with respect to methods for data collection and data treatment, with respect to research strategies, and with respect to which type of variables to emphasize. In this connection it is important to express the self-evident conviction that fruitful research does *not* presuppose the use of only *one* method for data collection (e.g., the interview), nor only one method for data treatment (e.g., factor analysis or Markov models), nor one strategy (e.g., longitudinal studies), nor one class of variables (e.g., cognitive factors). Many approaches and many new and creative strategies are needed. Fiske (Chapter 21) has suggested that effectiveness in the *formulation* of problems is decisive for the fruitfulness of research. Effective research on the diversity of problems that can be formulated in personality research (in terms of mediating variables, reaction variables or data, for different kinds and sizes of research units) presupposes a diversity of methods, strategies and submodels of psychological constructs. The essential point is, of course, the choice of the appropriate method, the appropriate strategy and the appropriate type of psychological constructs for the problem under consideration (see, e.g., Sarason, Chapter 20).

Conceptual Distinctions and Generalizations

In order for research and theorizing to be more effective and valid, the specification and clarification of the concepts and methods that are used are of decisive importance. Too often, the debate about issues has been based on misunderstandings and so has not been fruitful. Discussants of the issues and problems in personality research have not always made it clear whether they are focusing on mediating variables, reaction variables, or actual data. Another basis of confusion has been the failure to distinguish between a personality model and its measurement model. As was suggested earlier in this chapter (see page 6), each combination of reaction variable by data collection method has its own properties. These properties must be taken into account in discussing the consequences of the results of empirical studies for models of behavior. Block's review of the results (Chapter 2) from his longitudinal study, presented in *Lives through time* (Block, 1971), illustrates the point of relating reaction variables to methods of data collection. The importance of clear conceptual communication is illustrated by Lay (Chapter 8) in referring to a study by Bem and Allen (1974). As Lay points out, Bem and Allen use relative consistency (correlational view) and absolute consistency (lack of variability) interchangeably when, in fact, the two meanings of consistency are quite different.

With respect to making generalizations, researchers should be cognizant of the limitations of the results of empirical studies. For example, results of studies on within-situation interaction cannot be generalized to between- (across-) situations interaction; and results from studies investigating small units of behavior, as in dyadic communication, by objective methods, cannot simply be generalized to ratings of molar social behavior. Cronbach (1975) has discussed the difficulties inherent in attempting to generalize from one time period to another, even when one is investigating the same kind of relationships among psychological variables in both time periods.

Description of Individuals and Groups

In the traditional trait measurement model the adequate description of an individual is in terms of a personality profile based on a number of reaction variables. The position on each dimension for reaction variables is often used as an estimation of the individual's "true score" on a dimension for the latent trait, that is supposed to determine actual behavior. In an interactional model of behavior, the adequate description of an individual on the reaction level is in terms of a number of profiles across different kinds of situations; one profile for each of a number of significant reaction variables. The total pattern of cross-situational profiles, for an individual, reflects his or her idiographic pattern of stable and changing reactions across situations. The lawfulness and stability of that pattern is the basis for explanation and prediction of individual behavior (see page 70).

Multidimensional, cross-situational profiles can be used as a basis for classifying individuals into homogenous groups with regard to their specific patterns of reactions across significant situations (see Pervin, Chapter 27). One method by which individuals can be classified into homogeneous groups on the basis of their cross-situational profiles is latent profile analysis (see, e.g., Mårdberg, 1973). The method, which has been used by Magnusson and Ekehammar (1975a) in a comparison of groups of subjects that differ with regard to profiles for S data, on anxiety across situations that differ in their anxiety-evoking character, has the advantage that it does not require normal distributions or linearity of data.

Methodological Problems

The methodological problems encountered in personality research and the choice of methods for data collection and data treatment are closely related to the measurement model that is used to operationalize the concepts in the theoretical model of behavior (see Magnusson, 1974a). Traditional methods of data treatment, e.g., regression analysis, factor analysis, and analysis of variance, are primarily useful for a mechanistic model of man and his behavior. However, because we have not fully explored the nature of mechanistic interaction (see

Endler, 1975b) these techniques, in person by treatment designs, are useful in that they may enable us to get a better understanding of the person by situation interaction process (see, e.g., Endler, 1976; Takala, Chapter 6). The correlational approach is an appropriate one for investigating the relative consistency hypothesis (stable rank orders) in terms of the combinations of reaction variables by methods of data collection. An illustration of the usefulness of the ANOVA approach is offered in the study by de Bonis (Chapter 15) in this volume. Nelsen, in Chapter 5, discusses the potential use of factor analysis and multiple regression analysis in research on interactionism.

However, the main future interest in interactional psychology should be in dynamic interactions, and our understanding of these interactions is not illuminated by the traditional approaches mentioned above. Sarason, Smith, and Diener (1975) and Endler (1976) have indicated that typical variance components studies tell us *what* the state of affairs is but do not tell us *why*. Many of the chapters in this volume, when discussing methodological problems, emphasize the need to develop new methods that are appropriate for investigating dynamic interaction (see Alker, Chapter 19; Raush, Chapter 22, and 1965, 1972; Endler & Magnusson, 1974, 1976). Although there has been a call for new methods " . . . the appeal has not been matched with method . . . too vague and general technology has not favored its development" (Raush, Chapter 22, page 303). The lack of adequate methodological tools for studying dynamic interactions is an obstacle for future research. The development of such methods is one of the most urgent needs in terms of providing us with more effective research on the person by situation interaction issue (e.g., Fiske, Chapter 21, and Sarason, Chapter 20).

Suggested Strategies for Future Research

The change of focus in personality research from the person *per se,* as exemplified in the trait personality and dynamic personality tradition, to the continuous, dynamic (organismic) interaction between persons and situations requires new empirical research strategies. Many of the chapters in this volume suggest strategies for future research on interactional psychology. At this point we shall merely summarize a sample of these suggestions. For further details the reader is referred to the various chapters in this volume.

Several authors in this volume stress the importance of studying dynamic person by situation interactions instead of the mechanistic interactions that have previously dominated the empirical research on interaction (see Bowers, Chapter 3; Mischel, Chapter 25; Raush, Chapter 22; Reid, Chapter 12, Takala, Chapter 6; Wachtel, Chapter 24, among others). In that context many authors argue for additional research about *how* the interaction process is initiated and maintained in terms of theoretical explanatory concepts. In an earlier section in this chapter we discussed two types of dynamic interaction, within-situation interaction and between- (across-) situations interaction. The request for studies on behavior in natural settings (see Alker, Chapter 19; Bowers, Chapter 3; Fiske, Chapter 21) is relevant for both types of dynamic interaction, within and between situations. Argyle's proposition that we should analyze and study the generative rules of the situations and their effects on individual behavior is also valid for within- and between-situational analyses. Fiske's (Chapter 21) and Peterson's (Chapter 23) plea for careful observations of small units of behavior primarily concern within-situation interactions. Fiske (Chapter 21) argues for the objective measurement and observation of small units of behavior (e.g., verbal communication) as the basis for making psychology "a science." A somewhat similar approach is suggested by Argyle (Chapter 26) in his plea for "a generative rules approach" to social interaction, arguing for a "grammar" of behavior with reference to linguistic rules. Takala (Chapter 6) in his studies of "personal styles," argues for the use of more "low-order" concepts and a more molecular research strategy. Peterson (Chapter 23) and Raush (Chapter 22) stress the importance of analyzing the process in interpersonal (social) interaction. Argyle (Chapter 26), Bowers (Chapter 3), and Takala (Chapter 6) have all emphasized the importance of making careful observations of interpersonal behavior, *within* a situation, during the ongoing interaction process. Alker (Chapter 19) and Pervin (Chapter 27) are concerned with person by situation interactions *between* (across) *situations* and suggest the need for idiographic descriptions, as does Wachtel (Chapter 24), who emphasizes the importance of interaction cycles. Mischel (Chapter 24) and Wachtel (Chapter 24) suggest the need for more studies on *how* and *why* individuals select situations when they are free to make a choice, and Schalling (Chapter 7) emphasizes the need for examining physiological indicators of states during the interaction process.

The fruitfulness of making observations of individuals over long periods of time (longitudinal studies) has been eloquently demonstrated by Block in his book *Lives through time* (1971, and Chapter 2; see also Magnusson, Dunér, & Zetterblom, 1975). The importance of additional longitudinal studies in order to obtain a better knowledge of the person by situation interaction process is discussed by Alker (Chapter 19), Bowers (Chapter 3), Epstein (Chapter 4), Sarason (Chapter 20), and Wachtel (Chapter 24). Wachtel suggests a longitudinal approach to the study of cause and effect relationships, arguing that early personality has an indirect effect on adult behavior both in terms of its influence on the choice of life situations and in terms of provoking behavior by other individuals directed toward onself. The importance of studying earlier experiences as a basis for a better understanding of the individual's relationships to different situations is also discussed by Krau (Chapter 16) and by Reid (Chapter 12).

In an earlier section we have suggested that we need additional studies on different kinds of reaction variables using different methods for data collection.

Pervin (Chapter 27), in discussing the need for idiographic approaches that emphasize representative designs instead of systematic designs, argues for the use of "free-response" methods and for studies of the relationships among cognitive, affective, and reaction variables. Block (Chapter 2) emphasizes the need for well-planned studies using T data (see pp. 63—64).

Many of the previous empirical studies within the interactional frame of reference have been devoted to *descriptions* of persons by situation interactions. However, we obviously need *predictive* studies, which simultaneously incorporate personality and situational variables in the experimental design and make *predictions* based on theory (see Endler, 1976; Fiedler, Chapter 9; Spielberger, Chapter 11; Zuckerman, Chapter 13). An empirical study, in which an interactional model of anxiety (Endler, 1975a) was used to make *differential predictions* with respect to anxiety reactions in different situations, has been presented and discussed by Endler and Magnusson (1975). Nelsen (Chapter 5) suggests that predictions of actual behavior should be formulated in terms of *conditional probabilities,* based on careful analyses of situational cues. The problems raised by Sarason (Chapter 20) and by Pervin (Chapter 27), about representative designs and representative samples of individuals and situations, merit careful consideration. Sarason (Chapter 20) suggests that, as a first step, we focus on studies in well-defined situations in order to develop a better foundation for more generalizable studies.

Research on Situations

In the earlier discussion of consistency, we have suggested that coherent behavior is understandable and predictable under three conditions: (a) when we know how the individual interprets the kind of situation in which behavior is observed or to which predictions are made, (b) when we know how he or she usually reacts to situations that are interpreted in a similar way, and (c) when we have a theory linking the above two factors together. This implies that we need to know something about the situations in which behavior is observed, or to which behavior is predicted, in order to understand and predict individual behavior. Research on situations is therefore an important task for interactional psychology.

A number of chapters in this volume point to the need for systematic analyses of situations, both with regard to their meanings as wholes and with regard to the role of specific aspects of situations, in the ongoing within-situation interaction process (see Alker, Chapter 19; Argyle, Chapter 26; Epstein, Chapter 4; Krau, Chapter 16; Nelsen, Chapter 5; Pervin, Chapter 27; Reid, Chapter 12; Sarason, Chapter 20; Takala, Chapter 6). Raush (Chapter 22) suggests that we need a coalescence among behavioral, social learning, biocognitive, and psychodynamic viewpoints. Zlotowicz (Chapter 28) strongly emphasizes the situational aspects of interactions and advocates an empirical approach to the study of situations. He believes that interaction occurs primarily *between* situations and that the main task of psychology is to describe and classify situations. "An accurate knowledge of situations, their mutual relationships, and significance would tell us much about the persons involved" (Chapter 28, page 398).

Careful theoretical and empirical analyses are needed in order to arrive at an adequate and effective classification of situations. Classification serves a number of useful purposes in biological and social sciences, as recently discussed by Sokal (1974):

> The paramount purpose of a classification is to describe the structure and relationship of the constituent objects to each other and to similar objects, and to simplify these relationships in such a way that general statements can be made about classes of objects. The definition, description, and simplification of taxonomic structure is a challenging task. (p. 1116).

This statement also has validity when the objects of research are situations.

Epstein (Chapter 4) stresses that knowledge about the situational side of the person by situation interaction, in which behavior develops, is needed for a better understanding of the interactional process (see also Magnusson, 1971, 1974b; Krau, Chapter 16; among others). Descriptions and classifications of situations in terms that express their relevance for different kinds of reactions are useful as a basis for the selection of appropriate situations in empirical studies of between- (across-) situations interactions. Differential predictions about behavioral outcomes, with reference to the kind of situations to which behavior is predicted, would be assisted by appropriate classifications of situations (see Nelsen, Chapter 5; Spielberger, Chapter 11; Zuckerman, Chapter 13).

Different views on the analyses of situations have been presented in the chapters in this volume. In earlier theorizing and empirical research two main approaches have been evident (see Magnusson, 1976a). The *first* approach is characterized (a) by investigating situational differences in terms of *person variables* and (b) by using *empirical methods* to establish the situational factors of interest. In this approach most of the studies have been performed on situations as wholes. The *second* approach is characterized (a) by *theoretical analyses* of (b) *social and physical* properties of situations, by breaking down single situations into their effective components.

Analysis of Situations in Terms of Person Variables

With reference to the earlier discussion about mediating and reaction variables, the studies using person variables to describe and classify situations can be grouped into three main categories.

1. Situations can be studied in terms of the situational *input (content)* in the mediating process, that is, with respect to how they are *perceived* and *interpreted* by individuals. The importance of studying the meaning of situations has been stressed by many researchers (see e.g., Angyal, 1941; Koffka, 1935; Lewin,

1935; Murray, 1938; Murphy, 1947; Rotter, 1954; Raush, Farbman, & Llewellyn, 1960; Magnusson, 1971, 1974b; Bowers, 1973; Schneider, 1973; Mischel, 1973a; Endler, 1975b) and in this volume by Berkowitz (Chapter 10), Golding (Chapter 29), Krau (Chapter 16), Pervin (Chapter 27), Reid (Chapter 12), Sarason (Chapter 20), and Zlotowicz (Chapter 28), among others. Empirically this approach has been used by Pervin (1968), using a semantic differential technique, and by Magnusson (1971, 1974b), using a psychophysical multidimensional scaling technique.

An important assumption regarding the perception of situations is that there are individual differences in the perception of situations. This assumption has been empirically supported by Magnusson (1971, 1974b), who has analyzed situation perception data for both individuals and groups. He found that for some important situations the perceptions of these situations varied so much among individuals that the interpretation of group data was meaningless. It is therefore necessary to carefully determine when an analysis of situation perception data for situations as wholes can be made for group data and when the conditions for such an analysis do not exist. When the "cognitive maps" of situations differ markedly among individuals, for some important situations, meaningless groupings may be obtained, as is illustrated in the case described by Argyle (Chapter 26, page 362). In an interactional framework, the appropriate level of analysis for situation perception data is often in terms of individual data.

2. Situations can also be classified in terms of *mediating, motivational* variables, as for example in terms of the *press* they exercise on the individual or the *needs* they satisfy (see Murray, 1938; Rotter, 1954). Empirical research using the *need–press* approach has been presented by Stern, Stein, and Bloom (1956) and by Stern (1970) in their analyses of educational and work situations.

3. Situations can also be described in terms of the *reactions* they elicit (see Rotter, 1954; Frederiksen, 1972). Empirical studies expressing situational differences in reaction variables have been conducted by Sakoda (1952) and by Endler, Hunt, and Rosenstein (1962), among others (see also Levin, 1965; Frederiksen, Jensen & Beaton, 1972).

Of relevance to interactional psychology is the relationship between individuals' perceptions of situations and their reactions to the same situations. This relationship was investigated by Magnusson and Ekehammar (1975b), who studied the correspondence between individuals' perceptions of and their reactions to the same anxiety-provoking situations (see also Ekehammar, Schalling, & Magnusson, 1975). One important task for situational analyses is an investigation of the relationship between the important situational factors found on the basis of situation perception and situation reaction data, and the physical and social factors within situations, based on theoretical analyses of situations. How, for example, are individuals' *interpretations* of situations related to the *physical & social behavior* (e.g., hostility or anxiety) restrictions (or facilitations) exerted by these situations?

Situations can be described in terms of person variables. These variables can be operationalized using different kinds of methods for data collection, (compare for example Pervin's, 1968, and Magnusson's, 1971, studies on situation perception) and different kinds of methods for data treatment. The choice of methods for data collection and for data treatment should be related to the purpose of the study and to the theoretical behavioral model underlying the study. For example, as Magnusson (1974b) indicates, the classification of situations, based on individuals' perceptions, can be made in terms of a *dimensional* or a *categorization* model of cognitive functioning (see Bieri, Atkins, Briar, Leaman, Miller, & Tripodi, 1966). The appropriate methods for data treatment for the dimensional model of cognitive functioning are multidimensional scaling techniques (e.g., factor analysis), and the appropriate methods for data treatment for the categorization model of cognitive functioning involve cluster analyses. The strategy of using person variables to classify situations implies that both persons and situations can be classified in the same terms, for example, in terms of situation perception data (see Magnusson, 1976a, Ekehammar & Magnusson, 1973, for an empirical example).

Mischel (Chapter 25) warns about the potential dangers of research aimed at discovering situational dimensions. The search for dimensions of person variables (and the abuses of such dimensions) in differential psychology has often led us astray, and Mischel is concerned that we do not get into the same trap with respect to situational dimensions. However, the proper corrective for an abuse is not the abandonment of an approach that may be useful for some purposes. The dimensionalizing strategy is not good for every purpose, and every strategy can be misused. The basic criterion for the effectiveness of a strategy is whether or not it contributes meaningful answers to essential questions. There is a need for the dimensionalization and classification of situations as a basis for examining the person by situation interaction process.

Situational Analyses in Physical and Social Terms

The research tradition that stresses the importance of the description and classification of situations in terms of their social and physical characteristics, instead of in terms of person variables, is most clearly represented by Argyle (Chapter 26) in this volume. In his approach he follows a tradition earlier proposed by Sherif and Sherif (1956, 1963), who, working in a social psychological context, have suggested four main classes of characteristics (e.g., factors related to the individual, the task, etc., that can be used for describing and classifying situations. (See also Sells, 1963a, who presents a comprehensive system of taxonomic dimensions, and Barker, 1965, 1968, who discusses behavior settings.)

Assuming that social situations are discrete entities instead of continuous ones and that each situation, say a dinner or a committee meeting, is "a structural system of interdependent parts" (page 362), Argyle stresses the need for analyses of the basic components of situations that determine behavior within a situation. On the basis of a theoretical analysis he suggests that the following basic components should be considered in descriptions and classifications of situations: special moves, goals, structural—motivational themes, rules, pieces, and concepts (see pages 363—365).

An Integrated Personality Theory

We have earlier in this chapter advocated that future research be based on sound, fruitful psychological theories. Such theories will be helpful and effective for reaching one of the realistic goals of psychological research, namely " . . . to develop explanatory concepts, concepts that will help people use their heads" (Cronbach, 1975, p. 126). Trait psychology and psychodynamics, on one hand, and situationism, on the other, locate the main causal factors in the person and the situation, respectively, each neglecting the importance of factors on the other side of the interaction:

> Historically, the situationist's failure to recognize the importance of an intrapsychic organization as a stabilizing influence on behavior has its counterpart in the dynamic psychologist's underestimation of how the environment can modify a person's ongoing behavior. Fortunately, both traditions seem to be alerted to the crackers in their bed and a reconciliation of sorts may be in the offing (Bowers, Chapter 3, p. 75)

The interactional view of behavior seems to be a natural next step in theory and research (see especially Raush, Chapter 22; Sarason, Chapter 20). The consequences for psychological personality theory of the empirical studies on the person—situation interaction issue are not clear. However, the empirical results and the viewpoints discussed earlier in this chapter may form the basis for an outline of an integrated personality theory in which models for information processing, including cognitive and motivational factors on the person side and the meaning of situations as wholes, as well as within-situations components on the situation side, are integrated in a personality model that can explain the ongoing process in which individual behavior occurs. In the iterative research process in which theory and empirical studies influence each other, a focus on the person by interaction process may lead to a more functional personality theory than presently exists. This is a challenge to researchers in the personality field.

Part II

CONSISTENCY—
COHERENCE (TRAITS)

Part II contains seven chapters (Chapters 2–8) that are organized around the theme of consistency–coherence (traits).

Block (Chapter 2) questions Mischel's (1968, 1969, 1971, 1973a) critique of empirical personality research regarding the consistency versus specificity issue. Block's evaluation is that the failure to find consistency arises because many of the personality studies are weak conceptually and inadequate methodologically. He believes that there is a lawfullness and coherence (see Chapter 1, pages 45-50.) with respect to personality and provides some impressive evidence for longitudinal consistency correlations across similar situations using ratings (R data in Table 1.1, Chapter 1) and self-reports (S data in Table 1.1, Chapter 1) and strong relationships between the R data and the S data. However, the evidence for personality consistency using objective behavioral measures (O data in Table 1.1, Chapter 1) is erratic. Block emphasizes the need for good *theories* about person by situation interactions instead of mere demonstrations that interactions exist.

Bowers (Chapter 3) points out that personal consistency and behavioral specificity are not necessarily mutually exclusive. The reason investigators have failed to appreciate this is a tendency to confuse *phenomena* with their *explanations*. (See also our discussion of the distinction between mediating variables and reaction variables in Chapter 1.) Bowers, like Block, suggests a correlational strategy for discerning coherence and emphasizes the need for examining consistency in concrete interpersonal behavior and investigating consistency longitudinally in terms of context-specific behaviors. He points out that clinical contexts can provide us with significant data and that in dynamic interactions people not only respond to situations but also create the situations to which they respond.

Epstein (Chapter 4) contends that when appropriately measured there is strong empirical support for consistency and for the existence of traits. He points to the limitations of the variance components approach with respect to drawing conclusions about behavioral stability (see also Olweus, Chapter 17; Magnusson & Endler, Chapter 1, for a discussion of the limitations of the variance components approach). Providing empirical evidence from correlations (ranging from .80 to .90) across behavioral samples, over 24–34 days, Epstein finds support for intrasubject as well as intersubject reliability. He concludes that persons, situations, and their interactions are important areas of psychology investigation.

Nelsen (Chapter 5) emphasizes the distinction between dispositional (personality characteristics) constructs and occurent (occurence of behavior as a specific event) constructs, and the distinction between short-term versus long-term constructs with respect to consistency. Nelsen proposes that predicting behavior, according to a conditional probability model, may enable interactional psychology to integrate dispositional and occurent (behavioral) constructs. He discusses the relative merits of various statistical techniques (e.g., analysis of variance, factor analysis, regression analysis, cluster analysis) in terms of their implications for explaining person by situation interactions and outlines a program for investigating person by situation interactions, using both correlational and experimental techniques.

Takala (Chapter 6), using a correlational strategy, demonstrates the existence of consistency with respect to individual psychomotor styles. Although there is consistency within a class or category of psychomotor acts, there is little consistency across graphomotor, gross motor, and interpersonal modes of action. The nature and generality of psychomotor consistencies are related to maturity and social skills to the development and changes in these psychomotor skills. Takala advocates a molecular approach (see also Fiske, Chapter 21) and underlines the importance of using cognitive constructs for the understanding of interaction processes. Methodologically he suggests various correlational strategies (e.g., multitrait–multimethod, factor analyses) for investigating interactions.

Schalling (Chapter 7) suggests that there is room for a few broad trait concepts in personality and proposes that they have an implicit interactionist character. She favors a correlational strategy and suggests that psychopathology research and neurobehavioral research are important vehicles for developing trait constructs. She emphasizes the need for investigating the physiological correlates of traits (e.g., such traits as impulsiveness and anxiety proneness) and provides data on trait–situation interactions. Schalling recommends a trait–situation interaction strategy on behavior (where one investigates the joint influences of psychological and physiological states, and other dispositional constructs, and the meaning of situations) for investigating important problems in personality research.

Lay (Chapter 8), in the final chapter in Part II, makes an important distinction between two interpretations of cross-situational consistency: the correlational view of consistency (see our discussion of relative consistency in Chapter 1) and the variability or lack of difference view (see our discussion of absolute consistency in Chapter 1). He suggests that investigations often fail to distinguish between consistency conceived as low intrasubject differences in behavior between situations (absolute consistency), and consistency conceived as high correlations in behavior across situations (relative consistency) independent of absolute differences. Lay discusses the link between personality and cross-situational consistency and offers an alternative viewpoint.

Although all the chapters in Part II accept the assumption of coherence (in the sense of lawfulness), not all of them favor the trait position (e.g., see Nelsen, Chapter 5, which emphasizes interactionism).

2
Advancing the Psychology of Personality: Paradigmatic Shift or Improving the Quality of Research?

Jack Block

University of California, Berkeley

PERSONALITY ASSESSMENT UNDER SIEGE

In the last half dozen years or so, the field of personality psychology has been asked to reconsider certain premises that traditionally have guided conceptualization and research. The most influential questioner and critic of personology has been Mischel (1968, 1969, 1972, 1973a) but also expressing their concern have been Peterson (1965, 1968), Bem (1972), and Fiske (1973, 1974), among others.

The critique of personality psychology has been broadly put and has ranged widely. The essential criticism, advanced and buttressed in a number of ways, is an empirical one: The research evidence accruing over the years supports only weakly or not at all the assumption of personologists that traits or dispositions importantly govern behavior. Mischel (1968) develops this conclusion in a widely read review of the personality assessment of literature. He then goes on to suggest that the disappointing accomplishments of personality psychology after so many years of extensive effort may well have a larger implication, that the "paradigm" (Kuhn, 1962) traditionally employed in personality psychology is fundamentally inadequate and should be replaced by newer conceptualizations rising above the limitations set by earlier, now demonstrably unproductive assumptions.

For Mischel, the immediate issue confronting personality psychology is not necessarily a conceptual one but derives instead from undeniable empirical insufficiencies: "The initial assumptions of trait–state theory were logical, inherently plausible, and also consistent with common sense and intuitive impressions of personality. Their real limitation turned out to be empirical — they simply have not been supported adequately" (Mischel, 1968, p. 147). In Mischel's view, this inadequate empirical support cannot be ascribed solely to faulty (but in principle, remediable) research methodology; instead, he is inclined to believe this "basic dilemma of evidence" calls into question the very paradigm personologists have been employing.

This sense of paradigmatic crisis has proved challenging; other psychologists now have responded to various issues underlying the several arguments brought together by Mischel. For example, Bowers (1973) considers more closely some of the implicit assumptions underlying alternative approaches to psychology; Averill (1973b) and Wiggins (1974) discuss the logical status of the concept of "disposition"; Alker (1972) and Wachtel (1973a, b) elaborate various conceptual complications that may explain disappointing empirical relationships.

Much of what is said in these several articles I can myself endorse. However, these responses all seem to start from (and thereby implicitly accept) Mischel's assessment of the state of personality assessment. Excepting only Craik's (1969) brief demurral regarding the evidential basis for Mischel's highly negative evaluation of assessment accomplishments, the discussions to date of Mischel's diagnosis have adopted, without question, his 1968 interpretation of the empirical symptoms. Furthermore, although in later articles Mischel has importantly qualified (and thereby softened) certain implications of his position, he has continued to reference his 1968 book to support his critical evaluation of the state of personality psychology. Of perhaps largest significance, Mischel's (1968) conclusions have become widespread and are cited frequently and with bland acceptance in texts and by journal editors as the received view of the field. It therefore becomes important and even required to indicate some of the ways in which his negative evaluation can be countered. The present essay reads the research differently and, in addition, introduces some recent pertinent findings that permit a different structuring of the accomplishments and deficiencies characterizing personality research.

MISCHEL'S EMPIRICAL CONCLUSIONS

The three main interrelated conclusions of Mischel assert:

1. "[There is] impressive evidence that on virtually all of our dispositional measures of personality substantial changes occur in the characteristics of the individual longitudinally over time and, even more dramatically, across seemingly similar settings cross-sectionally" (Mischel, 1969, p. 1012). (See Mischel, 1968, Chapter 2, for his review of the evidence he brings to bear.)

2. Traits and states are largely constructs of the observer. The available evidence indicates that, more than a little, the personality traits and states observed by psychologists are the constructions of the observers instead of being strongly related to independent information about the subject's actual behavior (see Mischel, 1968, Chapter 3).

3. Inferences from traits and states are not predictively useful. Efforts to use trait and psychodynamic concepts in psychological prediction have not consistently demonstrated useful increments over easier, cheaper procedures for prediction (see Mischel, 1968, Chapter 5).

The first of Mischel's conclusions is the crucial one and accordingly is the primary concern of this essay. If the first summary evaluation by Mischel can be replaced by another perspective, then his second and third corollary conclusions also change in their significance because, as shall be seen, the evidence to be brought forward for the existence of appreciable personality consistency is also evidence both that the traits and states viewed by observers derive in fundamental ways from qualities residing within the individuals observed and that observer assessments are predictively useful.

A WORLDLY VIEW OF THE STATE
OF PSYCHOLOGICAL RESEARCH

In order to respond to Mischel's pessimistic conclusions with more optimistic perspectives, some prefatory remarks are necessary about the quality of contemporary psychological research and the inferences to be drawn from this research.

The Quality of Psychological Research

To support a positive view of the possibilities residing within the trait and psychodynamic view, it is necessary to berate with little mercy much of the research in personality psychology. This is an ironic position, reluctantly but I believe realistically advanced. I hope I will not be viewed as putting myself forward as a lordly, *non pareil* judge or critic. (simply (simply?) wish to assert that an intelligent, informed, vigilant evaluation of recorded personality research can quickly reveal that perhaps 90% of the studies are methodologically inadequate, without conceptual implication, and even foolish. Without recognition of the many kinds of deficiencies characterizing personality (and other psychological) research, it is impossible to make sense of the "litter-ature." Paradoxically, critical evaluation will permit a meaningful view of the field; uncritical acceptance of current empiricism will lead to a nihilism.

What is the basis for this indictment of so much personality research? Only some general remarks are feasible here, addressed to problems in operationalizing concepts, problems in formulating hypotheses, and problems of methodology and data analysis.

1. Many concepts have not been well represented by their operational indicators. Psychologists have been extraordinarily casual and even irresponsible in developing measures to represent concepts. In coordinating a concept with a measure, it is incumbent on the psychologist to justify, via construct validation procedures, the propriety of this assigned correspondence (Block, 1968). Too often, psychologists will award an implicative, even flashy name to a particular measure without supporting convergent and discriminant evidence for the label being employed. Whereupon, given the sociology of psychology, if the measure is a convenient one other psychologists are likely to employ it in a mountainous mass of studies of molehill significance. So, unless a trait or psychodynamic concept has been provided with a fair and supported operational translation, research involving these concepts is without implication.

2. Behavioral hypotheses derived from concepts should reflect the complexity and the implications of the concept being studied. Concepts have to be thought about; they often have complicated or contingent or interactive implications that should be but are not respected in psychological research. For example, psychological conceptualizations of the development of an ethical sense posit the gradual progression of the individual through a number of moral stages (Loevinger, 1966a; Kohlberg, 1964) Ethical consistency, according to these conceptions, cannot be manifested until certain ego or moral stages have been achieved. With this recognition in mind, the well-known Hartshorne and May (1928) studies of grade school children, which frequently have been interpreted as evidence for the inconsistency of moral conduct, become largely irrelevant because these children were too young to have achieved the character stages required before consistency in moral behavior properly could be expected. The rejection of an unwarranted hypothesis obviously carries no implication for the usefulness of a concept or for the separate likelihood of supporting a warranted hypothesis.

3. The reliability of many of the measures employed in personality research and the power of the research designs employed is often poor, unnecessarily so. It makes no sense to use measures so unreliable that subsequent intercorrelations among measures are constrained to be close to zero. It also is unreasonable to interpret research, by oneself or by others, when the reliabilities of the measures used is unknown or not taken into account. One cannot know, in this latter circumstance, whether low intercorrelations are interpretable as such or are first ascribable to the poor quality of the measures involved. It is not enough to know in the abstract of the attenuating effects of reliability; instead, *this recognition should be explicitly and specifically applied in the evaluation of each and every study.* By taking attenuation effects into account, the research evaluator will develop a wiser perspective on the relationships involved.

Similarly, the embarrassingly frequent use of inefficient designs, as noted, for example, by Cohen (1962, 1969), also attenuates the possibility of discerning relationships. Psychologists often employ research designs almost guaranteed to obscure relationships that may be residing in the data. Furthermore, they are often misinformed regarding the way chance operates in statistical decision-making situations and biased to expect relationships where they should not exist (Tversky & Kahneman, 1971). When power-deficient research designs are further conjoined with unreliable measures and then evaluated by psychologists with rash expectations, it should not be surprising if strong and reproducible relationships emerge only rarely.

The Inferences to Be Drawn from Contemporary Personality Research

If one accepts current research evidence in personality largely at face value, it is understandable why disappointment in empirical achievements to date has become widespread; whereupon the search for alternative, potentially more successful approaches is launched. The positive suggestions by Mischel draw on the empirical state of affairs but in a way that should be recognized as inductive rather than deductive, as tenable rather than required.

An equally sound induction from the empirical literature reasons that if personality research is poorly executed, then personality is likely to appear inconsistent. If it is the case that personality research frequently is operationalized poorly and that appropriate hypotheses often are tested in insensitive ways, what can be concluded regarding the usefulness of the trait and psychodynamic approaches from the variety of weak and certainly erratic relationships generated over the years? Rather little, I suggest. Only after appropriate testing of the trait and psychodynamic approaches has failed does abandonment of this conceptual view seem due.

In the meanwhile, and as a supplementary consideration, it may well be that the current dismal assessment of the personality literature depends too heavily on the poor "batting average" our sloppy empiricism has attained. Home runs have been averaged with strikeouts, and clearly there have been many of the latter. However, some people know how to play ball and others do not. What if the home runs are hit by competent, resourceful athletes, whereas the strikeouts come from the blind and the infirm? Surely, it is not elitist or beyond practical possibility to suggest that the "batting average" of personality psychology must be evaluated more closely, to see whether a pattern of quality or relevance can be said to characterize the order-implying findings reported, in contrast to a pattern of methodological insufficiency or conceptual irrelevance characterizing the results suggesting behavioral incoherence.

There are many kinds of problems in applying critical standards to research. It is difficult and often impossible, from published accounts, for a reader to separate the empirical wheat from the empirical chaff. There can be selective, projective reading of the evidence, seeing virtue in the research reporting preferred relationships and seeing deficiencies in the research reporting relationships unassimilable to one's conceptual position. Great responsibility is required in the "empirical integrator" (Underwood, 1957). The job, however, is worth attempting (indeed, is there an alternative?) and has the promise of discerning an order or structure that cannot otherwise be seen.

MISCHEL'S APPRAISAL OF THE CONSISTENCY AND SPECIFICITY LITERATURE

The first argument of Mischel is that the postulated and widely accepted notions using traits or psychodynamic "genotypes" to account for the consistencies of behavior beg the question — in his opinion, there is little empirical evidence of these consistencies for the trait or psychodynamic approaches to explain.

In my own view, there is decent and sometimes even impressive empirical support for the trait and psychodynamic approaches. Moreover, I believe there is a structure to the evidence. The pattern of where the findings are strongly positive and where they are discouraging has strong and even ironic implications for understanding the problems besetting personality psychology. Later sections of this chapter bring forward some of this evidence and its implications; here, some remarks are offered on why Mischel's negative evaluation of the literature on behavioral consistency need not be discouraging to personologists. A detailed, point by point countering evaluation is not delivered because it is not required. What is required is an indication of how the thrust of his assessment can be parried by certain recognitions or alternative perspectives.

To begin, note that Mischel's summary regarding the consistency and specificity of behavior relating to personality variables is quite brief, 5,507 words and less than 16 pages (Mischel, 1968, pp. 20–36). Within these few pages, he touches on attitudes toward authority and peers, moral behavior, sexual identification, dependency and aggression, rigidity and tolerance for ambiguity, cognitive avoidance, conditionability, moderator variables, and the temporal instability of personality (612 words per topic). Mischel did not intend these pages to be viewed as a sufficient or close evaluation of the available literature in the tradition of the lengthy reviews that appear in the *Psychological Bulletin*. Instead, these pages served Mischel as a vehicle to illustrate his perspectives and conclusions on the issues involved, albeit in a highly distilled form. Obviously, Mischel's conclusion, whatever its degree of correctness, cannot be truly supported by so brief, selective, and undetailed a literature presentation. Instead, as Bowers (1973) has noted, we must view Mischel's conclusions as deriving from certain larger premises and orientations he holds regarding psychology.

Consider now the very first example Mischel offers of a representative personality disposition for which the evidence of cross-situational generality is disappointing, the issue of attitudes toward authority and peers (Mischel, 1968, pp. 21–23). In Mischel's view, the trait and psychodynamic approaches have assumed the existence of highly generalized reactions to the various authority figures encountered in life. I myself believe, along with Wachtel (1973a), that at least the psychodynamic viewpoint regarding authority relationships and transference is far more complicated in its position and should not be operationally reduced to the empirical hypothesis that all measures of attitudes toward authority should interrelate. Surely, this hypothesis is wrong; there are patterns of identification. One may like one's father but not want to be like him; one may hate one's father but want very much to be the powerful person he appears to be; and so on. Of more immediate import, however, is the cogency of the Burwen and Campbell (1957) research, the only reference cited by Mischel to evaluate this certainly disputable hypothesis. Space limitations here prevent going into the onerous detail required to describe this study; this burden should be assumed by the motivated reader if he or she is to evaluate this research instead of simply accepting its summary conclusions.

Briefly put, the Burwen and Campbell study employed 73 officers and 82 enlisted men from 17 bomber crews. Burwen and Campbell reported "perfunctory complicance and occasional humorous sabotage of the test purpose" (p. 24), with the result that 10–15% of the answer sheets were discarded. Compulsory interviews were held with 57 of the subjects. "Particularly for enlisted personnel, this setting created a guarded, diferential attitude that was difficult to overcome during the one hour period involved" (Burwen & Campbell, 1957, p. 25).

All the measures were constructed for the purposes of the Burwen and Campbell study; there was no prior evidence for their construct validity. Furthermore, there has been no subsequent research to demonstrate the validity of the measures employed. Reliabilities, when available or inferrable, tend to be low.

What shall we say of this study? Clearly, the testing situation was an unfortunate one. Clearly, reliabilities were often so low as to preclude the finding of appreciable cross-measure relationships. Clearly, too, the operational translations of the authority concept were not validated and are highly contestable.

What were the results? There is a significant instrument component (i.e., method variance) underlying the measures. However, of 169 correlations not involving the same instrument, 143 (or 85%) are positive, a highly significant finding suggesting some degree of commonality rising above method variance in the host of measures employed. Overall, it is possible to argue that this study, given its unfortunate testing circumstances and the poor reliabilities associated with its *ad hoc* controversial measures, has issued results that are astonishingly supportive of the notion of trait consistency. My own preference, however, is to set this study aside as simply irrelevant to the issues supposedly being studied. In my view, the "totally negative" conclusion advanced by Burwen and Campbell (1957, p. 31) and reiterated by Mischel (1968, p. 23) is premature because of the many methodological and operationalizing problems afflicting the study.

It is readily possible, were space here available, to challenge or to counter other aspects of Mischel's appraisal of the literature on personality consistency and specificity. Clearly, Mischel has certain unacknowledged presumptions about trait or psychodynamic conceptualizations which cause him to anticipate certain behaviors should be related. This anticipation, when disappointed, permits him to conclude that trait or psychodynamic variables have failed. This gloominess, however, need not influence the mood of other personologists with different anticipations.

Most personologists are aware that conceptual issues and understandings become complex very quickly. An evaluation of empirical insufficiencies must be attentive to attendant conceptual complexities if it is to be relevant and therefore compelling. However, perhaps the best response to the view that empirical findings do not square with conceptual expectations is to attempt to show where and when they do and where and why they do not.

To this effort we now turn.

CONSISTENCY WITHIN AND BETWEEN PERSONALITY DATA DOMAINS

As Cattell has noted (Cattell, 1957, 1973), it is useful to distinguish among three kinds of personality data — R data, S data, and T data — through which traits or dispositions can be operationalized.[1]

1. R data are data derived from observers' evaluations of individuals leading more or less natural lives. Generally, these data take the form of personality ratings.[2]

2. S data are data derived from the self-observations of individuals regarding their behavior, feelings, and characteristics. Self-ratings and responses to personality inventories or questionnaires exemplify these kinds of data.[3]

---

[1] In accordance with the suggestion made in the introductory chapter in this book the first kind of data is referred to as R data.

[2] What I call O data in this essay Cattell labeled L (for *life*) data. I prefer the O designation because it is a continual reminder that this data domain depends quintessentially on the use of an *observer* as an active, filtering, cumulating, weighting, integrating instrument.

[3] What I call S data Cattell labeled as Q data when making these data distinctions. I prefer to use the letter S (for *self*-reporting), as a more general tag for this kind of data and also to avoid the confusion that arises because the letter Q, before Cattell, has been preempted by Stephenson (1953) to identify the ipsative approach (e.g., as in Q sorting).

3. T data are data derived from standardized, objective, more or less artificial test or laboratory situations wherein selected, specific, readily identified or enumerated behaviors are focused on, unbeknownst to the participating subject.

I wish to call attention to the nature and extent of the disposition or trait consistency existing within and between these three data domains. It is my contention, to be supported by some recent or unrecognized research results, that:

1. Well-done R data studies demonstrate undeniable and impressive personality consistency and continuity residing within the individuals being studied.

2. S data studies using carefully constructed personality inventories also show indisputable and appreciable personality coherence and stability within the individuals studied.

3. There are strong relationships between the dispositional qualities of individuals as studied via R data and as evaluated using S data.

4. The evidence for personality consistency as derived from studies using T data is extremely erratic, sometimes positive but often not.

5. As a corollary of the inconsistency manifested by T data, it follows that the relationship between T data, on the one hand, and either R data or S data, on the other hand, must also be uneven.

The above five recognitions can place a different perspective on the state of personality assessment. In particular, the deficiencies or irregularities existing within the T data domain carry implications and directives of great consequence.

There is appreciable personality consistency and continuity as studied within the R data domain. Ratings of personality have, over the years, earned an unfortunate reputation. They are costly, require the rater to live with uncertainty, and have been generated often in confounded, biased, subjective, unreliable ways. However, costs must be judged relative to goals, observer—judges can accept the necessity of decision, and there is no reason why prior practice must control rather than inform subsequent efforts to improve the quality of R data. Complicated and burdensome although they may be observer evaluations of personality can be employed in fully rigorous ways, meeting the usual scientific criteria of data reproducibility within any data set and independence among the data sets subsequently related (Block, 1961, Chapter 3). What are some such studies and what results issue from them?[4]

---

[4] I report primarily my own research because it is easiest for me to do and because the task of finding and evaluating a goodly portion of the relevant evidence in an unorganized literature is beyond my energies and particular interest. I claim, however, that because of my preoccupation with some of the issues surrounding the consistency—specificity controversy, my research has been sensitive to past concerns and has tried to respond to them. Other psychologists are certain to be able to cite other research that also deserves mention in support of the arguments I am collecting and advancing here. This essay should by no means be considered a survey of extant evidence.

The well-known longitudinal studies at Berkeley over the years collected an enormous amount of naturalistic information on a large number of boys and girls, men and women. My book, *Lives through time* (Block, 1971), integrates this material in an account, to date, of the personality characteristics and personality development of the individuals under study. The research design imposed on the archival material relied heavily on R data carefully developed.

For each subject, the naturalistic information available for the junior high school years was collected as one data set. Separately, naturalistic information for the senior high school years was assembled to construct a second data set. Finally, information available from an extensive interview of the subject during his or her fourth decade became a third data set. These three data sets were strictly independent, no data in one set being carried over into another.

The material for a particular subject at a particular age was evaluated by (usually) three clinical psychologists, each functioning independently. No psychologist evaluated a subject at more than one age and, moreover, the combinations of psychologists judging each particular age were permuted extensively, using the large pool of psychologists—judges available, to prevent the possible introduction of systematic judge effects. Psychologists expressed their descriptions or formulations of each subject using the California Q-set procedure (Block, 1961). The California Q set provides a basic and reasonably well-established set of variables for the psychodynamic description of personality, conjoined with an improved rating methodology that prevents the intrusion of extraneous and obfuscating differences between judges in their categorizing tendencies. Interjudge agreement in their CQ formulations was generally acceptable and consequently, for each subject at each time period, the several CQ formulations were arithmetically averaged. A consensually based and reproducible composite CQ description was therefore available for each subject, at each of three time periods — during junior high school, during senior high school, and as an adult. Further extensive information regarding the research design, the procedures employed, and the quality controls applied as the data were developed is available in *Lives through time* (Block, 1971).

Given the care and logic underlying these R data, it appears difficult to explain away substantial and conceptually expectable relationships empirically found to exist between time periods. Such relationships cannot be attributed to the effects of common data, common subjects, or the subtle influences of stereotypes. Instead, such relationships if obtained can be most readily (and perhaps only) understood in terms of enduring qualities within the subjects studied, qualities that were manifest in diverse ways but recognizable in their implications by experienced clinical psychologists.

Just what, in fact, are the findings? Over the 3-year period from junior high school (JHS) to senior high school (SHS), 59% (67/114) of the personality variables (CQ items) characterizing the male sample display consistency significant at the .001 level or better (correlations of at least .35, uncorrected for attenuation). For the female sample, the corresponding figure is 57% (65/114). Over the period from senior high school to the mid-thirties, an interval averaging close to 20 years, 28% (25/90) of the CQ items show consistency significant at the .001 level or better (correlations of at least .35, uncorrected for attenuation). Within the female sample, the corresponding figure is 30% (27/90). The correlations, *uncorrected,* range as high as .70 and .61 for the junior high school—senior high school and senior high school—adult intervals, respectively. If the unreliabilities of the individual CQ items are allowed for, many of the correlations exceed .6 or .7.[5]

To sketchily sample the psychological nature of the temporal consistencies observed, the CQ item "Is a genuinely dependable and responsible person" correlates .58 in the male sample from JHS to SHS and .53 from SHS to adulthood; the CQ item "Tends toward undercontrol of needs and impulses, unable to delay gratification" correlates .57 from JHS to SHS and .59 from SHS to adulthood. The CQ item "Enjoys aesthetic impressions, is aesthetically reactive" correlates .35 from JHS to SHS and .58 from SHS to adulthood.

Within the female sample, the CQ item "Basically submissive" correlates .50 from JHS to SHS and .46 from SHS to adulthood. The CQ item "Emphasizes being with others, gregarious" correlates .39 from JHS to SHS and .43 from SHS to adulthood. The CQ item "Tends to be rebellious and non-conforming" correlates .48 from JHS to SHS and .49 from SHS to adulthood. The CQ item "Is concerned with philosophical problems, e.g., religion, values, and the meaning of life, etc." correlates .45 from JHS to SHS and .42 from SHS to adulthood. All of these correlations are uncorrected for attenuation; many more can be cited. The consistencies relate to personality qualities, not simply or primarily to intellectual or cognitive characteristics, where Mischel does acknowledge consistency exists.

When it is further recognized that over these extended period of time, appreciable character change and transformation must have been involved in many of the individuals studied and that an overall correlation coefficient is a most inefficient and easily misled index of relationship, it seems to me that these R data results provide altogether impressive evidence of personality consistency. The findings of identifiable personality transformation become even more striking, in my view, if the analytical approach becomes more differentiated. Using these R data, I derived via inverse factor analysis a number of homogeneous types of personality development. Certain types of adult character structure can be identified with astonishing fidelity in early adolescence. For details as to these findings, many concomitant relationships, and the rationale for this approach, the reader should consult *Lives through time* (Block, 1971, Chapters 7—10).

---

[5] Appendices E, F, and G of *Lives through time* (Block, 1971) contain in detail the data here being summarized; Chapter 5 places this information into a psychological context.

In an ongoing longitudinal study of ego and cognitive development being conducted by my wife, Jeanne H. Block, and myself, we have been studying more than 100 children during their fourth, fifth, sixth, and eighth years of life.

The California Child Q set, an age-appropriate modification of the California Q set (Block, 1961, 1971), was used to develop personality characterizations of each child. The California Child Q set consists of 100 widely ranging, personality-relevant items that are ordered, using a forced-choice method, by a trained judge to express the judge's characterization of the personality of the child. The judges employed to characterize each child were his or her nursery school teachers; three teachers for more than half the children and two different teachers for the remaining children. In judging a child, each teacher worked completely independently of the other teachers and based her personality formulations on 5–9 months of observation of the child's behavior in the nursery school seeting for 3 hours each day. Each child was therefore well known to each judge, and the salient, consistent qualities of each child's personality had an opportunity to become manifest. All five nursery school teachers received training and calibration in using the Q set before they contributed their evaluations of these children. With the completion of the many Q sorts, for each child the two or three Q descriptions independently formulated by his or her teachers were averaged, resulting in one composite personality characterizations for that particular year. This procedure was followed during the child's fourth year and also during his or her fifth year. The five nursery school teachers contributing their personality formulations during the fourth year were an entirely different set from the five nursery school teachers contributing characterizations during the fifth year.

These data are most simply compared normatively rather than ipsatively by evaluating for each Q item the orderings of the children developed independently and a year apart. Within the convergent–discriminant framework (Campbell & Fiske, 1959), these across-time correlations can be viewed as evidence of convergent validity of the trait ratings because the usage of different and independent sets of judges employing different information at two different times in effect results in different "methods" of measurement of the personality variables being studied. The discriminant validity of each variable can be evaluated by noting whether it correlates higher at another time with differently named variables than it does with its correspondingly named variable.

With these conceptions of convergent and discriminant validity in mind, consider our results. For the 100 Q items, the average across-time correlation, calculated via the z transformation, is .48, uncorrected for attenuation. This average level of correspondence, by contemporary standards of psychological research, is rather high. With respect to discriminant validation, for 45% of the Q items the correlations between the Q item as rated during the fourth year and that same Q item as independently rated during the fifth year was higher than any of the correlations of that fourth year rating with the 99 other Q ratings for the fifth year. Therefore, not only appreciable convergence but also appreciable discrimination characterize these R data. The absolute independence between these personality characterizations developed a year apart means that the relationships observed derive from qualities and consistencies within the children being studied and cannot be attributed to the personal constructs or attribution tendencies of the judges offering their ratings.

Some further analyses of these data strikingly improve their convergent and discriminant validity. Apparently, a number of the Q items, when applied to young children, were redundant or beyond the ability of the judges to discriminate. We were exceeding the psychological resolution capacity of the judges. It therefore seemed sensible to bring together these correlated, unreliably different Q items in order to develop broader and better variables. Accordingly, we factored and varimaxed the fifth-year Q items and decided that 12 factors could be said to encompass the data. Beyond these 12 factors, we had only a few doublets and residual items. For each of the 12 factors, factor scores were derived by standard scoring the several factor-loading Q items and then averaging the standard scores, both for the fifth-year Q data on which the factor analyses were based and for the entirely independent fourth-year Q data. Thus, the pattern of the factor results from the fifth-year data determined how scores were derived from the fourth-year data, an arrangement that from one perspective (e.g., canonical correlation) is less than optimal when maximal correspondence between the two sets of data is sought. The advantage of applying the factor scoring or weighting arrangement based on the fifth-year data to the fourth-year data as well is that there is absolutely no capitalization on chance to bolster unfairly the relationships between age levels and that fully equivalent sets of variables exist at both ages.

What is the discriminant and convergent validity of the set of 12 factors, intermediate level variables presumably better meshed to the discrimination possibilities available from our personality characterizations?

For the 12 factors, identically measured in the fourth and fifth years, the discrimination validity is 100%. Each factor from the fourth year displays its highest correlation with its corresponding factor as measured in the fifth year. The *mean* across-time correlation or convergent validity for these 12 factors is .56, a figure most can agree to be impressive.

Again, for illustrative purposes and to breathe life into these summary figures, the factor "compliance," as rated during the fourth year correlates .72 uncorrected for attenuation, with "compliance" as independently rated during the fifth year. The factors, "undercontrol," "resilience," and "empathic relatedness" as rated during the fourth year correlated, respectively, .71, .46, and .64 with their corresponding factors during the fifth year. These figures are also uncorrected for attenuation. Although these data can readily be improved on, if simply by using more judges, these convergent validities are already and impressively high. Because they are based on independent sets of data, they are difficult to ascribe to artifact or to the workings of constructs solipsistically held by the observers involved. Instead, the results indicate that even with young children, recognizable and perduring qualities of personality have been formed.

Summarizing now our presentation regarding R data, it has been shown that good quality and independently established R data displays appreciable and encouraging convergent and discriminant validity. Other illustrations beyond those cited here can be culled from the literature (e.g., Gormly & Edelberg, 1974). My strong impression is that unpublished data in the archives of the Institute of Personality Assessment Research will also support the general findings advanced here regarding R data. It should also be recognized that the data reported, although of decent quality, can well be improved on, with the consequence that the convergent and discriminatory relationships reported can be expected to become better.

There is appreciable personality consistency and continuity, as studied within the domain of S data. Self-report questionnaires and personality inventories have a long history in psychology (Goldberg, 1971) and widespread usage. The dominant inventory still is the Minnesota Multiphasic Personality Inventory (MMPI) but the California Psychological Inventory (CPI), which derives substantially from the MMPI, has had extensive usage as well. Rising in popularity in recent years are Cattell's 16 Personality Factor Questionnaire (the 16 PF) and Jackson's Personality Research Form. A variety of studies have shown that the dimensions measured by one inventory or questionnaire usually can be measured impressively well by alternative inventories. For a summary of these studies, together with a demonstration of the interchangeability of the CPI and the 16 PF, see the report by Campbell and Chun (1976). These findings, which indicate that alternative and independent inventory-based measurements of personality dimensions are highly related, are a first and extensive indication that individual differences in personality, as quantified by S data, are consistent. Let me add some additional evidence, of a different kind, to this essential conclusion.

1. The CPI has had a long and productive history since its introduction by Gough (1957, 1964). As typically employed, 18 scales are scored. The extended meaning of these well-known scales, the basis of their derivation, their reliabilities, validities, and associated relationships may be found in other sources (Gough, 1964; Megargee, 1972).

The CPI was administered to adult subjects in the Berkeley longitudinal studies on two separate occasions, 10 years apart. It would be difficult to argue that 10 years later the subjects remembered their specific responses to the 480 CPI items. When the two sexes are separated within each of the two longitudinally studies samples, four independent samples can be identified: men (N = 39) administered the CPI at ages 38 and 48; men (N = 59) administered the CPI at ages 31 and 41; and women (N = 43) administered the CPI at ages 38 and 48; and women (N = 78) administered the CPI at ages 31 and 41. What is the convergent and discriminant validity of the 18 CPI scales over the 10-year period involved?[6]

For the four separate samples, the discriminant validity (meaning an inventory scale correlates higher with itself 10 years later than it does with any other scale 10 years later) are 89% (16 of 18 scales), 100% (18 of 18 scales), 89% (16 of 18 scales), and 100% (18 of 18 scales). The very few failures of discriminant validity are by small amounts and make obvious psychological sense. The mean convergent validities are .68, .70, .72, and .73. Recognizing the effects of unreliability and of genuine personality change over the 10 years involved, it appears that these figures can hardly be higher. I also suggest that these findings are probably of general applicability in the S domain; they are not unique to the CPI. The evidence on inventory interchangeability indicates that other substantial inventories would have done as well had they been employed.

2. Many of the subjects in the longitudinally studied sample had been administered the What I Like To Do questionnaire (WILTD) during their junior high school and senior high school years in the 1930s. The WILTD questionnaire consisted of 50 questions regarding the subject's preferences and tendencies in a number of life situations. No special rationale underlies the questions employed and the wording of the questions as formulated in those early days leaves much to be desired. For the purposes of *Lives through time* and as reported therein, I factor analyzed the WILTD questionnaires, separately and combined for the sexes and the time periods involved, with the result that two primary and overriding factors were identified. The factor that concerns us here is the one subsuming items that impressed me as clear expressions of "overcontrol." I developed scores for each subject by simply summing across the 17 items loading on this factor for each subject. To convey quickly a sense of the items involved in this scale, here are two examples: "Can you stick to a disagreeable work for a long time though no one makes you do it?" (scored for a True response) and "Do you get angry easily?" (scored for a False response).

For this chapter, the WILTD overcontrol scores derived during the high school years were correlated with the CPI ego control scores derived from an administration of the CPI about 25 years later. The CPI ego control scale was constructed some years ago on the basis of adult criterion groups. The measures being related were therefore independently constructed and based on data widely separated in time.

In the male sample, from junior high school to senior high school, the WILTD

---

[6] The earlier CPI protocols were collected and developed for *Lives through time* (Block, 1971); the latest CPI protocols were collected in a subsequent follow-up assessment of the subjects conducted by the Institute of Human Development. The correlations between the early and later CPI protocols were computed under the auspices of Dr. Jane Brooks, who will be reporting in detail on her analyses and their implications. I am most grateful to her for permission to report these data in summary form.

overcontrol scales correlated .48. From senior high school to adulthood, the WILTD overcontrol score correlated .52 with the CPI ego control scale. In the female sample, from junior high school to senior high school, the WILTD overcontrol scales correlated .66. From senior high school to adulthood, the WILTD overcontrol score correlated .53 with the ego control scale. None of these figures allows for attenuation resulting from unreliability. Considering the nonoptimal nature of the measures involved and the time span of a quarter century, the findings of these appreciable and conceptually required correlations is further firm evidence of personality continuity in the S data domain.

3. *There are strong relationships between the qualities of individuals as studied via R data and as evaluated using S data.* It has already been shown that R data developed to describe subjects longitudinally studied display good personality consistency over time and that S data collected longitudinally also reveal impressive personality continuity. Now it remains to be seen whether these two data domains are strongly or at least sufficiently related, as they must be.

The group of individuals studied continues to be the sample from *Lives through time,* for whom Q composites and CPI protocols exist. It is not entirely clear just what the best way of connecting the personality Q ratings to the CPI protocols may be. An orthodox multivariate statistician might suggest canonical correlation or multiple regression techniques, but these methods capitalize on chance, require larger sample sizes that psychologists usually have available, and provide results in a form usually not psychologically conveyable. I prefer, at least for the present purpose, a simple, ostensive, and therefore readily understandable method. Specifically, what are the particular personality ratings significantly associated with the various CPI scales?[7] If these ratings are numerously and appropriately correlated with the CPI scales, it becomes clear enough that the two data domains are related.

When the personality ratings characterizing the subjects during adulthood are related to the CPI scales administered at about the same time, the significant correlations observed across the R- and S-data domains are both plentiful and psychologically relevant. These results are too voluminous to report here, but an indication of the strength and conceptual validity of these across-domain associations earlier was presented in Chapters 8 and 9 of *Lives through time,* where the many CPI scales significantly associated with a variety of rating-defined personality types are listed.

In this chapter, for dramaturgical reasons, I elect to report the connections between the CPIs administered when the subjects were in their mid-thirties and

[7] The reader will recall that the CPI was given on two separate occasions separated by about 10 years. Logically, we expect that if CPI scores from one time relate well to early O data, then CPI scores from the second administration also should relate to the early O data, and such is the case. Dr. Jane Brooks will be reporting these findings, based on a period approaching 35 years.

the personality ratings formulated to characterize the personalities of the subjects during adolescence, some of 20 or 25 years earlier. I also report the connection between a questionnaire or S data measure developed during adolescence with personality ratings formulated a *generation later,* when the subjects were in adulthood. Because of the absolute independence of the data domains and the great time spans involved, because of the many attenuating factors that operated, and because of the characterological changes that must have been present, correlations having statistical size and making psychological sense should be especially persuasive evidence for an essential coherence of personality.

TABLE 2.1

Personality Rating Correlates in Adolescence of CPI Dominance Scores Gathered When the Male Subjects Were in Their Mid-Thirties

JHS r^a	SHS r^a	Q item content
.31b	.29b	Has a wide range of interests
.32a	.23c	Is a talkative individual
.30b	–	Appears to have a high degree of intellectual capacity
–.24b	–.26b	Is uncomfortable with uncertainty and complexities
–.28b	–	Basically suqmissive
–.21c	–	Feels a lack of personal meaning in life
–.21c	–	Tends toward overcontrol of needs and impulses
.25b	–	Shows condescending behavior in relations with others
.21c	.22c	Is turned to for advice and reassurance
–.26b	–.25c	Gives up and withdraws in face of frustration, adversity
–.26b	–.28b	Vulnerable to real or fancied threats
–.38a	–	Reluctant to take definite action
–	27b	Is facially and/or gesturally expressive
–.24c	–.23c	Is basically distrustful of people, questions motivations
.27b	–	Genuinely values intellectual and cognitive matters
.33a	.25c	Behaves in assertive fashion in interpersonal situations
.25b	.27b	Is an interesting, arresting person
–.21c	–	Concerned with body and adequacy of physiological function
.29b	–	Has high aspiration level for self
–	–.23c	Has clear-cut, internally consistent personality
–	–.24c	Appears straightforward, forthright
.21c	–	Is cheerful
–	–.30b	Handles anxiety, conflicts by repression or disassociation
–	.39a	Tends to proffer advice
–.38a	–.38a	Is emotionally bland/has flattened effect
.31b	–	Is verbally fluent/can express ideas well
.21c	.25c	Is self-dramatizing/histrionic
–.31b	–.25b	Does not vary roles relates to everyone in same way

^{a}Correlations followed by an a are significant at the .01 level; if followed by a b, at the .05 level; if followed by a c, at the .10 level. Ninety Q items were evaluated for significance.

TABLE 2.2

Personality Rating Correlates in Adolescence of CPI Dominance Scores Gathered when the Female Subjects Were in Their Mid-Thirties

JHS r^a	SHS r^a	Q item Content
.29b	.39a	Is a talkative individual
.24c	–	Appears to have a high degree of intellectual capacity
–	–.33a	Is uncomfortable with uncertainty and complexities
–.35a	–	Anxiety and tension find outlet in bodily symptoms
–.32a	–.35a	Basically submissive
.33a	.39a	Has rapid personal tempo
–	–.31a	Arouses nurturant felling in others of both sexes
–	–.35a	Feels a lack of personal meaning in life
–	–.35a	Tends toward overcontrol of needs and impulses
–	.24b	Is turned to for advice and reassurance
–.25b	–.39a	Gives up and withdraws in face of frustration, adversity
–	–.26b	Is calm, relaxed in manner
–.34a	–.32a	Vulnerable to real or fancied threats
–	.23c	Is moralistic
–.25b	–.40a	Reluctant to take definite action
.22c	.31b	Is facially and/or gesturally expressive
–.28b	–.39a	Has brittle ego-defense system, maladaptive under stress
–.21c	–.41a	Tends to feel guilty
–	–.25b	Aloof, avoids close interpersonal relationships
–	–.25b	Is basically distrustful of people, questions motivations
.22c	.41a	Behaves in assertive fashion in interpersonal situations
–	.28b	Emphasizes being with others, gregarious
–.24b	–	Is self-defeating
–	.24c	Responds to humor
.35a	–	Is an interesting, arresting person
–.29b	–.21c	Concerned with body and adequacy of physiological function
–	.25b	Socially perceptive of wide range of interpersonal cues
–	.22c	Pushes, stretches limits, sees what he can get away with
–	.24b	Has high aspiration level for self
.21c	–	Consciously unaware of self-concern
–.28b	–	Projects own feelings and motivations onto others
–	–.32a	Feels cheated and victimized by life
–	–.22c	Ruminates and has persistent, pre-occupying thoughts
–	–.35a	Handles anxiety, conflicts by repression or disassociation
–	.21c	Is power oriented, values power in self and others
–	.43a	Has social poise and presence
–	.21c	Expresses hostile feelings directly
–	.34a	Tends to proffer advice
.22c	–	Values own independence and autonomy
–.34a	–.31b	Is emotionally bland, has flattened effect
–	.30b	Is verbally fluent, can express ideas well
–	.21c	Is self-dramatizing, histrionic

aCorrelations followed by an a are significant at the .01 level; if followed by a b, at the .05 level; if followed by a c, at the .10 level. Ninety Q items were evaluated for significance.

In relating the CPI taken during adulthood to earlier personality ratings formulated in adolescence, again a profusion of statistically significant findings was observed. For economy of presentation, only the results surrounding two CPI scales are reported. The two scales, the Dominance Scale and the Socialization Scale, are central scales of the CPI; they have been carefully developed and they were designed to measure quite different psychological dimensions. For our male sample, the correlation between these two scales was −.01; for the female sample, the correlation was −.09. Table 2.1 through 2.4 present the Q-item rating correlates from both the junior high school and senior high school periods with the dominance and socialization scales of the CPI taken 20−25 years later, for both the male and female samples.

TABLE 2.3

Personality Rating Correlates in Adolescence of CPI Socialization Scores Gathered when the Male Subjects Were in Their Mid-Thirties

JHS r^a	SHS r^a	Q item content
.53a	.48a	Is a genuinely dependable and responsible person
−.22c	−	Is a talkative individual
.41a	.29b	Behaves in giving way toward others
.30b	.33a	Is fastidious
.50a	.24c	Is protective of those close to him
.43a	.47a	Behaves in a sympathetic or considerate manner
.34a	−	Arouses nurturant feeling in others of both sexes
−.21c	−.34a	Feels a lack of personal meaning in life
−.23c	−.23c	Extrapunitive/tends to transfer or project blame
.22c	.23c	Prides self on being objective, rational
−	.35a	Tends toward overcontrol of needs and impulses
.44a	.52a	Is productive, gets things done
.38a	.33a	Tends to arouse liking and acceptance in people
.23c	.30b	Is turned to for advice and reassurance
.27b	−	Is satisfied with personal appearance
.29b	.25c	Seems to be aware of the impression he makes on others
.25b	.37a	Is calm, relaxed in manner
−.23c	−.47a	Over-reactive to minor frustration/irritable
.33a	−	Has warmth, is compassionate
−.34a	−.29b	Is negativistic, tends to undermine/obstruct, sabotage
−.49a	−.25c	Is guileful and deceitful, manipulative, opportunistic
−.36a	−	Has hostility toward others
−.37a	−.24c	Has brittle ego-defense system, maladaptive under stress
−.27b	−	Is basically distrustful of people, questions, motivations
−.37a	−.48a	Is unpredictable and changeable in behavior and attitudes
−.25b	−.44a	Undercontrol of needs, impulses
−.40a	−.33b	Is self-defeating
.29b	−	Has insight into own motives and behavior
−.35a	−.38a	Tends to be rebellious and nonconforming
−.22c	−	Judges self and others in conventional terms

continued

TABLE 2.3 *continued*

JHS r^a	SHS r^a	Q item content
−.35a	−.25b	Pushes, stretches limits, sees what he can get away with
−.25b	−.24c	Is self-indulgent
−.24b	−.27b	Bothered by anything that can be construed as a demand
−	.27b	Has high aspiration level for self
.30b	.29b	Consciously unaware of self-concern
.35a	−	Has clear-cut, internally consistent personality
−.29b	−	Projects own feelings and motivations onto others
.37a	−	Appears straightforward, forthright
−.34a	−.30b	Feels cheated and victimized by life
−.24c	−	Ruminates and has persistent, preoccupying thoughts
−.22c	−	Interested in members of opposite sex
−	.23c	Is physically attractive, good looking
−.26b	−.44a	Has fluctuating moods
−	.31b	Is cheerful
−.30b	−	Interprets simple, clear-cut situations in complicated ways
−.25b	−	Compares self to others
−	.28b	Has social poise and presence
.23c	−	Behaves in a masculine or feminine style or manner
−	−.39a	Expresses hostile feelings directly
−.29b	−.23c	Is self-dramatizing, histrionic

aCorrelations followed by an a are significant at the .01 level; if followed by a b, at the .05 level; if followed by a c, at the .10 level. Ninety Q items were evaluated for significance.

TABLE 2.4

Personality Rating Correlates in Adolescence of CPI Socialization Scores Gathered When the Female Subjects Were in Their Mid-Thirties

JHS r^a	SHS r^a	Q item content
−	−.29b	Is critical, skeptical, not easily impressed
.42a	.39a	Is a genuinely dependable and responsible person
−.25b	−	Is a talkative individual
.32a	−	Behaves in giving way toward others
.30b	.39a	Is fastidious
−	.27b	Is uncomfortable with uncertainty and complexities
.25b	−	Is protective of those close to him
.33a	.34a	Basically submissive
−	−.24b	Is introspective
.33a	.28b	Behaves in a sympathetic or considerate manner
.37a	−	Arouses nurturant feeling in others of both sexes
−	−.24c	Extrapunitive/tends to transfer or project blame
.34a	.37a	Tends toward overcontrol of needs and impulses
.37a	.41a	Is productive, gets things done
.24c	.26b	Tends to arouse liking and acceptance in people

—	.24c	Is satisfied with personal appearance
—	.34a	Is calm, relaxed in manner
−.21c	−.46a	Over-reactive to minor frustration, irritable
.27b	—	Has warmth, is compassionate
−.33a	−.40a	Is negativistic, tends to undermine, obstruct, sabotage
−.30b	−.26b	Is guileful and deceitful, manipulative, opportunistic
−.29b	−.31b	Has hostility toward others
—	−.25b	Thinks and associated ideas unusually
—	−.31b	Is basically distrustful of people, questions motivations
−.40a	−.51a	Is unpredictable and changeable in behavior and attitudes
−.39a	−.39a	Undercontrol of needs, impulses
−.31a	−.36a	Is self-defeating
—	−.21c	Is an interesting, arresting person
−.27b	—	Enjoys sensuous experiences
−.50a	−.53a	Tends to be rebellious and non-conforming
.21c	—	Socially perceptive of wide range of interpersonal cues
−.56a	−.34a	Pushes, stretches limits, sees what he can get away with
−.35a	−.23c	Is self-indulgent
−.21c	−.21c	Bothered by anything that can be construed as a demand
—	−.23c	Perceives different contexts in sexual terms
—	.38a	Consciously unaware of self-concern
.24c	.37a	Has clear-cut, internally consistent personality
—	−.21c	Projects own feelings and motivations onto others
—	−.33a	Feels cheated and victimized by life
—	.28b	Is physically attractive, good-looking
−.29b	−.46a	Has fluctuating moods
—	.37a	Is cheerful
—	.30b	Handles anxiety, conflicts by repression or disassociations
−.23c	−.36a	Expresses hostile feelings directly
−.25b	—	Values own independence and autonomy
—	.27b	Is emotionally bland, has flattened effect
−.23c	—	Is self-dramatizing, histrionic
—	.30b	Does not vary role, relates to everyone in the same way

[a]Correlations followed by an a are significant at the .01 level; if followed by a b, at the .05 level; if followed by a c, at the .10 level. Ninety Q items were evaluated for significance.

I suggest that the reader who peruses the numerous correlates in these tables will recognize and will not dispute the existence of constellations of personal qualities that accord well with the generally held meanings of dominance and socialization. Many of the correlations, although low, serve to augment the interpretation and implications of these concepts. Certainly, there are some differences between the sexes in the personality precursors of these dimensions as later measured. Overall, however, considering the many obstacles to discernment of relationship affecting these analyses, it seems fair to conclude that rich and required connections exist between these personality ratings and the CPI scales studied.

In relating questionnaire or S data from adolescence to personality ratings or R data developed during adulthood, the only available questionnaire scale score was the WILTD overcontrol scale, earlier described. Tables 2.5 and 2.6 report the Q items from the personality formulations of the subjects as adults that correlate significantly with the WILTD questionnaire measure of overcontrol, administered when the subjects were in senior high school.

Again, I suggest that the tabled relationships demonstrate a strong correspondence between overcontrol as measured via questionnaire in adolescence and rating-based personality characteristics of subjects evaluated in their mid-thirties. As has been noted earlier, the manifestations of ego control are different in males than in females because of differences in the prescriptive and proscriptive properties of sex roles (J. H. Block, 1973). Because of this recognition, better questionnaire measurement of ego control is available when sex-specific inventory scales can be employed (Block, 1965). However, even though this desirable approach has not been feasible within the present data constraints, the findings

TABLE 2.5

Personality Rating Correlates in Adulthood of the WILTD Over-Control Score Gathered When the Male Subjects Were in Senior High School

Adult r^a	Q item content
.40b	Is a genuinely dependable and responsible person
.38b	Is fastidious
.45a	Prides self on being objective, rational
.52a	Tends toward overcontrol of needs and impulses
−.36b	Thinks and associates ideas unusually
−.38b	Is facially and/or gesturally expressive
−.39b	Is unpredictable and changeable in behavior and attitudes
−.42b	Undercontrol of needs, impulses
−.30c	Is an interesting, arresting person
−.48a	Enjoys sensuous experiences
−.35b	Tends to be rebellious and nonconforming
−.35b	Pushes, stretches limits, sees what he can get away with
.32c	Has high aspiration level for self
−.41b	Perceives different contexts in sexual terms
.42b	Has clear-cut, internally consistent personality
.36b	Is physically attractive, good looking
−.32c	Has fluctuating moods
.43b	Handles anxiety, conflicts by repression or disassociation
.32c	Is power oriented, values power in self and others
−.31c	Expresses hostile feelings directly
−.41b	Is self-dramatizing, histrionic

^{a}Correlations followed by an a are significant at the .01 level; if followed by a b, at the .05 level; if followed by a c, at the .10 level. Ninety Q items were evaluated for significance.

TABLE 2.6

Personality Rating Correlates in Adulthood of the WILTD Overcontrol Score Gathered When the Female Subjects Were in Senior High School

Adult r^a	Q item content
−.51a	Has a wide range of interests
−.38a	Appears to have a high degree of intellectual capacity
.37c	Is uncomfortable with uncertainty and complexities
.38c	Tends to be self-defensive
.35c	Extrapunitive, tends to transfer or project blame
.44b	Is negativistic/tends to undermine, obstruct, sabotage
.43b	Is moralistic
.34c	Is self-defeating
.41b	Responds to humor
−.58a	Has insight into own motives and behavior
−.33c	Socially perceptive of wide range of interpersonal cues
−.35c	Appears straightforward, forthright
−.37c	Is verbally fluent, can express ideas well
.48b	Does not vary role, relates to everyone in same way

^{a}Correlations followed by an a are significant at the .01 level; if followed by a b, at the .05 level, if followed by a c, at the .10 level. Ninety Q items were evaluated for significance.

testify to an enduring congruence between questionnaire and rating evaluations of overcontrol.

Recognizing the less than optimal nature of the data and measures being employed, but recognizing too the strict separation of the data between domains and across time, I believe there are grounds for encouragement and even a sense of security about certain principles and practices of personality psychology and personality assessment. It should also be noted that the findings just reported are by no means unique. With respect to the first two dimensions of the Minnesota Multiphasic Personality Inventory (MMPI), dimensions that are different from the CPI dominance and socialization dimensions here evaluated, R data or personality rating correlates have been identified in five different samples (Block, 1965, Table 19–28). Again, the connections between the R and S domains were plentiful and concordant. Finally, R data or personality rating correlates of broad arrays of MMPI, CPI, and Strong Vocational Interest Inventory scales can be found in now old reports (Block & Bailey, 1955; Block & Petersen, 1955; Block & Gough, 1955). It appears fair to conclude that the R and S domains have been linked in ways that, although improvable, are already quite substantial. No prestidigitation is required to achieve the results reported, simply the straightforward but careful application of procedures so well known as to be prosaic. Reasoning from past accomplishments, there is little reason to doubt that well-based and well-quantified R data will continue to be strongly related to well-developed S-data scales.

4. *The evidence for personality consistency as derived from studies using T data is extremely erratic, sometimes positive but often not.* This assertion should require little documentation, for in large measure the currently held despondent views of personality consistency derive from such evidence. Repeatedly, investigators have observed that putatively equivalent or related measures in the T-data domain do not manifest their conceptually required correspondence. For example, Coie (1974) concludes there is little empirical support for the characteristic of "curiosity" as a behavioral disposition operating in different, supposedly curiosity-evoking situations. Chown (1959) in her evaluation of the concept of "rigidity" found little evidence of coherence among a variety of purported rigidity measures. Measures of "reflectivity—impulsivity" (Kagan, Rosman, Day, Albert, & Phillips, 1964), "motor inhibition" (Maccoby, Dowley, Hagen, & Degerman, 1965), and "delay of gratification" (Mischel, 1961) should, for conceptual reasons, be linked together but they are not (Shipman, 1971). Many of the studies cited by Mischel (1968) further exemplify the frequent failure of T-domain measures to interrelate as, conceptually, is to be expected. At will, one can wander through the pages of personality journals and find instance after instance of the absence of expected correlations among T measures. It is because this point has been and can be documented so extensively that I elect not to make the case, in any detail, again here.

5. *It follows as a corollary, therefore, of the erratic relationships among T measures that the relationships between T-data on the one hand, and either R data or S data, on the other, will also be uneven.* Again, it is necessary only to exemplify rather than to document this conclusion. For convenience, I illustrate the problem by some data from the ongoing study by my wife and myself, previously mentioned, wherein we were interested in measuring "delay of gratification." One of the measures employed was a modification of the delay of gratification procedure earlier developed by J. H. Block and Martin (1955). In this experiment, the subject child worked for M&M candies and was permitted to accumulate as many M&Ms as desired before stopping to eat and enjoy any. However, once having stopped to partake of the pleasures of sweetness, the child could not resume work to acquire more candy. Therefore, a child presumably able to delay gratification could acquire many candies before stopping; a child presumably unable to delay gratification would acquire only a few candies before stopping. A second experimental procedure designed to tap the child's ability to delay gratification involved the child's reaction to a gaily wrapped package identified as a present for him or her. The present, contents unknown, was shown to the child and then ostentatiously set to the side by the experimenter who directed his or her attention to the completion of a jigsaw puzzle task. After 4 minutes, during which time the experimenter as required assisted

the child to complete the puzzle, the child waited a further 90 seconds while the experimenter busied herself. During all this time, the package identified to the child as a present was in the child's sight. At the end of the 90 seconds, the child was told he or she could have the present, if he or she had not already taken it. The child's delay time before taking the present during the 90-second interval constituted the score of interest, to represent delay of gratification. Both the candy acquisition experiment and the gift delay experiment were administered to the children at ages 3.5 and 4.5 years.

From one age to the other, the correlation between candy acquisition scores was .24 for the boy sample and .30 for the girl sample. For the gift delay procedure, the across-time correlations were .23 for the boys and .03 for the girls. The correlations between the two procedures at 3.5 years were .01 and −.29, for the boys and girls, respectively, and at 4.5 the correlations were .07 for the boys and −.08 for the girls.

Of greater interest for the present purposes, however, are the correlates between these T-domain measures of delay of gratification and the R-domain personality ratings previously described. For the candy acquisition scores, at both ages 3.5 and 4.5 years, there were fewer significant personality correlates for either boys or girls than would have been expected on the basis of chance. The specific CCQ item "Is unable to delay gratification" correlated .09 and .11 (nonsignificant and in the wrong direction) with candy acquisition scores for the boys and girls respectively at age 3.5; at age 4.5, the correlations were, respectively, .20 and .11 for boys and for girls.

For the gift delay time scores, however, at both ages 3.5 and 4.5, there were many and conceptually congruent correlates with the CCQ personality ratings. The specific CCQ item "Is unable to delay gratification" correlated −.43 in the sample of boys and −.50 in the sample of girls at age 3.5; at age 4.5, the corresponding correlations were −.30 and −.35 for the boys and girls, respectively. For illustrative purposes, Table 2.7 represents all the CCQ-item correlates of gift delay time for the boys and girls at age 3.5. The pattern of correlates at age 4.5, when the procedure was repeated, is not quite so strong although it is by no means weak.

Although there are some interesting and perhaps suggestive discrepancies between boys and girls in their respective patterns of CCQ correlates with gift delay time, overall there appears to be good correspondence. A richly elaborated picture of the boy and of the girl who is unable to delay gratification is to be found in Table 2.7, a constellation of findings that suggests the gift delay time procedure is indeed "getting at" the concept intended. However, why did not the candy acquisition procedure, also carefully designed and previously used, fail to generate the correlates needed to support its aspired to validity? We do not really know, although we have some conjectures on the matter. For the moment, however, the only point requiring recognition is that this kind of anomaly, of

TABLE 2.7
CCQ Correlates of Gift Delay Time in 3-Year-Old Boys and in Girls

Correlation in sample of boys[a]	Correlation in sample of girls[a]	CCQ Item
.19	.26b	Is considerate of other children
−.34b	−.09	Seeks physical contact with others
.32b	.20	Tends to keep thoughts and feelings to self
.08	.29b	Develops genuine and close relationships
−.19	−.37a	Has transient interpersonal relationships
−.31b	−.43a	Attempts to transfer blame to others
.35b	.08	Shows concern for moral issues
−.23	−.26b	Expresses negative feelings directly and openly
−.37a	−.25c	Tries to take advantage of others
.47a	.12	Uses and responds to reason
−.49a	.12	Is visibly deviant from peers
.32b	.21	Is protective of others
.35b	.08	Shows a recognition of others' feelings; empathic
−.28b	−.05	Cries easily
−.38a	−.14	Is restless and fidgety
.27b	.15	Is inhibited and constricted
−.08	.26b	Is resourceful in initiating activities
.35b	.07	Tends to withdraw or disengage self under stress
−.30b	.01	Tends to go to pieces under stress
−.42a	−.23c	Has rapid shifts in mood; emotionally labile
−.38a	.20	Is afraid of being deprived; concerned about getting enough
−.36a	−.05	Is jealous and envious of others
.19	−.40a	Tends to dramatize or exaggerate mishaps
−.09	−.36a	Tends to be judgmental of others' behavior
−.33b	−.13	Has a rapid personal tempo
−.43a	−.50a	Is unable to delay gratification
.35b	.26b	Is attentive and able to concentrate
.39a	.34b	Is planful, thinks ahead
.01	.30b	Daydreams, tends to get lost in reverie
.22	.40a	Becomes strongly involved in what (s)he does
−.30b	.03	Is a talkative child
−.30b	−.34a	Is aggressive (physically or verbally)
−.23	−.26b	Is stubborn
−.36a	−.15	Emotional reactions are inappropriate
−.18	−.33b	Overreacts to minor frustrations; easily irritated
.34b	.15	Has an active fantasy life
.33b	.21	Is shy and reserved; makes social contacts slowly
.37a	.33b	Is reflective; thinks and deliberates before acting

[a]Correlations followed by an a are significant at the .01 level; if followed by a b, at the .05 level; if followed by a c, at the .10 level. One hundred CCQ items were evaluated for significance.

erratic relationships between R data and T data, arises often, and because we have shown R data can function impressively well, the fault must lie with the insufficiencies of T data.

Having shown that within the domains of R- and S-personality data, given good methodology, indisputably strong relationships exist and that within the domain of T-personality data, the evidence for lawfulness and coherence is far more difficult to attain, it is now incumbent on us to consider why this pattern of law and disorder exists and what strategies are likely to extend the realm of coherence so as to include as well the domain of T data.

Space constraints prevent a proper discussion here of the implications of the kind of data I have reported. There is one large recognition, however, to be declared quickly and without elaboration that I should like the reader to carry away.

We have seen that strong and coherent relationships can abound in the R and S domains. In an extended version of this essay, I will be bringing together some further relationships between, on the one hand, the R and S domains and, on the other, real-life indicators (the L domain), such as divorce, accident proneness, alcoholism, bachelorhood, grade-point average, voting tendencies, parental qualities, and the like. The number of nature of these relationships conjoined with the general inability to relate real-life indices to T data is certain to lend further urgency to the need to closely study why it is that psychologists have fared so badly in their T domain research.

In the meanwhile, it would be a misreading of the state of the evidence to conclude that the often (but not always) poor lawfulness observed within the T domain is immediate evidence for an exquisite behavioral discriminativeness of individuals within situations, a discriminativeness that defies conceptual encompassment. Perhaps this theoretical anticipation regarding the T domain, articulated currently by Mischel (Chapter 25) and by Cronbach (1975), will gain support in time. That time, however, is not until T research alerted to the requirements of measure reliability, cogent operationalization, and contextual dimensionalization has failed.

For me, endless fact gathering in the T domain without the possibility of finding generalizations to subsume these facts is a dismal prospect for the science of psychology. At the present juncture of personality psychology, I believe so much has not been done or done well that a foreclosure on efforts to seek lawfulness based on the results so far achieved by T-domain research is simply premature. "Objectivity" alone is not enough. T-domain research in personality, to become pursuasive, must achieve psychological depth and technical sophistication in a number of ways, some of which already have been mentioned on preceding pages.

My own wager on the future is that the personality coherence observed within and between the R and S (and L) domains will, as well, be found when T data are well created.

3

There's More to Iago than
Meets the Eye:
A Clinical Account of Personal
Consistency

Kenneth S. Bowers

University of Waterloo

It is sometimes difficult to distinguish a phenomenon from its explanation. For example, the acronym ESP designates not simply a phenomenon but an extra-sensory interpretation of it. In an earlier day, mesmerism referred not only to a dramatic and observable seizure or swoon but also to a magnetic explanation of the so-called mesmeric "crisis." When a phenomenon and its explanation are more or less indissolubly linked, a successful critique of the latter can discredit the former as well. For example, when the Franklin Commission conclusively demonstrated the inadequacy of a magnetic explanation of mesmerism, the phenomenon of mesmerism was also discredited (Bowers, 1976).

In the current trait–situationism controversy (Mischel, 1973a; Bowers, 1973; Wachtel, 1973a; Bem & Allen, 1974) we have something like a confusion of a phenomenon and its explanation. Traits (and/or dispositions) are generally regarded as explanations of personal consistency, and a concerted attack on this trait explanation (Bandura & Walters, 1963; Mischel, 1968; Peterson, 1968) has largely discredited the very consistency that traits purportedly explained. Consequently, in place of the trait-determined personal consistency of yore, we now have environmentally determined behavioral specificity (Bowers, 1973).

Surely, however, there is something wrong here. Consistency *qua* phenomenon does not disappear simply because a trait account of it has been found wanting (cf. Wallach & Leggett, 1972). Assuming for the moment that personal consistency is not simply an illusion, the question becomes what should *count* as consistency in personality and behavior, and how much of it is there?

CONSISTENCY AND CHANGE: SOME EXAMPLES

Simply asking this question suggests that what constitutes consistency (and change) in personality and behavior is not self-evident but requires a decision. Of course if such decisions were easy to make to everyone's satisfaction, they would have been made long ago. It is clear, however, that there are some important unresolved issues at the level of the phenomenon to be explained. Consider, for example, the important contributions of Moos. In one study, Moos (1969) and his collaborators focused on topographic features of behavior, such as talking and smoking, and found, not surprisingly, that their subjects did not talk or smoke across all situations — that smoking, for example, was more apt to occur in some circumstances than others. Bem and Allen (1974), in contrast, began with topographically different behaviors (e.g., promptness in submitting evaluations and expedition in completing homework assignments) and found considerable evidence that some people are consistently conscientious.

Now it seems clear to me that Bem and Allen would have been able to find consistency in some of Moos' subjects, and that in turn, Moos would have no problem in finding evidence for change (specificity) in Bem and Allen's subjects. If that is true, however, it is partly because the two sets of investigators are concerned with different phenomena. Bem and Allen are less interested than Moos in the changing topography of behavior and are more interested in the consistency expressed by different situation-specific behaviors.

Consider another example. In his 1968 critique of personality traits, Mischel specifically (if somewhat qualifiedly) excepted intellectual behavior from total situational specificity. Yet clearly, a person of even modest intelligence changes his answers from one WAIS item (i.e., situation) to another. Furthermore, the testee (and not the environment) gets credit for correct answers. Evidently, variability and change in test behavior reflects an inferred characteristic (intelligence) that is considerably more stable than the behavior by which it is revealed.

The notion that variability in behavior expresses an underlying consistency is rather nicely illustrated in an engaging book by William Powers (1973a), entitled *Behavior: The control of perception.* Take two rubber bands and tie them together. Have Joe hook his forefinger inside one rubber band, and have Jane hook her finger in the other rubber band. The knot joining the two rubber bands is now centered between the two facing participants. Then whisper instructions into Joe's ear. Jane is then told to pull and otherwise move her end of the rubber band in a way that permits her to figure out what Joe has secretly been told to do. This "game" situation leads to a lot of stretching and tugging by both parties, and what is generally noted by Jane is that Joe moves his hand in an opposite and equal direction vis a vis Jane's hand movement. Thus, if Joe moves his hand back and to the right, Jane moves her hand back and to her right. If Jane moves her hand left forward, so does Joe. Impressed with such clear evidence of her own stimulus control over Joe's responses, Jane generally

concludes that Joe has been told to move his hand symmetrically vis-à-vis her own hand movement. In so saying, Jane may be accurately describing Joe's outward behavior, but she has *not* identified what Joe has been told to do. In fact Joe was instructed to keep the knot joining the rubber bands directly over an inconspicuous spot on the table. To do so, of course, Joe must vary his overt behavior in a way that directly opposes Jane's movements. In other words, Joe's variable hand movements conserve a relatively inconspicuous but constant relationship between the spot and the knot.

That variability in overt behavior preserves an underlying stability is a key if implicit assumption of those people espousing personal consistency, whereas advocates of specificity are ordinarily more impressed with the conspicuously changing topography of visible behavior. These two orientations to the study of personality are rooted in quite different assumptions about nature and how it gets known. Consequently, the next section of this chapter briefly considers two different approaches to the problem of "objective" knowledge. Subsequently, we shall consider the implications of our analysis of objectivity vis-à-vis the study of personality.

OBJECTIVITY AND ABSTRACTION

In more behavioral or situationist approaches to psychology, the term "objective" typically refers to an observable property of the world. According to this view, such observed features provide a nonproblematic basis for objective knowledge. It follows, then, that close and controlled observation yields a veridical, i.e., an objective account of nature. To the extent that inference and abstraction replace observed "facts" in our knowledge claims, the account is more problematic and less objective. For example, references to the frequency of bar presses presumably provide a more "objective" account of behavior than inferential and abstract references to ego control.

The assumption that objectivity flows naturally from close and controlled observation of nature is not so much incorrect as incomplete. The mandate to observe closely and carefully becomes suddenly mute just when we need to know what it is about nature that is important to observe. Decisions on that critical question seem to derive from some prior understanding of the phenomenon in question.

A particularly instructive example of how close observation is insufficient for an objective view of the world involves the switch from an Aristotelian to a Galilean account of a bob swinging free at the end of a string. According to Aristotle's theory of inertia (Butterfield, 1957; Kuhn, 1962), all terrestial bodies come naturally to rest as close to the center of the earth as they can get. By this understanding, a bob swinging at the end of a string was simply falling with difficulty. Constrained by the string, the bob achieved its natural state of rest only after a great deal of motion and time had elapsed. By this Aristotelian view, the critical feature to observe in this complex of events was the length of time it took for the swinging bob to reach its natural resting state.

When Galileo observed a bob swinging at the end of a string, he saw something quite different. Instead of seeing a stone seeking its natural state of rest, he saw a pendulum, that is, a body that almost succeeded in repeating the same motion over and over again. Galileo thus intuited that a body in motion tended to stay in motion and, from this perspective, the important feature was the time per swing.

According to a noted historian of science (Butterfield, 1957), this shift from an Aristotelian to a Galilean view of a swinging bob was one of the most important events in the history of science. Yet:

> It was supremely difficult to escape from the Aristotelian doctrine by merely observing things more closely.... In fact, the modern law of inertia is not the thing you would discover by mere photographic methods of observation – it required a different kind of thinking-cap, a transposition in the mind of the scientist himself. (Butterfield, 1957, pp. 16–17)

The point is, of course, that a phenomenon under consideration does not tell the scientist what to observe. Inevitably, therefore, our conceptualization of a phenomenon, however implicit or unarticulated, has a profound and tenacious impact on what we decide to measure and record. In other words, what man brings to nature in the form of intuition, ideas, and (pre)conceptions is as important to an objective understanding of the world as what nature presents to man (Polanyi, 1964). This must be in part what Bruner (1957) means by his felicitous phrase "going beyond the information given," and this process certainly involves an abstract attitude toward concrete phenomena. As we have already suggested, however, abstraction is often viewed as the natural antagonist of objectivity, and it is perhaps important to pause at this troublesome possibility.

Psychologists often regard abstraction as a summarizing, foreshortening operation. Thus, for Mischel (1973a), "Traits are constructs which are inferred or abstracted from behavior" (p. 262). Later on he states that "while the traditional personality paradigm views traits as the intrapsychic *causes* of behavioral consistency, the present position sees them as *summary terms* (labels, codes, organizing constructs) applied to observed behavior" (p. 264). In other words, a trait is a mere abstraction in the observer's head that summarizes the behavior of the person observed, and that serves as a convenient and conventional way of talking about concrete behavior. However, according to Mischel, these memory-based, abstracted traits distort as much as they describe the behavior which the observer has seen. This view implies that the concrete behavior observed is more objective than the observer's summarizing abstract of it, because after all, it is the world that is objective, and our subjective view of it can only introduce distortions.

I do not wish to dismiss this summarizing view of abstraction as incorrect, but I do wish to place it in tension with another view of abstraction. This second view maintains that abstraction is a *condition* for objectivity, not simply a distorted summary of "objective" facts. By this view, the scientist's powers of abstraction facilitate a deeper seeing, a more penetrating vision that goes beyond superficial appearances to the order underlying them. It is easiest to see my point here by remembering that a brain damaged person's loss of an abstract attitude (Goldstein & Scheerer, 1941) makes him or her more concrete but *less* objective in the way he or she understands and deals with the world. This illustration nicely (if implicitly) conveys that the word "objective" refers as much to a condition of a discerning person as it does to a property of the world he or she observes, and that powers of abstraction are presupposed in any attempt to view the world objectively. By this second view, therefore, abstraction allows one to reveal and probe reality, not simply to summarize it.

The difference between identifying objectivity with worldly appearances, on one hand, and with an abstract understanding of them, on the other, is neatly exemplified in the field of taxonomy.[1] The great taxonomist Linnaeus simply appealed to various morphological similarities in animals as the objective basis for his taxonomic categories. Indeed, these class-defining similarities, so persuasive to the eye, were what counted as "real" for Linnaeus. In fact, the taxonomic class to which an animal belonged was more "real" than any animal classified in it. Ironically, it was the relative immutability of these species categories that made it difficult for pre-Darwinian taxonomists to appreciate the orderly and evolutionary change in various animal species.

Darwin, in contrast, although seeing similarities and differences in animal morphology, was not seduced by them. In effect, he looked beyond such appearances and attempted to understand how they came about. Thus, according to Ghiselin (1969):

> Instead of finding patterns in nature and deciding that because of their conspicuousness they seem important, we discover the underlying mechanisms that impose order on natural phenomena, whether we see that order or not, and then derive the structure of our classification systems from this understanding. . . . Classification ceased to be merely descriptive and became explanatory. (p. 83)

The natural classification system that resulted was based on "propinquity of descent," and a species became a:

> population, a unit of evolution and of reproductive activity — a kind of social entity. It comprises all those biological individuals which exchange genetic material with one another. . . . It is thus an integrated unit of biological function, rather than a mere class of similar things.
>
> But to so define "species" requires a high level of *abstraction*. . . . (p. 90, emphasis added)

[1] In the comments that follow, I shall be drawing heavily on a book by Michael Ghiselin (1969), *The triumph of the Darwinian method.*

Several summarizing comments are in order here. Darwin's achievement was a penetrating insight into an order underlying and generating the observable similarities and differences in the animal (and plant) kingdom. The pre-Darwinian appeal to such topographic features as a satisfactory objective basis for taxonomic classification had evidently impeded a more abstract, that is to say, a more penetrating consideration regarding the significance and origins of the similarities and differences in question. Finally, it is clear that the concept of species, although abstract, depends on a relational and interactional pattern of concrete animal behavior, a point that will not be lost on us as we proceed.

IMPLICATIONS FOR PERSONALITY

We are now in a position to make several comments regarding current theoretical issues in personality.

A Contextual Account of Reality

Many psychologists are, like Linnaeus (and Othello), persuaded only by what meets the eye, identifying it with the "objectively real," little appreciating that nature is more like Shakespeare's Iago — sans malice. According to this "Iago view," it is simply naive to appeal to observed features of behavior as the final court regarding an objective account of nature (or of personality). This appeal tends to presuppose a clean dichotomy between the "objective" world of behavioral facts and the subjective way we interpret them. Such a distinction is convenient and even important to make for many purposes, but it is misleading to imply that objectivity about personality and behavior depends on the "immaculate perception" of a concrete behavioral datum unimpregnated by human thought (Bowers, 1973; T. Mischel, 1971). Such an "innocent" realism seems to provide a safe harbor from the successive waves of "grand" personality theories — but the safety is in many ways more illusory than real. (See in this context recent articles that indicate problems with observer reliability even when rating physicalistic features of behavior, e.g., Johnston & Bolstad, 1973; Romanczyk, Kent, Diament, & O'Leary, 1973.) Specific behaviors are not only engendered by specific contexts, they must be understood in terms of the particular context and person under consideration — and such understanding oftentimes requires going beyond the immediate situational and behavioral givens (Holt, 1961; Wilson, 1973).

Consider, for example, a woman whose presenting complaint of agoraphobia has rendered her a virtual prisoner in her own home. Suppose she further states that the sexual relationship with her husband is virtually nonexistent. Two such unusual facts about the same person are apt to be related, yet it is unclear what the connection between them may be. In the course of discussion, it is perhaps further revealed that the patient has a history of premarital promiscuity about which she feels considerable shame and guilt. Suddenly, the agoraphobia seems understandable as a defense against the possibility of further sexual misadventures that may exacerbate current feelings of shame, unworthiness, and depression. Although this understanding may be limited or simply wrong, its plausibility is enhanced significantly when the patient rather hesitantly but suggestively remarks that the therapist's interest in her is sure to wane unless he receives something more than money for his time.

Each such incident and revelation seems to fit an emerging pattern of sexual conflict that is expressed in a variety of apparently different behaviors. As Wilson (1973) phrases it, "the observer necessarily constructs an underlying pattern that serves as the essential context for seeing what the situations and actions are, while these same situations and actions are a necessary resource for seeing what the context is" (p. 704). An objective account thus begins to emerge out of a pattern of interconnected evidence that points beyond itself to the order and organization underlying it.

The problem of discerning such patterns vis-à-vis a therapy patient is similar to that of an archeologist confronted with a bewildering variety of bones and teeth from extinct protomen. After long and laborious study, the various characteristics of the fossils begin to suggest a pattern and organization from which certain reasonable inferences can be made about the structure and life style of our ancient predecessors. And "the more evidence that can be assembled leading toward one kind of creature, the more likely it becomes that further evidence will fit" (Howell, 1970, p. 38). Thus, as the evidence about our agoraphobic accumulates, it becomes less and less likely that her presenting complaint is finally to be accounted for in terms of some simple history of conditioning.

Of course, a clinician or archeologist must remain open to the possibility that he or she is wrong. However, the attempt to avoid error by a simple enumeration or description of bones or behavior will not ultimately lead to a more objective account of reality. Objectivity involves discerning how the immediately given is embedded in a continuously evolving pattern and organization that is as much inferred as observed. Admittedly, this is a hazardous enterprise, but it is fatuous to suppose that serious inquiry could be otherwise.

The Subtle Reciprocity of Evidence and Conception

In somewhat different ways, the traditional trait and experimental approaches to personality tend to impose an order on nature by constraining behavioral diversity, instead of by discerning the order and organization in the diverse and variable behavior or particular persons. For example, the trait view typically presents a standardized (i.e., constraining) protocol on which people respond variously. By limiting the study of personality to the ordering of different people on a particular trait or personality dimension, the order underlying a particular person's diverse behavior and functioning can remain quite obscure.

Two people scoring high on trait anxiety can differ profoundly regarding the frequency with which they are exposed to threatening situations, how effectively they deal with anxiety, their typical mode of anxiety expression, and so on. Differences of this kind can make all the difference regarding how two highly anxious persons manage their lives.

In an experimental paradigm, in contrast, artfully arranged circumstances are devised in the hope that all the subjects in the experiment can be constrained to behave in the same predicted manner. Quite reasonably, a successful experimental outcome is attributed to how the environment is organized and arranged. Indeed, to the extent that everyone in an experiment behaves in nearly the same way, one can attribute little, if anything, to a particular person in the treatment group (Kelley, 1973). By contrast, in more permissive circumstances, planned constraints are less pressing and a person can engender as well as respond to an interpersonal environment in a way that is discernibly characteristic of him (Wachtel, 1973a). Hence, we can more readily attribute a pattern of emerging interactive behavior to the *person's* psychological and behavioral organization (cf. Raush, 1969).

It is at the level of more naturalistic observation, therefore, that personal consistencies begin to emerge. Over a variety of novel situations, Bill may typically hold back, letting others go first, discovering vicariously the consequences of involvement. Jill, in contrast, may jump into novel situations with both feet, apparently relishing the opportunity to see for herself just what surprises are in store.

In no time at all, however, problems arise. Should we describe Bill as reflective and realistically cautious, or is he instead vigilant and untrusting? Is Jill impulsive and uncautious, or trusting and accepting? We can speedily conceptualize too far beyond the evidence and, when we do so, it is generally in terms of some favored construct system or psychological theory whose hold on us exceeds our grasp on reality. At some point, unless we are very careful, theory and abstract conceptualization can begin to dominate our thinking and perception, so that everything we observe collapses into ready made conceptual categories. This tendency to "give up" on reality while "giving in" to theory provides ample grounds for the frequent charge that characteristics claimed for the person perceived actually reflect more faithfully the implicit personality theory of the observer (Cronbach, 1955; Mischel, 1968).

Make no mistake, this tendency constitutes a formidable epistemological dilemma. In a trenchant comment about psychoanalytic research, Meehl (1973) poses the difficulty as follows: "How do we get the advantages of having a skilled observer, who knows what to listen for and how to classify it, without having the methodological disadvantage that anyone who is skilled in this way has been theoretically brainwashed in the course of his training?" (p. 115). The problem is of course not unique to psychoanalysis but is endemic to all knowing. However, it seems especially problematic for the social sciences.

Perhaps we can never escape the conundrum altogether, but surely we can avoid cynical or silly solutions to it. It is cynical to suppose that the knower's conceptual framework is a prison that necessarily and inevitably bars access to nature – a position recently popularized by Kuhn (1962).[2] Nature and man's conception of it have conjugal rights, and from that turbulent union issues forth the possibility of warranted claims about nature (and persons), not simply clever and persuasive propaganda (see criticisms of Kuhn's position, e.g., Lakatos, 1970; Scheffler, 1967; Shapere, 1964). And as I have argued earlier and elsewhere (Bowers, 1973), it is silly to suppose that conception can be avoided as mind continuously penetrates nature – seeking her out at the joints (see also Kaplan, 1964; especially Chapter 4).

Part of the solution to this epistemological dilemma surely inheres in appreciating its existence, continuously reaffirming our commitment to understanding nature, and keeping our conceptual framework corrigible to evidence. Johann Kepler, for example, was finally "forced" by evidence to give up his theological attachment to the perfect symmetry of spheres and circles in accounting for planetary motion, and he reluctantly replaced circular with oval orbits.[3] Darwin, for his part, resisted his own conceptual framework by keeping a special notebook of observations that violated his expectancies. Behavioral scientists and clinicians would surely be well advised to emulate Darwin in this practice.

In short, we cannot escape conception, nor can we afford to be imprisoned by it. (There is something vaguely reminiscent in this seeming paradox of Bohr's famous comment that the opposite of a profound truth is also true; Holton, 1973, pp. 148–149.) Surely, progress in science depends in part on successfully negotiating this difficult dilemma, and in judging persons some similar sort of balancing act is required.

Consistency, Specificity, and Levels of Organization

I have argued that "objectivity" refers to a condition of the observer as much as it refers to topographic features of the world. More specifically, objectivity involves embedding observed features of the world into an emerging pattern or organization of which they form a part. This approach to objectivity has some significance for the specificity—consistency issue in personality that should now be made explicit.

---

[2] "We may, to be more precise, have to relinquish the notion, explicit or implicit, that changes of paradigm carry scientists and those who learn from them closer and closer to the truth" (Kuhn, 1962, p. 169).

[3] According to Koestler (1964), this shift was a personally traumatic one for Kepler:

It destroyed the dream of the "harmony of the spheres", which lay at the origin of the whole quest. At times [Kepler] felt like a criminal, or worse: a fool. All he had to say in his own defence was: "I have cleared the Augean stables of astronomy of cycles and spirals, and left behind me only a single cartful of dung." (p. 129)

According to the view being forwarded here, consistency and specificity are not exclusive features of personality and behavior but find their respective places in an emerging pattern of person—environment interchanges. For example, the fashion plate who is always changing clothes to fit the specific occasion is being consistently fashionable. Such a consistency may reflect an overdriven striving to be socially acceptable, which may also be expressed by topographically quite different behavior, viz., the person's coy and flirtatious manner. This need for approval may, pending other behavioral evidence, suggest that the person is very insecure regarding his worth and personal identity. Just where one stops resolving apparent differences (i.e., behavioral specificities) into superordinate similarities (i.e., personal consistency) depends in large part on one's purposes, not upon an appeal to one, indubitably "real" level of behavior. If one's purposes involve therapeutically changing a specific problem (such as obesity), it may be unnecessary to become directly involved with the patient's sense of isolation and low self-esteem. Indeed, success in treating the obesity may indirectly lead to dramatic amelioration of the latter problems. For didactic purposes, however, it may be important to make the connection between obesity and low self-esteem explicit, the better to distinguish this patient's problem from another obese person, for whom fat functions largely to placate a husband threatened by having a wife who is attractive to other men.

Recognizing the coexistence of specificity and consistency at different levels of organization highlights a sort of expositional sleight of hand in the literature, wherein the consistency of *personality* is often juxtaposed with and discredited by references to the situational specificity of *behavior.* One simply cannot automatically and uncritically assume that behavioral specificity excludes a less conspicuous but coexisting personal consistency (Alker, 1972).

Consider in this context Mischel's (1973b) comment that "people may proceed quickly beyond the observation of *some* consistency which does exist in behavior to the attribution of greater perceived consistencies which they construct" (pp. 341–342). Surely Mischel is correct in pointing out the possibility of attributing too much consistency to people; but surely he is incorrect in the implication that the only place to look for consistency is in overt behavior. As I have already argued, a variety of different, context-specific behaviors can reflect consistency at a higher level of organization. To reserve the word "consistency" to describe topographically similar behavior vastly underestimates the degree of consistency that can reasonably be attributed to people. Of this more later.

If it is true that topographically different behaviors can express one individual's personal consistency, it is even more obviously the case that two quite different people can behave in topographically similar ways. People of all sorts eat lunch, make love, brush their teeth, and go to work — irrespective of how they respond to the Rorschach. For many psychologists, this state of affairs seems to undermine the very need for a "personality organization": Why should something so particular (and invisible) be required to account for observable behavior so generally characteristic of different people; some combination of context and role prescription seems sufficient to this end.

Yet, the way a person performs a common behavior is sometimes quite revealing. One person ordinarily eats and makes love fastidiously; another person is given to gluttony in both circumstances. The more idiosyncratically expressive a common behavior is, the less one can attribute its performance solely to the context and/or to role demands; it is precisely the expressive aspects of a person's behavior that often seem most characteristic of him or her and most attributable to a relatively stable personality and behavioral organization.

However, it is not only the expressive aspects of behavior that are stabilized by being embedded in an internalized organization and system of control; more emphatically adaptive behaviors are also subject to the same internal guidance. This point has been rediscovered almost by default, i.e., by the insufficiencies of external control over behavior. It has slowly dawned on us, for example, that the ABA design (see, e.g., Leitenberg, 1973), although demonstrating the ability of external contingencies to minimize maladaptive behavior during treatment, has also demonstrated the *ineffectiveness* of such "objective" external controls to create therapeutic changes that endure beyond treatment termination. A host of recent research has confirmed that explicit external control over behavior can undermine the behavior's posttreatment persistence (e.g., Bowers, 1975; Levine & Fasnacht, 1974; Kazdin & Bootzin, 1972). A particularly dramatic illustration of this problem is evident in an as yet unpublished study on female adolescent delinquents. Nine months after they left a training school, girls who had participated in a token economy had worse after-care reports and a higher recidivism rate than matched controls, and they were much worse in these respects than a matched group of girls who had received a therapeutic regimen emphasizing peer instead of token control (Ross, Meichenbaum, & Bowers, unpublished manuscript, 1974). Results such as these underline the wisdom of Strupp's (1973) comment that: "The problem of how external controls are transformed into internal controls is one of the most basic issues of psychotherapy as well as child rearing . . . " (p. 7).

Implied in the preceding paragraph is the importance of an internal (and relatively invisible) organization that guides even "normal" context-specific behavior. Historically, the situationist's failure to recognize the importance of an intrapsychic organization as a stabilizing influence on behavior has its counterpart in the dynamic psychologist's underestimation of how the environment can modify a person's ongoing behavior. Fortunately, both traditions seem to be alerted to the crackers in their bed and a reconciliation of sorts may be in the offing.

An Interactional View

The key word summarizing this reconciliation is "interaction" (Ekehammar, 1974; Endler, 1975). This one word serves more than one purpose, however, and it is important to distinguish two quite different meanings of the term. One meaning of interaction has a statistical heritage. When the Subject × Treatment interaction in an analysis of variance design is large, the generality of main effects is obviously qualified. This statistical notion of interaction, although recognizing the predictive limits of traits and situations taken alone, nevertheless maintains intact what Overton (1973) has called the *additive paradigm.* According to this view, interaction refers to something that various antecedent variables do with each other to help produce an experimental outcome. Notice that in this additive paradigm the investigative emphasis is on various groups of individuals confronted with various levels of treatment (although the group data may well enhance the predictability of a particular subject receiving a particular treatment).

The *interactive paradigm* (Overton, 1973) is quite a different story. In this second paradigm, interaction refers to something that the organism and his environment do with each other. The emphasis is on behavioral feedback as an important determinant of perception and action (Powers, 1973a, b). Because the organism affects the environment affecting the organism in ongoing sequences of exchange, the interaction paradigm has little truck for hard and fast distinctions between antecedent conditions and behavioral outcomes. Behavioral outcomes are the antecedents for subsequent perception and behavior. Moreover, the investigative focus in this paradigm is on the individual's adaptation to the world, (although close study of a particular person's adaptations may considerably enhance the understanding of other similar people).

It is obvious that both the so-called additive and interactive paradigms have their adherents and their place in psychology. However, it appears that even those long wedded to the additive paradigm are beginning to have some second thoughts regarding its relevance to the complexity of human behavior (e.g., Cronbach, 1975; McGuire, 1973), and there seems to be a growing awakening to the virtues of the interactive paradigm. The primary insight of this latter view is a recognition that people not only respond to environments but also create the environments to which they in turn respond (Wachtel, 1973a; Bowers, 1973; Patterson & Reid, 1968). A particularly dramatic example of this tendency for people to create their environments has been reported by Gil (1970). This investigator cited a clinical report suggesting that at least some "battered children" are characterized by constant fussing and a particularly grating cry. By way of confirmation, in a large-scale epidemiological survey (Gil, 1970) found that 24.5% of battered children were marked by persistent behavioral atypicality, e.g., hyperactivity, and high annoyance potential. Clearly, this is not a reason for a normal parent to abuse his or her child, but such a pattern of behavior might elicit aggression from an undercontrolled, highly stressed parent. Two other clinical findings support the notion that some battered children may provoke parental attacks: (a) Frequently, only one child in a family is abused, and (b) some of these battered children, as they move from one foster home to another, are subjected to repeated abuse, even though the foster parents have had a "clean" record up to the time they have received the child in question. In some cases of child abuse, therefore, "deviance in the child was at least as substantial a factor in explaining the incidents as was deviance in the parent" (Bell, 1974, p. 6).

Watzlawick, Beavin, and Jackson (1967) have developed a whole theory of communication around the interactive sequences in which people become enmeshed. They provide the following instructive example:

> Suppose a couple have a marital problem to which he contributes passive withdrawal, while her 50 per cent is nagging criticism. In explaining their frustrations, the husband will state that withdrawal is his only *defence against* her nagging, while he will label this explanation a gross and willful distortion of what "really" happens in their marriage: namely, that she is critical of him *because* of his passivity. Stripped of all ephemeral and fortuitous elements, their fights consist in a monotonous exchange of the messages "I withdraw because you nag" and "I nag because you withdraw" (p. 56). (See also Haley, 1963, and Carson, 1969, for a similar interactional analysis.)

The prototype of such circular interpersonal behavior is the paranoid individual, who accurately perceives that he or she is surrounded by angry people but who remains unaware of the extent to which he or she creates this angry surround. A really "talented" paranoid can engender uncanny feelings of alarm and anger in the most benign interlocutor, and for this reason, such a person can be very difficult even for a skilled therapist to deal with.

It is no accident that all the above illustrations are derived from clinical contexts. Clinicians have been way ahead of academic psychologists in recognizing the pervasiveness of interbehavior patterns that typify an individual's conduct. Indeed, it is one of the ironies of twentieth century psychology that scientific investigators of human behavior have been in significant ways *less* empirical than clinicians by being more experimental in their approach. Heavy emphasis on classical experimental methodology (to wit, the presentation of a standard situation to all persons in a treatment group) has made it almost impossible to see, let alone investigate, the standard sort of situations that a person ordinarily generates for himself (Bowers, 1973; Wachtel, 1973a). In other words, the always critical decision regarding what to observe has been (implicitly) determined more by methodological preferences than by a genuine concern for how people ordinarily function.

Fortunately, this emphasis on classical experimental procedures is currently being balanced by a more eclectic approach to personality and behavior (e.g., Block, 1971; Lewis & Rosenblum, 1974; Willems & Raush, 1969). One of the crucial features of this "new look" in personality research involves an investigative focus on the patterning and organization of an individual's behavior over time. The time frame can vary enormously from a few minutes' observation of a subject's interchange with his environment, to genuinely longitudinal studies of many years' duration. Interestingly enough, the importance of time has also been propounded in recent archeological studies of man. Marshack (1972) has emphasized that the emerging ability to notate time and, therefore, to think in terms of seasons and places not immediately present was even more important to man's evolutionary advance than toolmaking. If thinking in time was so important to man's evolution, then surely it is important to include time-ordered behavioral patterns in our psychological study of man (Carlson, 1971).

It is true that B. F. Skinner has long espoused a time-course behavioral analysis on single organisms, but he has done so in highly simplified environments in which the effective response options are fixed by a *deus ex machina,* thereby limiting the subject's ability to engender environments characteristic of him or her. The interactional approach, in contrast, focuses precisely on the (unprogrammed) effects that the subject ordinarily engenders from his or her environment.

Although the study of dyads *per se* is often identified with an interactional approach (e.g., Secord & Backman, 1961), it is perhaps important to note that the interactional paradigm does not necessarily limit investigative focus to the study of dyads as an end in itself. Instead, the study of dyads can be in the service of understanding a particular individual. After all, a person is more enduring than any dyadic relationship he or she enters into, and ultimately the various dyads he or she generates and maintains often reveal a pattern of personal consistency that may be difficult to appreciate if the person's behavior in only one dyad is investigated. For example, knowing that a baby has been battered ordinarily reflects badly only on his or her parents. Knowing that this same child is battered by a succession of foster parents begins to refocus our interest on enduring characteristics of the child as someone who has a consistently adverse impact on his or her caretakers. Moreover, if a policeman is charged with police brutality, it can be difficult to determine the complaint's warrant. However, if such charges are leveled at the same policeman with disproportionate frequency, it may mean that he consistently engenders imprudent behavior from his antagonists — behavior for which he is vigilant, and to which he overresponds (Edward Renner, personal communication, 1974). In other words, enduring characteristics of the policeman are revealed in an emerging pattern of untoward behavior vis-à-vis the citizenry.

This chapter began with a quest for personal consistency, and the above comments and examples have implied that such consistency is perhaps most apparent in concrete interpersonal behavior. It was difficult for psychology to appreciate such consistency as long as it assumed a passive organism that only reacted to externally imposed forces (Overton & Reese, 1973). Like Aristotle, who thought bobs were naturally at rest, we were prevented from adopting a more Galilean view that people (like pendulums) continuously succeed in almost repeating themselves.

Block on Consistency

I have argued that personal consistency is a fact of life, and that it can be discerned in an accumulation of context-specific behaviors. The questions remain: How much consistency is there? And how is the answer to that question best (i.e., most objectively) determined? There may be better answers to both questions than those offered by Jack Block (1971) in his excellent book *Lives through time,* but I am unaware of them. Because I consider Block's methodology and results to be a major contribution to the study of personality, I should like to dwell on his contribution briefly.

Basically, Block employed a Q-sort methodology to describe each of more than 150 subjects (participants in the Oakland Growth and Berkely Guidance Studies) at three checkpoints in their lives, viz., at junior high school (JHS), senior high school (SHS), and in their middle thirties. Because Block's association with the two longitudinal studies began long after their inception, he had to deal with data collected by his predecessors, which meant there was heterogenous data for different subjects seen at the same age and for the same subject at different ages. A vast array of data — from news clippings, to teacher reports, to a synopsis of a 12-hour interview (obtained only when subjects were adults), to performance on standardized tests — served as grist for a judge's forced-normal Q sort of each subject in the investigation. However, a different set of judges used different data to Q sort the same subject at the JHS, SHS, and adult checkpoints. Consequently, only the subject and the Q-sort items themselves were continuously represented throughout the course of the study.

It is the adroit harnessing of clinical acumen by this Q-sort technique that is responsible for the success of Block's ambitious venture. The judges, for example, could use their clinical skills to evaluate whether a particular datum was of superficial or probing importance to an understanding of the subject at hand. The business of separating the wheat from the chaff is terribly complex (and hazardous), but it seems to involve letting what is now background data emerge into focus — informed by its embeddeness in a particular context and enriching the context into which it again fades — as yet another background feature comes into focus against a now more richly textured backdrop. For example, knowing that a subject dropped out of college is evaluated against a backdrop of whether he or she did so solely for financial reasons or to pursue a conflicting interest, such as drama. The decision to pursue thespian interests can in turn be judged against a backdrop of whether the decision was precipitate or long thought about and prepared for. If precipitate, the decision can be viewed against a background of other ill-considered ventures, which together convey an impression of a person bouncing erratically from one sudden interest to another — with typically little follow through and with no apparent concern for the likelihood of success. If this latter pattern emerges as somehow characteristic of the person, it can in turn be viewed against a background of inadequate parenting and discipline — and so on. In sum, a subject's status as a college dropout may be relatively uninformative about him or her *qua* person when viewed against a backdrop of financial hardship but fairly telling in the context of a tendency to make abrupt and frequently abortive life decisions.

Notice that this clinical decision about the importance of dropping out of college is different than simply entering the person into an IBM punch card as either a college graduate or dropout. The latter process does not avoid a decision somewhere along the line that education is a variable of potential interest, but it presupposes that such categorical information is equally important and probing for everyone. Such an assumption seems unlikely, even in a psychometrist's Camelot; in effect, it forces one into a normative instead of an idiographic approach to personality.

The Q-sort technique, in contrast, permits judges to proceed "from an *ipsative* frame of reference, that is, the saliency or decisiveness of the variable in shaping or characterizing the subject's behavior was . . . the criterion for item placement" (Block, 1971, p. 46). The Q-sort items themselves were carefully preselected to include a broad range of human conduct and proclivities, and they were sufficiently abstract so that topographically different *behaviors* could exemplify the same behavior *pattern*. Examples of Q-sort items are: (a) is self-defeating; (b) tends to be rebellious and nonconforming; (c) behaves in an ethically consistent manner, is consistent with his own personal standards; (d) is emotionally bland, has flattened affect.

The Q-sort items require the judge to make a *series of decisions* about the person at hand, a process that involves determining the adequacy of each particular item as a "container" for the clinician's emerging understanding. I have emphasized the sequential aspect of the above process, because it differentiates the Q-sorting judge from a clinician who makes more singular and global judgments about a subject's personality organization. The danger in the latter approach is that the judge more readily "sees" the person in terms of a limited number of favored psychological constructs and dimensions. The Q-sort items "force" the clinician to consider a broad range of behavioral patterns and to decide on their relative importance vis-à-vis the person being judged. In effect, a personality organization emerges from the accumulation of interdependent decisions made about the subject under consideration.

Such a process seems to permit theory to remain more in the back of one's mind instead of in front of one's eyes. The subject's record of behavior and the judge's discernment of it are in better than ordinary balance, codetermining each decision and disallowing an overweening use of theory to organize the profusion of data at hand. The entire approach seems a remarkably adroit way of preserving objectivity without identifying the "objective state of affairs" with a simple description of topographic behavior. In effect, it permits the clinician to penetrate appearances by his emerging understanding of them. Caveat, Iago.

Perhaps the reader has already anticipated the outcome of Block's ambitious investigation. The interjudge reliability of the Q-sort composites averaged about .75. Corrected for attenuation, the average correlation of Q-sort composites from JHS to SHS was approximately .75; from SHS to adult years, the analogous correlation was about .55. Because the latter correlation was obtained over a span of 15 years or so, it represents an impressive degree of personal consistency over a considerable period of time. Of course, the .55 correlation represents an average figure across all the subjects in the experiment, so some people were much more consistent and some much less so from their SHS to their adult years.

CONCLUSION

Well — personal consistency has been empirically confirmed. It is amazing how badly we have needed Block's investigation as an antidote to specificity accounts of behavior. Which all goes to show that you can fool most psychologists some of the time, and some psychologists most of the time — but it is damn hard to fool a good poet any of the time. And Robert Frost was a very good poet indeed. He saw this entire consistency—specificity issue with glistening insight in a poem he wrote about a king who gave up his crown to travel with his son. Indeed, the king sold himself into slavery, so as to support his son's desire to be a poet. The (former) king ends up as a cook in the court of King Darius, whose ability to rule was seriously compromised by his less than kingly origins and attributes. In no time, the cook distinguishes himself in so many diverse ways that Darius is soon abject before him. Continually asking his slave for advice on matters of character, freedom, and creativity, Darius finally orders himself beheaded for ineptitude, and the cook replaces Darius on the throne. The punch line (and the title) of this poem is as good a place as any to end this chapter: "How hard it is to keep from being king when it's in you and in the situation."

4

Traits are Alive and Well

Seymour Epstein

University of Massachusetts, Amherst

It has recently become popular to disclaim the existence of traits or, at the very least, to note that their reliability is so low that they have little predictive value and therefore are not very useful constructs (cf. Bem, 1972; Mischel, 1968; Peterson, 1968). What is the case for and against traits? Traits refer to *relatively* stable behavioral dispositions that individuals exhibit over time. To take physical height as an example, people can be characterized as short, average, or tall because their height remains relatively stable over time compared to the variation in height among different people. If individuals were much shorter than others on one day and much taller on the next, height would be useless as a dimension for characterizing individuals. Likewise, height would be of no value in characterizing individuals if individuals remained as stable in height as they currently do but all individuals were of identical height. As it is, variations in height within individuals over days are in the realm of minute fractions of an inch, whereas variations among people are in the realm of inches and even feet. Consequently height is a very effective measure of individual differences. Note that to establish that such as the case it is necessary to consider an adequate sample of measurements over time as well as an adequate sample of individuals.

In real life, we identify people by their behavioral attributes much as we do by their physical attributes. If we failed to do so, or did so inaccurately, we would pay a serious price as we would not know what to expect of individuals and how to act toward them. We would be recognized as insensitive or as poor judges of character. Traits, as judged in everyday life, are informal assessments of relatively broad and enduring response dispositions, hopefully inferred from a large sample of behavior. They imply the ability to predict, on the average, what can be expected of an individual over many events. To the extent that an observer can make such assessments accurately, he or she has extremely important information. It is not necessary for the observer to predict accurately in every situation for his or her construct to be useful. There is a considerable payoff, whether one is gambling for money or taking one's chances in interpersonal relationships, in being right most of the time. I considered the woman I was to marry to be a warm, considerate person. This does not mean I believed she would never get angry at me or would never misunderstand me. If her behavior were that invariant across situations, she would be rigid, a robot. It does mean that according to my assessment, her behavior, in general, would place her high on these attributes, high enough to make me willing to gamble my future happiness on my estimates, which fortunately were accurate. Note that in essence what was involved was being exposed to a sample of events from which a prediction was made of the average behavior in another sample of events.

What is the argument against traits? It is that psychologists have not been able to demonstrate that traits have sufficient reliability for them to be useful in prediction. Bem (1972) has noted that measures of consistency in personality rarely produce correlations as high as .30, indicating that a measure on one occasion cannot be expected to account for as much as 10% of the variance of the same behavior on another occasion. How have psychologists gone about attempting to establish the reliability of traits, however? They have generally proceeded by computing correlation coefficients across a group of people tested on only two occasions. Even the most extreme trait theorist would consider it foolhardy to infer the existence of a trait from a single instance of behavior and to use such information to predict another single instance of behavior. It is therefore apparent that opponents of trait theory have been having a good time knocking about a straw man.

A further line of development, which has been equally misguided in its application to assessing the reliability of traits, has been the use of analysis of variance for apportioning total variance according to the contribution of individuals, situations, and their interaction. This is particularly unfortunate, as the studies that have used this technique have investigated a sample of more than two events. On the basis of these studies it has often been concluded that the percent of total variance contributed by individuals is relatively small, accounting for less than 10% of the total variance. From this, the further conclusion has been arrived at that the reliability of individual differences can be no greater than .32, as a correlation of .32 accounts for 10% of the variance. This conclusion is unwarranted, and is based on a misunderstanding of the statistics that are involved. A reliability coefficient amounts to a comparison of variance contributed by individual differences to error variance, not to total variance. By selecting the appropriate error term in an analysis of variance, when one is available, it is possible to obtain a measure of the reliability of individual differences, but this is not the procedure that has been followed. It is actually possible for the reliability of a measure of a trait to be perfect, that is, for the reliability coefficient obtained by the standard procedure of correlating one set of responses from a sample of individuals with another set of responses from the same individuals to be 1.00, and yet to have individual differences contribute only a small proportion of the total variance. This is so because percent of total variance is influenced by sources of variance other than individual differences, and to the extent that the sum of other sources are large, the contribution of individual differences must necessarily be small.[1]

In order to illustrate the above argument, let us examine, for the moment, an extremely reliable kind of behavior, running speed. Assume that a number of runners compete in several races of varying distances, from 100-yard to 500-yard dashes. Assume further that all runners retain the same rank order in all races. This allows perfect predictability of behavior solely on the basis of knowing who is the runner. Now, as can be expected for short races of the type involved, differences among runners for any race can be anticipated to vary, at most, by no more than a few seconds. No runner on any race is likely to beat another runner by anywhere near half the distance that is being run. Furthermore, consider that the mean time to run races of different lengths varies markedly. The mean time for running the 500-yard dash can be anticipated to be slightly more than five times the mean time for running the 100-yard dash. It is therefore apparent that the variance contributed by differences among situations, in this case races of different length, is far greater than the variance contributed by differences among runners within races. It may be concluded that despite perfect predictability of individuals in the absence of knowledge about events, the proportion of total variance contributed by individual differences can be made as large or as small as one wishes by simply manipulating the variation among events.[2]

It follows from the above discussion that an adequate test has yet to be made of the stability of personality. If our reasoning is correct, it should be possible to demonstrate that when correlations are based on single events, reliability coefficients tend to be low, in the vicinity of those reported in most studies to date. As the number of events is increased, reliability coefficients should increase,

---

[1] For other comments on the misuse of analysis of variance in the evaluation of behavioral consistency, see Golding (1975a), Magnusson (1974a), and Olweus (Chapter 17).

[2] It should be noted that the same argument can also be applied to interaction variance. So long as the interaction does not involve a crossover effect, in which individuals obtain higher scores than others in some situations and lower scores than others in other situations, it is possible for all individuals to maintain their rank order despite a large interaction effect. In fact, in the example given above, a large interaction would occur as the result of runners being more closely bunched in the shorter than in the longer races.

until the upper limit of the reliability of the measure under investigation is reached.

Data for evaluating the above deduction were fortunately available to me from a study I had conducted on emotions in everyday life. In that study, subjects kept records of their significant emotional experiences each day for a period of a month. In order to obtain information on the issue in question, events were treated as equivalent to items in a test, and split-half reliability coefficients were determined for all possible sample sizes. That is, first the data of Day 1 were correlated with the data of Day 2, then the mean of Days 1 and 3 was correlated with the mean of Days 2 and 4, and so on, until the mean of all the odd days was correlated with the mean of all the even days. This procedure made it possible to determine the extent to which the stability of individual behavior, as indicated by a correlation coefficient, was dependent on the size of the behavioral sample that had been obtained.

METHOD

Fourteen undergraduate men and 14 undergraduate women kept records of their most positive and negative emotional experience each day for 24–34 days. The record forms contained three sections. The first was a blank page for describing the incident in narrative form. The second page contained an adjective check list with 90 adjectives identifying different feeling states. Subjects responded to the adjectives by entering a double check for items that described their feeling state most accurately, a single check for items that were somewhat accurate, and a question mark for items that were questionably accurate. The remainder of the items were left blank. These responses, in effect, comprised a four-point rating scale. Scales were obtained for emotions by combining items into scales derived from a factor analysis of the adjectives. There were eight scales for negative emotions, each consisting of three or more adjectives. The scales were as follows: depressed, frightened, angry, tense, tired, unworthy, frustrated, and fragmented. The scales for positive emotions were: happy, secure–calm, energetic, kindly, worthy, and unified. As an example of the items comprising a scale, worthy contained the adjectives "adequate," "competent," "appreciated," "respected," "pleased-with-self," and "proud." The third section contained 66 response tendencies, or impulses, that had been extracted from the narratives of a preliminary study. Examples of items are "to gratify your senses, live life to the full," and "to be with a loved one." Subjects used the same four-point scale for impulses as they used for the adjectives to note the degree to which they had experienced a particular impulse. They also noted whether they carried out the impulse. The latter comprised items of "behavior carried out." Impulses, like adjectives, were grouped into scales by factor analysis. Following are the scales for impulses associated with negative experiences: *achievement, affiliation, aggression, problem solving, mental escape, physical escape, nurturance, counteraction, self-punishment, withdrawal, stimulus reduction,* and *tension discharge.* The scales for impulses following positive experiences were: *achievement, affiliation, problem solving, expression of exuberance, nurturance, pleasure seeking,* and *stimulus seeking.* The scales for "behavior carried out" were the same as those for impulses.

Narratives were scored by two judges for the stimulus or situational factors that appeared to them to be responsible for the emotions that were reported. An initial attempt was made to use Murray's system for scoring presses in TAT protocols. This was not entirely satisfactory and modifications had to be introduced. Even with the modifications interscorer reliability was low. A good part of the difficulty was that at the time interviews had been conducted to elucidate the narratives a scoring system had not been decided on and information that later turned out to be necessary was often unavailable. At one point, it was decided to abandon analysis of stimulus factors because of the low interscorer reliability. However, it was finally decided to retain the measure, realizing that the reliability of the averaged ratings would be greater than the reliability of single ratings and that whatever results were obtained could be considered an underestimate. In order to increase reliability, the number of scales was reduced by examining the intercorrelations of the scales and combining scales of low frequency with other scales with which they were correlated. This resulted in the following 10 scales for negative experiences: *loss of love, negative evaluation, lack of consideration, accidental injury, failure, moral transgression, frustration, lack of stimulation, noxious physical stimulation, threat to values.* There were nine scales for positive experiences: *love and affection, positive evaluation, affilitation, success, pleasant physical stimulation, esthetic stimulation, freedom, relief, entertainment.*

RESULTS

Between-Subject Correlations

For each variable, responses on odd days were correlated with responses on even days. As already noted, this was first done using only the data of the first 2 days. Next, the mean of Days 1 and 3 was correlated with the mean of Days 2 and 4, and so on, until the mean of all the odd days was correlated with the mean of all the even days. Figure 4.1 presents mean correlations arranged by scoring category for pleasant and unpleasant experiences, as a function of the number of days included in the odd and even samples. Table 4.1 presents the range and mean of the correlations for the maximum number of days sampled, with the

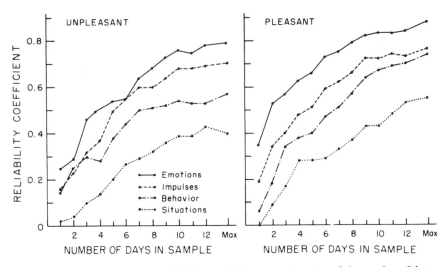

FIGURE 4.1. Between-subjects reliability coefficients as a function of the number of days included in the odd–even samples. Figures plotted represent the mean of the correlations for the variables within a category.

data arranged by scoring cateogry. It can be seen in Figure 4.1 that mean correlations when two days are compared vary between .00 and .40. The overall mean correlation is less than .20. These results are comparable to the results widely cited by others as evidence that personality traits are unreliable. With an increase in the number of days in the odd–even samples, the reliability coefficients increase until highly respectable coefficients are obtained when the mean of the maximum number of odd days is correlated with the mean of the maximum number of even days. In Table 4.1, it can be seen that the mean correlation for the six pleasant emotions is .88. A considerable number of variables produced reliability coefficients over .80, with some over .90. It is noteworthy that a sample of six events is sufficient to yield correlations over .50 for most emotions and impulses (see Figure 4.1). In view of the low interscorer agreement for rating situational variables, it is not surprising that situations yielded the lowest reliability coefficients. However, even these are considerably higher than those customarily reported for single events correlated with each other. The highest correlations for situational variables are quite respectable, being over .70.[3]

In an attempt to obtain information on the factors that influence the reliability of personality variables, the two variables with the highest correlations,

---

[3] The finding of highly significant correlations for situational variables provides support for the view that the tendency to experience a certain environment is itself a relatively stable personality characteristic (cf. Bowers, 1973; Alker, 1976; Wachtel, 1975, Chapter 24).

TABLE 4.1

Mean and Range of Between-Subjects Odd—Even Reliability Coefficients for Maximum Number of Days Sampled (24—34) (N = 28 Ss)

Category and number of variables included		Least reliable variable within category		Most reliable variable within category		Mean reliability
Unpleasant experiences	Emotions (8)	Tired	.61	Frustrated	.91	.79
	Situations (10)	Accidental injury	-.06	Loss-of-love	.70	.40
	Impulses (12)	Withdrawal	.51	Problem-solve	.88	.70
	Behavior (12)	Physical-escape	-.05	Affiliation	.87	.57
Pleasant experiences	Emotions (6)	Energetic	.86	Happy	.92	.88
	Situations (9)	Aesthetic stimulation	.25	Entertainment	.78	.55
	Impulses (7)	Achievement	.58	Pleasure seeking	.92	.76
	Behavior (7)	Achievement	.40	Nurturance	.95	.74

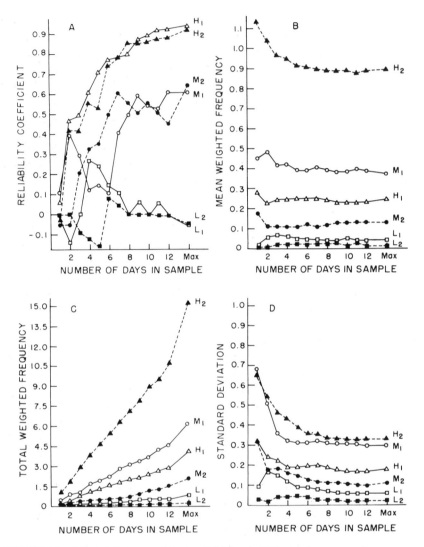

FIGURE 4.2. Selected between-subjects reliability coefficients, frequency of occurrence, and standard deviations as a function of the number of days included in the odd–even samples. The six curves represent the findings for six variables, which include the two that have produced the highest coefficients (H_1 and H_2), the two that have produced the lowest coefficients (L_1 and L_2), and two that have produced moderate coefficients (M_1 and M_2).

the two with the middlemost correlations, and the two with the lowest correlations were compared. In Figure 4.2A each of these correlations is plotted as a function of the number of days correlated. Not surprisingly, the lowest correlations, L1 and L2, produce curves that fluctuate around zero. It therefore appears that these variables would not produce coefficients reliably greater than zero, no matter how large the sample of events. The middlemost correlations, M1 and M2, show a continuous rise until a coefficient of about .60 is reached. However, there is relatively little increase from a sample of 7 days to the maximum sample size, suggesting that these variables probably would not increase much beyond .60 with a further increase in sample size. For the most reliable variables, H1 and H2, there is a continuous increase in reliability to over .90. An extrapolation of the curve suggests that the reliability may rise even higher should the sample size be further increased.

In Figure 4.2B, the mean frequency for the above variables is plotted as a function of sample size. It is evident that the variables with the lowest frequency have an extremely low rate of occurrence per day. In Figure 4.2C, which presents the cumulative frequency over days, it can be seen that the total frequency of occurrence for the least reliable variables is so low that even for the maximum number of days sampled the average subject produced fewer than one incident. Given this information, it is necessary to revise the previous conclusion that an increase in sample size would probable have had no effect on the reliability of these variables. The reliability may have been limited by the extremely low frequency and it is possible that a considerable increase in the number of events sampled would have made a difference.

As for the medium and high correlations in Figures 4.2B and 4.2C, it is noteworthy that they overlap in frequency of occurrence. Apparently, a high incidence of events does not guarantee high reliability, nor does a low incidence guarantee low reliability, so long as it is above a critical minimum.

Figure 4.2D presents the standard deviations of the variables as a function of the number of days in the sample size. The two variables with lowest reliability have very small standard deviations. Obviously, a certain minimum amount of variation must be present in order to produce respectable reliability coefficients. Beyond that minimum, there appears to be no clear-cut relationship between the size of the standard deviation and the reliability coefficients, as there is overlap in the variance of the high and medium reliability coefficients. It is noteworthy that the standard deviations tend to decrease as a function of the increasing number of events sampled. This can be attributed to a decrease in the noise of measurement as a result of averaging over many events.

It may be concluded that whereas a certain minimum mean frequency and variance is necessary for a variable to achieve high reliability, beyond that minimum the increase in reliability that was observed as a function of increasing sample size cannot be attributed to increases in the means or variances of the variables under consideration. Instead, it appears that some personality variables are intrinsically more reliable than others, either because the concepts they identify are more stable or because they have been more adequately operationalized. The reader who is interested in the kinds of variables that were found to be most and least reliable is referred to Table 4.1 and Figure 4.1. Emotions were more reliable than the other categories of variables, and situations were least reliable, which, as previously noted, to some unknown degree was a consequence of low interscorer agreement. For all categories, pleasant experiences produced higher reliability coefficients than unpleasant experiences. This has been replicated in further work, but we are at a loss to account for it other than to speculate that defensiveness toward, or confusion about, unpleasant reactions may in some manner contribute to inconsistency.

Within-Subject Correlations

Personality implies an organization of variables within the individual. To examine the reliability of personality, it is not sufficient to examine the stability of single variables among subjects, as in the preceding section, but it is necessary to also examine the stability of the patterning of variables within individuals. This can be accomplished by computing within-subject correlations across variables. This was first done by comparing an individual's profile of variables within a category for Day 1 with his profile for Day 2. The process was repeated, comparing the profile based on the means of Days 1 and 3 with the profile based on the means of Days 2 and 4, and so on, until the mean profile for the maximum number of odd days was correlated with the mean profile for the maximum number of even days. This was done separately for each category and for each subject, with pleasant and unpleasant experiences treated separately.

Figure 4.3 presents average within-subject correlations for the 28 subjects as a function of number of days. Table 4.2 presents the range and the mean of the correlations within a category for the maximum number of days in the odd—even samples. It can be seen in Figure 4.3 that when the data are derived from a

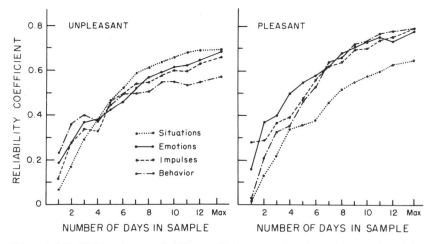

FIGURE 4.3. Within-subjects reliability coefficients as a function of the number of days included in the odd—even samples. Figures plotted represent the intrasubject correlations across the dimensions in a category averaged over all subjects.

TABLE 4.2

Mean and Range of Within-Subjects Odd–Even Reliability Coefficients for Maximum Number of Days Sampled (24–34) (N = 28 Ss)

	Category and number of variables included	Least reliable subject within category		Most Reliable subject within category		Mean reliability
Unpleasant experiences	Emotions (8)	S28	.24	S16	.96	.68
	Situations (10)	S10	−.05	S28	.95	.69
	Impulses (12)	S14	.18	S20	.95	.66
	Behavior (12)	S 2	−.17	S25	.97	.60
Pleasant experiences	Emotions (6)	S12	.13	S 3	.95	.78
	Situations (9)	S 2	−.04	S 7	.97	.65
	Impulses (7)	S 2	−.15	S23	.99	.79
	Behavior (7)	S10	.24	S28	1.00	.79

single event the intrasubject correlations across variables average less than .20. From this one may be tempted to conclude that there is no stability in the organization of personality. However, as the number of observations is increased, the profiles become increasingly stable. When mean profiles derived from all odd days are correlated with mean profiles derived from all even days, the average subject obtains reliability coefficients that, depending on the category, vary between .60 and .79. Table 4.2 reveals that there are marked individual differences in the stability of such personality profiles. Within each category there are subjects who exhibit coefficients that are not significantly differnt from zero and others who exhibit nearly perfect stability.

It may be concluded that the overall evidence attests to a respectably high degree of stability in the organization of variables within most individuals but also indicates that individuals differ considerably in this respect, with some exhibiting very little stability and others exhibiting close to perfect stability.

DISCUSSION

Can the Finding of High Reliability Be Dismissed Because it Is Based on Self-Report Data?

Given the frequent assertion that there is a .30 barrier for cross-situational reliability coefficients, the findings in this study are no less than dramatic. When adequate data samples over time were obtained it was demonstrated, over a wide variety of variables, that correlations much higher than those normally reported were obtained. When results that are so much at variance with previous conceptions are uncovered, the question must be raised of whether they are as good as they appear or whether they have been produced by some artifact. Considering that the findings of others have been reproduced when the data have been analyzed by correlating single events, that the magnitude of the reliability coefficients has risen systematically as an increasing number of events has been averaged, and that we have since obtained similar results in other studies, it appears that artifacts can be ruled out. There remains the possible objection that the findings are based on self-report. After all, personality tests, which are also self-report measures, have characteristically yielded high reliability coefficients. The high reliability of personality tests has not been impressive because it has simply demonstrated that people's views about themselves are stable. This is a far cry from demonstrating that people react consistently in everyday life. In what way, then, can it be said that the present findings, which are also based on self-report, contribute something beyond what has been demonstrated by personality inventories?

First, it should be considered that the data in the present study are considerably different from what is obtained from a personality inventory. In personality inventories people are required to make vague estimates to indicate what they believe they are like. In this study actual records of specific incidents were kept. It is one thing to state "I am an anxious person" and another to keep a record of one's actual anxiety reactions. That the two are very different was made evident to us when we administered identical forms to the same individuals, once to be filled out as a personality inventory on a single occasion and again to be used as data sheets for recording specific events. A comparison of the profiles based on estimates of how often people believed they had certain reactions with actual records frequently revealed a lack of correspondence, often to the surprise of the participants.

Second, the most meaningful judgments about certain kinds of reactions, such as the experience of emotions, are those of the subjects themselves. Assume that an individual records as his or her most unpleasant experience of the day that he or she failed a test, and feels sad as a consequence. Who is to say that he or she did not fail and is not really sad but just thinks he or she it? How can failure better be judged than through the eyes of the person who experiences it? Of course, one can argue that psychology should not study inner phenomena, such as feelings and dreams, but the cost of this is to restrict personality research to a narrow and superficial domain.[4]

Third, within this study, not all variables referred to inner states. Highly respectable reliability coefficients were found for reports of behavior carried out, comparable to those for the inner variables. It was also noteworthy that situational variables, which were scored by judged other than the subjects, produced mean coefficients well over .30, with some as high as .78, despite limitations imposed by low interjudge reliability.

Fourth, in studies by others, self-observation and observations by external observers have produced comparable reliability coefficients (cf. Bem & Allen, 1974; Moos, 1969). In fact, in one study (Moos, 1969), observation by others of the subjects' smoking behavior identified a more stable variable than all but one of many measures that employed self-ratings. The overall evidence provides no support for the view that self-ratings of specific reactions produce spuriously high reliability coefficients in comparison to ratings by judges.[5]

[4] Even from such a constrictive viewpoint, the findings of this study are of considerable interest, for the ratings themselves constitute a sample of the overt behavior of raters. It must then be acknowledged that such behavior, which may be described as rating style, has been demonstrated to be highly reliable when the behavioral sample for each individual has consisted or a large number of events but has been unreliable when the behavioral sample has consisted of single events.

[5] Since completion of this paper, a study by Barry Leon (1976) has supplied information on daily observations by external judges of 30 individuals over 28 days on eight variables relating to sociability and impulsivity. Split-half correlations were obtained as a function of sample size in the same manner as in the present study. The mean correlation for the eight variables in the study for a 1-day sample was .37 and the mean split-half correlation for a 14-day sample in each half was .81. When the data were arranged by the degree of inference

Finally, it was demonstrated in the present study that when reliability coefficients were derived from a comparison of single events, the findings of others were replicated and reliability coefficients averaging about .20 were found. Because it was shown that adequate data sampling raised many of the coefficients to .80 and higher, it must be concluded that the original limits on the correlations were imposed by error of measurement as the result of single observations. Therefore, the procedure that others have employed all but guarantees reliability coefficients to be low. It may be concluded that those who have argued that personality is unstable have simply not used procedures that can establish its stability.

The Relative Importance of People, Situations, and Interactions

As a reaction to the presumed lack of reliability of personality traits, a number of psychologists have stressed the importance of situations and the interaction of situations and individuals. This has resulted in some lively debate as to which is most important, individuals, situations, or their interaction. Depending on the studies cited, all views can be supported, including the interesting additional observation (cf. Sarason, Smith, & Diener, 1975) that none of the above accounts for a high proportion of total variance.

It is logically inescapable that, depending on how studies are conducted, any one of the three sources of variance can be demonstrated to be most important. To return to the analogy of people running races, by selecting races that vary little in distance and runners who vary greatly in speed it can be shown that individuals account for almost all of the variance. By selecting runners of close to equal ability and varying the lengths of the races (within limits, so that no new attributes are required, such as endurance, which would contribute to an interaction) it can be shown that situations account for almost all of the variance. By varying the type of race (e.g., dashes, long-distance events, and hurdle races) and the specialties of the runners so that some excel in some races and do poorly in others, it can be shown that interactions account for almost all of the variance. It is therefore apparent that the general question of which source of variance is most important is a meaningless one. This is not to deny that the technique of apportioning variances in an analysis of variance can have value for special purposes.

The argument as to which source of variance, in general, is most important is reminiscent of the older argument about whether intelligence is general or

---

required to make the ratings, it was found that the highest reliability coefficients were produced by variables requiring the least inference, thereby indicating that scorer bias was not very likely a source of spuriously high correlations. It may be concluded that the finding that there is a high degree of behavioral consistency in personality variables when the data are based on an adequate sample of events is not specific to self-report data.

specific. The answer has turned out to be that it is both. For some purposes it is useful to have a general index of overall ability that covers a variety of mental performances, whereas for other purposes it is more useful to have a diagnostic instrument. In like manner, the answer to the question of whether behavior is determined by the person, the situation, or their interaction, is that it is determined by all three. How important each is can only be established with reference to the purposes of the investigator.

There is obviously both theoretical and practical value in identifying relatively enduring response dispositions, or traits, that can be used to predict long-term behavior averaged over many situations without having to specify the nature of particular situations. To accomplish this, one needs to develop a classification system for individuals, and to investigate individuals in depth by observing them in a representative sample of situations. It is also important for some purposes to know the effect certain kinds of situations have on people, in general. To this end, it is necessary to develop a classification system for situations and to investigate the situations with an adequate, representative sample of people. Finally, one may wish to determine how certain kinds of people behave in certain kinds of situations. To this end, one needs both a classification system of people and of situations and procedures that simultaneously vary situations and people alone meaningfully related dimensions. It then becomes important to obtain an adequate number of observations of certain kinds of people in certain kinds of situations. The principle holds that whether one wishes to study people, situations, or their interaction, error of measurement can be reduced by appropriate sampling and averaging.

The Implications of Error of Measurement for Personality Research

One of the most crucial issues in personality research has centered around the inability, with a few exceptions (e.g., Block, Chapter 2; Olweus, Chapter 17), to demonstrate consistency of behavior in individuals. This has ushered in widespread criticism of personality theories that have attempted to conceptualize stable response dispositions in people. Given the absence of stability in human behavior, the existence of personality, as a meaningful concept, is, in itself, called into question. Mischel (1969), after a purportedly extensive review of clinical, developmental, experimental, and correlational studies, stated: "I am more and more convinced, however, hopefully by data as well as on theoretical grounds, that the observed inconsistency so regularly found in studies of noncognitive personality dimensions often reflects the state of nature and not merely the noise of measurement" (p. 1014).

It now appears that the low reliability coefficients that routinely have been reported have very likely been the result of error of measurement produced by inadequate sampling of the behavior of the individuals who have been studied. In those few studies that have provided evidence of stability of behavior, error of measurement has been reduced either by using multidimensional criteria (cf. Fishbein & Ajzen, 1974), by obtaining relatively enduring samples of behavior (cf. Block, Chapter 2; Olweus, Chapter 17), or by averaging many observations, as in the present study. Such findings provide renewed hope for personality research. They suggest that instead of attempting to find reliability by turning to molecular levels of behavior, or complex statistical procedures, or increasingly complicated theories, such as ones that assume that individuals do not share the same behavioral dimensions, investigators of personality should first obtain adequate samples of the behavior of individuals. Ironically enough this suggests that the laboratory experiment itself, at least as normally conducted, although the sin qua non of scientific method to many, is a questionable source of personality data.

Carlson (1971) has charged that in the course of a desperate search for objectivity and reliability the person has been abandoned in personality research. It now appears that the person can be reintroduced into personality research and that he or she will be a better person for the ordeal — more reliable, and therefore more respectable to psychologists than her or his predecessor.

Acknowledgments

The preparation of this paper and the research reported in it were supported by NIHM Research Grant MH-01293.

5

Interactional Psychology: Some Emerging Features of an Integrated Scientific Discipline

Edward A. Nelsen

North Carolina Central University[1]

In his Presidential Address to the American Psychological Association in 1957, Lee Cronbach brought into focus a long-standing schism within scientific psychology. He noted that research methods had become so sharply differentiated that distinct scientific disciplines could be identified. Thus, Cronbach (1957) delineated:

> ... two historic streams of method, thought, and affiliation which run through the last century of our science. One stream is *experimental psychology*; the other *correlational psychology*. [In 1938] Dashiell [had] optimistically forecast a confluence of these two streams, but that confluence is still in the making. Psychology continues to this day to be limited by the dedication of its investigators to one or the other method of inquiry rather than to scientific psychology as a whole. (p. 671)

After contrasting the strategies and methods of the experimental and correlational disciplines, Cronbach took note of the potential contributions of the disciplines to one another. He declared:

> It is not enough for each discipline to borrow from the other. Correlational psychology studies only variance among organisms; experimental psychology studies only variance among treatments. A united discipline will study both of these, but it will also be concerned with the otherwise neglected interactions between organismic and treatment variables (Shen, 1942). Our job is to invent constructs and to form a network of laws which permits prediction. From observations we must infer a psychological description of the situation and of the present state of the organism. Our laws should permit us to predict, from this description, the behavior of organism-in-situation. (p. 681)

---

[1] Now at Arizona State University, Tempe, Arizona.

Thus, nearly two decades ago Cronbach exhorted psychologists to focus on interactions of organisms and situations, and he sketched a rough outline of a new, integrated discipline.

During the 18 years since Cronbach's address, substantial progress has been made in studying person–situation interactions. Cronbach (1975) himself characterized the study of Aptitude X Treatment interactions as a "hybrid discipline [that] is now flourishing" (p. 116). An historical survey of personality concepts also led Ekehammar (1974) to conclude that "conceptions have converged and are converging toward an interactionist conceptualization" (p. 1044). A survey of personality and social psychological research over a span of three decades by Sarason, Smith, and Diener (1975) showed a substantial increase in the percentage of studies that permitted determination of interactions between individual and experimental effects.

Despite movement toward interactional psychology during the past several decades, however, there remain within present day psychology many adherents to the separate disciplines. For example, Bowers (1973) and Golding and Reid (in their chapters in this volume) cite examples of noted researchers who state interactional assumptions yet differ markedly in emphasizing either personality or situational variables as the primary bases for predicting behavior. Also, the aforementioned survey of personality research by Sarason, Smith, and Diener (1975) showed that in 1970 fully three-fourths of the studies they surveyed did not permit determination of S X P interaction effects. Moreover, the new types of constructs envisioned by Cronbach have not been invented. If interactional psychology is now flourishing as a hybrid displine, therefore, its identity is still that of a stepchild. Its distinctive features are still obscured by vestiges of the segregated disciplines, and certain disparities inherited from its parent disciplines are yet to be resolved.

Accordingly, in this chapter the basic concepts of the two disciplines will be examined in juxtaposition and logical distinctions between fundamental constructs of experimental and correlational psychology will be drawn. A distinction will be drawn, first, between broad, long-term constructs common to correlational studies and focal, short-term constructs characteristic of experimental research. A more basic distinction will then be drawn between dispositional constructs and constructs signifying response occurrences. This latter distinction is critical because it is basic to derivation of a unit of analysis that can subsume both situational and personality variables. Accordingly, a new type of conceptual unit is proposed — one that focuses on the conditional probability of behavior as a function of both dispositional and situational variables. Such a unit may better serve interactional psychology because it is conducive to analysis of the conjoint interaction of the two kinds of variables.

CONSTRUCTS AND METHODS OF MEASUREMENT
WITHIN THE TWO DISCIPLINES

As Cronbach (1957) noted, the experimental and correlational disciplines were differentially committed to investigation of situational versus organismic variables and distinct methods of measurement were developed within each discipline. Moreover, fundamentally different types of concepts and constructs emerged in relation to these measurement approaches.

Experimentalists developed and applied their concepts and measures in a laboratory context while studying hypotheses concerning situational determinants of behavior and/or changes that could be observed within a relatively short span of time, e.g., learning a particular response or skill under different conditions. They developed such concepts and measures as "stimulus," "stimulus intensity," "response," "response frequency," "response intensity," "error," and "performance." In general, it should be noted, these concepts and measures refer to specific events of limited duration, that is, *narrowly categorized, short-term phenomena.* These constructs accordingly carry connotations of concreteness as well as of behavioral, situational, and temporal specificity.

Correlational psychologists, in contrast, studied relatively broad and general characteristics of individuals, and measures of these characteristics have been presumed, if not demonstrated, to be relatively consistent across situations and over time. For example, differential psychologists have developed concepts and measures of such behavioral phenomena as "ability," "skill," "interest," "attitude," "trait," and "motive." These concepts and measures, in contrast with those of experimentalists, generally refer to *broadly categorized, long-term behavioral phenomena.* Accordingly, the constructs of correlational psychology have acquired broad behavioral, cross-situational, and long-term connotations.

This distinction between the long- and short-term constructs that evolved within each discipline, although elementary and quite obvious, has often been overlooked by psychologists, and efforts to apply the language and constructs of the laboratory experiment to the broad phenomena of personality and development have sometimes resulted in serious distortions of meaning. For example, a study by Bandura and McDonald (1963) was designed to test the invariance (stability) of "objective" and "subjective" moral stages postulated by Piaget (1948). After observing data which showed that children who initially gave "subjective" responses could be influenced by models to give "objective" responses and vice versa, Bandura and Walters (1963) concluded: "The so-called developmental stages were readily altered by the provision of adult models who consistently adopted moral orientations that run counter to those displayed by the child" (p. 209). In other words, they observed specific behavioral changes in one situation and concluded from this that a "stage" had changed. However, the fact that behavioral characteristics similar to those of an alternative stage can be elicited under a particular situational condition certainly does not mean that a stage has been altered, just as drug-induced sedation of a violent person does not mean a long-standing disposition toward violence has been altered except for a few hours. Recreation of particular conditions could very well reveal that the behaviors in question would occur with the original probability.

Another illustration of confounded concepts comes from an analysis of social behavior by Staats and Staats (1963) in their book, *Complex Human Behavior.* After they cited several operant conditioning studies that demonstrated generalization within a class of responses, they concluded:

> The results ... do support the contention that what are called personality traits may be considered to be classes of responses which have developed according to the principles of operant conditioning. (p. 269)

They went on to say:

> It is suggested that the application of learning principles to the behaviors under discussion in the book are all dealing with "personality" behavior: social behavior, language, intelligent behavior, problem solving behavior, and so on. (p. 285)

In this analysis, as in the Bandura and Walters' interpretation, long-term constructs of individual psychology were reduced to ostensibly equivalent short-term concepts of stimulus—response psychology. Such attempts probably do have some heuristic value. However, ordinary standards for scientific explanation are violated when researchers draw inferences, conclusions, or implications regarding broad and enduring dispositions from experimental data on narrowly defined, short-term responses. Such inferences tend to becloud scientific analysis and explanation because they may lead others to overlook important parameters of individual variation, for example, to lose sight of a situational or temporal dimension that implicitly defines and describes certain psychological phenomena.

Such confounding of constructs is, in part, a natural consequence of 50 years of conceptual and linguistic inbreeding within the separate disciplines. Many investigators have become insensitive to the long-term or short-term connotations of their basic constructs because they have been typically applied only to the organismic or situational phenomena that are indigenous to the research domains of each discipline. When writers who are not cognizant of the differing connotations apply the concepts of their discipline to exogenous phenomena, contradictory meanings may become apparent. For example, when Staats and Staats used the phrase " 'personality' behavior," the long-term connotations of the term "personality" apparently contradicted the narrow, short-term connotations of "behavior." The authors resolved the apparent contradiction by enclosing the term "personality" in quotation marks, a writer's device that indicates a term is being qualified or used in an unusual manner.

However, the basic issue here is not just a matter of semantic usage. It is not enough for the scientist to employ terms according to their conventional denotations and connotations. Scientific analysis rests on formal definitions, logical specification, and systematic measurement of relevant properties. Moreover, the long-term and short-term distinction is not the whole story. The distinction is only relative and somewhat arbitrary, and it does not sufficiently differentiate the constructs of the two disciplines on logical grounds.

It is necessary, therefore, to further sharpen the distinction between the types of constructs that have been cultured within the separate disciplines. Accordingly, psychologists should note that certain philosophers (e.g., Alston, 1971; Ryle, 1949) have drawn a fundamental distinction between constructs that characterize dispositions and those that refer to particular occurrences. Specification of the differing logical properties, contexts, and uses of dispositional constructs and constructs referring to response occurrences may help clarify differences between the differing types of concepts and the different levels of analysis indigenous to the correlational and experimental disciplines.

RESPONSE OCCURRENCES AND DISPOSITIONS

The distinction between constructs referring to occurrences versus dispositions was originally posed and sharply drawn by the British philosopher, Gilbert Ryle (1949), in his book *The Concept of Mind*. He argued convincingly against the "dogma of the ghost in the machine," that is, the Cartesian myth that "mental happenings occur in insulated fields, known as 'minds' . . . " (p. 13). He posed that such words as "intelligence," "belief," "attitude," and "motive" do not refer to internal control mechanisms of the mind. Instead, he argued, such terms signify abilities, tendencies, or proneness toward various actions.

> Dispositional statements about particular things and persons are . . . like law statements in the fact that we use them in a partly similar way. They apply to, or they are satisfied by, the actions, reactions, and states of the object; they are inference-tickets, which license us to predict, retrodict, explain, and modify these actions, reactions, and states. (p. 124)

Such terms as "thinking," "solving," "reasoning," "feeling," "trying," and "obeying," in contrast, signify occurrences that pertain to qualities of intellect and character. Such terms, as well as action words, for example, "running," "hitting," "crying," or "eye blinking," signify actual events or episodes, that is, ones that occur in a particular situation within a specified time interval.

The distinction between dispositions and responses, as drawn by Ryle and other philosophers (e.g., Alston, 1971; Rozeboom, 1973), has a number of implications for psychologists. The differentiation implies not only different types of concepts but also distinct scientific—analytical rules and procedures for developing, validating, and interpreting measures relating to the two types of constructs. It also implies new conceptual schemas for analyzing interactive relationships between the two types of concepts and their correlated measures and procedures. These issues are considered in the following sections.

PROPERTIES OF DISPOSITIONS AND THEIR MEASUREMENT

In casual usage, a dispositional construct implies that the probability of a given form of behavior is relatively high (or low) for a given class of persons. For example, dispositional constructs, such as "schizophrenic," "inner directed," "aggressive," or "achievement oriented," are usually used to indicate a general propensity toward certain kinds of acts. Such concepts as "claustrophobic" or "test anxious" imply that *under certain conditions* a particular mode of responses is likely to occur; that is, if the organism is placed in a certain situation, then certain reactions may be expected.

Probabilitistic statements are abstract propositions that may forecast a class of events and in general they cannot be formulated or evaluated on the basis of a single instance of the class of events. A weather forecast that calls for a 5% chance of rain cannot on a given day literally be called "wrong" if it rains on that day. The forecast explicitly included the possibility that it would rain. In a similar vein, because dispositional constructs in psychology generally refer to patterns or regularities of behavior, a single behavioral episode is insufficient as a basis for inferences regarding dispositions.

In general, if probabilistic statements are proffered in terms of specified conditions that govern the occurrence of the class of events, then greater accuracy of prediction may be possible. For example, weather forecasts of a "20% chance of rain in Stockholm" and "a 70% chance of rain in Seattle, Washington" for a given day would be imprecise if they were based simply on average daily rainfall for each city. Presumably, however, the accuracy of these forecasts could be improved considerably if seasonal variations and/or daily climatic conditions were systematically appraised.

If dispositions are conceptualized in terms of conditional probabilities, definition and measurement of dispositions must consider not only general forms or modes of response but also basic factors that govern or limit the probabilities of the responses. Therefore, I propose that a three-dimensional classification scheme should be used to effectively characterize dispositions. I propose that dispositions may be dimensionalized according to (1) classification of response modes, (2) classification of situational variables, and (3) temporal parameters. Moreover, I shall suggest that from one point of view these three dimensions are integral to analysis of situation—personality interactions.

The first dimension, pertaining to covarying relationships among forms or modes of responses, has traditionally been recognized as the primary basis for differentiating dispositions. For example, Spence (1963) described traits, abilities, etc., as "generalized response characteristics." Conventional standards for measurement of traits, attitudes, etc., require that at least some degree of covariation among responses (i.e., internal consistency) can be demonstrated. Covariation among responses is an empirical matter and therefore not limited to phenotypically similar behaviors. In other words, certain dispositions may encompass seemingly divergent forms of overt behavior, whereas others may be limited to narrowly defined differences. For example, the scientific basis for characterizing an individual as "schizophrenic" requires demonstrated covariance among measures of frequency of delusions, hallucinations, social withdrawal, etc. The empirical basis for a dispositional construction of "hypochondriasis," in contrast, involves correlation among measures of complaints about physical symptoms and ailments.

While focusing on classes of response modes as a basis for classifying and measuring behavioral traits, psychologists for many years gave little attention to the classification of situational contexts within which response covariations were observed. However, it is apparent that a *situational dimension* may characterize and differentiate dispositions of given individuals according to the nature or class of situations that may elicit or facilitate (or suppress) a given type of action in the individuals. For example, one individual may be moved to angry aggressive behavior by various cues that are seemingly challenges to his status, whereas another may be aroused to similar behavior only by gross injustices or infringement on the wellbeing of helpless, innocent victims. Even though the *forms* of the overt responses may be similar in these differing situations, the dispositions must be recognized as psychologically distinct because the conditions under which the behaviors generally occur can be lawfully distinguished.

A third dimension for characterizing dispositions is based on a *temporal variable.* In the vast majority of theoretical and empirical accounts, the life span of traits, etc., is left unspecified and indeterminate. Most traits, abilities, motives, etc., are typically *assumed* to be relatively stable over time, but few investigators have actually concerned themselves with the issue of stability versus change. Indeed, the assumption of long-term stability is not essential to dispositional analyses. A dispositional statement may characterize a gradually (or rapidly) changing propensity or a short-term state, as well as a stable, long-term propensity. The essential point is that the individual's behavior must be predictable within a defined span of time.

The notion of developmental stage points to dispositional characteristics of particular periods of life. In sophisticated stage theories, such as Piaget's, issues of onset, termination, and sequential changes within stages are given formal consideration.

The temporal dimension of dispositional constructs is also integral to the state—trait distinction, drawn by Cattell (1966) and by Zuckerman and Spielberger in their chapters in this volume. "State" constructs, as distinguished from "trait" constructs, generally signify either an occurrence or a disposition of relatively short duration. For example, such notions as "arousal of an anxiety state," "set," "adaptation level," and "cognitive dissonance" imply short-term, perhaps momentary, occurrences or dispositions. In contrast, trait concepts are generally used in the form of long-term dispositional statements, e.g., as Zuckerman and Spielberger use the "trait anxiety" concept to characterize a measure developed to predict occurrences of "state anxiety."

In general, "state" concepts represent occurrences when employed to describe dependent variables (e.g., Spielberger and Zuckerman use the notion of "state anxiety" to characterize a dependent variable, i.e., an observed anxiety level). Studies in which an "anxiety state" is induced as an independent or mediating variable and consequent response measures are observed as dependent variables, however, concern dispositional aspects of anxiety states, because various consequences may be predicted from the manipulation of the disposition. (See Alston, 1971, for a further analysis of alternative and conflated uses of dispositional and occurrent constructs.)

RELATIONSHIPS AMONG DISPOSITIONS AND SITUATIONS: PREDICTION OF BEHAVIOR IN TERMS OF CONDITIONAL PROBABILITIES

Their inability to predict particular behaviors from measures of attitudes and traits has plagued psychologists for decades. This issue has never been satisfactorily resolved. For example, Cronbach (1975) argued:

> Propositions about traits are actuarial statements, valid over situations in the aggregate. Thus, a total score on a religious attitude questionnaire turns out to be a fine predictor of response in real life, when the criterion is an average over 100 kinds of relevant activity — saying grace, voicing conscientious objection, etc. (Fishbein & Ajzen, 1974). The trait measure, however, has negligible power to forecast what the high scorer is likely to do in any one situation. (p. 120)

Thus, Cronbach shows that predictions of particular behaviors are necessarily imprecise, to the extent that the measures of traits and attitudes are assumed to encompass any and all varieties of situations, as well as a broad range of religious behaviors.

If propositions about dispositions are conceptualized in relation to functionally equivalent classes of situations instead of "situations in the aggregate," however, then greater accuracy of prediction may be possible. In other words, if one can specify and measure the situational conditions that elicit, inhibit, or modulate a given class of behavior, the occurrence of specific responses may be reasonably predictable.

Therefore, I am suggesting that analyses and predictions of behavior should be formulated in terms of conditional probabilities. A conventional formula[2] from

---

[2] This formula is adapted from Hays and Winkler (1971) and Rozeboom (1973). Rozeboom qualifies his advocacy of this schematization on the grounds that the pattern of

probability theory schematizes the type of statement I am advocating:

$$Pr\,(R_x|D_x \cdot S_x) = r$$

Thus, the probability of the response (R_x) is a function of the interaction between the disposition (D_x) of the individual (toward R_x under a particular situational condition) and the strength of situational press (S_x) at a given moment.

According to this schematization, a number of personality measures might jointly comprise a measure of the disposition (D_x) and a number of situational and/or environmental variables could likewise jointly constitute the index of situational press (S_x). Note especially that *it is the form of the functional relationship(s) between* D_x *and* S_x *that represents the person by situation interaction;* or one might say more properly, the *disposition by situation interaction.* The functional relationship is assumed to be multiplicative instead of additive, so if the value of D_x or S_x is zero, $r = 0$. Of course, unknown (unmeasured) variables and measurement error would necessarily become factors in the equation.

An example of mechanical phenomena, borrowed from Ryle (1949) may serve to illustrate this analytic—predictive framework in a simplistic manner. Consider a sheet of glass of given molecular structure, strength, thickness, and brittleness. Jointly, measures of these properties may be combined to predict the probability of shattering under certain circumstances. This disposition toward breakage is an enduring property, although it may change slightly over time or under certain environmental conditions. We can predict, even though the particular sheet of glass has never broken, that given a particular situation, this sheet of glass, with a certain level of probability, will break. Of course, the probability is contingent not only on the characteristics of the glass but also on particular situational events or conditions that may affect the glass, for example, the weight, speed, thrust, and angle of an object impinging upon the sheet of glass. Given accurate assessment of the relevant dispositional and situational variables, the prediction in a single situation might be quite accurate and certainly more accurate than a general (unconditional) prediction based on an aggregate of all naturally occurring situations. Unknown factors or imprecise measures, of course, would reduce the accuracy of the forecast. This example avoids many of the complexities and viscissitudes of human and even subhuman behavior, and the extent to which actuarial predictions of human behavior can be improved under this general schema remains to be seen. The paradigm seems more

---

statistical probabilities represented by the formula does not suffice to identify lines of nomic (causal) determination, nor does it discriminate statistical dependencies that are purely nomic from those that are all or in part logical. Nevertheless, the formula represents a useful tool for predicting behavior and for representing situational and dispositional variables that are interacting. The reader should consult Rozeboom for his formulation of dispositional constructs in causal analysis.

promising, however, than paradigms based on prediction in the aggregate without regard for situations.

METHODOLOGICAL IMPLICATIONS

This conceptualization of behavioral prediction implies that the conventional research strategies of the older experimental and correlational disciplines must be modified and/or replaced with more complex and varied strategies. The research strategies for a new integrated discipline of interactional psychology, I submit, must be based on innovative approaches toward personality measurement, multivariate experimental designs, and sophisticated statistical—analytic strategies.

Personality measurement has until recently been limited to the development of theoretically or empirically derived measures of broad traits. Internal consistency among test items has been the primary formal requirement for developing personality scales. Little consideration has been given to the specific behaviors encompassed by the trait measures, and even less consideration has been given to the situational parameters affecting the behaviors.

The analysis of disposition—situation interaction in this chapter clearly implies that conceptualization and measurement of dispositions (traits, abilities, etc.) must include systematic consideration of situational, behavioral, and temporal parameters as they moderate interrelationships among test items or test scales. Several general measurement strategies may be suggested, although the broad scope of this chapter precludes detailed consideration of methodological issues and procedures.

First, the most obvious and direct approach to measuring dispositions involves summating or averaging given types of responses over time, within specified types of situations. The response measures may be based on objective behavioral or physiological data, self-report data, or observational report data. The chapters in this volume by Epstein, Spielberger, and Zuckerman discuss and illustrate the fruitfulness of this approach.

Second, innovative test item formats should be devised to assess systematically the situational scope of dispositions. Instruments developed by Sarason, Davidson, Lighthall, Waite, and Ruebush (1960), by Endler, Hunt, and Rosenstein (1962), by Ekehammar and Magnusson (1973), and by Spielberger, Gorsuch, and Lushene (1970) might be cited as prototypes for such instruments. The instruments developed by these investigators all focused on self-report measures of anxiety responses in specified situations. Comparable measures for aggressive, dependent, achievement, cooperative, competitive, and other forms of social behavior also need to be developed, although previous efforts in this direction should be noted, for example, Endler and Hunt (1968) and Zuckerman (1976).

Third, virtually all personality measures that purport to predict behavior should be scrutinized, analyzed, and revised if necessary, to determine the situational as well as the temporal boundaries of the measures. Standards for instrument validation should include requirements for data analyses that clarify and delimit the scope of situations in which the scale may be applied for behavioral prediction. Likewise, even though longitudinal test–retest data are recognized as legitimate for validating scales, such data are only rarely reported and even more rarely are they reported for different age levels, sexes, socio-economic groups, etc.

These suggestions should not be taken to indicate that the S–R format is the only legitimate means of measuring personality, or that all other existing instruments are relatively useless for predicting behavior. On the contrary, some personality measures, may, in fact, be demonstrably useful for predicting behavior in a wide variety of situations; for example, measures of field dependence–independence (Witkin, Dyk, Faterson, Goodenough, & Karp, 1962) and approval motivation (Crowne & Marlowe, 1964) have demonstrated predictive power across a range of situations. However, the nature and scope of relevant situations need to be further clarified and documented in relation to almost every scale.

As situations are defined and assessed systematically, issues concerning statistical analysis of situational effects become critical. For example, when behaviors of several persons are observed and measured in various situations, a variance component technique may be used to determine proportions of variance from persons, situations, and person–situation interactions (Endler & Hunt, 1966). A plethora of studies (e.g., see Bowers, 1973; Cronbach & Snow, in press; and Endler & Magnusson, 1974, for reviews) has shown that substantial behavioral variation is attributable to person–situation interaction.

Although such convincing demonstrations of the relative significance of person–situation interaction may be necessary to impress diehard situationists and/or trait theorists, however, the heuristic and theoretical value of the variance components technique is limited. This limitation of the variance partitioning procedure, as traditionally used for assessing sources of variation, results from the lack of conceptual specification and statistical independence of measures of the personality and situational parameters that may be operating in particular situations. For example, several years ago we published a paper (Nelsen, Grinder, & Mutterer, 1969) which showed that about 24% of the variance in measures of honesty was attributable to persons, about 14% to situations, and between 0 and 62% to P X S interactions. In retrospect, I feel that this study yielded relatively little insight concerning either situational, dispositional, or S X P interactive determinants of behavior. The findings do not provide a basis for predicting or explaining which personality factors and situational factors are relevant or how they interact.

Among various alternative strategies I now recommend as more fruitful are factor analyses and multiple regression analyses. The latter method is closely akin to the variance partitioning technique in that it allows assessment of the contribution of personality measures in toto, as predictors or "sources" of behavioral variation. It offers the added advantage of allowing for separate assessment of the contribution of each personality variable or situational variable that has been independently measured and entered into restricted models of the regression equation (e.g., in a stepwise procedure).

The regression procedure may be easily conceptualized in terms of the conditional probability model previously mentioned. Although regression analysis has not commonly been applied to the prediction of specific (narrowly defined) response occurrences, the application is straightforward and readily interpretable in terms of probabilities and predictive accuracy. Predictions under different situational conditions can be compared on the bases of the slopes and intercepts of the regression equations for each situation. Moreover, the computed value for a predicted score (conventionally signified Y') can represent the term D_x in the formula suggested above.

In addition to this device for computing D_x, procedures for determining the situational press, i.e., the value of S_x, would need to be determined. Methods for classifying situations and for analyzing the joint (additive and interactive) effects of situational variables are less developed than methods for studying relationships among response variables. Nevertheless, the analysis by Patterson and Cobb (1971b) of the conditional probability of hitting under various situational conditions is noteworthy as a pioneering effort in this area.

Among the types of research strategies that may enable investigators to classify situations systematically are some that have been technologically extant for several decades but utilized only rarely by personality and social psychologists until recently. I am referring to methods for classifying stimuli and/or studying similarities and differences among stimuli. Among these methods are multidimensional scaling (Richardson, 1938) and variants thereof (see Young, 1975); P-, O-, S-, and T-factor analysis (Cattell, 1966); and cluster analysis (see Bailey, 1975). The format employed in George Kelly's (1955) role repertory test also deserves mention in this context. The work of D. Magnusson and his co-workers (e.g., Magnusson & Ekehammar, 1973) illustrates the potential utility of factor analytic studies of categories of situations. For further discussion of this issue, see Hake (1966) and Heise (1975).

The question of behavioral criteria for validating regression equations as indices is also problematical from a practical as well as a conceptual viewpoint. The conceptual problem concerns the determination of coherent classifications of situations and responses that can be approached according to the aforementioned procedures. Once meaningful classes of situations and behaviors are determined, the problem of accumulating sufficient data to represent an adequate criterion of the disposition (the Y in the regression equation) becomes a practical problem of gathering more or less vast quantities of behavioral measures on large samples of persons.

These methodological suggestions are presented only in general, tentative terms. Many more complex methodological issues are yet to be raised by the notions of disposition, conditional probability, and Disposition $\times$ Situation interaction. Efforts to clarify and resolve these complex methodological issues, as well as theoretical issues implied by the notions herein, may eventually shape interactional psychology as an integrated scientific discipline for the psychology's next generation.

6

Consistencies and Perception of Consistencies in Individual Psychomotor Behavior

Martti Takala

University of Jyväskylä, Finland

Discussions about the generality, constancy, and structure of personality traits reflect different concepts of man and different uses of psychological knowledge. The criticism of trait approach has not been determined only by the disappointment with the previous empirical results. It also indicates a reorientation or a new emphasis in the application of psychological science: Were there no use for accurate descriptions of interindividual differences in the society, no trait concept might be needed for the psychological theory.

The data discussed in this chapter are mainly concerned with psychomotor styles and perception of these styles. The point of view of interaction between "individual characteristics" and "situations" is emphasized in the approach. Some introductory comments may connect this chapter with the other contributions to this volume, although no detailed arguments are included.

Person and Environment

The relationship between person and environment, in the most general form, was described by Lewin (1935). All theorists agree that behavior represents the result of some kind of interaction between organism and environment (Sells, 1963b). Accordingly, all psychological theories should be "interactionistic," except for those that are definitely wrong. Yet, within this general frame, there are great differences in the relative emphasis of "person" and "situation." What is more important, although sometimes neglected in the debate, is that various theories differ radically in the conceptualization of both "trait" and the environmental variables. The pure trait theories are limited to the classification of individual characteristics, and they cannot be compared with other types of personality theories. Systematic analyses of situations are required (Endler & Magnusson, 1974). However, a taxonomy is not enough in itself. Its principles should be derived from theoretical understanding. The recent discussions are concentrated on an ahistorical interpretation of individual behavior across situations — interactions between "present person" and "present situations" — and the taxonomies of traits and situations offer a superficial solution in the choice of experimental variables for such designs. The interpretation of the process of development and change as an interaction between individual goals and capacities, on the one hand, and personal, social, and cultural environments, on the other, is important for a theory of personality. "Person" and "situation" should not be considered as mutually excluding or contrasting classes of determinants. What is regarded as "person" at time x consists of the cumulative learning experiences of an individual in his mutual interplay with previous environments until time x.

The Data

The nature of the data that are available for personality description may vary greatly, from naive observation to actuarial material, self-reports, and controlled behavioral measures. As a theoretical concept, trait is considered to be independent of the particular mode of measurement. The dimensional descriptions of personality involve a complex network of inferences from tests to traits and from traits to predictions (Cronbach, 1956). The gap between the data that are highly specific to the procedure used and the conceptualization of traits is extremely wide (Fiske, 1971, 1974). Similar data can be coded by using specific categories or by ascribing a broad meaning to each episode of behavior. The psychological processes of both the subject and the examiner, provoked by the assessment situation, obviously depend on the mode of measurement. Different situational determinants can be assumed to contribute to the individual scores in, say, personality inventories and miniature situation tasks.

In addition, the aspects of response which are examined, e.g., routine skill performance, choice among alternative preferences, expression of feeling, construction of conceptual hierarchies, or social initiation, certainly represent different psychological processes. One can hardly assume that similar descriptions of the interaction between person and environment would apply to all of them. According to this view trait descriptions are rather specific to particular data, although some broad categories are of limited value for practical purposes. Attempts toward a unique, scientifically correct classification of personality traits may be fruitless and the interactions may consist of extremely varying and complicated processes.

Interindividual Differences

The major part of personality measurement is concerned with the assessment of interindividual differences. The empirical data applied in the theoretical discussion of trait psychology or "situationism" are mainly concerned with the consistency or lack of consistency in interindividual differences which, however, tends to be confused or identified with intrapsychical consistency of individual personality in the interpretation. In principle, the structure and content of personality may be consistent and stable, regardless of whether any interindividual differences exist.

Psychometric Evidence

Psychometric evidence is emphasized in the criticism of trait approach, in the same manner as the main evidence for trait theory has been based on psychometric interpretation. The criticism has been concerned with low "average" correlations between "corresponding" measures or responses made in different types of situations (e.g., Mischel, 1968). The observation of low correlations and the disappointment with expectations is common and essential. However, the conclusions made from this observation tend to be overgeneralized. If the psychological processes associated with various kinds of personality variables are widely different, if the variables are selected and coded at different levels of inference, and if the sources of situational variation are complex, the problem of consistency should not be treated as a global issue.

Correspondingly, the emphasis on interaction effects, both in general, and especially in connection with the S—R Inventory of Anxiousness (Endler & Hunt, 1966) has been fruitful; anxiety has been a vague label for different kinds of experience and response and yet helpful as a global concept and it can be provoked by various stimuli and situations. If, however, generalizations are made from the relative strength of interactions found in anxiety-provoking situations to other aspects of behavior, the particular characteristics of respective psychological processes should be considered. The demonstration of the contribution of stimuli, response modes, and their interactions to the total variation of the behavioral measure provides a starting point for further research but it does not produce a theoretical explanation. In addition, the S—R scheme cannot be applied to all aspects of individual behavior.

If data consist of self-reports, an interpretation of Person X Situation interaction in terms of personal constructs should be attempted. The cognitive constructs of the subject; the discrimination among cues, situations, and responses; and the attempts toward maintaining cognitive consistency certainly exert an influence on the responses in verbal self-reports, and this effect depends on whether the questionnaire items are couched in behavioral terms or in more general statements.

For data based on actual behavior or observation of particular aspects of behavior, the amount of inference required in coding may determine what is considered to be important: behavior that is consistent at one level of inference (e.g., stereotypic responses or "honest" behavior in different tasks) is less consistent at another level (similar forms of behavior as indications of adaptation and coping strategies). The level of inference is crucial for the definition of similarity among the forms of behavior or the situations.

An essential question for any explanation of interaction is whether the modes of behavior to be studied are cognitively controlled and what kind of cognitive mediation has been decisive for learning a certain mode of behavior.

Situation Sampling

Sampling of situations seems to be one of the most difficult problems for a study of the relative contribution of person and situation to the total variance of behavior. Bowers (1973, pp. 321–325) has discussed the relevance of the sampling of conditions for the interpretation of experimental results. It may be possible to cover a reasonably large proportion of different situations by the items of self-reports. In the observation of behavior only relatively small samples of subjects and situations can be employed. The experimental studies should therefore be concentrated on the systematic effects of such situational variations that can be theoretically meaningful. Overall statements concerning the relative contribution of person or situation are less relevant.

The comments presented above − including the critical remarks − are relevant to the experiments on psychomotor expression and nonverbal communication, which are briefly reported below.

SYSTEMS OF PSYCHOMOTOR EXPRESSION
AND NONVERBAL COMMUNICATION

The studies to be reviewed have not attempted to give any general solution to the problem of the relative weight of the components of variance in the total variation of psychomotor behavior. Only such aspects of psychomotor behavior have been considered that traditionally have been subsumed under the concepts of "psychomotor expression" or "nonverbal communication." The experiments have looked for such consistencies of individual behavior that may be important for a description of a person and that may serve as cues for the impressions formed by other persons in interpersonal interaction. Accordingly, the examination has been mainly limited to correlational analyses. The procedure may be defended, provided that the dimensions of consistency are simultaneously considered. Various theoretical explanations emphasize different aspects of the communication process and they may predict generality in regard to different aspects of the variation of tasks or situations.

The process of expressive behavior and nonverbal communication can be approached in terms of *three systems of descriptions.* Two are intrapersonal systems: the system of the sender and the system of the receiver of the message. In the early studies of expression (Klages, 1913, and others; see Holzkamp, 1965) the *system of the sender* was strongly emphasized. Practically all the experimental problems judged to be relevant were concerned with eliciting and emitting expressions. Attempts were made to explain the variance of expression in terms of the temporary or permanent characteristics of the sender, while recognizing the (unanalyzed) situational context. The process of decoding the expressive message was ignored or "explained" by intuition or empathy interpretations.

Studies of the intrapersonal *system of the receiver* developed independently of those concerned with the system of the sender. Experiments on the attribution of intent and affective states to other persons, on intuitive personality theories, etc., concentrated on the process of decoding. Many descriptive systems of personality traits presented previously were, in fact, dimensions of the subjective discriminations among word meanings made by the decoder. Various kinds of interaction effects between the decoding situations and decoders are involved in the studies of social perception.

Whereas the intrapersonal approach tended to regard psychomotor behavior of the sender solely as an expressive act, later studies opened new possibilities by examining expression as communicative behavior. The *interpersonal* nature of psychomotor behavior became a central issue in the observational studies of small groups, as well as in the analysis of paralinguistic phenomena.

Both the intrapersonal system of the sender and that of the receiver can be examined in terms of Person X Situation interaction. Accordingly, the interpersonal system consists of more complex interaction effects that seldom have been considered simultaneously.

The hypothetical psychomotor styles could be described as individual characteristics of either expressive or performance-oriented behavior. Different levels of inference included in the interpretation of responses could be exemplified (Takala, 1975) as follows: physical measures ("size," "speed," "angular" versus "curvilinear movement pattern"); physiological measures ("tonic contraction of postural extensors," "preference of abduction versus adduction movements of hands"); coding the meaning of the movements – the meaning can be inferred from individual or interpersonal acts ("expansiveness," "aggressive movements," "autistic gestures") or as a part of the total process of communication. Cross-situational consistency would be indicated by a regular occurence of a specific response or by a general class of behavior in widely varying conditions (Alker, 1972), such as scratching the skin or impulsivity (sudden acceleration or deceleration of movements).

Some theoretical expectations can be spelled out on the basis of the general interpretation of psychomotor expression but they do not suffice to fill the gap between theory and observations, mentioned by Fiske (1974). They may, however, be fruitful, provided that different theoretical concepts call forth somewhat differing empirical assumptions. The explanations of the development and the functions of psychomotor styles have been partly overlapping and they have represented different explanatory power (Takala, 1963, 1975; Konttinen,

1968). It should be admitted that the explanations of the development of psychomotor styles do not, as such, suffice to explain the interindividual differences of these styles. For the present purpose, the explanations are classified as follows.

Psychomotor Styles as Overlearned Habits

The response level or "sampling" interpretation of individual behavior is restricted to the description of consistencies that have developed through instrumental or model learning. The explanation does not specify the contribution of various factors to learning. Consequently, the nature and generality of habits may be most directly determined by physiological background factors, by interpersonal interaction, or by the requirements of adaptive performance (coping strategies), but the explanation is not extended to a comparison among them.

The meaning of the task to the subject may be an important determinant of the generality of the individual style. If cognitive control or cognitive—affective mediation are important for individual performance, the generalization and discrimination of individual styles is likely to be closely associated with the similarity of the meaning of the task. However, psychomotor styles may represent such overlearned routine performances that are individually consistent and generalized on the dimensions of motor characteristics, regardless of the meaning of the task. Accordingly, the habit interpretation could be further divided into two main classes of explanation. The first hypothesizes that psychomotor styles are relatively autonomous routine performances and the second considers the cognitive—affective mediation essential. The second alternative is related to the symbol interpretation of psychomotor styles (page 113).

The interpretation of psychomotor styles as overlearned habits means an expectation of high consistency within at least narrow classes of behavior. The individual quality of skilled performance is often considered an overlearned coping style. Autistic movements (automanipulation, etc.), characteristic of an individual, and other recurrent indications of tension are usually interpreted as overlearned stereotypes. The habit interpretation was provisionally suggested already by Allport and Vernon (1933) who, however, stressed personal styles with broad generality. The interpretation is not sufficiently specified for predictions. It is useful at the exploratory stage but should be later supplemented with other assumptions.

Physiological or Dispositional Interpretations

Individual variation in psychomotor behavior is determined by anatomical and physiological structures and by products of learning that are built on these structures and that also modify them. The most complex dispositional explanations, for example, those based on general individual properties of the CNS or autonomic activity, are very vague, because they presuppose extensive chains of explanations in terms of structure—learning interaction.

The physiological and dispositional explanations would be most pertinent in regard to indications of arousal, activeness, impulsive movements, or to temperamental characteristics (Davis, 1948; Eysenck, 1952; Nebylitsyn & Gray, 1972). The temperamental variables should be rather general classes of behavior and relatively independent of the meaning or the interpersonal nature of the task. The experimental studies by Davis on extreme types of psychomotor styles in stress or fatigue situations were most closely related to the temperamental interpretation. Lately, there has been increasing scepticism about the relevance of general dichotomies. Experimental evidence concerning expressive movements and temperament, as a whole, has been judged to support the disposition interpretation (Talmadge, 1958; Brouchon, 1973).

Communication Interpretation

Psychomotor acts serve mainly to communicate such emotions, intentions, and other characteristics as are relevant for social interaction. The important interpersonal relationships prevailing in an environment and the particular acts that are fundamental for developing and maintaining these relationships provide models for an individual's early learning, which results in individually consistent patterns of communication. As far as psychomotor behavior maintains its adaptive nature, the consistency of individual psychomotor behavior depends on (a) the permanent expectations and goals of the actor in interpersonal situations, and on (b) the expectations and goals of the observers. It means that psychomotor styles should be most consistent across such social situations in which the mutual roles of the participants are fixed, and least consistent if the expectations and goals of the actors and those of the observers are simultaneously changed. Because the psychomotor acts have different functions in the communicative process (Frijda, 1965; Ekman & Friesen, 1969), the individual consistency may be concealed by other factors or limited to narrow sets of behavior.

The communication interpretation of psychomotor styles suggests that the characteristics that regulate the flow of social interaction are consistent as long as the interpersonal relationships and expectations remain the same: social initiative, glancing at others, smiling, avoiding mutual visual contact, interruption of other persons' speaking, and the utilization of space in interpersonal settings. Individual consistency would not extend to other kinds of tasks or to radically different interpersonal relationships.

Symbol Interpretation

The trait names, used for the description of other persons or oneself, often include some notion of psychomotor behavior, especially the typological descriptions of temperament (Jaensch, 1930; Kretschmer, 1951) integrated psychomotor behavior with global personality characteristics, by using broad generalizations by analogy.

Some aspects of person perception may be determined by simple psychomotor cues that are perceived and generalized by ascribing trait labels metaphorically related to motor behavior (Takala, 1972). The impression of a "fast person" may either be reduced to the perceived speed of speaking or walking or it may represent a global impression of cognitive and motor patterns. Movement may also serve as an additional cue in cases where it alone is not sufficient to create a definite impression (Tagiuri, 1960). A person who draws large figures can be called "expansive," that is, he or she tends to cover a large physical area with his motor response. But the interpretation may be extended further. It is supposed that a person who makes "expansive" drawings has many social contacts, he or she tries to dominate others by occupying a large portion of common space, etc. (Sommer, 1969). Such analogies are intuitively promising and they refer to the meaning of acts. However, they are very vague. The metaphorical use of words inevitably occurs in person description of everyday life (Cohen, 1973, pp. 155–159).

The theory of expression by Klages (1913) focuses on the results of an expressive act, which are perceived by both the sender and the receiver as a visual pattern and which, therefore, may be more controlled by intention than is the movement itself. Another kind of symbol interpretation is developed from Darwin's theory of expression, which states that expressions are primordial reactions, based on original approach, avoidance, etc., responses. Although the starting point seems to be unambiguous, the metaphoric meanings of approach and avoidance extend the possible symbol interpretations beyond any definite limit.

Some aspects of the symbol interpretation can be examined within the second alternative of habit explanations (page 118). If the individual psychomotor styles are generalized according to the metaphoric meanings of movement characteristics, this may indicate the relevance of symbol interpretation. The applications of this interpretation is more frequently limited to specific and idiosyncratic symbols and meanings.

The recent experimental studies have concentrated on studying psychomotor styles at the behavioral level instead of abstract constructs. Psychomotor expression is considered important as such. It does not call for a justification beyond itself (Wallach & Leggett, 1972). The importance is related to the fact that psychomotor acts are decoded by other persons as an indication of intentional or unintentional expression of either temporary or permanent characteristics, moods, temperament, adoption of conventional social skills, etc.

This chapter emphasizes the studies carried out at the Department of Psychology of the University of Jyväskylä, Finland, because not all of the results are easily obtainable. They are, however, complemented with examples from other experiments. The types of "psychomotor" acts included in the encoding tasks can be listed as follows:

1. Graphomotor performances
2. Gross motor performances
3. Interpersonal acts

The decoding tasks have been restricted to the interpersonal variables.

PERSONAL STYLES IN GRAPHOMOTOR AND GROSS MOTOR TASKS

Generality of Graphomotor Styles across Tasks

In our studies (Takala & Rantanen, 1964; Konttinen & Olkinuora, 1968) the tasks administered to the subjects varied on the dimension from sensorimotor to "open," which means the degree to which performance is determined by the instruction (and stimulus). Sensorimotor tasks are determined by the instruction (e.g., copying) far more than "open" tasks (e.g., expression of fantasy). Six graphomotor variables were scored in each task (size, pressure, nuance, reinforcement, continuity, angularity). The intercorrelations were examined by means of both the multitrait–multimethod technique (Campbell & Fiske, 1959) and factor analysis. The main result of the replicated study indicated that four or five central graphic variables were independent of each other and interindividually consistent across various tasks, and no method factor occurred. Some more complex, although weak, relationships were found. The nature or the meaning of the task was not essential for the grouping of variables. The results suggest that these graphomotor styles are overlearned routine performances that remain interindividually consistent regardless of the content of the task to be performed.

Area Factor and Personal Space

Various types of explanation have been suggested for the interindividual differences in the size of area covered by one's movements: development of spontaneous versus controlled motor habits, imbalance between the extensor and flexor muscles; interpersonal attitudes ("expansive" versus "restricted"). The communication and symbol interpretations would be most relevant to social encounters where the personal territories of individuals were invaded and where the tendency to expand or defend one's own area created conflicts between the actors.

In our studies of graphomotor tasks it was shown that the individual size of graphic movements was relatively consistent across tasks, including tasks that differed greatly from those trained in daily life and where no visual control was possible. The intercorrelations of single tasks frequently exceeded +.50 (Takala, 1953; see also Talmadge, 1958). In addition, it was shown (Takala, 1972, and unpublished results) that the interindividual differences were not radically changed when speed stress was introduced, when the subjects were fatigued or satiated, or when the possibility for controlling one's graphomotor performance was in other ways decreased. The results did not correspond to those found by Davis (1948) and others in more complex choice tasks in which the changes of arousal ("overreaction" versus "inertia" types of response) are more important than psychomotor acts.

In another series of experiments (Takala, 1972) it was shown that the individual consistency found in graphomotor tasks did not extend to performances requiring large hand movements or to placement tasks that provided visual feedback of the results of motor performance.

Accordingly, the generality of the "area factor" is more limited than suggested by Allport and Vernon (1933). It is probably based on individual routine habits that are generalized within narrow sets of performances. The effect of individual preference for impulsive versus controlled movements may be found in some tasks but, in general, individual style is not sensitive to the changes of situation or the affective nature of the task. The replicated experiments by Konttinen (1968) did not support the assumptions of any consistent contribution of moderator variables, proposed by Wallach (e.g., Wallach & Gahm, 1960).

Personal Tempo

A person's natural speed of acting is called his personal tempo. In typological studies the extreme types of temperament were shown to differ in various simple tests of preferred tempo (Enke, 1930; Kretschmer, 1951) and the results were explained in dispositional terms (Kretschmer, 1951; Mishima, 1965). No evidence of any general tempo factor was found in the other studies (Harrison, 1941; Rimoldi, 1951). The experiments of our laboratory (Takala & Partanen, 1964) showed that the average intercorrelations among the personal tempo tests were close to zero in the younger age groups (9–12 years), whereas in age group 13–14 years they were systematically positive with an average of +.36. The (low) positive correlations among the tempo tests were interpreted as indications of the preference of fast versus slow working speed.

In a study of hyperkinetic children (Stevens, 1970) it was found that these children always tended to work close to their maximum speed. They were unable to adapt to changing incentive conditions. A physiological explanation, concerned with the regulation of arousal and concentration, was suggested by the author for this extreme group. The interpersonal meaning of the speed of acts has not been varied in any of these experiments.

Evaluation of the Consistency of Personal Styles Within
Individual Psychomotor Performance

In the correlation studies reviewed above the effects of (a) the meaning of the
task (sensorimotor—open, simple—complex), (b) response mode (graphomotor,
gross motor, placement), and (c) the state of the subject have been varied. In
·other experiments, in addition, the subject have modified their drawing performance intentionally (simulation of social roles, Konttinen & Karila, 1969) and
the developmental differentiation of the graphomotor styles of girls and boys
has been examined (Kaartinen, 1960). As a whole, the results support the view
of high consistencies of individual style, regardless of the nature or the content
of the task and the state of the subject. In most graphic variables included, the
consistency is not related to the meaning of the task or to the individual
meanings of graphomotor performance; accordingly, the symbol and communication explanations were considered irrelevant for these style variables. The
individual psychomotor style was consistent only within relatively narrow sets of
behavior and within a particular response mode. It seems to represent a motor
routine performance that is generalized to other performances requiring approximately similar types of skill. The psychomotor style is, in these cases, the
personal quality of *motor* performance. In some experiments, and especially in
extreme cases, it is related to *temperamental* factors (high versus low activation).
In the simulation experiment, the *communication* interpretation is supported in
a restricted sense: The social role of the personal orientations or preferences
adopted by the subject may be expressed and communicated intentionally. The
examination of psychomotor styles presented here has been limited to nomothetic description.

THE PROBLEMS OF PERSONAL STYLE
IN INTERPERSONAL BEHAVIOR

Styles in Dyadic Communication

The experimental studies of the temporal patterns on conversation are relevant
for the theoretical discussions of the consistency and modifiability of personal
styles. Some aspects of speech behavior are individually consistent from a
particular conversation to another for the same individual, provided the participants of the dialog are the same (Jaffe & Feldstein, 1970; Matarazzo & Wiens,
1972). An individual is able to modify his temporal pattern when successive
conversations involve different partners. Mutual pacing is referable to a bilateral
adjustment of silence intervals, and this may correlate with such phenomena as
empathy or communication of mood (Jaffe & Feldstein, 1970). The unexperi-

TABLE 6.1
Consistency Correlations for Interviewer Behavior

Total speaking time	+.79	Facial expression (tension excluded)	+.59
Length of utterance	+.33	Head nod	+.65
Interruption	+.42	Gesture	+.21
Gaze direction toward the interviewee	+.73	Facial tension	+.88
Smiling	+.60	Hand tension	+.53
Gross bodily movement	+.62	Change of posture	+.79

enced interviewers are less able to modify their individual tempo (Feldstein, 1972). In an experiment, carried out in our laboratory, 15 interviewers interviewed four 9- to 10-year-old children. Different children were interviewed by each. The psychomotor characteristics of the interviewer were coded from a videotape. The average correlations among the four interviews are given in Table 6.1.

Highest consistency was found for categories of speaking time, tension, and postural changes, and regulation of social interaction (gaze, smiling, facial expression, and head nod). The experimental situation obviously increases the individual consistency, because the interviewer tends to maintain a similar general attitude toward all children.

The experimental studies concerning the individual style in dyadic communication may be interpreted in terms of an interaction between person and situation: some characteristics of individual speech and nonverbal behavior are stable under normal conditions, provided the role of the individual and his or her attitude toward the others remain the same. *Social skill* partly consists of an adjustment to the rhythm of conversation created by both participants. The skilled interviewers are "situationists" who are able to modify their personal pattern of speaking, whereas those less experienced are bound to behave according to their "traits." This interpretation is valid when the forms of behavior are coded at a low level of inference (page 115). If another level of inference is applied in coding, the skilled interviewers show more competence in adapting to different situations, and competence may be defined as a "trait." To express it more simply, qualified interviewers are able to discriminate between situations and partners and they act according to it (Mischel, 1973a). The limitation of this interpretation is that skilled discriminativeness and unskilled fluctuation of behavior according to occasional cues cannot be distinguished from each other.

Consistency of Styles in Interpersonal Tasks

Individual, dyadic, and small-group action were videotaped in a series of experiments (Pölkki & Takala, 1975; Takala, 1972, 1973, 1974a, b; Takala & Pölkki, 1974). The number of tasks (acting, interview, group decision making, etc.)

varied from two to five in each experiment. The forms of behavior, coded from the videotape, were divided into three main groups according to the assumptions of their style characteristics.

1. *Movements regulating social interaction*: glancing at others, avoiding gaze contact, smiling, utilization of extensive space, restriction of personal space to a minimum.

2. *Psychomotor indications of tension*: automanipulative movements of different parts of the body; rigid versus relaxed posture.

3. *Temperamental acts*: number of motor acts initiated; speed of movements.

Originally, it had been assumed that the psychomotor categories concerned with the regulation of social interaction would be relevant from the point of view of the communication interpretation of psychomotor styles: They had been expected to change according to the mutual roles and the interpersonal nature of the tasks. Nevertheless, both the indications of tension and the temperamental acts may also be directly associated with the interpersonal meaning of the condition.

As a whole, it was found in these experiments that *activeness* (number of self-initiated acts) represented a rather broad individual style of behaving. Whether it was mainly related to a general orientation toward the tasks (actively involved versus passive) within a set of experiments or a pervasive "disposition" could not be decided from the evidence of encoding studies. The results of decoding and peer rating experiments indicated that activeness may be the most central variable of psychomotor styles for interpersonal communication (Takala, 1974b; Takala & Pölkki, 1974; see also Davitz, 1964). The total tension scores were relatively consistent, regardless of the task, but the separate indicators of tension did not reveal a similar pattern. It was concluded that the individual habits of expressing tension were relatively specific and idiosyncratic. They may represent alternative modes of responding and show Person X Situation interactions, whereas the compound score of tension indicates a more general aspect of behavior.

With regard to the categories of interaction regulation some consistency was found that was not accounted for by the change of group composition. Personal styles were more sensitive to specific conditions and the type of the task than to group composition. Space utilization was most consistent and gaze direction least consistent across different types of social interaction. In any case, the individual interpersonal style is much more modifiable by external conditions and arrangements than graphomotor expression.

For a more general interpretation of the results, they may be compared with those obtained by Pitkänen and Turunen (1974), who recorded the psychomotor acts of 8-year-old boys during various types of individual and small-group tasks.

The consistency of psychomotor behavior was very high in space utilization and impulsiveness in the group tasks and after an interval of 7 weeks (+.50 to +.82 in space utilization). Psychomotor consistency was much higher than the consistency of coping strategies adopted in various tasks. One might assume that at an early age the utilization of space would be closely associated with general activeness and also indicate more dispositional individual behavior. Increased control of impulsive movements with increasing age and the social skill consisting of considering other persons' need of space in mutual interaction may decrease the generality of individual differences in spatial behavior and activeness and change their meaning. Again, increased "discriminative facility" with increasing skill or maturity (Mischel, 1973a) would be in question.

Perception of Consistencies in Interpersonal Behavior

At one level of consideration, personality traits may be defined as constructs created by the observers (e.g., Fiske, 1974). Decoding expressive behavior includes an interaction between the observer's person and situational factors (p. 117). The stable characteristics of the decoder are his cognitive constructs, whereas his role in interpersonal encounters may be the most central situational factor affecting person perception. The categories used for the description of others are determined by the intimacy of relationship and the observatory versus participatory role (Jones & Nisbett, 1971; Pölkki & Takala, 1975). The relatively high agreement among the decoders in their naive descriptions of first impressions, regardless of the amount of information (Takala & Pölkki, 1974), implies the existence of common association and identification rules (Cook, 1971) which are basic for these ratings.

This chapter does not attempt to describe the Person X Situation interactions in person perception. The examples of experiments are concluded by some references to the relationship between the psychomotor styles of the actors and the perceptions of naive observers about the actors. It may provide information concerning the importance of interpersonal psychomotor styles as cues for person perception. The individual psychomotor styles, as coded by means of the analytical coding procedure (p. 125), were correlated with the average impressions formed by the decoders on the basis of the visual presentation of videotape (silent film condition, Takala & Pölkki, 1974). Samples of the recording of each task were shown to different groups of observers.

The observers' rating of activeness correlated positively with the psychomotor style categories of space utilization, smiling, initiation of new activity, and gaze direction, but there were great fluctuations between the tasks. The rating of stability was most consistently related to indications of tension (−.27 to −.63), whereas the meaning of postural cues seemed to depend decisively on the particular condition. The rating of consciousness was associated only with rigid posture in one task (+.55); a similar relationship has been found previously (Takala, 1972). It should be added that among the external and physical characteristics of the actors no consistent connection with the ratings of the observers were found, except between that of wearing glasses and the impression of conscientiousness.

Accordingly, the impressions formed by naive observers can be partially predicted from some encoded style characteristics. The result supports the evidence of the generality and importance of these interpersonal styles. Simultaneously, however, it is obvious that the meaning of psychomotor style to the decoder may change with the change of the context. Here is an extreme example: Even though indications of tension are essential cues for the first impression of instability, they are no longer relevant for ratings that are based on long acquaintanceship. The present examination was limited to psychomotor styles. However, the cues for activeness and tension are redundant across the psychomotor, vocal, and verbal content channels of information (Takala, 1974b), and they are integrated in person perception, provided information on all channels is available.

CONCLUSIONS AND SUMMARY

The empirical data included in this chapter have demonstrated the existence of individual psychomotor styles or consistencies of various aspects of psychomotor acts. The dimensions of generality of these consistencies have been examined, and different theoretical frames have been applied in the analysis of psychomotor expression and communication. According to our approach, it is not considered essential what percentage of the variance of psychomotor behavior is accounted for by "person," and "interaction," because the results of such comparisons are decisively determined by the choice of methods and measures as well as by the level of describing behavior. Mechanistic adoption of an interactionistic view would not assist theoretical understanding of either traits or situations.

According to the present results, little consistency can be expected across graphomotor, gross motor, and interpersonal modes of action, whereas within each mode either narrow or broad categories of psychomotor style can be found. In interpersonal behavior, the amount of activeness, indications of tension, and utilization of space represent broad categories with significant consistency. These aspects of individual style are also essential for the impressions formed by external observers.

The generality and the nature of consistencies in psychomotor styles is associated with maturity and social skills, and different explanations for interindividual differences are required simultaneously to understand the development and change of psychomotor styles. Idiographic description of individual psychomotor styles has not been discussed in this chapter.

7

The Trait—Situation Interaction and the Physiological Correlates of Behavior

Daisy Schalling

University of Stockholm
  and
Karolinska Institute,
Stockholm, Sweden

Recent trends in psychology, especially the rapid growth of social learning theory with its emphasis on the environment and the great interest in person—situation interactions as determinants of behavior (Endler & Magnusson, 1976), have lead to a critical reassessment of the trait model. Mischel's 1968 book *Personality and assessment* has frequently been cited in support of a view that trait concepts are virtually useless and that there is very little evidence for the consistency of behavior that is assumed to be required for the trait model to be valid. Both these views are eloquently and convincingly rejected in chapters in this volume, for example, by Epstein (Chapter 4) and by Block (Chapter 2). Mischel himself later clarified his position in pointing out (Mischel, 1973a) that his main target was the lack of efficiency of trait assessment methods, their poor reliability, and their lack of ability to predict behavior in specific situations. His objections in this respect are worth attention. It appears, however, that Mischel has overestimated the importance of predicting specific behavior in a specific situation. In theoretical personality research, at least, one is more interested in estimating how individuals *tend* to perceive, react to, behave in, and cope with some relevant ranges of situations.

The classical trait model has been criticized for neglecting situational influences. As a matter of fact, according to the trait measurement model, variations in behavior across situations are regarded as error, as pointed out by Magnusson (1974a). It seems, however, that many modern trait theorists have disregarded the strict trait measurement model implications while keeping the trait model, using a set of hypothetical mediating variables to account for behavior. Most of them are implicitly interactionistic, at least in the more general sense of the word. On the theoretical level, situations are taken into account in many different ways (see, e.g., Klein, Barr, & Wolitsky, 1967). A trait score indicates the probability of a certain type of behavior's occurring in certain situations relevant for that particular trait. In predicting behavior, the intensity or provocation value of the situation must be taken into account, as well as the strength of the predisposition in the individual. As pointed out by Klein, Barr, and Wolitsky (1967), "there is no contradiction in viewing such readiness to act as autonomous aspects of personality which at the same time are locked into situational conditions" (p. 476). A position on a trait may therefore be described in terms of the degree of situational provocation required for a certain type of behavior or reaction to occur. A coherent pattern of behavior over situations is a sufficient basis for a trait conceptualization (Block, 1968a), and there is no need to assume a stable rank order of individuals across situations as to specific behaviors (cf. Magnusson, 1974a). For example, high-impulsive individuals may behave conspicuously different from low-impulsive only in situations requiring consistency, planning or vigilant attention to detail.

In this chapter, some aspects of a personality research project are described, within which trait—situation interactions have been systematically studied. We have found it useful to work with a few broad trait constructs, chosen on the basis of their theoretical relevance. However, an indiscriminate application of trait concepts is rejected. There is certainly no reason to assume that any behavior, in any situation, can be interpreted in terms of a trait. What can be used as a guide for the selection of some important personality areas in which fruitful trait conceptualizations are possible? Lykken's (1971) criticism against using factor analysis for "dimensional discovery," as a "taxonomic tool," seems well taken. However, the use of factor analysis for testing hypotheses of structures, based on theoretical assumptions, appears more interesting, although proper techniques for this purpose have only recently become available (Rosén, 1976).

Useful sources of hypotheses about potentially important trait concepts are clinical observation, and theory and research in psychopathology. Patients with anxiety neurosis, obsessive—compulsive symptoms, and psychopaths all give examples of behavior that may be conceptualized as traits of potential importance (Eysenck & Eysenck, 1967). In such extreme cases the disposition may be so strong that it manifests itself even in neutral, nonprovocative situations, which makes it easier to study (Klein, Barr, & Wolitsky, 1967). Neurobehavioral animal studies constitute another source of hypotheses concerning potentially interesting "consistent patterns of individual differences" (Gray, 1973).

The personality constructs with which we have been working in our laboratory have been chosen on the basis of such considerations. They are broad dimensions on a high level of abstraction and are regarded as mediating variables that are assumed to have certain physiological correlates.

IMPULSIVENESS AND ANXIETY PRONENESS
AND THEIR PHYSIOLOGICAL CORRELATES

This chapter focuses on two constructs for which there is some evidence that they are associated with coherent patterns of individual differences concerning (1) the modulation of sensory input and level of vigilance and (2) the modulation of emotion. Both are assumed to be involved in the attractiveness or aversiveness of different classes of stimuli or situations and in the "choice" of situations, which is an important aspect of an interactionist approach (Endler & Magnusson, 1974).

The first construct, *impulsiveness,* is assumed to have its physiological correlates partly in the brainstem reticular activation structures, and their associated neurochemical processes, having to do with modulation of sensory input (attenuation versus amplification) and maintaining the level of vigilance. We have used, somewhat inadvertently, the term "cortical arousal" as a common denominator for the underlying physiological processes.

Impulsive individuals are assumed to have a low habitual level of cortical arousal, although this level of course varies with circumstances. Their everyday behavior is assumed to reflect the tendency toward lowered vigilance, and efforts to counteract the rapid decrease in vigilance by sensation-seeking behavior. It should be noted that impulsiveness in the sense it is used here does not imply yielding to strong inner impulses as in the psychoanalytic use of the term. Instead, it implies weak restraints, lack of inhibitory self-control, lack of foresight and anticipation, acting on the spur of the moment, without much consideration of alternative choices or strategies (cf. Schalling, 1970). In personality inventories, impulsiveness has appeared as one of the two aspects of the more comprehensive extraversion factor (Eysenck & Eysenck, 1967).

The second construct, *anxiety proneness,* is assumed to have its main physiological correlates in some of the limbic structures and hypothalamus, in the autonomic nervous system, and in their associated neurochemical processes. We have used the term "autonomic arousal," again somewhat inadvertently, to denote the assumed physiological correlates of anxiety proneness. The underlying processes are involved in the evaluation of external and internal stimuli as potentially dangerous, and in the concomitant feelings of worry and concern, as well as more vague feelings of distress and panic. They are therefore related to differences in anxiety and sensitivity to threat. Anxiety-prone individuals are assumed to overreact emotionally and be more sensitive to stressful stimuli than less anxiety-prone individuals.

In our research we have tested various aspects of a trait model postulating a specific pattern of relations between components of anxiety and impulsiveness, and between these and the physiological arousal constructs (see Schalling, Cronholm, & Åsberg, 1975; Schalling, 1976).

This trait model is based on the assumption that man is a self-regulative system in constant interaction with his environment. A continuously active nervous system with varying patterns of arousal determines what will be selected as cues and what will be disregarded in each situation. Cognitive processing of stored information and of sensory input is of course of central importance for the person–situation interaction although not elaborated on in this chapter (cf. Schalling, 1975b). The model is influenced by neuropsychological, psychiatric, and psychophysiological research (e.g., Eysenck, 1967, 1975; Lacey, 1967; Lader & Wing, 1966; Routtenberg, 1968).

The main difference between this model and the Eysenck personality theory is that he works with the broader dimension of extraversion, including two correlated factors, sociability and impulsivity. The reasons for choosing to focus on impulsiveness have been outlined by Schalling (1970, 1975c). The predictions made on the basis of assumptions regarding physiological processes underlying extraversion have been found in our studies to be more valid for impulsiveness scales (e.g., Schalling, 1971). Among the evidence that favors a distinction between sociability and impulsivity may be mentioned a study on a group of criminals. According to Eysenck's hypothesis criminals are high in extraversion (Eysenck, 1967). When criminals were compared with matched controls on scores in inventory scales giving separate measures for the two aspects of extraversion, the criminals were found to score higher in impulsivity, but lower in sociability, both differences significant (Schalling & Holmberg, 1970). In several studies from our laboratory, these two variables have shown correlations with different signs with external variables. Furthermore, Eaves and Eysenck (1975) found that genetic factors contributed to a large extent both to the variation and covariation of sociability and impulsivity and concluded that there was some justification for regarding sociability and impulsivity as "distinguishable genetically."

The scales used to measure the *impulsiveness* construct are Solidity in the Marke–Nyman Temperament Scale, an impulsivity subscale of the EPI Extraversion scale, and two scales in a recently constructed inventory, Impulsiveness and Monotony Avoidance.

The scales used to measure the *anxiety proneness* construct are the EPI Neuroticism scale, the Validity scale of the MNT, and scales in a recently constructed inventory, the Multi-Component-Anxiety inventory (MCA), including in its last version three scales, Psychic Anxiety, Somatic Anxiety, and Muscle Tension. Detailed descriptions are given in Schalling, Cronholm, and Åsberg (1975) and Schalling, Tobisson, Åsberg, and Cronholm (1975).

Factor analyses on data from many different groups of students, conscripts, psychiatric patients, and criminals, have supported the classification of the scales (Schalling, 1975b; Rosén, 1975).

In addition to the two constructs described, a third construct has been studied in our laboratory, *socialization,* measured by means of the Gough CPI socialization scale (Rosén & Schalling, 1974).

There is empirical evidence linking both laboratory performances and some everyday behavior (e.g., smoking and traffic accidents) to inventory measures of *impulsiveness.* In a series of studies in our laboratory the construct validity of impulsiveness has been studied in various ways. Impulsive subjects have shown higher pain tolerance for electrical pain stimulation (Schalling, 1971, 1976; Schalling, Rissler, & Edman, 1970). Differences between more and less impulsive subjects in line with the theory have been obtained in a study on semantic generalization of skin conductance responses. The more impulsive subjects generalized more to homonyms than to synonyms of conditioned stimuli, i.e., they showed a pattern typical for subjects with low cortical arousal (Schalling, S. E. Levander, & Wredenmark, 1975). Furthermore, criminals and narcotic addicts, as well as heavy smokers, have been shown to be more impulsive than control subjects.

It should be noted that some American researchers have worked with similar constructs. Among these are Barratt (1972), Kagan (1966), and Kipnis (1971). Block (1965) has used the construct overcontrol versus undercontrol to cover behavior tendencies that seem in important respects similar to those implied in our impulsiveness construct.

Corresponding evidence for *anxiety proneness* has come from many studies (Eysenck, 1967; Lader & Wing, 1966; Martin & Sroufe, 1970). Comprehensive accounts of the anxiety concept and of the physiological basis for anxiety have been given by Epstein (1972), Lader (1972), and Spielberger (1972b). Anxiety-prone subjects tend to have, for example, a slower rate of habituation of psychophysiological responses to simple stimuli, and they have more difficulty in relaxing after stimulation. They appear to be more vulnerable, especially to ego threat (Spielberger, 1966) than less anxiety-prone subjects.

In a series of studies, it has thus been shown that subdividing experimental groups according to measures on these traits has made the results of manipulating situational variables interpretable and meaningful.

IMPULSIVENESS, ANXIETY PRONENESS, AND THE AVERSIVENESS OF DIFFERENT TYPES OF SITUATIONS

One of the problems in studying interactions between persons and situations is that the influence of situations on behavior does not only depend on certain "objective" features of the situations but also, maybe predominantly, on the perception of the situation by the person (Magnusson, 1971; Ekehammar, Schalling, & Magnusson, 1975). Furthermore, this perception and the state of arousal or mood that is induced by a certain situation may vary, according to the position of a person on a relevant trait. This trait–situation interaction is an important aspect of interactionism (cf. Endler & Magnusson, 1974).

When studying interaction between personality trait variables and situations, the choice of situations is important. Situations may be classified as predominantly activating, characterized by a large amount and variety of input and thus augmenting the level of cortical arousal, and as predominantly monotonous, with a small amount and variety of input, and thus lowering the level of cortical arousal. Impulsive subjects may be hypothesized to prefer the first type, the "overstimulation," "thrilling" situations, whereas they would find the second type, the "understimulation," "boring" situations aversive.

Furthermore, situations vary with regard to degree of stress, danger or frustration that is involved. Some situations are predominantly neutral or relaxed, others more stressful. Anxiety-prone subjects may be hypothesized to find situations of the latter type especially aversive. Finally, there are different kinds of stressful situations. According to Spielberger (1966), trait anxiety is related to sensitivity to ego threat but not to physical stress. Findings in line with this hypothesis have been reported by Hodges (1968), Hodges and Felling (1970), and Lamb (1973).

These hypotheses regarding the interaction between individual differences and situational characteristics have been tested in a series of studies in our laboratory. In a preliminary study on criminals (Schalling & Levander, 1964), psychopathic, impulsive subjects tended to report more discomfort in boring situations, and less in pain situations, than did anxiety-prone subjects. The findings were therefore in line with the trait–situation interaction hypothesis.

In later studies, the aversiveness of a number of situations has been studied on groups of students, conscripts, and criminals. The descriptions of the situations are included in a rating scale, denoted the "Situational Unpleasantness Sensitivity" scale (SUS). Each situation is rated on a nine-point scale for degree of attractiveness versus aversiveness ("How unpleasant or pleasant do you think you would feel if you were in the situation?"). The situations included in the first version of the scale (SUS I) were classified, on the basis of item content, into four subscales with six items in each: Anticipation, Pain, Thrill, and Boredom. The items were chosen to reflect different kinds of "stressfulness," as well as overstimulation (Thrill) and understimulation (Boredom). (For a description of SUS I, see Schalling, 1970, 1971, and Schalling, Rissler, and Edman, 1970). The a priori classification of the items was largely supported by factor analyses (Ekehammar, Schalling, & Magnusson, 1975). The SUS has features in common with the Endler S–R scales (Endler & Hunt, 1966), but does not involve different response modes.

SUS I was modified by two graduate students, Pettersson and Sköld (1972). The new version, SUS II, has seven subscales, each including four items (Table 7.1). The scales are Anticipation, Criticism, Aggression (different aspects of ego-involving, interpersonal stressfulness), Pain–Medical, Pain (physical stressful-

TABLE 7.1
Situations in SUS II Grouped into Scales According to a priori Classifications

Anticipation
   Waiting for your turn to take a driving test
   Waiting to be interviewed for a job
   Waiting for the boss to introduce you to your new fellow workers
   Waiting for a TV reporter to interview you about your place of employment

Criticism
   Not being invited to a party arranged by your fellow worker
   Being interrupted by your friends, who change the subject, when you are going to tell
   something
   Being told that a friend of yours has unjustifiably criticized you behind your back
   Being criticized by your boss, who thinks you are careless

Aggression
   Seeing a man being shot on the TV news
   Seeing a fight on the street
   Seeing a man being attacked in a detective film
   Seeing a fox killing a hare

Pain–medical
   Getting stitches for a wound
   Getting an inocculation shot against polio
   Treating a wound with iodine so that it hurts
   Having a tooth filled without freezing

Pain
   Getting stung by a wasp
   Pricking your finger on a thorny bush
   Stepping on a sharp stone while walking barefoot
   Getting something in your eye that irritates you for a while

Thrill
   Sailing in a severe storm
   Being on a runaway horse
   Riding a canoe down the rapids
   Skiing down a steep hill

Boredom
   Peeling 20 pounds of potatoes
   Weeding a large garden plot
   Checking goods on an assembly line
   Waiting for a train that is several hours late

ness), Thrill (overstimulation), and Boredom (understimulation). Factor analyses have supported the classification, although some overlap has been noted (Pettersson & Sköld, 1972). In a group of 70 students, Aggression and Criticism items received the highest mean ratings for unpleasantness. However, there were sex differences. The men tended to give higher unpleasantness ratings in the Boredom scale than the women and lower ratings in the Aggression, Thrill, Pain–Medical, and Criticism scales.

Correlations between the SUS ratings and scores in anxiety proneness and impulsiveness inventory scales have been studied in many different groups in our laboratory (Hultberger, 1974; Molin, Schalling, & Edman, 1973; Pettersson & Sköld, 1972; Schalling, 1971, 1975a; Schalling, Rissler, & Edman, 1970). For SUS I the findings may be summarized so that more anxiety-prone subjects tend consistently to rate Anticipation and Thrill situations as more unpleasant than do less anxiety-prone subjects. More impulsive subjects tend to rate Thrill situations as less unpleasant than do less impulsive subjects.

The correlations obtained between the SUS II variables and personality variables are in the same direction. In a group of 70 students scores in anxiety proneness scales were associated with high ratings of unpleasantness in situations involving criticism and anticipation, but they were not related to unpleasantness in situations involving physical pain. These findings support the hypothesis by Spielberger, according to which ego threat, but not physical stress, is associated with trait anxiety. However, Neuroticism and Somatic Anxiety correlated with unpleasantness in Pain–Medical situations. It may be assumed that in this type of situation, other aspects than the physical pain are important. Unpleasantness in Thrill situations was positively related to anxiety proneness measures but negatively to impulsiveness and other extraversion measures, which was in line with the hypotheses outlined above. Extravert subjects rated less unpleasantness in Anticipation situations.

Preliminary results from two groups of criminals show the same trends, in general more pronounced. More anxiety-prone subjects consistently rated Anticipation and Criticism situations higher in unpleasantness than less anxiety-prone ones. More impulsive subjects tended to rate lower unpleasantness in Thrill and Aggression situations and higher in Boredom situations. The results are in line with the hypotheses and seem to be in agreement with what can be expected in view of the assumed physiological bases for these personality variables.

PERSONALITY AND SITUATIONAL DETERMINANTS OF SMOKING: AN EXAMPLE OF INTERACTION

Smoking is an everyday behavior that is interesting from an interactionist point of view. There are large individual differences both in the amount and in the situational patterns of smoking. The attractiveness of smoking may be mediated by psychological factors (e.g., by its ritual, psychosocial, and sensory–motor aspects) or pharmacological factors (presumably by nicotine absorbed in inhalating smoke). Smoking has effects on physiological measures and on certain laboratory performances (see, e.g., Frankenhaeuser, Myrsten, Post, & Johansson, 1971). The effects are inconsistent – both "stimulant" and "depressant" behavioral and electrocortical effects have been noted. This discrepancy may be dose dependent and perhaps also situation dependent. There is evidence for a self-regulating of dosage of nicotine. At least heavy smokers have been shown to consume more cigarettes and smoke with more frequent puffs when the nicotine content of the cigarettes has been lowered in double-blind experiments (Ashton, Watson, & Sadler, 1970).

Increased laboratory stress is followed by increase in amount of smoking. Schachter (1975) suggested that the increase might be a compensation for a stress-induced increase of nicotine excretion (reflected in decrease of urinary pH). Blocking the renal excretion of nicotine by administering high doses of bicarbonate had the effect of eliminating the increase of smoking during stress. Schachter concluded that at least in heavy smokers the smoking appeared to be largely determined by inner cues; they might have a sensitivity to the content of nicotine in the body. The finding of increased cigarette smoking during stress, by itself, would typically be interpreted as a situation effect. However, if you change the physiological state of the person, the influence of the situation may change. Therefore, many apparently simple demonstrations of the effects of situations on behavior may turn out to be instances of complicated interactions between the person and the situation.

There is some evidence that the varying effects of smoking may be related to the arousal-regulating mechanisms underlying the personality constructs of impulsiveness and anxiety proneness, as described above. Smoking may be used as a tool to reduce the distance to the "optimal" level of arousal for each person–situation combination. Results in that direction have been obtained in some animal experiments, and also in a recent EEG study on humans (Ashton, Millman, Telford, & Thompson, 1974). It was found that "the rate of nicotine intake in extraverted smokers was slower and associated with a stimulant effect, while in introverted smokers, the rate was faster and associated with a depressant effect in terms of changes in CNV magnitude" (p. 69).

If smoking is thus involved in arousal-regulating mechanisms, it may be related to situations inducing or demanding different levels of arousal. Frith (1971) studied the desire for smoking in different situations, described and classified into "high-arousal situations," concerned with stress and anxiety, and "low-arousal situations," concerned with relaxation and boredom. He found higher smoking desire in low-arousal situations, which he interpreted as being in line with an assumption of nicotine as a predominantly stimulant drug.

Myrsten, Andersson, Frankenhaeuser, and Mårdh (1975) divided a group of smokers into those who preferred to smoke in low-arousal situations and those who preferred to smoke in high-arousal situations. They were tested under smoking and nonsmoking condi ions in a low-arousal situation (a vigilance test) and a high-arousal situation (a complex sensory—motor test). Performance and general wellbeing were favorably affected by smoking only in the preferred situation type. As hypothesized, the effects of smoking were influenced by the type of situation in which it occurred, in interaction with the characteristics of the person.

The person—situation interaction in the area of smoking behavior and smoking motivation has been the object of a series of studies in our laboratory by two graduate students, M. Hultberger (1974) and D. Waller (1975). In a study on a large group of students (n = 156), smoking desire was studied in a range of situations. They were subdivided on the basis of classifications made by a group of psychologists into four types: emotional stress and concentration (high-arousal situations), relaxation and monotony (low-arousal situations). As in the following studies, arousal was used in the more general sense (Lindsley, 1951) as a dimension varying from deep sleep to extreme excitement. Self-rated smoking desire was highest in situations of monotony and emotional stress. The anxiety proneness variables were highly related to smoking desire in the emotional stress situations. Men who preferred to smoke in low-arousal situations had conspicuously low scores in Psychic Anxiety and in Neuroticism (Hultberger, 1974).

In later studies on students (Waller, 1975) a large number of situations were rated for smoking desire, and also for degree of arousal. Cluster analysis of smoking desire ratings for each situation gave seven types of situations. Among the situations belonging to each cluster, five were chosen in such a way as to insure homogeneity within each cluster with regard to degree of arousal. Care was also taken not to include situations in which smoking might interfere with a demand for motor activity. The following situation clusters were included in a Smoking Situation Preference scale (SSPS): low-arousal clusters (relaxation and monotony), moderate-arousal clusters (social occasions and concentration) and high-arousal clusters (anticipation and vague distress). The means and standard deviations for ratings of arousal in these situation clusters are given in Table 7.2. In addition to the SSPS, subjects also rated how often they smoked to achieve certain states. The smoking motives were classified as increased concentration, increased energy, increased relaxation, and increased sociability. Finally, positive and negative smoking effects were studied.

In SSPS, consistently higher smoking desire ratings were obtained for high-arousal situations (anticipation and vague distress) than for low-arousal situations (relaxation and monotony). High smoking desire was also reported for social occasions (Table 7.2). The results are therefore not consistent with Frith's results. The discrepancy might be caused by the greater care in the construction of the SSPS scale; for example, situations with demands of motor activity had been avoided and the degree of perceived arousal had been empirically controlled.

TABLE 7.2

Means and Standard Deviations of Ratings of Arousal and of Ratings for Smoking Desire in Situation Clusters in the Smoking Situation Preference Scale (SSPS) and Correlations (r) Between Ratings of Smoking Desire and Amount of Smoking (cig/day) in a Group of Students ($n = 45$): Ratings of Smoking Desire Are also Given for a Second Group of Students ($n = 75$)[a]

SSPS	Arousal ratings (0–25) $n = 45$		Smoking desire ratings (0–20) $n = 45$		Smoking desire ratings (0–20) $n = 78$		Corr. ($n = 45$)
	$\bar{X}$	SD	$\bar{X}$	SD	$\bar{X}$	SD	
Low-arousal situations							
Relaxation	5.60	1.64	8.89	3.98	10.19	3.88	.45**
Monotony	7.29	4.58	12.16	4.18	10.11	3.40	.49**
Moderate-arousal situations							
Social occasions	8.29	2.16	13.80	2.65	13.63	2.87	.41**
Concentration	12.49	2.56	8.50	4.43	7.59	4.31	.29*
High-arousal situations							
Anticipation	15.38	3.02	12.47	3.57	11.79	5.27	.14
Vague distress	16.58	1.99	13.53	3.36	11.69	3.95	.26

[a]Modified from Waller (1975).
*$p < .05$.
**$p < .01$.

Rated arousal and smoking desire were highly related for anticipation situations. Smoking desire in vague distress and anticipation situations was highly related to reported calming effects of smoking.

Heavy smokers rated more smoking desire in low- and moderate-arousal situations than light smokers, whereas there was no relation between amount of smoking and smoking desire in high-arousal situations (Table 7.2). Heavy smokers reported as motives for smoking increased concentration and increased energy more than light smokers. Furthermore, heavy smokers tended to be more impulsive, which is in line with many earlier studies (Smith, 1970). Scores in impulsiveness were related to the motive to increase concentration.

The pattern of these results is in line with the assumption that more impulsive subjects and more heavy smokers seek to increase their vigilance level and concentration by smoking. It is an intriguing hypothesis that the stimulant properties of nicotine may be more effective in impulsive extravert individuals who tend to become drowsy especially in monotonous situations. Experimental findings that give some support to such an interpretation have been reported by Ashton, Millman, Telford, and Thompson (1974), as mentioned above. Of course, other interpretations are possible. Monotonous situations may lead to suboptimal levels of cortical arousal and a concomitant increase of autonomic arousal (London, Schubert, & Washburn, 1972). A special kind of "tranquillizing" might thus be involved.

More anxiety-prone subjects rated higher smoking desire in anticipation and vague distress situations than less anxiety-prone subjects. The anxiety proneness variables were also related to smoking motives of increased relaxation. Surprisingly, however, the more anxiety-prone subjects rated the effects of smoking more negatively, e.g., reported getting "more irritated." To complete the picture, the anxiety-prone smoker had also significantly more often tried to quit smoking.

Smoking behavior illustrates the interaction between personality traits and characteristics of situations and appears to be associated with the regulation of arousal. Anxiety-prone individuals try to use smoking as a tranquillizer in stressful situations. In other situations, their self-reported smoking desire does not differ from that of less anxiety-prone subjects. However, the therapy appears to fail. According to self-ratings of effects, the anxiety-prone individuals do not achieve calm but become more irritated and stressed. Why do they continue? One explanation suggested by Jarvik (1970) is that smoking has some immediate positive effect. Furthermore smoking may facilitate short-term attenuation of unpleasant stimuli. It is possible that the heart rate increase induced by smoking is involved in this attenuation. There is some evidence that increased heart rate contributes to such "coping" effects (Hare, 1975; Schalling, 1976). The paradox may also be accounted for in terms of Schachter's (1973) attribution hypothesis. Anxiety-prone subjects may get some relief by attributing the inner turmoil they experience as being caused by smoking instead of by the stress of the situation. This hypothesis, however, appears tenuous.

The mechanisms mediating the trait–situation interaction in the area of smoking are still obscure. Further studies are needed, combining experimental manipulations of situations, trait measures of relevant personality variables, and psychological and physiological recordings of smoking effects.

Acknowledgments

The work reported here has been supported by grants from the Medical Research Council (26 X-4545), from the Swedish Council for Social Science Research (588), and from the Swedish Tobacco Company (7408:7610).

8

Some Notes on the Concept of Cross-Situational Consistency

Clarry Lay

York University

The concept of cross-situational consistency in behavior is central to the person–situation issue. Consistency is typically viewed as evidencing the person position; inconsistency as supporting the role of situations. The very concept and its implications have often been oversimplified, however. This chapter addresses itself briefly to two of those oversimplifications.

My first indication that the term "cross-situational consistency" has been used in a deceptively simple manner came in the course of preparing a paper on the actor–observer bias (Lay, Ziegler, Hershfield, & Miller, 1974). What we met at that time was a basic problem in defining the term. More specifically, we were faced with the question of what was meant by "consistency" (the complexities in defining situations is a point dealt with by others in this volume). There are two basic interpretations of cross-situational consistency in the literature and one is often used without acknowledgment of the other.

In one, consistency is viewed in terms of intrasubject differences in behavior between situations, the lack of differences implying consistency. This view is implicit in all studies employing a variance components analysis. In contrast, cross-situational consistency may be defined in terms of the relationships of behavior across situations (over subjects), high correlations between situations implying consistency regardless of absolute differences. This latter view is entailed in any correlational analysis of behavioral consistency. People may then exhibit differences in their level of behavior across situations but nevertheless still be "consistent" in the sense of maintaining relative ranks across those situations (cf. Golding, 1975a). In our paper we chose the correlational view as the more fitting definition of cross-situational consistency. We then proceeded, however, to treat our data to reflect both definitions, employing a correlational analysis first and then a percentage of variance components analysis. The latter was intended to supplement the correlational data and to provide, uniquely, some information regarding the Person X Situation interaction.

We reflected on what a simple and basic definitional distinction we were dealing with and attributed our initial difficulties to our own backwardness. We soon discovered, however, that the distinction was not always an easy one to comprehend. More importantly, many investigators in the area seemingly failed to appreciate this distinction and its implications. I have one good, recent example.

Bem and Allen (1974) were concerned with the validity of our intuitions, as against our research, in the person—situation issue. They noted "the discrepancy between our intuitions, which tell us that individuals do in fact display pervasive cross-situational consistencies in their behavior, and the vast empirical literature, which tells us they do not" (pp. 507—508). In exploring this point, they unfortunately switched back and forth from the correlational view of consistency to the variability (lack of difference) view. For example, they introduced the term "scalability" as a requirement of consistency imposed by the traditional research paradigm, that the sample of subjects must all rank order the "difficulty levels" of the behaviors in the same way. This is clearly a correlational approach to defining consistency. Bem and Allen made this very clear in their paper, describing exceptions where the relative ranking of "friendly" behavior over situations is not maintained by them, the second author adhering to a "people in general" ranking, the first author disrupting that ranking (as illustrated, in fact, in the "interactional" model in Figure 1 of Argyle & Little, 1972). In then going on to suggest how one could conduct research based on an idiographic approach leading to nomothetic principles, the reader was advised to "separate those individuals who are cross-situationally consistent on the trait dimension and throw the others out . . ." (p. 512). They continued, however, with the puzzling statement that "Unless an individual's variance on a particular trait dimension is small, it makes no sense to attach psychological significance to his mean on that dimension" (p. 512). Did they really mean variance? Their view of consistency had moved from a correlational approach to a variability interpretation within the same paragraph. Furthermore, in their empirical assessment of their recommended "idiographic" approach, variance scores across situations were computed and respondents were asked "How much do you vary from one situation to another in how 'friendly' and 'outgoing' are you?" To this question, did the Bem and Allen naive subjects respond on the basis of the "lack of differences" model of cross-situational consistency or on the basis of the correlational view? Unfortunately, until this question is answered the Bem and Allen empirical analysis is questionable.

To consider the perceiver's point of view, the correlational view of consistency would first have to be restated as the degree of congruency between the direction of differences in the behavior of an individual across situations and the direction of differences across those situations in people in general. Returning to the question Bem and Allen asked their subjects, in considering how much one varies across situations on a particular dimension, do we reflect on absolute differences in the level of our behavior between situations or do we consider the degree to which we maintain our relative ranking with others in general? At first glance it is more likely the former, variability view, although Bem and Allen have recommended the need for an idiographic approach on the basis of the latter, correlational interpretation. On second thought, when considering how variable our behavior is between situations, perhaps we make adjustments in perceiving differences between situations on the basis of our relative ranking or the "difficulty level" of the situations. If you are more anxious when traveling on an airplane than on a train, you very well may not see this as inconsistent behavior on your part.

I have obtained some unpublished data concerning this question. Unfortunately, the data offered no clear-cut answer. Depending on the behavior being assessed (in this case, *anxiety* and *hostility*), subjects apparently viewed consistency across situations both in terms of the variability interpretation and in terms of the correlational approach. Further empirical work is required on this question.

Regardless of how it is viewed, cross-situational consistency in behavior is linked to the concept of personality, the lack of consistency being deemed to invalidate the concept (Mischel, 1968). In the second part of this chapter I would like briefly to reconsider this link. Simply, could the consistency implying personality link not be viewed the other way around? Could we not just as well view the maintaining of relative ranks over situations of people in general (or the lack of intrasubject variability) as reflecting something about the nature of the situations, and inconsistency as reflecting something about the nature of people? When a person behaves in an expected manner in terms of the direction of differences between situations, does this consistency not tell us more about the situations than about the person? This reasoning implies that it is the Person X Situation interaction (i.e., cross-situational inconsistency) that reflects the person and personality. The person would also be reflected in his levels of behavior in each situation relative to others (i.e., intersubject differences within situations). This would certainly be consistent with attribution theory. Here the more atypical the person's behavior across (and within) situations, the greater the person or dispositional attribution. As Jones and Davis (1965) and Jones and Gerard (1967, pp. 264–265) have indicated, observed behavior of a low base rate, in relation to high base-rate behavior (or in our case, patterns of behavior across situations), increases the likelihood that an enduring disposition will be inferred from that behavior. Therefore, cross-situational inconsistency or incongruency, as opposed to consistency, might lead us to a dispositional attribution.

Going back to the Bem and Allen (1974) paper, a differing conceptual link between consistency of behavior and personality might well be at the root of the discrepancy they noted between our intuitions and our research regarding the state of personality. Miller and Norman (1975), in interpreting their data which countered the typical actor—observer bias, inferred that "indicating that one's behavior varies across situations does not mean that one does not perceive himself as having a personality, just as it does not mean that one perceives himself as being entirely under situational control" [p. 513].

Finally, the topic of cross-situational consistency might better be examined at this time independently of its possible implications for the concept of personality. The questions of consistency and the degree to which persons interact with situations, along with such related endeavors as providing a taxonomy of situations and of units of behavior are worthwhile in their own right. Their complex link to personality has often served to obscure these questions. The intent to study the degree of consistency of behavior in some specified domain at some specified unit of behavior over some delineated situations need not bring about abrupt defensive replies and maneuvering from those who hold a firm belief in the existence of personality.

Part III

PERSONALITY BY TREATMENT
EXPERIMENTAL DESIGNS

Part III contains eight chapters (Chapters 9–16) that are organized around the theme of personality by treatment experimental designs, in the field of personality research.

Fiedler (Chapter 9), using an analysis of variance person by treatment experimental design has demonstrated that group (and organizational) effectiveness is a function of the interaction of the leader's motivational structure (a person variable) and the degree to which the situation provides the leader with control and influence. The situation serves as a moderator variable, which interacts with the leader's personality in producing group effectiveness. Although the Fiedler studies are an example of mechanistic interaction, they are based on a sound theory that enables one to *predict* person by situation interactions.

Berkowitz (Chapter 10) is concerned with the interaction of internal qualities (person variable) and external conditions (situations) in effecting aggressive behavior. He suggests that impulsive aggressive responses are influenced by the interaction of the person's internal qualities (emotional states or thoughts), or persistent traits and various conditions, including situations (e.g., the strength of previously aggressive habits, the meaning attributed to the environmental details, and the aspects of the situation that are singled out for attention). These conditions themselves are influenced by both situational factors and relatively persistent personal characteristics. Berkowitz essentially uses a person by treatment experimental strategy and is concerned with mechanistic interactions.

Spielberger (Chapter 14) discusses the implications of the state–trait conception for interactionist psychology. He discusses the shortcomings of the extreme situational-specificity position and within the context of an interactional model of personality suggests that behavioral consistency over time is a function of the interaction of situation-specific personality traits and situations that reoccur over time. He provides empirical support for his contentions on the basis of his research on state and trait anxiety. For a similar interaction model of anxiety, with a somewhat different perspective the reader is referred to Endler (1976). Like Fiedler's and Berkowitz's research, Spielberger's research is congruent with the person by treatment experimental design research strategy.

Reid (Chapter 12) points out that in the past there has been a false over-emphasis on both persons and situations as determinants of behavior. He proposes the use of person–situation concepts that seriously consider both persons and situations and the complex interaction between the two. Reid favors broad band or global personal and situation concepts. This will enable us both to be situational specific and to use these concepts in a wide variety of situations. Reid believes that the concept of locus of control meets his criteria, because it can be used as an interactional concept within such areas as stress, crowding, intrinsic motivation, and helplessness. Like Mischel (Chapter 25), Reid is concerned with cognitively based individual differences. Reid's approach involves a person by situation experimental research strategy.

Zuckerman and Mellstrom (Chapter 13) suggest that the investigation of person by situation interactions would be facilitated if we defined traits (a personal variable) in terms of mean level of states instead of by general trait measures. Their approach is different from Spielberger's (Chapter 11), in that Spielberger suggests that we focus on situation-specific traits. Zuckerman and Mellstrom studied responses to actual fear situations. They conclude that although transsituational consistencies of responses within classes of situations exist, the general trait measure is not a fruitful one for assessing individual differences. Zuckerman and Mellstrom used a variance components strategy, derived from the analysis of variance, to investigate anxiety in college students.

Nuttin (Chapter 14) conceptualizes personality as a mode of behavioral functioning. *Personality functioning implies "objects" that are behaviorally dealt with. The totality of these objects constitute man's behavioral world.* The world (situations) of these objects is itself a function of psychological activity. Nuttin proposes that the personality–world unit (person–situation interaction) should be the unit of analysis. The flexibility of these units is related to the notion that humans can construct and represent their worlds independently of the objective environment. Using a person by situation experimental design, Nuttin discusses his research *on man's perception of his behavioral outcomes (successes and failures)* as a function of personality and situational variables.

De Bonis (Chapter 15) discusses the convergence and divergence of modes of anxiety responses with respect to the interaction of sex differences on trait anxiety (persona variable) and stressful situations using a person by treatment experimental design. She suggests, among other things, that sex differences with respect to trait anxiety are dependent on the type of situation being investigated and that degree of similarity between situations is a function of the type of mode of response being investigated (e.g., physiological or verbal).

Krau (Chapter 16) in the last contribution to Part III, is concerned with the role of set with respect to the perception of situations. Although situations have objective and socially patterned dimensions, the subjective and objective dimensions do not coincide because of psychological factors. Set influences the subjective perception of situations; however, objectively existing dimensions of reality provide strong stimulants and this corrects for misperceptions caused by subjective factors. Krau suggests correlational techniques and variance components technique as means of studying interactions of set (a person variable) and objective aspects of situations.

9
What Triggers the Person—
Situation Interaction
in Leadership?

Fred E. Fiedler

University of Washington

The statement that an individual's behavior is the product of the interaction between the situation and his personality is now a well-accepted truism that has long ceased to startle us. However, this is a completely empty phrase unless we are able to state explicitly what particular aspect of the situation and which particular personality variable interact in producing a given behavior. This chapter deals with the interactions between an index of an individual's motivational structure, measured by the Least Preferred Co-worker, or LPC, score, and the degree to which the situation provides control, influence, and structure. Most of the data relevant to this interaction were obtained in the context of leadership research.

In many respects, the leader—member interaction is particularly appropriate for research of this type. Most emotionally intense interpersonal relationships are private affairs. These are, of course, the only ones in which we can expect strong effects. For example, the interaction between husband and wife is by nature intimate and largely hidden from view. To a substantial albeit somewhat lesser degree this is equally true of the relationship between parent and child, between close friends, and between partners in a business venture. In contrast, the relationship between a leader and his group is by definition open to public observation. Except for the relatively isolated instances in which a leader takes one of his or her subordinates aside for a private conference, or for the rare eyeball to eyeball confrontation, most behaviors of the leader are usually under the close scrutiny of all others who are in his or her group.

Authority relations in groups and organizations tend to be of considerable emotional importance to all participants in the interaction. Leaders tend to worry a great deal about the performance of their groups, about the way in which they are seen by their subordinates, and how they are evaluated by their own superiors. Most subordinates are extremely concerned with the leader's evaluation of them, and their relationship with the leader. A cross word or a scowl from the supervisor is usually enough to bring discomfort to an employee, and a reprimand is seen by many subordinates as a severe blow to their ego. Neither can there be any doubt that the superior's judgment may greatly affect the subordinate's fate in the organization. Not surprisingly, therefore, the leader tends to be closely observed and watched by those who are his or her followers and subordinates.

Over the last two decades, leadership has gradually emerged as an area of research that is almost exclusively devoted to the study of the interaction between the leader's personality or behavior and the situation (Hollander & Julian, 1969). The leadership and management field is currently full of books and scientific papers that speak about contingencies, and I am pleased to think that our research had something to do with this trend.

Practically all current leadership theories and models now say that the same leader does not necessarily perform equally well or poorly in all situations and that different types of individuals perform better in some situations than in others. Few, if any, major leadership research programs today assume one magic leadership trait that determines success, although there are still a number of positions which hold that there is one ideal type of leader behavior or one ideal type of leadership strategy. Some say, for example, that a permissive or participative type of leadership is better than one which is autocratic. There is, however, little empirical evidence to support these views (Stogdill, 1974).

In the contingency model of leadership effectiveness (Fiedler, 1964, 1967) the interaction of leader personality and situation is the crucial element for understanding leader performance and leader behavior. This theory is briefly described below, followed by a discussion in greater detail of the nature of the interaction and the underlying bases that seem to explain the particular findings of our research program.

THE CONTINGENCY MODEL

The theory holds that the effectiveness of a task group or of an organization depends on two main factors: the leader's motivational system (leadership style) and the degree to which the situation gives the leader control and influence. Leaders can be classified into two distinct types on the basis of the Least Preferred Co-worker (LPC) score. This score is obtained by first asking an individual to think of all persons with whom he or she has ever worked, and then to describe the one person in his or her life with whom he or she has been able to work least well on a short bipolar eight-point scale of the semantic differential format. For example,

Friendly	:__:__:__:__:__:__:__:__:	Unfriendly
	8 7 6 5 4 3 2 1	
Cooperative	:__:__:__:__:__:__:__:__:	Uncooperative
	8 7 6 5 4 3 2 1	

High-LPC persons, that is, individuals who describe their least preferred co-worker in relatively positive terms, are called relationship motivated. The relationship-motivated leader under stressful conditions needs to relate to others and is primarily concerned with maintaining close interpersonal relations.

Low-LPC persons, those who describe their least preferred co-worker in very unfavorable terms, are called task motivated. Task-motivated leaders are primarily concerned with more concrete evidence of achievement, that is, the accomplishment of the group task (Fiedler, 1972).

The second variable, "situational favorableness" (Fiedler, 1964, 1967, 1970), indicates the degree to which the situation gives the leader control and influence. It is generally measured on the basis of three subscales. These are the degree to which (a) the leaders are, or feel, accepted and supported by their members (leader–member relations); (b) the task is clear-cut, programmed, and structured as to goals, procedures, and measurable progress and success (task structure); and (c) the leaders position provides them with power to reward and punish and thus to obtain compliance from subordinates (position power). Reasonably reliable measures for each of these dimensions are available.

We scale situational favorableness generally by categorizing group situations as being high or low on each of these three subdimensions by dividing the groups at the median into those with good and poor leader member relations and high and low task structure and position power. This leads to an eight-celled classification shown on the horizontal axis of Figure 9.1, with the most favorable octant (I) shown on the left and the least favorable octant (VIII) to the right of the scale. An alternative method (Nebeker, 1975) entails standardizing each of the subscales and then computing situational favorableness by the formula

$$4(LMR) + 2(TS) + (PP)$$

where LMR = leader–member relations, TS = task structure, and PP = position power.

The theory assumes that a leader has most control and influence in groups that fall into Octant I, that is, where he or she is accepted, has high position power, and a structured task. He or she will have somewhat less control and influence in Octant II, where he or she is accepted and has a structured task but little position power; and so on to groups in Octant VIII, where control and influence

154 FRED E. FIEDLER

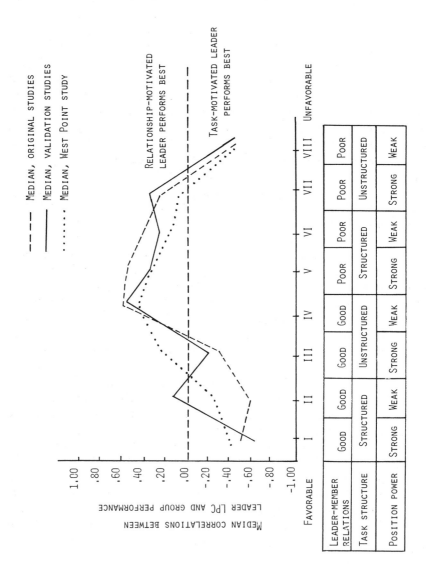

FIGURE 9.1 Median correlations obtained in original and validation studies of the contingency model.

are very small because the leader is not accepted by his or her group, has a vague, unstructured task, and has little position power. This assumption has now been supported in various empirical studies (e.g., Nebeker, 1975).

The research based on the contingency model has consistently shown that the task-motivated leaders perform best in very favorable or in unfavorable situations, whereas the relationship-motivated leaders tend to perform best in situations that are moderately favorable. Individuals who are in the middle of the LPC scale also tend to perform around the average on various types of tasks.

The vertical axis of Figure 9.1 shows the median correlation coefficients between leader LPC and group performance. A positive correlation indicates that relationship-motivated (high-LPC) leaders have performed better; a negative relation shows that task-motivated (low-LPC) leaders have performed better. The broken line in Figure 9.1 indicates the results of the original studies conducted between 1951 and 1963, whereas the solid line indicates the median correlations of the validation studies conducted since 1963. The coefficients of the original and of the validation studies correlate quite highly (rho = 0.75, $p < .05$) and show that the model does indeed predict group performance (Fiedler, 1971).

The dot–dash line shows the results of a major validation study conducted by Chemers and Skrzypek (1972) at the United States Military Academy at West Point. In this experiment, groups were assigned to each of the eight octants of the situational favorableness dimension by giving them high or low position power and one structured and one unstructured tasks in counterbalanced order. Most important, these teams were assembled on the basis of LPC scores and sociometric preference ratings that had been obtained 3 weeks prior to the experiment. The experiment accounted for 28% of the variance in performance scores (Shiflett, 1973). The magnitude of the correlation coefficients obtained in this study correlated .86 with the coefficients reported in 1964 for the original contingency model.

The contingency model shows clearly first, that both the relationship-motivated and the task-motivated leaders perform well under some situations but not others. Second, it is not accurate to speak of a "good" leader or a "poor" leader. Instead, one must think of a leader who performs well in one situation but not in another. Third, the performance of a leader depends on the interaction of the situation and the leader's personality.

It seems obvious that this theory is based on an important and very powerful interaction which has considerable relevance for the individual. In real-life situations, the outcome of this interaction may well influence the course of a person's career and professional life or the success of an organization. Let us now turn to the more specific behaviors and situational characteristics that this interaction involves.

THE PERSONALITY–SITUATION INTERACTION
AND LEADER BEHAVIOR

When we talk about the situation what do we really mean? In this context, at least, it seems to be the circumstances in the leader's situation that affect his or her degree of control and certainty versus lack of control, uncertainty and the concomitant threat and anxiety which he or she faces. One important factor that affects the nature of the interaction is the different way in which different types of individuals cope with this situationally aroused stress and anxiety. One major group, the relationship-motivated people, cope by seeking support from others and by attempting to strengthen the interpersonal bonds. These individuals become more dependent on those with whom they interact. In contrast, the task-motivated group becomes more concerned with the security that comes from achievement. In effect, "If I do the right thing, if I do my job, then "I'll be safe."

However, when the relationship-motivated individuals are secure in their environment, when their support from others is assured, then they want the "luxuries" of interpersonal relations, their secondary goals, not just to have the acceptance and approval of their subordinates but also of their superiors and others. This secondary goal generates behavior that is approved by the boss, which shows that the individual is efficient and concerned with the organization's work.

Task-motivated individuals in a condition that provides them with a great deal of control and influence also seek a secondary goal. When in the favorable situation the achievement of the task is assured by virtue of the leader's knowing what to do and having the support of the group, they can then relax and devote themselves to rewarding their subordinates for providing security and acceptance.

I want to show in this chapter that the increase and decrease of control and the attendant changes in security and certainty which this brings with it modify behavior in predictable and nonobvious ways. Let us, therefore, look first at the typical interactions between LPC and situational favorableness that affect leader behavior and then go on to some of the less obvious relations that these interactions permit us to predict.

The basic behaviors with which we are concerned in this discussion are related to the two major leader behavior dimensions, namely, the leader's attempts to develop a close, cohesive, and willing group and his or her attempts to accomplish the assigned tasks. The first set of behaviors is variously called by such terms as maintenance, social–emotional, or considerate behavior, or employee centeredness; the second set is variously called task-centered, job-centered, or structuring behavior.

In one of our early studies (Meuwese & Fiedler, 1965) we compared the behavior of relationship-motivated (high-LPC) and task-motivated (low-LPC)

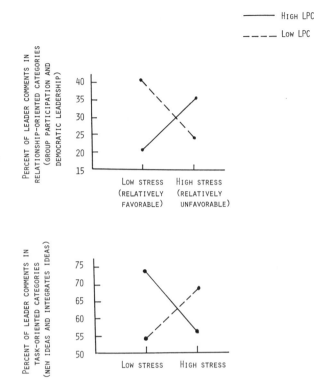

FIGURE 9.2   The effect of leader motivation (LPC) and situational stress on interpersonal, social–emotional, and job-relevant leader behavior.

leaders in a study that involved a low-stress condition and a condition of relatively high stress. Figure 9.2 shows this relationship for social–emotional behavior and for task-relevant behavior. The three-man groups in this study consisted of Reserve Officer Training Corps (ROTC) cadets who worked in three-man teams on tasks requiring some creativity. In the low-stress condition the groups were given to understand that this was a laboratory experiment without any consequences for their own military careers. In the high-stress condition the groups performed their work in front of a senior officer with rank of major, lieutenant colonel, or colonel, who took copious notes throughout the exercise. Observers rated the leaders' behaviors.

As can be seen, the relationship-motivated leaders manifested more task-relevant behavior in the relaxed condition and more social–emotional behavior in the stressful condition, whereas the task-motivated, low-LPC leaders were rated as higher in social–emotional behavior in the relaxed condition and higher in task-relevant behavior in the stressful condition.

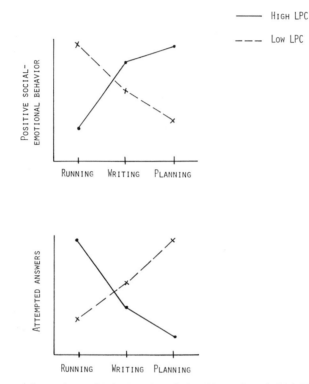

FIGURE 9.3 Comparison of behaviors by relationship-motivated (high-LPC, ——) and by task-motivated (low-LPC, – – –) leaders in three phases of an experimental task involving a class project of running a rat maze study. (Sample & Wilson, 1965, data, reanalyzed by Shirakashi.)

This relationship is also illustrated in a study by Sample and Wilson (1965). These investigators made up three-man teams of students in a large introductory psychology class. Each of the teams was given a rat and the assignment to plan, run, and report on a rat learning experiment. Unknown to the students, the subject of the experiment was not the rat but the team's leader, who was observed throughout the experiment.

Sample and Wilson showed that the high- and the low-LPC leaders behaved quite differently in the planning, reporting, and running phase of their study. This relationship is shown on Figure 9.3. The planning phase, of course, is the least structured of these and therefore the least favorable to the leader. The running phase is the most structured and therefore the most favorable situation for the leader. The interaction is again quite obvious. Moreover, this study is especially interesting because the same individuals were observed as behaving quite differently toward their group members in the three phases of the experiment. A number of other field studies and experiments have yielded similar findings (see Fiedler, 1972; Larson & Rowland, 1973).

The next logical step is to see whether a deliberate or incidental change in the leadership situation results in a corresponding change in leader behavior. One study that shows this to be the case has been conducted by Chemers (1969) in Iran. He developed a culture training program that was designed to provide information about the Iranian culture and specific guidance in how to interact with Iranians.

The experiment used three-man groups with American leaders and Iranian group members. These groups were given tasks involving negotiations and the development of recommendations on the employment of women and training of low-status supervisors. Both of these were controversial problems in Iran at that time. At the end of the task sessions the Iranian group members described the group climate, the leader's consideration for them, and their evaluation of the leader.

Specifically, we would expect a leadership training program of this type to increase the leader's control and influence by providing greater structure and thus to decrease his or her uncertainty and anxiety. This should then result in relatively more considerate, social–emotional behavior on the part of the task-motivated, low-LPC leader, but it should result in less considerate, social–emotional behavior on the part of the relationship-motivated, high-LPC leader.

Half the leaders were high-LPC and the other half low-LPC persons. These leaders were again subdivided and randomly assigned to a condition involving culture training or a control condition in which the leaders were given comparable training in physical geography of Iran. As noted above, the culture training is, of course, designed to increase the leader's control of the interpersonal situation.

Figure 9.4 shows the results. It is quite clear that the task-motivated leaders with culture training were seen as having developed better group climate and, although this is not shown on this figure, they were also rated as having been more considerate and as more esteemed. The relationship-motivated leaders were seen as significantly less considerate, less esteemed, and as having developed a less pleasant group climate.

A similar effect can be seen when we observe the behavior of leaders in relatively stable and relatively unstable environments. A longitudinal field study was conducted by Bons and Fiedler (1976) in which we obtained behavior ratings by infantry squad members of their squad leaders both at the beginning of the organization's training cycle and again 8 months later, just after the units had passed their combat readiness test.

We would expect here that a leader who retains both his unit and his superiors to have a more secure and structured environment. In this situation the stable organizational environment will typically enable the leader to consolidate his

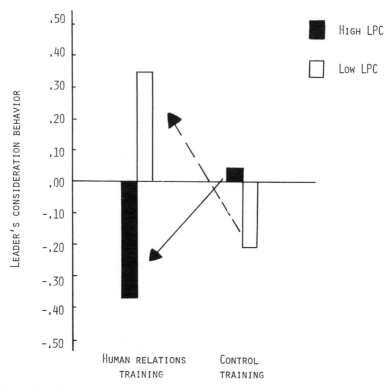

FIGURE 9.4 Effects of human relations training for high-LPC (filled bars) and low-LPC (empty bars) leaders.

control and influence. A leader who must adjust to a new set of subordinates and to a new superior has a more uncertain situation. He must first earn the respect and loyalty of his new subordinates because his ability to rely on them obviously tends to be less if he has worked with them only a short time than if he has gone through the entire training period with them. Likewise, the leader has to learn the expectations and standards of his new superiors, and he needs to develop a relationship with his new boss that enables him to judge with some certainty how far the superior is likely to back him in his dealings with his group members.[1]

We therefore expect the relationship-motivated leader in a stable environment to decrease his dependence on his subordinates. He will therefore be seen as less

[1] There is evidence, however, that the relationship-motivated leader essentially withdraws from the task and his group in situations in which his control is extremely low and his anxiety is very high.

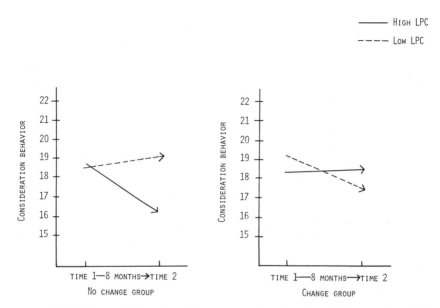

―――― H<small>IGH</small> LPC

‑ ‑ ‑ ‑ L<small>OW</small> LPC

FIGURE 9.5 Effect of change in job environment on behavior of high- and low-LPC leaders. (――), High LPC; (‑‑‑), low LPC. Change = boss change and/or job change.

considerate, whereas the task-motivated leader, secure in the knowledge that he can get the job done, tends to relax and develop a more pleasant, considerate relationship with subordinates. In the unstable condition, however, the reverse will occur. The task-motivated leader will become primarily concerned with task to the detriment of his interpersonal relations. The relationship-motivated leader will become more concerned with the support from his subordinates, and he will, therefore, become more considerate in his dealings with them. These findings are shown in Figure 9.5, and similar findings have been reported by Bons and Fiedler (1974).[2]

DISCUSSION

Our data throw some important light on the nature of a critical dimension in the leader–situation interaction, that is, the aspect of the situation which triggers different types of interpersonal behaviors in different personalities. Our research

[2] The situation is actually more complex than is here indicated. As one may expect, the old hands, those with many years of military service, are less affected by changes in unit and changes in superiors, and although there are a substantial number of relations in the expected direction, many of these were not quite significant at the 5% level. The general trends, however, are quite clear and follow the predictions of the model.

suggests that this critical aspect is related to the control and influence, and the certainty of outcomes, which the individual perceives in the situation. The interaction probably occurs because uncertainty and the attendant anxiety about the outcomes of the interactions in which he or she is involved evoke different coping mechanisms.

The aspect of personality, with which we are here concerned, can be interpreted as a motivational hierarchy, with relationship- and task-motivated leaders having different goal structures. For the relationship-motivated person, the goal of being related to others, and especially to his or her subordinates, is primary. His or her goal to be admired by others and respected by his or her boss is secondary. For this reason, anxiety-arousing conditions, such as unfavorable leadership situations in which the individual lacks assurance that he or she can achieve his or her primary goal, evoke behaviors designed to cement the individual's relations with others. A favorable situation, which is in part defined by good leader–member relations, allows the relationship-motivated leader to turn his or her efforts to the achievement of his or her secondary goal, that is, concern with how his or her boss feels about him or her (Fiedler, 1972; Larson & Rowland, 1973).

In like manner, the task-motivated person depends for his or her self-esteem on some tangible accomplishments, for example, completion of the task. Uncertainty and concomitant anxiety then focus attention on task accomplishment rather than on the secondary goal of pleasant interpersonal relations, which can be pursued once the performance of the task is secure.

That anxiety should play a major role in this interaction is no surprise. First of all, we do find that the reported anxiety of leaders in unfavorable situations is significantly higher than it is in favorable, high-control situations. Second, it has been known for a long time that anxiety is a very powerful motivator of behavior, and that many individuals behave quite differently when they are calm and in control than when they are anxious and uncertain because they have lost control over the situation. Under these conditions some people tend to become quite calm and collected whereas others tend to fall apart; some function much better under the challenge of an uncertain situation whereas others perform more poorly.

One major dimension, if not perhaps the most important, is then the structure of the environment that permits the individual to know what hangs together with what and what consequences his or her behavior will have on the outcome of a particular interaction. The situational favorableness dimension in leadership situations provides one measure of this certainty dimension, that is, of the perceived structure in the environment. We need to determine how this dimension can be adequately measured in other interpersonal contexts, and some of our recent research has dealt with this problem.

Finally, the interaction between the leader's motivational structure and the control he or she has over the situation throws important light on the processes that determine whether the leader is effective or ineffective. If the situation evokes a type of behavior that the particular leadership problem requires, the leader is successful. If the situation evokes the inappropriate behavior, the leader meets with failure.

How then, can the leader influence whether he or she succeeds or fails? Practically all leadership theorists have taken the position that we can improve leadership performance by changing the leader's personality or at least his or her interpersonal behavior in various leadership situations. Our prescription is quite different. Our faith that we can change the leader's personality is rather small. Our faith is considerably greater that we can teach the leader to identify the types of situations in which he or she is likely to be successful, and if necessary, to modify his or her control and influence to match it to his or her motivational structure. A recently developed leadership training program (Fiedler, Chemers, & Mahar, 1976) teaches the leader how to match the situation to his or her personality. The efficacy of this approach for improving leadership performance has now been supported.

Acknowledgments

The research reported in this paper was in part supported by Contract NR 177-472, N00014-67-A-0103-0012, with the Office of Naval Research and ARPA Order 454; Contract NR 177-473, N00014-67-A-0103-0013, with the Advanced Research Projects Agency (Fred E. Fiedler, Principal Investigator); and in part by Department of the Army contract No. DAHC 19-74-G-0005 (Fred E. Fiedler, Principal Investigator). The author is indebted to Claude Steele for his helpful comments.

10

Situational and Personal Conditions Governing Reactions to Aggressive Cues

Leonard Berkowitz

University of Wisconsin

Many explanations of the violence in our society emphasize a single source: either the aggressor's personal qualities or the situational conditions that have driven or permitted them to attack others. In the first category aggression has been attributed to various characteristics within the individual: an aggressive instinct or a murderous mind or a hostile personality. Likewise, we sometimes hear about the aggressors' need to prove their masculinity and protect their image of themselves. If we do not like any of these accounts we may prefer to say that the attackers have acquired aggressive habits because their aggression has been frequently reinforced in the past. To get to the second category, however, we may favor a situational explanation and trace the violence mainly to frustrations or other aversive events or perhaps to group norms calling for aggressive action.

Most of these factors undoubtedly do affect the likelihood of aggression. Nevertheless, whether they refer to persistent individual traits or to the surrounding environment, the chances are that they are neither necessary nor sufficient in themselves to produce a violent outburst. In aggression, as in other aspects of human conduct, the behavior is governed by the interaction of internal qualities and external conditions. What people do, even their attacks on others, depend on the interplay between their psychological characteristics and the situation confronting them.

Some of the research conducted by my associates and myself as well as by other investigators shows how aggressive behavior can be influenced by the interaction of internal conditions (whether long-lasting habits or personality traits or short-lived emotional states) with specific environment stimuli. I shall

neurotic

165

summarize several of the findings here because I think these studies have implications going well beyond the matter of aggression. They can suggest which particular features in the surrounding situation can interact with an individual's existing qualities to affect his actions and why this happens. Here is how I interpret the research results. As I have proposed elsewhere (Berkowitz, 1973, 1974), the environmental details function much like conditioned stimuli to elicit those associated reactions the person is disposed to perform at that time because of the set he or she has or the habits he or she possesses or the emotion he or she is feeling.

Toch (1969) has an illustration of the interplay of these internal and external factors in his discussion of the behavior of extremely violent men. Like many of the people he studied, one of Toch's cases, a man named Sam, became highly assaultive when he thought his self-esteem was threatened. Confronted by what he regarded as a challenge, Sam could convince himself he was really worthwhile by beating up his opponent. Some types of encounters were particularly likely to enrage him. Apparently because he had been victimized a number of times by much bigger people when he was younger, even the slightest provocation at the hands of a physically larger person now infuriated him. In other words, it is not enough to say that Sam's aggression had been frequently reinforced or that he wanted to preserve his picture of himself. We also have to recognize that particular kinds of situations were apt to set him off and that he had learned to react violently to specific stimuli. His personality predisposed him to respond aggressively to certain kinds of situations.

Investigations carried out in my own laboratory and elsewhere have demonstrated how particular environmental stimuli can intensify an individual's attacks on others. For Sam a provocation associated with earlier pain (a physically big person) produced an extremely violent reaction. He was disposed to think of ambiguous encounters with others as threats, i.e., as painful events, and then to respond aggressively to these situations. Animal research has shown that pain-connected situational stimuli can increase the strength of the aggression displayed by an aroused organism. In one animal experiment (Ulrich, Hutchinson, & Azrin, 1965), for example, an innocent victim who had just happened to be nearby when the subject was first given shocks later drew the strongest attacks when the subject was again hurt. The victim associated with the previous pain elicited the strongest aggression the next time the subject was provoked. Similarly, at the human level, when young boys who had been deliberately defeated in a card game were then given an opportunity to shoot at various targets, their first attack was typically directed at the target most resembling their earlier frustrator (Moore, 1964). Again, this particular target was connected with the prior aversive event.

This type of pain-elicited aggression is not confined to the victims of aggression. Aggressors can become highly assaultive when they are in the presence of stimuli that have been paired with aversive events. For example, people tend to be more punitive if the object they use to deliver the punishment is associated with earlier pain than if the punishment apparatus does not have this pain connection (Fraczek, 1973).

Situational stimuli that are associated with aggression can also intensify aggressive reactions (Berkowitz, 1973, 1974). As one early demonstration of this, in one of our experiments (Berkowitz, 1965), university men who were required to shock someone after they had watched a violent movie actually administered more shocks to this person when they believed he was a college boxer than when they thought he was a speech major. Labeling the victim as a "boxer" had apparently connected him with the notion of "aggression," thus defining him as an aggressive cue and causing relatively strong attacks to be made on him.

Before I proceed further, I should again note that the aggressor's response to the situational cue depends on both the external stimulus and his or her existing internal condition. A habit is a readiness to respond in a certain way to particular stimuli. The person who has acquired the habit of extreme violence, an internal quality, has actually learned to react aggressively to certain cues, the situational factor. Geen and Stonner (1971) have given us an example of how this can operate. In their experiment they rewarded some of their subjects verbally for shocking a fellow student. After the initial training the men were told to shock this person again whenever a word appeared on the screen before them, supposedly in order to disrupt that individual's learning of the word. They had to deliver a shock each time but could vary the intensity of the punishment. Geen and Stonner found that the previously rewarded subjects administered more severe punishment to their partner in response to a word having aggressive meaning (such as "stab") than in reaction to a nonaggressive word (e.g., "wash"). They were also more punitive in response to the aggressive cues than were the nonreinforced subjects. The subjects' aggressiveness was therefore a joint function of both their reinforcement history and the environmental stimuli associated with aggression.

All this indicates that a major task confronting those who should like to predict someone's behavior is to determine what cues evoke emotional conduct. In the specific case of aggression, a fair number of studies have now dealt with one kind of aggression-associated situational stimulus: weapons. Although some investigators have obtained negative results (e.g., Buss, Brooker, & Buss, 1972; Page & Scheidt, 1971), other evidence indicates that the mere presence of guns does at times heighten the intensity of an individual's attacks on another person. For example, in addition to my original experiment (Berkowitz & LePage, 1967), Frodi (1973) demonstrated that angered Swedish high school boys administered reliably more shocks to their frustrater if weapons were nearby than if guns were not present, whereas the sight of a baby bottle and the picture of a mother nursing her child led to fewer shocks. Going south, Leyens and Parke (1975) exposed their Belgian university students to slides portraying various objects and then asked the subjects to report the level of shock intensity they wanted to give to their partner. The investigators found that the provoked men wanted to give their insulter more intense punishment after they had looked at highly aggressive slides, such as pictures of a machine gun or bayonet, than after they had seen less aggressive objects, such as a box of matches or a box of dessert. Meanwhile, back in the United States, Charles Turner and his students at the University of Utah have also shown how the sight of weapons can increase the level of an individual's aggressiveness. In one of their experiments (Turner & Goldsmith, 1976) male and female nursery school children displayed more antisocial behavior (not including makebelieve aggression) when toy guns were available than when novel, nonaggressive toys were present. The youngsters in this study, we might note, did not have to be angry in order to be affected by the guns. This was also the case in another experiment involving male University students at a college spring carnival (Turner, Layton, Fenn, & Simons, 1976). Whether or not they had been previously insulted by the target person, the nearby presence of a rifle increased the number of times the men participating in one of the carnival games threw wet sponges at him.

Still, this evidence certainly does not mean that weapons always enhance aggressiveness. Other conditions obviously influence the degree to which guns stimulate aggression-facilitating reactions. In the remainder of this chapter I should like to consider some of the factors that can affect these reactions to aggressive cues. At least some of these factors may operate in other forms of emotional behavior as well, activating dormant emotional dispositions.

Inhibitions against aggression are clearly exceedingly important. The play settings in Turner's experiments (in the nursery school and at the spring carnival) had probably lessened the subjects' restraints so that they could more readily display socially disapproved behavior. Many of the subjects in the experiments obtaining negative results were probably strongly inhibited. Turner and Simons (1974) have demonstrated that subjects tend to hold back on their aggression when they believe that the investigator is testing their psychological adjustment and/or is interested in observing their response to weapons. If people are concerned about showing how "healthy" or "normal" they are, they are apt to restrain their socially disapproved tendencies, including their inclination to attack someone.

Of course, there are individual differences in the readiness to inhibit aggression. Those who frequently crave social approval are likely to suppress any actions that may cost them the goodwill of onlookers. They want to avoid doing anything that may incur the bystanders' displeasure. Fear of acting improperly may also be aroused by a strong urge to behave in a socially questionable fashion. Whether or not we habitually seek approval, we may also restrain our aggressive inclinations when we are solely tempted to attack someone and believe our aggressive desire is inappropriate or perhaps even unjustified in the particular situation (Berkowitz, Lepinski, & Angulo, 1969; Berkowitz & Turner, 1973). Awareness of the improper urge generates anxiety and produces an inhibition of the disapproved behavior. Fraczek and Macaulay (1971) evidently observed this type of phenomenon in their study of reactions to weapons. On dividing their subjects into those who had many or relatively few emotional ideas (as previously measured), the researchers found that these two groups responded differently to the presence of guns. Only the less emotional men were reliably more punitive to their previously insulting tormentor when weapons were nearby. The highly emotional subjects, in contrast, were fairly aggressive after the provocation with or without guns present. These people may have restrained the strong aggressive inclinations stimulated by the sight of the guns, thinking that they had to keep their punishment within acceptable bounds; they were afraid of seeming too hostile.

These particular emotional individuals inhibited their aggressiveness because of the way they viewed their own hostile urge and not merely because they were aroused. Indeed, they probably would have attacked their victim fairly strongly if it was only a matter of their internal excitation. Psychologists have demonstrated in a variety of ways and with many different kinds of responses that a high arousal level energizes the dominant action tendencies operating at that moment. We can see this in an experiment by Geen and O'Neal (1969). Some of their subjects heard a moderate white noise after seeing a brief fight movie. These persons were then much harsher to the individual they had to punish soon afterwards than were others not given either the film cues or the white noise. In other words, the noise-engendered arousal had intensified the aggressive reactions stimulated by the aggressive cues on the screen, heightening the punishment administered. If we extend this finding to personality reactions, it appears that the excitement generated by loud noises, or other sources as well, increases the chances of people with aggressive dispositions responding violently to some aggressive stimulus.

The Fraczek and Macaulay experiment, as well as the Turner and Simons study, indicates that people are not mere puppets responding passively and automatically to the stimuli surrounding them. They think about their actions and judge the propriety of their conduct. They also assign meaning to what they see. We must keep this last point in mind when considering the weapons effect. Contrary to some criticisms, I have never assumed that weapons always serve as aggressive stimuli. A stimuli is a construction established by the beholder rather than an objective event in an absolute sense. Many people associate guns with anxiety arousal. They think of guns as "bad," "horrible," "dangerous" objects and, consequently, the sight of weapons causes them to be inhibited instead of extremely aggressive.

I do not know of any studies that document this point directly, but we do have some relevant evidence. In keeping with Lazarus' work on the cognitive appraisal of emotional incidents (e.g., Lazarus & Alfert, 1964), two of our Wisconsin experiments have shown that the impact of movie violence depends to a considerable extent on the viewers' interpretation of the scenes they watch

(Berkowitz & Alioto, 1973). They have to view the action as "aggression" if the film event is to serve as an aggressive cue. As in the first of our studies, therefore, if they see a football game but think of it as an athletic contest between skilled players trying only to win they are not likely to be particularly aggressive afterwards. They are much more apt to be aggressively stimulated if they believe the contestants want to hurt each other. The meaning they give to the witnessed occurrence determines its cue properties and thereby controls its ability to elicit particular reactions. Some people, much like Toch's violent man Sam, are characteristically quick to define the events they encounter as "aggression," and so, these events can easily precipitate violent reactions from them.

The second experiment in this series also testifies to the importance of interpretations. It demonstrated that the observers' response to a violent movie can be influenced by two kinds of meanings: not only whether they regard the scenes as "aggressive" or not, but also whether they think the incidents are "real" or only fantasy. Here too in line with other research (e.g., Feshbach, 1972), we found that our subjects were stimulated to display the strongest aggression after seeing a war film when they focused their attention on the aggressive instead of anxiety-provoking aspects of the battle *and* believed the fighting was real and not fictional. My guess is that the observers distanced themselves psychologically from the scenes they were watching when they thought the movie was only makebelieve, and so the screen cues had less of an impact on them.

Other kinds of interpretations can also affect the viewers' response. Leyens and his colleagues at Louvain (Leyens, Cisneros, & Hossay, 1975) have reported that the sight of aggressive objects is less likely to have violence-enhancing consequences when the observers concentrate on the objects' nonaggressive features. The subjects, Belgian military recruits, first looked at a series of slides, either aggressive (e.g., a machine gun) or nonaggressive (e.g., flowers) in nature. Some of those in the former group were asked to judge the esthetic qualities of the slides. Shortly afterwards all of the men were insulted by the experimenters' accomplice and then were told they could give him electric shocks. The aggressive slides increased the intensity of the shocks the angry men wanted to deliver only if they had not been concentrating on the esthetic aspects of the pictures. Whether the meaning of the objects was altered or other thoughts interfered with the aggressive reactions, attention to the esthetic features caused the weapons slides to be no more aggressively stimulating than the nonaggressive ones. It is well worth determining whether this phenomenon has a counterpart in persistent individual differences. Are some people typically likely to think of the nonaggressive — or nonemotional — aspects of the otherwise emotion-generating situations they usually meet? Maybe they attend to certain nonemotional features of these situations or perhaps they are reminded of other nonemotional occurrences. If so, those thoughts could dampen their emotional responses.

All in all, various conditions determine how people respond to the mere presence of guns or, more generally, to aggressive cues. This chapter has listed a number of these factors: the strength of their aggressive habits, the level of their inhibitions against aggression, how excited they are at the time, their judgment of the propriety of their hostile inclinations, the meaning they attribute to these cues, how realistic the objects or events are to them, and what aspects they are attending to at the moment. Many of these conditions can be situationally induced or they may be affected by relatively persistent personal characteristics. However they arise, these internal factors influence the aggressive reactions to details in the surrounding environment.

11
State—Trait Anxiety and Interactional Psychology

Charles D. Spielberger

University of South Florida,
Tampa

The relative importance of personality traits and situational factors as determinants of behavior has long been a source of controversy in psychology. With regard to the doctrine of traits, such personologists as Gordon Allport (1937) explain observed consistencies in behavior in terms of intrapsychic psychophysical dispositions. In Allport's (1937) view:

> In everyday life, no one, not even a psychologist, doubts that underlying the conduct of a mature person there are characteristic dispositions or traits. . . . Traits are not creations in the mind of the observer, nor are they verbal fictions; they are here accepted as biophysical facts, actual psychophysical dispositions related — though no one yet knows how — to persistent neural systems of stress and determination. (p. 274)

Although personologists generally acknowledge that both traits and situational factors influence behavior, proponents of situational specificity have questioned the usefulness of trait concepts (Bem, 1972; Mischel, 1968, 1969, 1973a; Peterson, 1968, Vernon, 1964). The major criticism of trait theory expressed by the advocates of situational specificity is that cumulative research findings over the years have revealed that behavior varies from situation to situation and that there is little empirical evidence of cross-situational consistencies which can be attributed to personality traits. In addition to asserting that trait measures have not proved useful in the prediction of behavior, Mischel (1968, 1969) further contends that traits are explanatory fictions based more on the observer's psychological need for consistency than on observed consistencies in behavior.

Although it is beyond the scope of this chapter to attempt to point out the shortcomings of the extreme situational-specificity position, in this volume Block (Chapter 2) provides an insightful critique and detailed refutation of

Mischel's earlier position,[1] in which he notes serious limitations in Mischel's review of the research literature on which his conclusions have been based. Block also reports impressive evidence from his own research of remarkable coherence in certain personality characteristics, extending over time periods as long as 35 years. An equally impressive case is made by Epstein on the basis of both logical considerations and empirical findings for the assertion that "traits are alive and well" (see Chapter 4, this volume).

TIME, BEHAVIORAL CONSISTENCY, AND INTERACTIONAL PSYCHOLOGY

Whereas the evidence of behavioral consistency reported by Block and Epstein is certainly impressive, the claims of Mischel and others are undeniable with regard to numerous studies in which investigators have failed to find cross-situational consistency in experimental research on personality traits. How can we account for the observations of substantial consistency and coherence in certain behaviors over time and yet little apparent consistency in many of these same behaviors over situations? The experimental evidence of both substantial consistency over time and lack of consistency across situations may be viewed as paradoxical, but a possible resolution of this paradox is suggested when it is noted that situations are completely confounded with time.[2]

The passage of time provides an opportunity for new situations to occur, and for the same or similar situations to reoccur. The fact that situations tend to vary over time gives rise to behavioral variability and inconsistency. However, most people live in more or less structured environments in which many activities (situations) are scheduled periodically, for example: a psychology course may meet on Monday, Wednesday, and Friday mornings; social engagements are often scheduled for Saturday evenings; and many people sleep late or go to church on Sunday. Over longer periods of time, there are obviously more opportunities to encounter similar situations, and it seems reasonable to expect that the greater the periodic occurrence of a particular situation, the higher the probability of an individual's developing consistent or coherent patterns of behavior to cope with such situations.

Over brief periods of time, we might expect new or different situations to occur more often than the recurrence of similar situations. Curiosity and boredom motivate people to seek varied experiences, in person or vicariously

---

[1] It should be noted that the extreme position taken in 1968 by Mischel with regard to situational specificity has been considerably modified (Mischel, 1973a). In Chapter 25, this volume, Mischel further clarifies his position with regard to the person versus situation controversy and appears to espouse an interactionist position.

[2] This important point was cogently noted by Clarry Lay at the Symposium on Interactional Psychology, held in Stockholm in June, 1975, on which this volume is based.

(e.g., Berlyne, 1950, 1954, 1965), which may account, at least in part, for the popularity of TV, the profitability of the tourist industry, and why psychologists attend conferences and symposia. Curiosity may also motivate undergraduate college students, in search of novelty and interesting experiences, to sign up for psychology experiments. Therefore, individual differences in curiosity and/or stimulation-seeking behavior (Zuckerman & Mellstrom, Chapter 13, this volume) may contribute to the erratic nature of behavioral responses to experimental laboratory situations and, especially, to the kinds of responses that are reflected in what Block refers to as T data (Chapter 2, this volume).

The trait versus situation controversy has stimulated a number of recent studies in which the investigators have ascertained the percentage of the total systematic variance attributable to individual differences, situational factors, and their interactions (Bowers, 1973; Endler & Hunt, 1969; Sarason & Smith, 1971). In these studies, more variance was contributed by person–situation interactions than by either traits or situational variables. On the basis of this research Endler (1973) contends that the person versus situation controversy is a pseudo-issue, and he suggests that the basic question should be rephrased: "How do individual differences and situations *interact* in determining behavior?" (Endler, 1975, p. 147). Endler and Magnusson (1975) have recently proposed a person–situation interaction model of personality and have reviewed the theoretical issues and empirical findings that support this position.

Within the context of an interactional model of personality, I shall argue in this chapter that behavioral consistency over time results from trait-determined consistencies in situations that recur over time. Fundamental to this view is the definition of a personality trait in terms of individual differences in the disposition to respond with specific types of behavior to particular classes or categories of situations. From this definition, it follows that consistency in behavior over time reflects the interaction of more or less situation-specific personality traits with situations that recur over time.

Consistency in trait-related behaviors can be observed in natural situations that recur over time, provided that the time sample is long enough for the situation to occur on a number of occasions. Such conditions and consistencies are clearly reflected in the research reported in this volume by Block and Epstein. Furthermore, if traits are situation specific, it should also be possible to observe consistencies in related behaviors in experimental laboratory situations that are trait congruent (Endler, 1975).

In this chapter, research findings for one particular trait and its associated behavioral and physiological correlates are examined for several experimental situations that were selected for investigation because of their presumed congruence with the trait in question. The trait to be considered here is anxiety and the situations in which the data were obtained were characterized by some degree of stress (Spielberger, 1966, 1972a; Spielberger, Gorsuch, & Lushene, 1970).

STRESS, ANXIETY, AND INTERACTIONAL PSYCHOLOGY

In general, personality traits reflect individual differences in acquired behavioral dispositions to view the world in a particular way and to manifest consistent responses to specified situations (Campbell, 1963). Trait anxiety (A-trait) is here defined in terms of relatively stable individual differences in anxiety proneness, that is, differences among people in the disposition or tendency (1) to perceive a wide range of situations as threatening and (2) to respond to these situations with differential elevations in state anxiety (Spielberger, 1966, 1972a). As a reactive disposition, trait anxiety remains latent until activated by the perceived dangers associated with specific situations. The Taylor (1953) Manifest Anxiety Scale (MAS) and the A-trait scale of the State–Trait Anxiety Inventory (Spielberger, Gorsuch, & Lushene, 1970) are representative measures of trait anxiety.

State anxiety (A-state) is characterized by subjective, consciously perceived feelings of tension, apprehension, nervousness accompanied by or associated with activation of the autonomic nervous system (ANS). Because it is widely accepted that most people respond to stressful situations with elevations in anxiety as an emotional state, A-states may vary in intensity and fluctuate over time as a function of the stresses that impinge on the individual. When A-state reactions are experimentally induced by stressful stimulation, the particular index by which the strength of these reactions are to be evaluated must be specified. Changes in heart rate, blood pressure, galvanic skin response, and muscle action potential have been used as physiological indicants of state anxiety (Martin, 1961). A number of self-report measures have also been developed to measure emotional reactions to stress (e.g., Spielberger, 1972a; Spielberger, Gorsuch, & Lushene, 1970; Zuckerman, 1960; Zuckerman & Lubin, 1965, 1968).

Two studies are reported in which the emotional reactions of persons who differed in anxiety proneness were evaluated in selected stressful situations. The fundamental question explored in these studies was the relative power of general and situation-specific measures of trait anxiety to predict changes in state anxiety under conditions in which the psychological or physical danger was more or less trait congruent.

Study I: The Effects of Threat of Shock on Heart Rate

Hodges and Spielberger (1966) evaluated the effects of threat of shock on state anxiety as measured by changes in heart rate (HR). The subjects were male college students who were high (HA) or low (LA) in trait anxiety as measured by extreme scores on the MAS. High-anxiety subjects had MAS scores of 21 or higher; low-anxiety subjects scored eight or lower.

The subjects in this experiment were also given a "Fear of Shock Questionnaire" (FSQ), which consisted of a single item: "How much apprehension or concern would you have about participating in a psychology experiment in which you received strong electric shock?" Subjects responded, from "none" to "extreme," on a five-point rating scale. The MAS and the FSQ were both given approximately 2 months before the beginning of the experiment.

High- and low-anxiety subjects were assigned, in equal numbers, to either a threat or a no threat (control) condition. In the context of a verbal conditioning cover task (Spielberger, Southard, & Hodges, 1966), the subjects in the threat condition were given the following instructions:

> That's fine. Now we want to see how a strong electric shock will effect the relationship between the verbal task and your blood pressure. During the remainder of the experiment you will receive electric shock. . . . Although the shocks you receive may be quite strong, they will not harm you. . . . After we attach these electrodes to your leg you will perform the same task as before. (Hodges & Spielberger, 1966, p. 289)

Electrodes were then attached to the subjects' left ankle as they continued to work on the verbal conditioning task while anticipating shock. No shock was ever given.

In the no threat condition, the experimenter paused for a rest period that ~vas equivalent in time to that required to give the threat instructions. Following this rest period, the subjects resumed working on the verbal conditioning task. HR was measured in beats per minute and recorded continuously throughout the experiment for all subjects.

Changes in HR for subjects in the threat and no threat conditions are shown in Figure 11.1, in which it may be noted that the no threat control group showed little or no change in HR as they continued to work on the verbal conditioning task. In the threat condition, the HA and LA subjects showed an immediate and substantial increase in HR of approximately 15 bpm but, contrary to expectation, no differences in HR were found for the HA and LA groups.

In Figure 11.2, changes in HR for subjects in the threat condition who had indicated little or no fear of shock (LFS) are compared with subjects who had reported moderate to high fear of shock (HFS). The increase in HR was more than twice as great for the HFS group (23 bpm) than for the LFS group (11 bpm); the linear correlation between FSQ scores and changes in HR was .43. The correlation of MAS scores with changes in HR was essentially zero, and the MAS and FSQ were also uncorrelated.

In summary, trait anxiety and fear of shock appear to be independent and unrelated personality traits, and only fear of shock predicted changes in ANS arousal in response to the threat of electric shock. These findings may be interpreted as indicating that students with high fear of shock, as measured by the FSQ, had appraised the stress situation as more threatening than had subjects who were low in the fear of shock trait. Therefore, the amount of ANS arousal induced by threat of shock was related to the situation-specific personality trait, "fear of shock," but not to more general anxiety proneness as measured by the MAS.

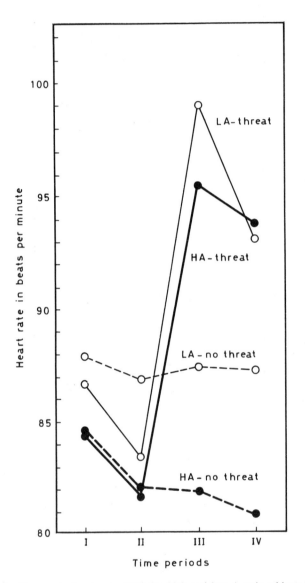

FIGURE 11.1 Changes in heart rate (HR) for high and low A-trait subjects in the threat and no threat conditions over time periods. During each period, HR was continuously recorded for 30 seconds. Reprinted with permission from Hodges and Spielberger (1966).

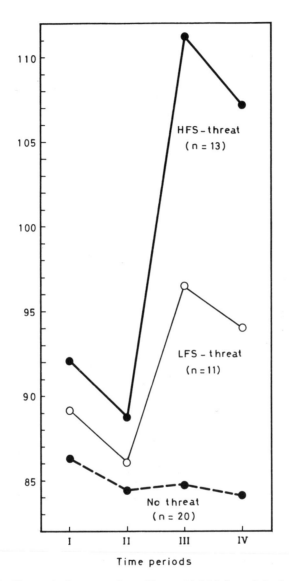

FIGURE 11.2 Changes in heart rate for subjects with high fear of shock (HFS) and low fear of shock (LFS) in the threat and no threat conditions. Reprinted with permission from Hodges and Spielberger (1966).

Study II: The Effects of Psychological and Physical Stress on State Anxiety

Lamb (1973) evaluated the effects of an ego-stress situation (giving a speech) and a physical stressor (blowing up a balloon until it bursts) on HR and self-report measure of state and trait anxiety. The subjects were undergraduate college students enrolled in a public speaking class who were selected on the basis of extreme Speech Trait Anxiety scores (Lamb, 1969, 1971). The Speech A-trait scale consisted of 20 items (e.g., "I am terrified at the thought of speaking before a group") to which the subjects were required to respond on a four-point rating scale which was the same as that used in the A-trait scale of the STAI (e.g., "almost never," "sometimes," "often," "almost always").

During an initial rest period, electrodes were attached to the subjects for recording heart rate, which was transmitted by telemetric procedures (Clevenger, Motley, & Carlile, 1967). The subjects were also administered the STAI A-state and A-trait scales, after which they were escorted into another room and given the following instructions:

> You are now to give a 2-minute speech on the topic "my most difficult class last quar-
> ter." You might want to include some discussion of why it was difficult, the content of
> the course, and the role of the teacher, but the content of the speech is completely up
> to you. Remember, the speech must last 2 minutes. I will stop you when you have
> talked for 2 minutes. Your speech will be televised with these cameras and the video
> tapes will be made available to your instructors in order to help them teach you to speak
> more effectively. You have 30 seconds to prepare your speech. When I give you the
> signal, go to the podium and begin. (Lamb, 1973, p. 119)

Each subject then gave a 2-minute speech that was recorded by means of a TV camera and videotape recorder. After the speech, the STAI A-state scale was readministered, first with instructions to "Indicate how you felt during the speech," and then with instructions to "Indicate how you feel now, at this moment." The STAI A-trait scale was also readministered during the postspeech period, with standard instructions ("Indicate how you generally feel").

After they had completed the self-report anxiety measures, the subjects were told, "When I give you the signal, blow up this balloon until it bursts" (Lamb, 1973, p. 119). Following the balloon burst, the subjects were given the STAI A-state and A-trait scales with essentially the same instructions as during the postspeech period of the study.

Changes in state and trait anxiety were examined as a function of speech A-trait and experimentally induced stress. The mean STAI A-state scores for the high (HSA) and low (LSA) speech A-trait groups in the rest, speech, postspeech, and balloon-burst periods are reported in Figure 11.3a. For both HSA and LSA subjects, A-state scores increased from the rest to the speech period, declined in the postspeech period, and increased again in the balloon-burst period. In contrast, as may be noted in Figure 11.3b, the A-trait scores, obtained at

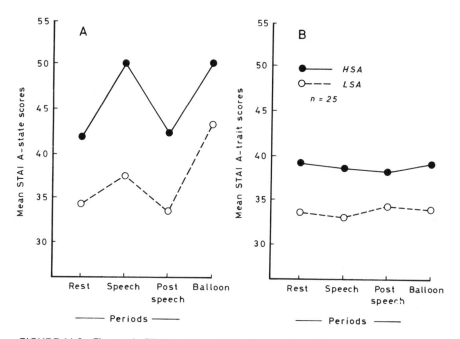

FIGURE 11.3 Changes in STAI A-state and A-trait scores for subjects with high (HSA) and low (LSA) speech anxiety scores in the rest, speech, postspeech, and balloon-burst periods. Reprinted with permission from Lamb (1969).

precisely the same time as the A-state measures, were remarkably stable across the experimental periods.

On the basis of Trait–State Anxiety Theory (Spielberger, 1966, 1972a), it would be expected that HSA subjects would respond with higher levels of A-state in the trait-congruent speech situation than LSA subjects but not in the balloon-burst situation. To evaluate this expectation, Lamb examined the A-state scores in two ways. First, changes in these scores from the rest to the speech period were evaluated for subjects who differed in speech A-trait. The significant A-trait by Periods interaction obtained in this analysis, when considered with the data presented in Figure 11.3a, indicated that the mean increase in A-state from the rest period to the speech period was greater for the HSA subjects than for the LSA subjects.

Next, changes in A-state scores from the postspeech to the balloon-burst period were examined for subjects who differed in speech A-trait. In this analysis, the main effects of A-trait and periods were highly significant but the A-trait by Periods interaction was not. These findings suggested that the magnitude of change in the A-state scores of the HSA and LSA subjects was comparable in the balloon-burst period.

As was found for the A-state scores, HR increased for both HSA and LSA subjects from the rest period to the speech period, declined in the postspeech period, and then increased in the balloon-burst period. However, in the analyses of the HR data only the main effect of Periods was significant. Changes in HR from the rest to the speech period and from the postspeech period to the balloon-burst period were therefore comparable for the HSA and LSA subjects.

In summary, the situation-specific measure of speech trait anxiety predicted the observed changes in STAI A-state scores in the speech situation but not in the balloon-burst situation. Greater increases in A-state scores were found in the speaking situation for the HSA subjects than for the LSA subjects, whereas changes in A-state scores in the balloon-burst situation were unrelated to speech A-trait. Heart rate scores increased in both the speech and the balloon-burst situations, but changes in this measure were unrelated to speech A-trait. Evidence obtained in research on computer assisted learning suggests that self-report scales may provide more sensitive measures of A-state in ego-threat situations than psychophysiological measures, such as HR and blood pressure (Spielberger, O'Neil, & Hansen, 1972). Such measures as the STAI A-state scale are specifically designed to evaluate changes in state anxiety, whereas physiological response measures may be influenced by other emotional states (e.g., anger) and by physical exertion.

SITUATION-SPECIFIC AND
GENERAL MEASURES OF TRAIT ANXIETY

In the two studies described above, situation-specific measures of speech trait anxiety and fear of shock predicted changes in state anxiety in trait-congruent stress situations but not in stress situations unrelated to the situation-specific A-trait measures. On the basis of evidence obtained in a number of recent studies on stress and anxiety, it has been demonstrated that changes in state anxiety are related to general measures of trait anxiety, such as the MAS and the STAI A-trait scale, under conditions of psychological stress but not in situations where stress has been induced by physical dangers, such as the threat of pain or imminent surgery (e.g., Auerbach, 1973; Hodges, 1968; Katkin, 1965; Martinez-Urrutia, 1975).

General A-trait scales predict greater elevations in A-state for high A-trait individuals in psychological stress situations that contain threats to self-esteem or ego threats. However, as Lazarus (1966) has pointed out, it is not the stressor that determines the emotional response, but the appraisal of the stress situation by the subject. In probabilistic terms, persons who score high on general A-trait measures are more likely than persons with low scores to (1) perceive situations that involve social and evaluative stress as more threatening and (2) experience greater elevations in A-state in such situations. Research evidence that has accumulated for the MAS and the STAI A-trait scales suggests that these general

A-trait scales actually measure individual differences in anxiety proneness in social-evaluative situations. Therefore, even so-called general A-trait measures are situation-specific although the situations involved are broadly defined.

More research has been conducted on test anxiety than on any other situation-specific A-trait measure. In the context of Trait–State Anxiety Theory, Spielberger (1972b) conceptualizes "trait test anxiety" as reflecting individual differences in anxiety proneness in evaluative situations. This conception implies that persons who score high on measures of test anxiety (Sarason, 1972, 1975a) perceive test situations as more threatening than individuals with low test anxiety scores. Consequently, highly test-anxious persons respond with greater elevations in state anxiety than low test-anxious persons to the evaluative threat inherent in most test situations (Spielberger, Anton, & Bedell, 1976).

Psychologically stressful situations, such as taking exams or giving speeches, involve the common attribute of posing threats to self-esteem. Therefore, measures of speech anxiety and test anxiety are moderately correlated with one another as well as with general A-trait measures. Whereas situation-specific test anxiety and speech anxiety are better predictors of A-state elevations in stressful situations that are trait-congruent, general A-trait scales tend to be better predictors of A-state reactions in stress situations that are not trait-congruent.

Evidence that has accumulated from research on situation-specific anxiety traits clearly supports the interactionist model of personality (Endler & Magnusson, 1975). By taking into account both individual differences in situation-specific anxiety proneness and the nature of the stressor situation, more systematic variance can be accounted for in personality research than when more general traits and more broadly defined situations are considered. From the interactionist point of view, consistencies in behavior would be expected for persons who differed with regard to a particular situation-specific personality trait but only in trait-congruent situations.

Over the past decade, the interactionist model of personality has received strong empirical support, and much progress has also been made with regard to the measurement of situation-specific personality traits. These advances have also served to make explicit the need for more systematic analysis and measurement of the major dimensions of situations. Magnusson and his colleagues (Ekehammar & Magnusson, 1973; Ekehammar, Schalling, & Magnusson, 1975; Magnusson, 1974; Magnusson & Ekehammar, 1975) have successfully applied multivariate statistical techniques in the analysis of stressful situations. Their research findings have demonstrated the importance of distinguishing between the perceptions of and the reactions to stressful situations, and they have shown that people perceive and respond to psychological stressors and physical dangers in different ways. Future progress in interactional psychology and in experimental personality research will require clarification of the complex relationships among situation-specific personality traits and more or less trait-congruent situations.

12
Locus of Control as an Important Concept for an Interactionist Approach to Behavior

David W. Reid

York University

With the increasing amount of research into the means by which personality and situational factors interact in affecting behavior (Magnusson, 1974a) there is an accompanying need for better theoretical models to explain person–situation interactions. Bowers (1973), Mischel (1973a), Endler (1975b), and several of the other contributors to this book have been leading the way toward developing these models. Many of these writers concur on two points of view: that greater consideration should be placed on the mutual interdependence between the individual and his or her environment and that greater consideration should be given to the way each individual cognizes his or her environment. A common position among these authors is to view each person's behavior as an ongoing *process* whereby changes in the environment can become intertwined with an individual's interpretation in such a way as to lead him or her to not only change his or her understanding of the situation, but also to change his or her behavior over sequences of time. The latter orientation of an ongoing process stands in contrast to previous trait models where individual behavior is expected to be rather rigidly consistent across all situations and over time.

Many of the foregoing points of view need to be much more rigorously refined and extended before they are going to be of much use to the research psychologist. Assuming the dynamic nature of person-situation interaction any theoretical models will have to be relatively global, allowing for application across many different behavioral contexts. Furthermore, they must be sufficiently malleable to allow their being operationalized in diverse ways to make them specific to the context in which they are being used. Consider the following as an example. Behaviorists are likely to concede that most behavior occurs only when there is an expected contingency (i.e., reward) or effect. Perhaps this should be viewed as two separate but interdependent concepts, with one being the subject's expected outcome of behavior and other being the desirability of the outcome. These should be called general concepts, but how they are specified should vary with the context in which they are used. In other words, the actual outcomes or rewards would differ from one situation to another, as would their desirability. The general concepts would be guidelines for the researcher, however, and, what is most important to emphasize, they would be measured as situation-specific person variables, not as enduring traits. Undoubtedly, there are instances where the same measuring instrument is applicable across situations and subjects responses on these instruments may also be stable across certain situations, but such cases are probably the exception.

A relatively recent concept that holds considerable promise for increasing our understanding of the interaction between person and situations is locus of control. This concept refers to the degree to which attribution of causality of behavior is made either to oneself or to sources external to oneself. From the already rather extensive literature involving locus of control it appears that behavior is strongly influenced by the degree to which the individual feels he or she is either in control of his or her outcomes or else is being influenced by various aspects of his or her environment.

SALIENCE OF LOCUS OF CONTROL
IN SOCIAL PERSONALITY RESEARCH

The remainder of this Chapter is devoted to delineating the salience of the concept of locus of control in current social personality research and to showing how this concept plays an integral part in interpreting the complex interplay between the person and his or her environment. It is important for the reader to realize, however, that in line with the earlier discussion, the concept of locus of control is treated in a very general way, allowing the specification and operationalization of the concept to take quite different forms depending on the behavior being studied.

In recent years a vast amount of research has been published on such topics as intrinsic–extrinsic motivation, attribution of causation, attribution of responsibility, psychological reactance, helplessness, stress, reactions to aversive stimuli, crowding, and individual beliefs in internal versus external control of reinforcement. Although this research is based on various theoretical models and uses quite divergent methodologies, each topic appears to deal with locus of control. A common theme among these topics is that the manner in which subjects attribute causality strongly affects their subsequent behavior. To illustrate this point the basic findings from most of these areas are briefly summarized.[1]

Intrinsic Motivation

One of the best applications of the locus of control concept is found in a series of studies on intrinsic–extrinsic motivation by Deci (1975), Kruglanski, Alon, and Lewis (1972), Lepper and Greene (1975), and Ross (1975). A general research paradigm followed throughout many of these studies was to give rewards to one group of subjects (often children) for doing an intrinsically interesting task and to omit rewards to another group doing the same task. Subsequently, the two groups of subjects were left alone with a number of tasks, including the intrinsic task. The experimenter measured intrinsic interest by recording which subjects played with the intrinsic task first, the length of time played with the task, and which task the subjects felt to be the most interesting. The general result was that those subjects who received an "external" reward for doing the task showed less intrinsic interest in the later session. These results have been interpreted in terms of attribution processes. Subjects in the reward condition are more likely to attribute their motivation for doing the task to the reward, whereas the subjects in the nonreward condition are more likely to attribute their motivation to the intrinsic aspects of the task. The point that has relevance in the present discussion is that the subjects in these studies have been sensitive to the existence of external sources of control even in relatively short-term, contrived situations.

Attribution to Causality

Many of the recent studies on attribution processes involve experimental manipulation whereby subjects may falsely see the cause of their behavior in external sources instead of in themselves. A good illustration of this is the study by Storms and Nisbett (1970) with patients suffering from insomnia. In this study, one group of insomniacs was given pills (placebos) with the instruction that the pills would produce alertness, mind racing, and other symptoms normally reported by insomniacs during periods of wakefulness. Another group of insomniacs was given the same pills with the expectation that they would produce relaxation. As predicted, subjects given the relaxation set reported greater difficulty with getting to sleep than did those subjects who could attribute their wakefulness to the pill. Although such studies as these (and those on intrinsic motivation cited above) demonstrate how subjects falsely attribute

---

[1] Space limitations have restricted the number of references and the amount of detail that can be given for each topic area. Consequently, only the most recent or more central references are given. Further references can be found within these sources.

their behavior or experiences to external causes there are other studies, such as those by Valins (1966) and Davison and Valins (1969), that also show how subjects can be deceived into falsely attributing causation to themselves.[2]

Helplessness

Seligman has succeeded in inducing what he refers to as learned helplessness by experimentally altering conditions. Learned helplessness has been demonstrated in a series of studies with dogs (Seligman, Maier, & Solomon, 1971) and more recently with humans (Herndon & Glass, 1975; Hiroto & Seligman, 1975; Thornton & Jacobs, 1971; Williams & Moffat, 1974). To induce learned helplessness a two-stage experimental paradigm is used. The paradigm involves first giving the subject a series of trials where it learns that no matter how it responds it has no effect on its circumstances. Later the subject is placed in a different situation where it must learn a new response. Usually the previous experience of having no effect (helplessness) impedes the subject from performing in the latter situation. Overmeier and Seligman (1967), for example, placed one group of dogs into a Pavlov harness and administered 64 unsignaled, inescapable shocks. A second group of dogs was also strapped into the harness but not given shocks. Twenty-four hours later each dog was placed in a different apparatus, where the experimenter attempted to condition the animal to first escape and then avoid signaled shock. A greater percentage of the preshocked group (63%) than the nonshocked group (6%) failed to learn to escape shock.

Weiss, Glazer, and Pohorecky (1974) have questioned Seligman's use of the learned helplessness concept to explain his data and have offered an alternative interpretation based on a chemical deficit rather than learning. They cite evidence to suggest that the experimental situations used by Seligman deplete norepinephrine in the brain. Norepinephrine is a neurotransmitter in the nervous system that can impede physical activity when normal levels of it are depleted. They postulated that when the dogs were exposed to inescapable shock the norepinephrine levels would be depleted, leaving the dogs in a somewhat immobile state where they could not make the necessary jump in order to escape shock. The depletion of norepinephrine is a temporary phenomenon, however, and the level reinstates itself over a period of time, thus explaining why Seligman's effects last little more than 24 hours. Weiss et al. acknowledge the fact that their interpretation does not explain all of Seligman's findings, but they point out that the learned helplessness concept may not be as viable as their own. No matter which theory is the better one, it still appears that the state of being without control leads to behavioral impairment; an interpretation supporting the importance of the locus of control concept.

[2] For further examples of locus of control and attribution of causation, the reader is referred to two excellent books by Jones, Kanouse, Kelley, Nisbett, Valins, and Wiener (1972) and by London and Nisbett (1974).

Perceived Control and Stress

Throughout most of their research, Glass and Singer (1972) have used a distinctive two-stage research paradigm to demonstrate the effects of stress. In the first stage subjects work at an abilities task, usually involving arithmetic computations. For the experimental condition the group works in the presence of an interfering aperiodic (unpredictable) stressor, such as noise, whereas in the control condition the group works without the stressor. Immediately following this there is a second stage where both experimental and control groups complete some additional performance tasks, but without the presence of any stressor. The general finding has been that no performance differences exist between experimental and control groups within the first stage, but within the second stage the experimental group does more poorly. Glass and Singer (1972) interpret these results in terms of Seligman's learned helplessness concept. Subjects in the aperiodic stressor condition are presumably more likely to experience being helpless, not only because they cannot arrest the noise but also because they cannot determine either onset or offset of the noise. This lack of perceived control subsequently interfered with performance on the poststress tasks.

To test this interpretation Glass and Singer (1972) ran a number of further studies. In one study using only two experimental groups, subjects received unpredictable noise bursts. Each subject in the first group was shown a microswitch on her chair and was told that he could terminate the noise anytime he wished by simply pressing the button. It was intimated, however, that the experimenter preferred that he not press the button, although the ultimate choice was entirely up to him. With this instruction subjects in the first condition could attribute more control to themselves than could subjects in the second condition where there was no microswitch or accompanying instruction. A postexperimental questionnaire measuring rated degree of control showed the manipulated perception of control had worked. On the poststress tasks the perceived control group did better.

Locus of Control and Reactions to Aversive Stimuli

Seligman, Maier, and Solomon (1971) and Averill (1973a), among others, have reported the effects of "perceived control" on the reactions of both humans and animals to aversive stimuli, such as electrical shock. Perceived control has been defined in many ways, two of which include being able to avoid the shock and being able to predict the onset of the aversive stimulus. It is generally concluded that perceived control over impending harm helps to reduce the noxiousness of the event. Although there is considerable support for this assumption Averill (1973a) cautions against overgeneralization. Additional variables must be taken into consideration. Yet it is interesting, in view of the current emphasis on interactionism, to note the substance for Averill's caution. He states:

> ... the relationship of personal control to stress is primarily a function of the meaning
> of the control response for the individual. ... The stress reducing properties of personal
> control depend upon such factors as the nature of the response and the context in which
> it is embedded and not just upon its effectiveness in preventing or mitigating the impact
> of a potentially harmful stimulus. (p. 286)

Crowding

Lawrence (1974) has recently reviewed the psychological literature on crowding
and human behavior. He reports that the results of research on the dire effects of
overcrowding on humans are inconclusive. It may be hypothesized that this type
of research suffers from a general failure to look at crowding from the
process-oriented frame of reference in which both the individual's perception of
crowding and the situational density are looked at concurrently.

   With crowding there is a greater likelihood that one has reduced control over
the events that occur to oneself. Perhaps in a densely populated situation those
people who feel crowded are those who also feel a greater loss of control because
of the density. Zlutnick and Altman (1972) have made a similar proposal
concerning tolerance of crowding. Sherrod (1974), using the Glass and Singer
stress paradigm, has shown that density is detrimental to subjects' performance
only when subjects feel they have no control over their crowded condition.

Individual differences in Locus of Control

Although the studies cited above demonstrate that locus of control affects
people's behavior they do not examine for individual differences. In other
words, some individuals may have a greater tendency to believe they have an
internal locus of control over their outcomes than others who more readily
attribute causation to external determinants. Yet a recent review of the literature by Lefcourt (1972, 1976) supports the existence of this tendency which has
usually been defined in terms of Rotter's social learning theory construct of
internal versus external locus of control for reinforcement. Reported validity for
the construct has been considerable and over a large number of studies it has
become increasingly clear that those subjects with a more internal orientation
react differently to certain situational variables than do those who are more
external. Research evidence suggests, for example, that the more internal subjects are more resistant to attempts to coerce them, are more sensitive to skill
challenging cues, and gain more information about what is going on around them
(Lefcourt, 1972, 1976).

   In the past the general tendency was to treat the locus of control construct as
a trait, even though Rotter (1966, 1975) never intended it to be used as such.
Furthermore, Rotter's I–E construct has generally been examined without

including measures of situational expectancies, values of reinforcement, etc., which are considered to be of equal importance in this theory. At last we are beginning to see a directional shift toward using nontrait-oriented, situation-specific measures of I–E (Lefcourt, 1976; Mischel, Zeiss, and Zeiss, 1974) which include theoretically relevant variables, such as value (Naditch & DeMaio, 1973) and situational confidence (Gilmor & Minton, 1974). In part, this trend began with the realization that Rotter's I–E scale was multidimensional and that the researcher could no longer assume people to be more or less consistently internal or external across all psychological contexts (Reid, 1975; Reid & Ware, 1973, 1974).

LOCUS OF CONTROL AS A PERSON–SITUATION CONCEPT

Although space limitations have restricted the extent of this review enough research has been cited to underscore the dominance of the locus of control concept in psychological research. Although many of the above studies operationalize locus of control in terms of experimental arrangement of events the authors invariably interpret their results in terms of the subject's perception and understanding of their particular situation. This latter approach is completely in line with the approach to interactional psychology outlined earlier. It is hoped, however, that future research can also be directed toward closer examination of individual differences in locus of control orientations within situations.

In order to apply the locus of control concept across these many topic areas it has been necessary to take a very general definition of the concept. Within each study the operationalization of the concept has taken a different form. In the intrinsic motivation studies, for example, locus of control was defined in terms of the salience of an "external" reward, whereas in the stress studies control was defined both in terms of predictability of a noise and an instructional set of being able to turn off the noise. Obviously, comparison between these studies is greatly limited because locus of control is not exactly the same thing in all studies. However, psychologists who require the operationalization of locus of control to be identical across different research topics are following an assumption of trait psychology that is not viable for the person–situation orientation being promoted in this chapter. In other words, although the situation-specific measures should be reliable and valid within the context that they are being used, there is no need for convergent validity across different behavioral contexts. The similarity shown across these studies has attempted to be conceptual in dimension and no more than that. Nonetheless the extent to which locus of control phenomena are applicable in most behavioral settings indicates how the concept functions as a guideline to measuring and predicting person–situation interaction.

13

The Contribution of Persons, Situations, Modes of Responses, and Their Interactions in Self-Reported Responses to Hypothetical and Real Anxiety-Inducing Situations[1]

Marvin Zuckerman
Martin Mellstrom, Jr.

University of Delaware

Endler and Hunt (1966, 1968, 1969) and Endler, Hunt, and Rosenstein (1962) have used their S—R inventories of anxiousness and hostility to attempt to provide answers to the old debate between personologists and situationalists as to which factors are of primary importance in determining behavior. These debates have been reactivated by social learning theorists, such as Mischel (1973a), and Endler's work analyzing the proportions of variance in response to the dimensions of his test has received critical scrutiny.

Bowers (1973) and Mischel (1973a) have conceded that the paradigm used by Endler and his colleagues cannot provide any conclusive answer to the broad question because the particular proportions of variance for persons, situations, or responses depend on the heterogeneity or homogeneity of the particular members of these classes selected for study. If one uses extreme situations one obtains large main effects from situations and the same obtains for the other

---

[1] This paper constitutes a portion of the paper presented by Marvin Zuckerman at the Symposium on Interactional Psychology in Stockholm, June 1975. The original paper was entitled: "General and specific traits as predictors of self-reported states and behavior in real situations."

classes, such as persons. Recently, for instance, Endler and Okada (1975) found that situational factors accounted for more variance in normals, whereas person differences across situations accounted for more variance in psychotics, with neurotics falling intermediate between the other two groups.

Recognizing this limitation of the Endler and Hunt paradigm we decided it might still be of value to apply it to the studies by Mellstrom, Cicala, and Zuckerman (1976) and Mellstrom (1976). These studies offered the unique opportunity to study the responses of the same groups of subjects to both hypothetical situations contained in tests and to the actual situations themselves. Endler's conclusions have been based on responses to hypothetical situations in tests rather than responses to real situations. Moos (1969) has been one of the few investigators to apply the Endler and Hunt paradigm to responses to real situations and he has found that persons, and persons by situations interactions, are of much greater importance than Endler's studies may lead us to believe.

In Mellstrom's studies we decided to limit our situations to a specific class of phobic ones and our responses to three self-report measures of different types: autonomic (heart beating), affect (fearful feeling) and behavioral (wanting to avoid or get out of situation). We used a relatively homogeneous group of college students. By limiting our variables we hoped to provide an answer to a more modest question than that one usually posed. Instead of the probably unanswerable question "What is more important in determining behavior?" we asked: "What is more important in determining fear responses in situations which are frightening to many?"

METHODS

Study I

Mellstrom, Zuckerman, and Cicala (1974) found that reported fear arousal and behavioral avoidance in female subjects exposed to a live snake were predictable from specific fear trait measures, such as the snake situation responses in the Zuckerman (1976) Inventory of Personal Reactions (ZIPERS), but not predictable from general fear measures, such as the Taylor Manifest Anxiety Scale (TMAS), or omnibus measures, such as the summed fear responses to all situations contained in the ZIPERS.

Mellstrom, Cicala, and Zuckerman (1976) extended this study with 76 females, who were each exposed to three potentially fear-evoking situations on three separate occasions. The situations included exposure to a live snake, looking down from a height on an open balcony, and being suddenly put into darkness in a totally lightproof room.

Prior to being exposed to these situations the subjects had been given the following trait anxiety measures:

1. General trait measures included the Taylor (1953) Manifest Anxiety Scale (TMAS); The Eysenck and Eysenck (1964) Personality Inventory Neuroticism scale (EPI-N); and the Spielberger, Gorsuch, and Lushene (1970) State Trait Anxiety Inventory (STAI). These traditional types of anxiety scales ask subjects about the frequency of typical affect and somatic anxiety responses without much specification of eliciting situations.

2. Specific Trait fear measures were obtained from (a) the standard snake situation in the ZIPERS and two situations for heights and darkness inserted into the test; (b) the fears of heights, snakes, and dark places in the Geer (1965) Fear Survey Schedule (GFSS); and (c) three Situational Fear Questionnaires (SFQ) constructed by Mellstrom to measure fears of snakes, heights, and darkness.

Fear responses were measured by verbal report measures, including the ZIPERS state test, and various objective or behavioral measures, including observers' ratings, task performance scores, latency, and duration of self-exposure. Because the model demands that the responses used be on a similar scale the present analyses are limited to three modes of self-report in the ZIPERS trait test (hypothetical situations), and in state tests given to the subjects as they were about to enter the actual situations. In the trait forms the situation is described and the subject is asked to recall how he has reacted to the situation in the past, or to predict how he is likely to react, if he has never been exposed to the situation or one like it. In the state form of the ZIPERS no situation is specified; the subject is simply asked to rate how he feels "now" on 13 items. The same 13 responses are used for each situation described in the trait form and in the state form. Three fear-relevant responses were used in the proportions of variance analyses for both forms: (1) "My heart is beating faster"; (2) "I feel fearful"; (3) "I want to avoid or get out of the situation."

Study II

The results of the first study (Mellstrom, Cicala, & Zuckerman, 1976) indicated that specific traits (responses to specific hypothetical situations relevant to the situations being predicted) were more predictive of responses to the actual situations than general traits. This was particularly true for the snake exposure situation. Because Spielberger (1972a) claims that such general anxiety tests as the TMAS and STAI are really tests of social anxiety instead of fear of physical harm we decided to include more situations clearly related to ego threat in the second study. Specifically, examination and interview stress situations were used along with a new physical harm situation, exposure to a live rat. Male as well as female subjects were used in the second study to assess the possible interaction between sex of subject and fear responses in the different types of situations.

The EPI neuroticism and STAI scales were used as measures of general trait anxiety and the ZIPERS trait and state scales were used. In this study an effort was made to write the specific situations in the ZIPERS trait form to resemble the actual situations used more closely than had been done in the prior study. Observer ratings and objective measures have also been used to measure fear responses in these situations but the analyses to be reported only deal with three self-reported responses in the trait and state ZIPERS forms for the reasons alluded to earlier.

The procedure for the rat exposure situation was similar to that used for the snake in the prior experiment. The subjects were informed that their task was to go and pick up the rat. Before they attempted the task, they were given two A-state scales (STAI and ZIPERS) with instructions to rate how they felt at the moment. At the same time they were rated on a behavior check list, describing objective signs of anxiety. The time it took for the subjects to touch the rat was recorded as their latency. The approach behavior was rated as a task score on a rating form describing a continuum of behaviors. The subjects then took the fear thermometer self-rating.

In the test anxiety situation the subjects were told that they would be given a difficult memory task that was a good indicator of intelligence. After the instructions they took the state tests and were rated on the checklist by observers. Performance on the learning task constituted the task score. The fear thermometer was filled out by the subject as the last step in the procedure.

An interview was used to create a social anxiety situation. While they were waiting for the experiment the subjects were observed and videotaped without their knowledge. Then the subjects were told they would be interviewed by three persons and their reactions would be videotaped. The subjects took the two state measures and this was followed by a nondirective interview with the subjects under observation from the interviewer sitting across from them and observers sitting to their sides. Another set of ratings was made during the interview.

RESULTS

Subjects Defined by Their Mean Levels of Response

In Table 13.1 we have presented the results of the proportions of variance analysis from Endler, Hunt and Rosenstein's (1962) S–R Inventory, Endler and Okada's (1975) new S–R Inventory, and Mellstrom's two studies, where proportions of variance were analyzed for both responses to hypothetical situations in the trait tests and the self-report state measures in the actual situations.

Looking first at Endler's studies of responses to situations in tests we see a marked change in results from his 1962 to his 1975 version of the S–R

TABLE 13.1
Percentages of Total Variation by Sources

Sources	Situations in tests				Actual situations, Mellstrom	
	Endler		Mellstrom			
	1962	1974	I	II	I[a]	II[b]
Persons (P)	7.3	3.8	29.5	35.2	28.0	29.0
Situations (S)	5.5	18.0	8.6	0.0	20.6	0.6
Responses (R)	24.3	2.5	0.4	4.6	0.5	5.7
P × S	9.7	19.2	21.8	14.0	22.7	21.5
P × R	10.9	8.1	2.6	16.8	10.1	11.7
S × R	6.4	6.1	0.6	2.5	0.9	0.7
Residual	35.9	42.2	36.5	26.8	17.2	30.8

[a]Exposure to snakes, heights, darkness.
[b]Exposure to rat, "intelligence test," interview.

Inventory: the variance from situations shows a marked increase, whereas that from responses shows a marked decrease. The proportion of variance from the interactions of persons and situations also shows a sizable increase. We suggest that the changes are largely a function of the change in the structure of the S–R Inventory. The reduction from 14 heterogeneous response categories to nine more homogeneous ones probably was influential in reducing the variance from responses. The 11 situations in the old inventory were also reduced in number to four, but as was pointed out earlier the situations now included two that elicited practically no anxiety and two that did elicit anxiety. There is maximum contrast between situations making for large variation in response, therefore, and, because the situations are stated vaguely, large person by situation interactions.

Mellstrom's studies, which used only three fear-relevant responses of the ZIPERS (heart beat, fearful feeling, and avoidance), found a much larger proportion of variance in test responses from persons and small proportions from the main effects of situations and responses. The persons by situations interaction accounted for substantial variance as it did in Endler's last study with the new S–R Inventory. In the second Mellstrom study the persons by responses interaction also accounted for a large proportion of variance.

Turning now to the actual state responses *in real situations* in the Mellstrom studies we see that the individual differences between persons still account for sizeable variance, as do persons by situations interactions. In both studies these two sources of variance account for about 50% of the total. The major change in the results of the two studies is that situations that account for a fifth of the variance in the first study account for an insignificant half a percent in the second study. The reason for this becomes obvious when the mean responses in the two studies are examined. In the first study the snake exposure elicited significantly more fear response than the heights and darkness experiences; in the second study, however, all three situations, rat, test, and interview, elicited almost equal amounts of fear and the differences between them were not significant. Responses that were an insignificant source of variance in the first study were a small but significant source in the second.

It is interesting to contrast the proportions of variance in test responses and those in the actual situations where the same response measures were used. In Study I it appeared that subjects showed less variation in response to test situations (8.6%) than actually characterized their differential responses to the real situations (20.6%). In Study II responses to situations in the test and in *actual situations* yielded similar proportions of variance except for a somewhat greater persons by situations proportion in the actual situations. In both studies the subjects reported significantly greater fear reactions to the hypothetical situations in the test than they actually reported when exposed to the real situations.[2]

Subjects Defined by General Trait Measures

The discussion about contributions of persons and situations to behavior is often confused with another issue: the usefulness of general trait definitions of

---

[2] Recently Golding (1975a) has argued that the generalizability coefficient is the appropriate technique to use, instead of the omega-squared ratio, to answer the questions concerning the influence of individual differences and situations. Whereas the omega-squared ratio used in the analyses by Endler and Hunt (1966, 1968, 1969) and Endler, Hunt, and Rosenstein (1962) reflects the percentage of total variation accounted for by persons and situations, the generalizability coefficient measures the percentage of observed score variation from persons or situations. The latter score reflects the degree to which an individual person responds consistently to all situations relative to other persons.

Mellstrom reanalyzed his data calculating the generalizability coefficients. Looking at the unit sample data he found coefficients of .33 for persons, .13 for situations, and .01 for modes of response on the responses to the test and .36 for persons, .34 for situations, and .02 for modes of response in the actual situations. These data led to similar conclusions as the omega-squared ratios in Table 13:1 where persons accounted for much more variance than situations in the hypothetical test situations, but situations were nearly as important as persons in the actual situations.

In Group II (rat, test, interview) he found coefficients of .38 for persons, 0 for situations, and .09 for modes of response in hypothetical situations and .31 for persons, .01 for situations, and .12 for modes of responses in the actual situations. These data are also consistent with the omega-squared ratios in Table 13:1, where persons were an important source of variance, whereas situations contributed little to the variance.

The generalizability coefficients, like the omega-squared ratios, indicate that individual consistency across situations was prominent in both hypothetical and actual situations in both studies, whereas situations were only consistent in their effects on subjects in the actual situations to which Group I was exposed.

persons. In the prior analyses the persons dimension was defined by their responses to hypothetical or actual situations. In the general trait measure the subject's level is assessed independently of his responses to situations. We decided to analyze the data in Mellstrom's studies by using the general trait tests to define three levels of persons: high, medium, and low. This procedure allowed us to compute a within-cells error term. The intercorrelations of the general trait anxiety tests in the first study were quite high: TMAS versus STAI, $r = .84$; TMAS versus EPI-N, $r = .86$; and STAI versus EPI-N, $r = .73$. Scores on the three trait tests were converted into standard scores and combined to provide one trait measure that was used to classify subjects. In the second study, the STAI and EPI-N tests did not correlate as highly as in the first study ($r = .46$) but they were combined in the same fashion to provide a more reliable measure of the trait.

Table 13.2 shows the proportions of variance using the trait scores to define three levels of subjects. The most striking aspect of the results is the high proportion of variance of the error term which accounts for 66–88% of the variance in test responses and 60–82% of the variance in responses to actual situations.

These results reflect the poor showing of the general trait measures in prediction noted in the prior paper (Mellstrom, Cicala, & Zuckerman), 1976). The findings of greatest interest are the proportions of variance accounted for by the A trait itself, as a definition of persons, and the persons by situations interactions. In the first study the A trait accounted for only 8% of the variance in the female subjects; in the second study it accounted for 13% of the variance in females but for only 4% of that in males. Although the A trait factor was a significant source of variance in both studies, its contribution was considerably

TABLE 13.2

Percent of Total Variance Contributed by Each Source Where Levels of General Trait Anxiety Constitute the Persons (P) Factor

	Situations in tests			Actual situations		
	I-F	II-F	II-M	I-F	II-F	II-M
A trait[a] (P)	4.0	19.9	0.0	7.6	13.2	4.1
Situations (S)	12.1	0.0	0.0	29.9	0.0	2.7
Responses (R)	0.0	6.8	7.6	0.0	7.2	9.2
P × S	0.7	1.6	0.0	0.7	0.0	0.0
P × R	0.0	1.3	0.0	0.0	2.0	0.0
S × R	0.9	3.7	4.3	1.3	0.0	2.4
P × S × R	0.0	.5	0.0	0.9	0.0	0.0
Error	82.2	66.3	88.1	59.6	77.6	81.7

[a]High, medium, and low defined by combining general trait measures (TMAS, STAI, EPI-N) into a single trait score.

less than when state responses themselves were used to define the person diminsion. The proportions for the persons by situations interactions were negligible and insignificant in both studies.

The results confirm what has been reiterated many times before: The general trait measure is a weak predictor of consistent individual behavior across situations (Mellstrom, Cicala, & Zuckerman, 1976) and time (Zuckerman, 1976) and relatively poor as a predictor of person—situation interactions. Therefore, Mischel (1968, 1971) may be correct in his attack on the conventional general trait measure as a generalized predictor of behavior, but he may be incorrect in assuming that relatively broad transsituational consistencies in human behavior do not exist. When we limit our study to a subset of fear responses in a subset of stressful situations we do find that persons (defined by their own mean levels of state responses) are an important source of variance, as are person—situation interactions. The influence of situation, in contrast, seems to vary widely depending on the arbitrary decision on which types of situations we select for comparison. The study of person—situation interactions could be facilitated if we defined traits in terms of individuals' mean levels of states rather than general trait measures, a possibility first suggested by Zuckerman, Persky, and Link (1967).

14

A Conceptual Frame of Personality—World Interaction: A Relational Theory[1]

Joseph R. Nuttin

University of Leuven,
Louvain, Belgium

THE PERSONALITY—WORLD UNIT

A major problem in studying the human person and his or her behavioral dealing with the environment is to construct a conceptual frame in which the personality—world interaction can theoretically be approached. Some well-known models have tried to solve the problem by giving priority to the environment and reducing it to the stimulus function, whereas the personality is a secondarily active organism reacting to the impinging stimulus. Other behavioral scientists have insisted on personality as a primary source of activity and have shown that man's behavioral "response" usually consists of *acting on* the environment in such a way that a continuously changing *inter*action process develops. In this chapter, I try to show that personality and environment or world are not to be considered as two autonomously preexisting units interacting with each other at a given moment, but that both, personality and world, only function and exist as two interdependent poles of a unitary behavioral process. This behavioral per-

[1] Originally, the text of this contribution consisted of two parts: a theoretical one, which is published here, and a report of a series of experiments written in collaboration with my associate, Dr. R. Vreven. The part actually presented at the symposium was the second one (Nuttin & Vreven, 1975); it was read by Dr. Vreven and describes the experiments, which are only very briefly referred to in the present contribution. This experimental part has been published in the *Journal of Personality and Social Psychology,* 1976, **34,** 734–745. It was assumed that the theoretical part of the paper would be of more interest to the readers of this volume.

sonality—world unit is the basic "entity" to be studied in psychology; it is functional and not "substantive" in nature. Our main points are made very briefly; for a somewhat more extensive exposition, the reader is referred to two earlier texts where the same conceptual frame is described in a different context (Nuttin, 1965, 1973).

First, personality is a mode of functioning that, essentially and intrinsically, implies an object or world. In other words, the psychological or behavioral functions[2] constituting personality, such as perceiving, imagining, thinking, planning, doing something, all imply and are an active reference to, and deal with, an "object." Therefore, personality as a whole, that is, as the hierarchical structure of behavioral patterns, is a mode of being actively or virtually related to a world. It is not sufficient to say that personality is "open to" the world, or that it is part of the interacting elements of the field. In fact, these statements imply that both, personality and world, previously and autonomously exist in and by themselves as substantive entities. It is claimed here that personality, functionally speaking, consists in a specific and active relatedness to a behavioral world, whereas this world itself is gradually built up in the process of personality functioning.

As to the behavioral world, our way of conceiving of it is connected with the concept of behavior itself. Admittedly, objects in our environment act on man along channels of chemical and physical processes influencing behavior, but behavior as a global act in a given situation is not primarily a reaction to physically defined stimuli, waves, and molecules; it can be explained only in terms of man's perception of, and dealing with, meaningful situations, objects, and people. This meaningful world gradually emerges from man's perception and understanding of behavioral relationships between people and objects, and from his behavioral participation in this functional network. In other words, the world is a construct of behavioral personality functioning. The world thus constructed is the "public" scene of people's behavior and the "object" they are acting on. Its meaning is more or less the same for all normal people living in similar cultural and physical conditions, that is, for people having particpated during the first stage of life in the same network of behavioral relations. For instance, this part of my perceptual space is a house for all of us, and this gadget is a telephone, that is, "something" that makes it possible to behave in a certain way, viz., to talk to people who are not present.

---

[2] The term "behavior" as used here includes all man's psychological functions; each of these functions can enter behavior either as its main component (as is the case for instance with perception when man's behavior at a given moment is looking at something), or as an ancillary or secondary component (as when one's behavior is going to a hotel; in the latter case, motor activity is the main component, whereas perception accompanies and guides one's steps). The term "personality functioning" is used in the same behavioral sense; it is identical with behavior as just defined.

THE WORLD AS PART OF PERSONALITY FUNCTIONING

Certain objects, now, play a more central role in the behavioral functioning of a given person. Suppose that a psychologist has organized the department of psychology at his or her university, or that he or she is the founder and manager of a factory in his or her home town. These parts of the public behavioral world are almost continuously the objects of the psychologist's thinking, feeling, and activity in general. As such, they constitute that person's *personal* world and have become integral parts of the functioning of his or her personality, including its development and history. The same applies to the family and other objects with which the person identifies. Thus, a person's personal world – the situations, people, and objects as he or she perceives and conceives them, strives for them – constitute the "objective" or "material" aspect of the personality, that is, its content. For other people, on the contrary, the same department of psychology or the factory just mentioned may be very peripheral or practically "nonexistent" items in the network of their behavioral activity; actually they are not parts of their personal world. In other words, the same public world gives rise to a great many different personal worlds. A person's personal world is to be conceived as part of his or her personality; the various "objects" in it belong to different, more or less intimate, layers of his or her identity.

In the context of this conceptual frame it is understood, for instance, why the acculturation process is usually deeply disturbing for personality functioning. Having to abandon one's culture and the "material" objects of personality functioning means shattering some "material" parts of the personality construct itself as it has developed through time. Something similar can be said of individuals who, in the course of a therapeutic process, "lose their past" in the sense that they gain insight in the pathological or inauthentic nature of the constructs they have built up in their behavioral life.

From what has been said it follows that, in the behavioral process, personality and world cannot be simply opposed to each other. In research, of course, some of the variables are called personality and others are called environmental variables, but it should be kept in mind that each of the two categories penetrates the other.

A most important point in studying the behavioral personality–world interaction is a person's relative independency from the "physical" and public environment actually given. Although precepts and concepts (i.e., the objects as perceived or conceived and integrated in personality functioning as mentioned above) essentially refer to situations and objects "out there," their physical presence is not required for their being "available" in personality functioning. Because of their higher cognitive functions (ideational processes and imagination), people are able to re-present behavioral worlds not actually "present"; moreover, they are able to deal with them in a great variety of ideational ways.

These imagined situations may modify a people's perception of the world actually given and their dealing with it. It follows that our control of the environmental data presented to people is limited. Situations not actually presented to them may function as the "environment" they are dealing with or responding to. For instance, a person's behavior at a given moment may be related to rewarding or punishing objects not environmentally given or expected but re-presented by that person in a context unknown to the observer. Space and time distances can be bridged in this way. Important characteristics of personality functioning (normal as well as abnormal) are to be explained as a function of this type of relationship with worlds and objects not actually given (e.g., long-term delay of reward). This flexibility of the world which a person is able to construct is also one of the reasons why, outside the realm of science fiction, psychologists should be less "optimistic" with regard to the environmental control of a person's real-life behavior.

PERSONALITY CONSISTENCY AND THE WORLD

Personality functioning is supposed to remain more or less consistent through time across a variety of situations. Once more, this characteristic is not to be attributed to the personality pole of the personality—world interaction process without taking into account the role played by its correlative component (the world). In fact, personality consistency implies the "material" element of personality functioning. People are consistent with their opinions, their concepts of themselves, their value hierarchies, their behavioral pasts, etc. Self-consistency in a variety of situations does not refer to an "empty" self; it implies much more than the relative stability of some formal characteristics. People tend to remain consistent with what they are and what they have done, thought, and said. This consistency is based, to a large extent, on the retention of their psychological activities and the intentional objects of these activities. In other words, a person's behavioral past, in the sense of what he or she has done and thought, is retained as a continuously present element; it constitutes an important component of personality consistency through time. It follows that it is inaccurate to conceive of personality consistency in terms of a relatively identical formal pattern, on the one side, and an ever-changing variety of situations, on the other. In our conceptual frame, the new and varying situations are gradually integrated in the accumulated personality content which is a component of personality consistency. The scene does not continuously change, therefore, as when various objects are successively introduced in an empty room. Generally speaking, what constitutes the fascinating identity, richness, and intimacy of a person, and also that person's consistency, or "remaining her- or himself," is the accumulated and retained content of the personality functioning through time: that person's steadily expanding ego—world unit. Personality development, therefore, is a steadily growing insertion of a person into his or her behavioral world. People assimilate their world and grow in and by it, whereas their personal worlds of experience are continuously growing with them.

A RESEARCH OUTLINE:
A PERSON'S PERCEPTION OF HIS OR HER
ACTING ON THE WORLD

Several years ago I started studying a rather unexplored field in which individuals' perceptions of their action on the world and their self-percept were closely interrelated. The general topic was the individual's perception of his or her own behavior and its outcomes as a function of some personality and situational variables. The theoretical frame in which this research program has been conceived can be briefly described as follows. Behavioral processes in the broad sense, as defined above, are conceived as processes by which a personality constructs his or her perceptual (and conceptual) world and acts on it. In acting, people try to realize some preferential relationships with their world according to the plans, projects, and goals they have in mind (i.e., some relationships they have constructed on the ideational level of dealing with the world). To the extent that a goal is reached, the behavior outcome is said to be more or less successful or unsuccessful. As to the personality side, people conceive of themselves (and others) not only in terms of physical appearance and similar variables, but mainly in terms of what they have done, what they plan or have to do, and how successful they have been and are in doing it. This viewpoint presents us with a behavioral concept of personality and a behavioral approach to personality investigation (Nuttin, 1969). In other words, in studying individuals' perception of their successful and unsuccessful acting on their world, one studies their perception of themselves (as a behaving subject) and of the world as "acted on" at the same time. A systematically distorted pattern in one's perception of behavioral outcomes (in terms of "overperception" of either successes or failures) may, therefore, be a promising area of research. Moreover, the individual's tendency to attribute his or her successes and failures either to her- or himself or to world variables (Heider, 1958; Weiner, 1971) is an additional major point fitting into the context of our conceptual frame. At the moment, however, our research findings in this area have not yet been related to the attribution issue. The "hope of success" and "fear of failure" problems (Heckhausen, 1963, 1975) may also be studied in the same context, whereas the impact of distorted success perception on serial learning and memory will probably be investigated in our laboratory.

As to the experimental results obtained until now, I may refer to some other publications (Janssens & Nuttin, 1977; Nuttin & Abreu, 1977; Nuttin & Greenwald, 1968; Vreven & Nuttin, 1976). Let it be mentioned only that some systematic distortions are found in the perception of the relative frequency of one's successes and failures as a function of personality variables as well as social and situational factors. Some of these findings with regard to personality variables have been tentatively explained in terms of a tendency to self-consistency. In some respects the frequency perception of neutral events is found to follow different laws from those established for the perception of ego-involved phenomena, such as successes and failures. It may be interesting to mention just one result with regard to what can be called the "level of aspiration" issue in the perceptual field. After there is induced in a group of subjects a heightened level of expectation on the basis of a high number of successes obtained by a socius, a tendency is found, in the same group of subjects, either to underestimate the number of their own successes in subsequent similar tasks (contrast effect, especially found in female and field-dependent subjects) or to "overperceive" their successes in the direction of the high performance previously made by the socius (assimilation effect, found to some extent in male and field-independent subjects). On the contrary, the frequency perception of neutral events is not at all influenced by subjects's higher expectations based on performances made by a socius.

On the basis of these and similar results it is necessary to distinguish between expectations as a purely cognitive and prognostic process, on the one side, and expectation with regard to ego-involved events (such as behavioral outcomes), on the other. The latter is assumed to be dynamically loaded and, therefore, may produce in a person more or less competitive comparisons leading either to assimilation or to contrast effects, or to a conflict between both. The purely cognitive expectation, on the contrary, does not produce a dynamic "level of aspiration" and more easily submits itself to objective environmental data. Dynamic variables, such as self-consistency and self-assertion or competition, are more likely to leave a personality impress on the world perceived within the personality—world unit.

15

Assessing Interactions between Trait Anxiety and Stressful Situations with Special Emphasis on the Coherence of Response Modes[1]

Monique de Bonis

Centre National de la Recherche Scientifique, Paris

The main criticism that has been leveled against trait theories in the discussion inaugurated by Mischel (1968) is based on consistency across time and generalization across situations. Little attention has been paid, however, in these speculative attacks, to the problem of coherence across response modes or response levels. If empirical studies of interactions between persons and situations are required (a task the feasibility and utility of which are not universally acknowledged), they must be carried out by considering several response modes. For it is important to note that consistency across time or situations may be found in respect to one level of behavior, but not to another. This does not mean at all that persons are inconsistent, or that situations lack specific effects, but it is probably related to some equivalence among responses in the behavioral repertoire of the subjects. Specification of the predictive value as well as assignation of situational influences involve taking into account several response modes, sampled across different levels of behavior, and considering not a sum but a combination of the latter.[2]

---

[1] A detailed description of the data presented here can be found in the paper read at the Symposium on Interactional Psychology, Stockholm, June 22–27, 1975.

[2] Some evidence of the fact that the degree of generality is related to the level of measurement is given in the field of the factorial model of personality developed by Cattell and Scheier (1961) showing that anxiety appears as a more or less general trait (first- or second-order factor) according to what he calls L or Q data.

Concerning the domain of anxiety, a good deal of research has been done in this direction by Endler, Hunt, and Rosenstein (1962) and Endler and Magnusson (1974). However, despite the advantages provided in these studies by the use of the S–R Inventory, which must be considered as a technical innovation compared to other methods (de Bonis, 1974a), it seems to me that interactions have not been clearly defined in terms of modes of responses — first, because response modes have been considered as main effects rather than as dependent variables and second because the use of questionnaires has restricted the range of response modes to the verbal one.

So, there is a need to move on to analysis in experimental settings in order to assess interactions at several levels of behavior. However, this shifting of research strategy from the study of imaginary responses evoked by imaginary situations to actual responses, given in actual situations, must be actualized under certain constraints. Information conveyed by the meaning attributed to the situation, as well as by the meaning the subject gives to his or her own internal responses, must be preserved.

In our work, our main concern has been to find out the level(s) where the effect of the situation or the importance of individual differences is to be located.

Interaction between trait anxiety, situations as they are, and situations as they are perceived has been investigated on responses as they are and responses as they are perceived. Sex differences have been used as a mean to vary anxiety trait level; indeed, results reported in the literature (Ekehammar, 1972) offer enough evidence of the consistency of such sex differences. Semantic differential has been chosen as a tool for assessing the meaning that subjects give to the situations. Instead of looking for some "absolute" meaning of the situations, we focused our attention on one limited aspect of the meaning: the semantic distance between situations.

The change of method parallels a shift of interest from a descriptive approach, in which interactions lead to an idiographic description of the individual, to the search for an explanation of individual differences.

Results summarized here are based on two studies in which the same following experimental paradigm was used. Each experiment includes three steps: In the first step subjects fill in anxiety questionnaires (de Bonis, 1973); then they are shown two short videotaped film situations during which certain physiological responses are continuously recorded. The third step includes (a) evaluation of the meaning of the two situations (semantic differential) and (b) evaluation of somatic subjective reactivity during the presentation of the two sequences.

The two experiments differ mainly in terms of the objective distance between situations. The first consists in a restful and a stressful film (de Bonis, 1974b), the second in a stressful film (severe burn cases) and a threat of shock situation.

The subjects were respectively two samples of 50 students equated for sex within each group.

TABLE 15.1

Perceived Distance between a Restful and a
Stressful Situation and Physiological or
Verbal Response Modes
(mean differences and standard deviations)

Males ($N = 24$) nonstress–stress[a]	Females ($N = 24$) nonstress–stress[a]	T
Semantic distances between situations ($\sqrt{\Sigma d^2}$)		
6.01	7.48	
(1.76)	(2.88)	2.23*
Response modes Physiological (HR)		
−0.87	1.69	
(5.29)	(3.06)	2.03*
Verbal (subjective reports)		
0.92	0.67	
(1.60)	(1.37)	<1

[a]Stress, circumcision films.

*$p < .05$.

Results of the first study show that sex differences in trait anxiety are associated with differences in perceived distance between situations. Females more anxious than males perceive the stressful situation as more distant from the restful one than males. This differentiation is accompanied by a physiological difference in reactivity (HR), but not by a difference at the verbal level (reported reactivity) (Table 15.1).

In the second experiment, the same sex differences in trait anxiety did not induce any difference in the semantic distance between the two situations. They were perceived as close to one another for males and females. To this perceived similarity corresponds a highly different physiological reactivity, the threat of shock situation provoking HR acceleration and an increased number of skin potential responses for *both sexes*. On the verbal responses sex differences appeared: females giving more verbal responses for both situations (a result in agreement with nondifferentiation), whereas males gave far more responses for the threat of shock situation (to which they were physiologically more responsive) than for the other (Table 15.2).

The main conclusion that can be drawn from these results must be briefly summarized as following:

1. Interactions between trait anxiety and situations have been shown either at a physiological or at a verbal level of response, depending on the situations

TABLE 15.2
Perceived Similarity between Two stressful
Situations and Physiological or Verbal
Response Modes (mean differences and
standard deviations)

	Males (N = 23) stress A−stress B^a	Females (N = 23) stress A−stress (B^a	T
Semantic distance between situations ($\sqrt{\Sigma d^2}$)			
	5.69	5.47	
	(1.49)	(2.09)	<1
Response modes			
Physiological			
HR			
	−11.82	−10.83	
	(8.66)	(9.81)	
SPR			
	−10.22	−6.10	<1
	(9.81)	(6.04)	
Verbal (subjective reports)			
	−10.48	1.21	
	(17.66)	(20.32)	2.38*

^{a}Stress A, severe burn case film; stress B, threat of shock.
*p < .05.

investigated. Among factors responsible for such apparent inconsistencies, the most important is probably the heterogeneity of measurement scales, i.e., differences in sensitivity as well as differences in temporal units proper to each response mode. Reducing this method factor appears to be the most important preliminary task. Besides scale heterogeneity, however, discrepancy between verbal and physiological response modes has probably another meaning that has to be investigated in a functional perspective.

2. Connection between perceived distance between situations and sex differences in trait anxiety seems to be modulated by some intrinsic intensive properties of the objective situation. Indeed, in our studies, the connection is closer in mildly stress-provoking situations than in stronger ones. Highly stressful situations seem to level down the effect of sex anxiety differences.

3. The notion of perceived similarity needs further specification. A perceived similarity can be accompanied by important differences between situations as they are reacted to. We must remember that situations can be similar in one dimension but not in another. The right choice of dimension for a given situation can hardly be achieved in experimental situations.

4. Concerning the assessment of "external events" (i.e., situations) or private ones (i.e., subjective or physiological reactivity), similarities and differences should be interpreted within some reference continuum.

In conclusion, the assessment of interactions between situations and personality must be actualized by taking into account a more integrated pattern of responses.

16
Subjective Dimension Assignment through Set to Objective Situations

Edgar Krau

University of Cluj-Napoca, Roumania

In their review on interactional psychology Endler and Magnusson (1974) refer to an objective versus a subjective approach. The latter studies situations with respect to how they are perceived by individuals. The authors assume that the meaning an individual assigns to a situation is the most influential factor affecting his behavior. To continue this thought, an adaptive and beneficial interaction can emerge only if the situation's subjective dimensions coincide with the objective ones.

Situational interaction therefore has a heuristic aspect, the gist of which lies in response conformity with the objective characteristics of the situation. Because the ultimate goal of science is to help optimize behavior, a major task of psychological research in this field therefore is to discover, primarily, how correct and incorrect situation perceiving and reacting takes place.

Existing psychological concepts do not explain the phenomenon of a person presenting false responses. In his theory or model regarding nervous stimuli, N. D. Sokolov (1960) presumed a cell system that conserved the information from recurring stimuli. Thus appears the most probable program of action concerning these stimuli. Such a system is compared with the real stimulus. If they are not identical an "orientation" reaction starts, facilitating the reception of new elements. This theory does not explain the psychophysiological process of elaborating the cell system of the nervous stimulus model. Primarily it has nothing to say about erroneous reactions. The same remark can be made regarding K. Pribram's (1961) TOTE units in which the control image successively approaches the real. The point is that the acknowledged exit reaction is sometimes improper and damaging. One could explain this deficiency of the models mentioned by referring to the laboratory environment from which they were drawn. The laboratory situation has a precise, unequivocal, and immediate sanctioning of activity that can not be found in the bulk of life situations, with its incomparable greater complexity, where stimuli are ambiguous, consequences do not follow immmediately, and their causation is difficult to establish.

This does not mean that situational interaction is hazardous and unpredictable. Life situations do have a socially and culturally patterned meaning which elicits typical attitudes on the part of the individual. Such situation dimensions were studied by Magnusson (1971), using a method of paired comparisons. In the case of interaction detrimental to the individual or to others, situational dimensions had been wrongly and idiosyncratically assigned. Distortions in situation perceiving and hence interacting point to a mechanism responsible for subjective dimension assignment to the objective situation. Our hypothesis, in an empirical study, was that *set* represents this mechanism.

The concept of set is not new but experiments concerning set have been carried out mainly in the laboratory. This has resulted in a somewhat artificial character of the concept, with the doubt, lingering in the background, whether inference to real-life situations is legitimate, and if so, to what extent? We therefore chose to organize the entire research project in the form of "natural experiments," embedded in real-life situations, that is, in the school situation. Experimental variants applied to situations in school and leisure time ranged from single perceptual tasks to the analysis of witnessed real-life events. To prevent sample bias we chose a class whose school results were distributed almost normally. Other classes were used as control units.

In interpretation, besides statistical data processing, a great emphasis was put on a twofold qualitative analysis: Clinical method, as described in French psychology, was used to detect antecedent corrolaries of manifest erroneous behavior; then the whole complicated phenomenology was transposed to a neurophysiological level, for only such an examination could shed light on the mechanisms involved, thus defining the phenomenon and its range of influence.

There were a total of five experimental series, each new variant growing out organically from hypotheses that led to the interpretation of the previous experiment.

1. The first series had to define the scope of set in simple perceptual tasks of school life.
*Variant A:*Writing a list of words under dictation. The words differed with respect to how well known they were to the pupils.
*Variant B:*Reading the text that had been dictated under A and explaining word meaning. Variant B followed a week after Variant A. This arrangement was necessary to verify the role of stimulus unfamiliarity in recognition errors.

Variance analysis of mistakes in familiar versus unfamiliar word categories revealed one very reliable factor, in encompassing 35–43% of the total variance.

However, which factor was this? The hearing ability of our subjects was normal, and Roumanian orthography is close enough to spelling. One might think that this fact indicated unfamiliarity of word meaning. However, one-third of the mistakes occurred in familiar words, whereas one-third of the unknown words with difficult spelling had been correctly written. If we included Variant B in this reasoning (i.e., where the dictated words were read and explained by the subject) we found a correlation of .29 between the errors in both variants, which for 1,000 word stimuli was significant. In the subsequent qualitative analysis, we could precisely trace the word with which the stimulus had been confused in 40% of the cases. Several of these misperceptions were so persistent that they did not vanish even after a second reading. (They disappeared only after a third or fourth lecture.)

These results indicated first, that task difficulty does not produce errors automatically and, second, that there is a psychological mechanism responsible for the misperception of situations. To test the first hypothesis the experimental task had to be simplified; to test the second it had to be sufficiently complex to represent real-life situations. Our experimental design followed this line.

2. Copying (in order for this not to be primarily automatic the text was in Russian, a foreign language studied in school).

Variant A: A well-known, learned text.

Variant B: An unknown text that was to be studied later in the year.

One would expect the bulk of errors to appear at the unknown difficult text but outcomes clearly indicated the opposite tendency, thus reinforcing our experimental hypotheses.

3. Picture description.

Variant A: Description while looking at the picture.

Variant B: Description from memory immediately after a presentation of 20 seconds duration.

Variant C: Description from memory (20-second stimuli presentation) after a delay of 4 hours of normal school program.

Each variant required the description of two pictures. Statistical data processing took account of the number of details described correctly.

The outcomes showed surprisingly little difference between the number of details described in Variant A compared to variants B and C. Reproduction errors indicate faulty recognitions of situations, and therefore, do not originate in transformations of previous perceptions in memory. To disclose the psychological mechanism of these misrecognitions we used the qualitative analysis of every error in all experimental variants, involving clinical interviews and the comparison between components of the perceived situation, the objectively existing one, and those of past experience with which they had been confounded.

4. Movie picture description.

5. Description by the subjects and observations by the experimenter of subjects' real-life behavior, followed by clinical interviews.

The common feature of all errors in paragraphs 3, 4, and 5 was the distortion of perception in the direction of some event of past experience (from very recently to early childhood) with a high tonus of physiological excitation.

We have known since the days of Wundt that perception is not a mere copy of outside stimulus but also includes knowledge we have of it from past experience. We cannot see that an apple is smooth and cold in touch, but still, looking at it, we perceive it that way. Physiologically it has to be assumed that excitation radiates from centers stimulated by the object present, to other ones, with which they have established connections in the past.

If, behavioristically we consider perception as a conditioned reflex, it is a reflex (i.e., a response) to a complex stimulus made up from the actual stimulation and vestiges of past experience associated with it. In his experiments Pavlov (1951) could prove, however, that components of a complex stimulus did not have equal importance in determining the final reaction. Although in simple experiments the effect of each component was proportional with the strength it impressed on sense organs, later research proved that excitation strength depended on reward and consolidation.

If perception is a reflex response to a complex stimulus, it follows that the character of this response depends on the dominant components of the cerebral mosaic aroused by the ouside situation, that is, on the components in which, for one reason or another, excitation is greatest. In correct perceptions the dominances of nervous constellations coincide with the essential features of the object, essential from the viewpoint of actual situation interaction.

Under certain conditions, the role of strong components in the complex stimulus is assumed by certain elements that, according to the objective situation, have had to stay in the background. They are not essential traits or dimensions of the objective situation but accumulate a maximum of physiological excitation by being linked to centers with a powerful latent excitatory process. How can all this be proved?

If the above-stated theory is true, then a delusive perception should disappear (a) if we could manage to decrease the latent excitation of the center that provoked the displacement in the repartition of physiological excitation between the components of the nervous cell constellation mirroring the outside object or (b) if we could increase the stimulation produced by the latter.

As far as the second proof is concerned, we observed that reading improved at the third or fourth lecture in the same way as in the copying experiment. A word written erroneously the first time was correct at its second or third occurrence. Thus, excitation produced by repeated presentation of the stimulus is summing in the nervous centers and reinforces the elements of the object's real image. Moreover, the first proving modality of our hypothesis is not as difficult as it may seem. In many cases latent excitation fades with the passing of time, as it has appeared only because of a recent interesting unfinished activity. This process could be followed in an additional experiment in which subjects described similar pictures after a 1-week interval.

In some cases, however, the arousal of such patterns of activity is caused by ego-involving experiences, and they do not vanish so easily. Yet we managed to intervene here through counselling. The subject's appeasement marked the fading away of aroused centers and correct reality perception was restored, enabling a correct and beneficial interaction with the social environment.

Dimension assigning to situations and the subsequent behavior are therefore dependent on dominance in nervous centers as to accumulated physiological excitation. Set expresses this dependence through which each behavioral act acquires its dimensionality. As a result set becomes a general phenomenon but not a separate state.

The strength in excitation of a nervous constellation through summation by repetitive stimulation is one way of producing dominance. There are two others, namely, tension provoked by an unfinished action, as described by Zeigarnik (1927) and the latent excitation of persisting ego-involving problems.

Perhaps we might add a fourth modality: dominance through imagination. It occurs in the creative process on the stage, when actors identify with the characters they play. This process also occurs in daily life. In this case there is no problem with respect to past experience but in the future events the subject pictures mentally.

All I have said so far must not create the impression that through set the perception and response to the outside world are determined from within; that we mentally "construe" the environmental situations we interact with. The outside world has an objective existence and if misperceptions appear they are distortions of this objectively existing world.

Such distortions of a correct reflection can occur only under special conditions that reduce the strength of outside stimulation and hamper the process of analysis. Under normal conditions, it is the mechanism of *set* that determines the correct orientation in objectively existing situations, because environmental objects used to produce an incomparably stronger stimulation of nervous centers than interactional vestiges, which constitute our past experience associated to these sensorial stimulations. Erroneous interactional responses are not indicating the arbitrary activity of the personality factor in the person—situation couple or the impossibility for the person to know reality as it is; on the contrary, they appear as natural, strictly determined phenomena that can occur only within limits defined precisely through the action exerted by the outside world.

Part IV

METHODOLOGICAL CRITIQUES

Part IV contains three chapters (Chapter 17–19) that are organized around the theme of methodological critiques. All three chapters criticize some of the current techniques in personality research and suggest some alternative research strategies.

Olweus (Chapter 17) after discussing the relationship among personologism, situationism, and interactionism, provides a logical–conceptual and methodological critique of interactionism (see Chapter 1 for a discussion of interactionism). He makes some important and useful distinctions among various uses of the concept of interactionism and discusses the limitations of the variance components technique with respect to interactionism (see also Epstein, Chapter 4, and Chapter 1). Olweus concludes that the person–situation interaction issue as usually formulated is intrinsically unanswerable. He suggests that a more useful question is "how" persons and situations interact in evoking behavior (see Endler 1973, 1975b; Endler and Magnusson 1974). Olweus suggests that studying correlations across real-life situations is a useful strategy for investigating issues relevant to interactionism in personality.

Nisbett (Chapter 18) states that because most of the classic studies in psychology are studies that report main effects and not interactions, the search for interactions is sterile and counterproductive. He states that it is not possible to predict all situations and that most findings of interactions are not replicable post hoc findings. Hisbett believes, that because it is difficult to disconfirm interactions we should focus on main effect studies. However, it should be pointed out that main effect studies can be based on "bad theories" to the same extent that interaction studies are based on "bad theories." What are needed are studies that are based on sound theories that can predict both interactions and main effects (see Endler & Magnusson, 1976, Chapter 1, in this volume). Cronbach (1975) and McGuire (1968, 1973) have suggested that many of the inconsistent research findings are caused by higher order interactions. In order to understand the complexity of human behavior we must develop theories that enable us to predict these interactions.

Alker (Chapter 19), after reviewing some of the controversies and relevant literature regarding personality consistency and situational specificity, discusses the practical (small periods of time and specification studies) and logical limitations (the requirement that persons and situations must be identified independently) of the parametric studies. He points out that analysis of variance procedures do not detect reciprocal interactions between situations and persons (or take into account the notion that people to a great extent help characterize the situation). Alker proposes a two-stage least-squares analysis as a means of estimating the strengths of a relationship, when it is assumed that two variables reciprocally interact. Alker also proposes the strategy of using correlations across large groups (aggregates), for personality research. He believes that the personological tradition can encompass the trait, situationist, and interactionist positions of personality research and theory.

17

A Critical Analysis of the "Modern" Interactionist Position

Dan Olweus[1]

University of Bergen,
Norway

The so-called person–situation issue – usually formulated as a question of whether individual differences or situations (or their interaction) are more important in the determination of behavior – has attracted a good deal of interest in the professional journals of psychology. In close association with this question there has been a lively discussion of the characteristics and relative merits of three different personality conceptions, designated as the personologist, the situationist, and the interactionist positions. In an article in the *Psychological Bulletin,* Ekehammar (1974) gives an overview of many of the questions involved. A good starting point for the following considerations is a quotation from Ekehammar's article, in which he briefly characterizes the three positions concerned:

Personologism is here used as a label for those views advocating stable intraorganismic constructs, such as "traits", "psychic structures", or "internal dispositions", as the main determinant of behavioral variation (e.g., Alker, 1972; Wachtel, 1973a). This position may generally be expressed as $B = f(P)$, where B stands for behavior and P for person. *Situationism* can be regarded as the antithesis of personologism and labels those views emphasizing environmental (situational) factors as the main sources of behavioral variation (e.g., Mischel, 1968). This position may generally be expressed as $B = f(E)$, where E stands for environment or some part thereof (e.g., situation). *Interactionism* can be regarded as the synthesis of personologism and situationism, which implies that neither the person per se nor the situation per se is emphasized, but the interaction of these two factors is regarded as the main source of behavioral variation (e.g., Bowers, 1973; Endler, 1975b). This position may generally be expressed as $B = f(P, E)$ in analogy with the preceeding expressions. (p. 1026)

[1] At the Department of Psychology, Box 25, N-5014 BERGEN - U, Norway.

221

In his article Ekehammar then goes on to demonstrate meritoriously that many of the thoughts and conceptualizations occurring in modern interactionist formulations in reality have a long history in psychology. According to Ekehammar, however, "the interactionist view has not flowered until now, partly because of the inaptness of earlier methodological tools" (p. 1027). It is, above all, the development of the analysis of variance approach directed toward the comparison of variance components that is said to have made possible adequate comparisons between the personologist, the situationist, and the interactionist positions. Moreover, it is clear that Ekehammar is strongly in favor of the interactionist view: "Thus, if interactionism is not the Zeitgeist of today's personality psychology, it will probably be that of tomorrow" (p. 1045).

It should be immediately pointed out that many of the thoughts and arguments presented in Ekehammar's article are derived from other authors' work, especially those by Endler (Endler, 1973, 1975b; Endler & Hunt, 1966, 1968, 1969). It should also be noted that although the technique of estimating components of variance has been known in psychology for some time (e.g., Gaito, 1960; Gleser, Cronbach, & Rajaratnam, 1965; Medley & Mitzel, 1963) Endler and Hunt seem to have been the first who have used it in an attempt to give answers to the person—situation issue (1966). The primary reason that only Ekehammar's article is taken as a point of departure is that it gives a good summary of how the three positions involved have been usually perceived in the present context.

The main focus of this chapter is a methodological and logical—conceptual critique of the so-called "modern" interactionist position. This critique concerns the common use of the analysis of variance components approach in comparing the interactionist position with competing theoretical views. Furthermore, the way of conceptualizing the "modern" interactionist position is critically examined, and it is also asserted that the person—situation issue, as commonly formulated, is probably best regarded as intrinsically unanswerable.

Because of space limitations it will not be possible to present a thorough argumentation regarding the use of the analysis of variance components technique in the present context. It has been given in detail elsewhere (Olweus, 1975a). Here only some of the main conclusions are stated, as they are of importance as a background for the general conclusions and views advanced in the final section of this paper. However, readers who want to follow the lines of reasoning leading up to the methodological conclusions should consult Olweus (1975a).

WHAT COMPONENTS OF VARIANCE
ARE TO BE EXPECTED
FOR THE DIFFERENT POSITIONS?

As suggested in the previous section it has been maintained that only the development of the components of variance analysis has made possible an adequate test of the three theoretical positions at issue, the personologist, the situationist, and the interactionist views. If this assertion is correct it implies that different outcomes in such analyses must be interpretable in a relatively unambiguous way in support of one or other of the positions. What are, then, the expectations, regarding the magnitude of the variance components, or, rather, regarding the relative (percentage) contributions to total variance from persons (individual differences), situations, and their interaction?

The common view in these contexts has been that personologism regards the individual's "traits" (or similar constructs) as the main determinant of the "behavioral" variation. This has generally been interpreted to mean that person factors (individual differences) are expected to account for the major portion of the variance. In contrast, the situationists are said to maintain that most of the variance should be contributed by situational factors. Finally, according to the interactionist position, neither individual differences nor situational factors are assumed to be of major importance per se; instead, it is the person by situation interaction that is expected to contribute most of the variance. Examples of formulations of this type are to be found in Endler's works (e.g., 1973, 1975b), in the previously mentioned article by Ekehammar (1974), and in an article by Bowers (1973), in which he reviewed 11 articles concerned with the relative magnitude of person and situational influences on behavior.

Because conceptions such as these have played an essential part in the discussions about the positions at issue it is important to determine their correctness. Do these statements about the expected (relative) contributions to total variance represent an adequate characterization of the positions involved?

Conclusions

In summary, it may be readily demonstrated (Olweus, 1975a) that *many common statements regarding the (relative) size of the variance components to be expected on the basis of a trait and a situationist position are obviously incorrect,* being the result of misconceptions of the positions in question and/or misconceptions of the analysis of variance components technique. Furthermore, an analysis of what variance contributions may be compatible with the three positions at issue clearly reveals that it is *impossible to institute adequate tests of these positions by means of the analysis of variance components technique (as commonly used): Several different outcomes are consistent with all three or with two of the positions.* The most important point, from this perspective, is that outcomes in which the person by situation interaction variance component is larger than the person variance component and/or situation variance component are compatible with all three theoretical views. In addition, according to a trait as well as a situationist position, it is conceivable that the situation accounts for more variance than the person or, conversely, that the person contributes more of the variance than the situation. It is therefore clear that the predictions that can be made concerning the variance contributions to be expected on the basis of the three theoretical positions are not precise enough to permit definite, differential conclusions about the positions at issue: A particular outcome can be taken as support of two or of all three theoretical positions.

It also follows that the variance component approach can hardly, from this viewpoint, be said to represent an improvement over other methodological tools, such as correlation measures, as has been implied by some authors (e.g., Endler, 1973, 1975b; Ekehammar, 1974). *The variance component technique as used in the present context appears to have brought about more confusion than clarity.* As suggested, however, the contention that the variance components approach has made possible adequate tests between the positions at issue also seems to follow from the fact that *the trait as well as the situationist positions have been presented in an inappropriate, overly simple way.*

A corollary of the preceding analyses is that many of the conclusions drawn in the recent literature regarding the three positions at issue cannot be accepted. Some examples (see also, e.g., Endler & Hunt, 1968, pp. 309–310):

... neither trait nor the situationist predictions are borne out. Far too little of the total variance ($\bar{X}$ = 12.71%) is due to the person to justify a thoroughgoing trait position. On the other hand, the percentage of variance due to situations is also meager ($\bar{X}$ = 10.17%). (Bowers, 1973, p. 321)

... almost all studies employing this approach have shown that Person X Situation interaction is more important than either individual differences or situational differences in explaining behavioral variance. This implies that the personologist and situationist views should be discarded in favor of an interactionist position. (Ekehammar, 1974, p. 1044)

ADDITIONAL METHODOLOGICAL CRITICISM

As has been demonstrated in detail elsewhere (Olweus, 1975a), the common practice of regarding the square root of the relative contribution to total variance coming from persons as an indicator of the upper limit to possible validity coefficients (e.g., Argyle & Little, 1972; Endler & Hunt, 1969; Moos, 1968, 1969) is incorrect, being a result of a misunderstanding of the relationship between reliability theory and the components of variance approach.

WHAT IS THE MEANING OF INTERACTION
IN "MODERN" INTERACTIONISM?

After these methodological considerations some semantic and logical problems associated with the "new" interactionist position will be critically examined.

It is possible to distinguish at least four different meanings of the terms *interact* and *interaction* (and, to some extent, related theoretical "positions" or viewpoints) as they have been used in the literature. Three of these meanings occur in older as well as modern interactionist positions (Ekehammar, 1974), whereas the fourth is especially attached to certain modern formulations.

1. The term "interact" has been used in a *general sense* as an equivalent to "combine or connect." An example: ". . . determines how situations and individuals interact in evoking behavior" (Endler, 1973, p. 300). Here it is a question of *unidirectional interaction,* namely how two or more independent variables (person and situation variables) are combined or connected in their relationship to a dependent variable, the individual's behavior or reactions. This relationship may be a causal or noncausal (see Overton & Reese, 1973, p. 78).

2. In a second sense the term "interaction" has been used to designate the interdependency between the person and his environment, perhaps in particular as regards his perception or cognitive construction of the situation. Here the inseparability of the individual–environment system is emphasized. A quotation from Bowers (1973) illustrates this interpretation: "In sum, the situation is a function of the person in the sense that the observer's cognitive schemas filter and organize the environment in a fashion that makes it impossible ever to completely separate the environment from the person observing it" (p. 328).

3. In a somewhat related sense the term has also been used as roughly equivalent to "reciprocal action." Here the individual and the environment are seen as mutually influencing one another and the emphasis is often on processes over time: Environmental events affect the person's responses, which in turn affect the environment, which again influences the person's responses, etc. In a similar vein, some authors have stressed the view that individuals tend to select and generate situations that are typical for them to which they then react in a characteristic way (Bowers, 1973; Mischel, 1973a; Wachtel, 1973a). This kind of interaction has been called transaction (Pervin, 1968) and dynamic or *reciprocal interaction* (Overton & Reese, 1973).

4. The fourth meaning of the term "interaction" is the conventional one as used in analysis of variance, for example, "the interaction of the subjects with situations contributes more of the variance than does either by itself" (Endler & Hunt, 1966, p. 341). As in the first-mentioned meaning it is here a matter of unidirectional interaction but of a quite special character.

As to "modern" interactionism its close association with the variance components approach has been stressed by several authors (e.g., Endler, 1973, 1975b;

Ekehammar, 1974). It has been contended that only the development of this technique has made it possible "to put the interactionist theory to a more direct empirical test" (Ekehammar, 1974, p. 1044). Moreover, "The empirical evidence supported almost without exception the interactional view, which means that the relative magnitude of the Person × Situation interaction variance was usually greater than the relative magnitude of the person or situation variance" (Ekehammar, 1974, p. 1034). The link between this interactional position and the variance component approach, in particular the relative magnitude of the person by situation interaction variance, is thus quite strong. From such writings as these it is clear that the existence of a considerable person by situation interaction variance component is a necessary prerequisite to this position. In a sense it is "defined" in terms of this interaction variance. It should be noted that interaction is used here in the fourth sense mentioned above.

On the other hand, it is maintained by the same authors that the question "how?" is the main question for the (modern) interactionist. As Endler puts it (1975b): "The appropriate and logical question is *How* do individual differences and situations *interact* in evoking behavior?" From the way in which the "how?" question is discussed it is clear that the term "interact" is used in the first, general sense given above. The question may be formulated as follows: "How do individual differences and situations combine in evoking behavior?" This question represents a general inquiry into the determinants of behavior, where the behavior (B) is seen as a function of the person (P) and the environment (E, or situation). $B = f(P, E)$. The exact nature of the function, f, however, is to be found by research.

In a particular case the functional relation may be of an interactive character (interactive in the sense of analysis of variance); that is, there is a joint effect of the person and situation, over and above their possible separate effects, on behavior. Such a case may be generally represented by the following equation:

$$B = a + b_1 X_1 + b_2 X_2 + b_3 X_1 \cdot X_2,$$

where B represents behavior, X_1 values on a "person variable," X_2 values on a "situational variable," $X_1 \cdot X_2$ is the product (interactive) term, and a and b are constants (see, e.g., Goldberg, 1968, p. 487).

The functional relation, however, may turn out to be even simpler, with no need for an interactive term:

$$B = a + b_1 X_1 + b_2 X_2.$$

In such a case an individual's behavior can be estimated as the simple sum of the "person value" and the "situational value," appropriately weighted, plus a constant. The "person value" and the "situational value" are thus combined in a simple, linear way in their "effect" on behavior. This is, of course, a description of the type of interaction (in a general sense) that characterizes the person and situation variables in this case. However, the interaction variance is small here (mainly random variation) and may even be zero, as in the hypothetical example

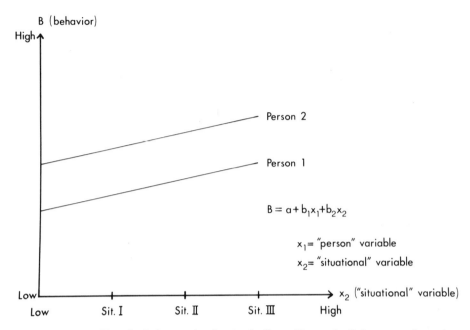

FIGURE 17.1 Hypothetical example of a simple, linear "interaction" (in a general sense) between person and situation variables with zero interaction variance.

in Figure 17.1. If such a relationship were found in a particular research situation, it no doubt would represent an adequate answer from the present perspective to the question "How do individual differences and situations interact in evoking behavior?" Before I draw the conclusions of the preceding argument it may be appropriate to examine more closely whether "interact" in the question above possibly has been used in the sense of the analysis of variance (the fourth sense). If this were the case, however, the implications for the "modern" interactionist position would be very peculiar. The "modern" inter-actionist would then be interested in finding answers to the question "how?" only when the relationship between the person and situational variables was of an interactive character (in the analysis of variance sense). This, of course, would constitute a very artificial restriction of the field of inquiry and also represent a serious break with the older interactionists whose main concern was to find out the nature of the interaction — in a general sense (and/or in the second and third sense) — between the individual and his or her environment.

Implications for the "Modern" Interactionist Position

Against this background, the only reasonable interpretation is that the term "interaction" has been used in two different senses which, in the present context, are incompatible. This is not, however, only a question of semantic obscurity; it also implied logical contradictions, which have far-reaching implications for this variant of "modern" interactionism. If, as has been maintained, "how?" is the central question for the "modern" interactionist, there is no a priori reason why the relative size of the person by situation interaction variance should be of particular interest to him. Also, a finding in empirical investigations that this variance is greater than the relative magnitude of the person or situation variance cannot be taken as support for an interactionist position.[2] As previously demonstrated (Figure 17.1), answers to the question "how?" may readily be found where there is no interaction (in the analysis of variance sense) between person and situational variables at all. The *"definition" of the "new" interactionist position in terms of a large interaction variance component therefore seems to be logically indefensible and should be discarded.* Such a conclusion also carries the implication that *this "new" form of interactionism in fact represents nothing new;* it is only a variant of the old inquiry into the determinants of behavior. The analysis of variance approach may be one technique among others to use in the search for functional relationships but, in the absence of definite theoretical expectations, there should be no particular interest attached to the person by situation interactions.

Other "Interactional" Approaches

What, then, about the other two meanings of the term "interaction" given above? Very little systematic empirical research seems to have been done within the framework of theoretical positions based on such interaction concepts, and the methodological implications of such views appear to be largely unexplored. Accordingly, these two meanings and their consequences will be discussed very briefly in the present context.

A theoretical position emphasizing the inseparability of the individual–environment system, as suggested in the quotation from Bowers (1973, p. 328), seems to postulate another model of man than that implied in the preceding discussion. Different types of questions are asked and different types of explanations are given (see Overton & Reese, 1973). Here the organism *and* its environment must be considered together rather than the organism per se or the environment per se. The individual's behavior is a function of the situation and the situation is a function of the individual.[3] Empirical research based on such premises seems to call for a "truly" interactive paradigm where behavioral events "are not decomposable into individual components" (Overton, 1973, p. 83; in

[2] Here, this assertion is largely based on logical grounds; in the first section of the chapter a similar statement has been made on the basis of methodological considerations.

[3] A conceptual scheme in which the individual's perception of the situation is a function of the individual (and the situation) and the individual's behavior is a function of the situation (and the individual) has been presented for the aggressive motive area in Olweus (1969, 1973a).

contrast to the linear model implied in the analysis of variance). Accordingly, a research technique permitting the separation of variance components from persons, situations, and their interaction would hardly be acceptable. Likewise, the calculation of proportional contributions to total variance would certainly conflict with the basic assumptions of such a position and therefore should be rejected, as has been the case in the nature–nuture controversy (Overton, 1973, p. 83). Although some research has been done on the basis of conceptions of this type, many methodological problems are obviously unsolved and it seems premature to judge the potential fruitfulness of such a position for empirical research in the field of personality.

Interaction in the third sense of the term, as equivalent to reciprocal action, is sometimes used in a way that is closely related to the one discussed in the preceding section (Overton & Reese, 1973). However, the focus may be on continuous processes over time, on chains of events, and the research models implied may involve quite different assumptions. Although analysis of variance may be of some help in studying selected aspects or sectors of these processes, other research approaches involving, for example, Markov chains (e.g., Raush, 1972) or conditional probabilities (e.g., Patterson & Cobb, 1971) are likely to prove more useful.

CONCLUDING REMARKS

Some General Conclusions

As was pointed out in the first part of this chapter, the variance components approach as commonly used does not permit an unambiguous test between the personologist, the situationist, and the interactionist positions. Several different outcomes are compatible with all three or with two of the positions at issue. It therefore seems impossible to make a clear empirical test of an interactionist position "defined" by the existence of a large person by situation variance. In addition, it was shown that such a "definition" of the interactionist position is associated with insolvable logical contradictions and it was proposed that this "definition" should be discarded. At the same time, however, such a conclusion implies that the "modern" interactionist position in fact represents nothing new. The main question for the "modern" interactionist of this type as well as for the older ones seems to be: "How do person variables and situational variables combine in their relationship to behavior?"[4]

Is the implication of these conclusions that components of variance analyses of the type discussed in this chapter should be avoided? From the perspective of a

---

[4] This somewhat clumsy formulation is preferred to "in evoking behavior" as formulations of the latter type imply a more definite view of the causal relations involved.

"truly" interactive position (see page 229) an affirmative answer would seem to be natural. In my opinion, however, such a standpoint appears unnecessarily restrictive. In brief, the position taken here is that such analyses may be of value to the science of personality psychology but that they should be interpreted in a different way from what has been common in the present contexts.

As has been emphasized by some authors (e.g., Mischel, 1973a; Olweus, 1974), estimates of the relative contributions to total variance from person, situations, and their interaction will vary markedly depending on the persons sampled and the situations selected. Obviously, studies could readily be arranged in which the situations or the persons or their interaction accounted for the overwhelming portion of the variance. Accordingly, it will never be possible to give definite answers in terms of relative variance contributions to the question of whether individual differences or situational factors or their interaction are more important in determing behavior. Furthermore, theoretical considerations suggest that this way of framing the question is inappropriate and that a more fruitful approach is to be found in the question "how?" (Anastasi, 1958). Actually, *it is probably best to regard the person–situation issue, formulated in this way, as intrinsically unanswerable or as a meaningless one,* as was maintained already in 1959 by Raush and his colleagues: "Neither component can be uncoupled from the other" (Raush, Dittman, & Taylor, 1959b, p. 373).

This is not to say, however, that estimates of relative variance contributions are not worth calculating in person by situation and similar designs. Of course, it may be of interest to know how much of the total variance can be predicted on the basis of information regarding individuals, situations, and their interaction or how much relative reduction in predictive uncertainty is obtained by specifying the different categories involved (Hays, 1963). And information about the components of variance may be valuable to the researcher for particular purposes, for example, in determining the degree of response consistency across a particular set of situations, $\sigma^2_p/(\sigma^2_p + \sigma^2_{ps})$, and/or within the framework of generalizability theory (see Cronbach, Gleser, Nanda, & Rajaratnam, 1972).[5] It

---

[5] In a recent article in the *Psychological Bulletin,* Golding (1975a) has argued that what he calls omega-squared ratios (that is, the relative contribution to total variance from a particular source of variance, e.g., $\sigma^2_p/\sigma^2_{tot}$) should be substituted by generalizability coefficients as these "indices carry the inferential weight desired . . ." (p. 279). Although I find myself in substantial agreement with some of Golding's general conclusions (1975a, pp. 285–287, see Olweus, 1975a), and it is obvious that generalizability coefficients may provide relevant information for particular purposes, it is contended here that the use of such coefficients does not represent a solution to the person–situation issue, as commonly formulated. In brief, it is difficult to make meaningful comparisons between the generalizability coefficients proposed by Golding and the relative sizes of such coefficients can hardly be taken as evidence of the relative importance of persons and situations in determining behavior. Furthermore, generalizability coefficients similar to omega-squared ratios for interaction terms are often difficult to interpret, as also suggested by Golding in his Footnote 6 (1975a, p. 283). In general, many of the arguments advanced in the first

should not, however, be regarded as an answer — not even a tentative one — to the person—situation issue, as commonly formulated.

Another general conclusion of the preceding analyses and considerations is that the term interaction — for instance, in interactionism and interactional psychology — has been employed indiscriminately in several different, partly incompatible meanings. It is recommended that in order to avoid confusion different terms be used for the different types of meaning intended.

Comments on a Typical Research Paradigm

Even if it is clear from the above that estimates of variance components may provide useful information for particular purposes, it should also be stressed that such estimates may give very little help in finding clues to the mechanisms involved, that is, in getting answers to the fundamental question "how?" In a sense, the typical research paradigm used (person by situation or person by situation by an additional factor, etc.) may be regarded as basically atheoretical. To a great extent this is a consequence of the fact that persons, not different values of a personality variable, constitute the "levels" of one of the factors in the design. The individuals under study may be different in a number of unknown ways and the design therefore does not permit the desirable linking of behavioral variation to particular personality dimensions.

If a large person by situation (or, e.g., person by response mode) interaction variance is found it may have arisen in many different ways. When the inter-action variance is considerable, it seems important to try to discover regularities in the person by situation (etc.) interaction patterns, for instance, by sorting the individuals into relatively homogeneous subgroups by means of multivariate classification procedures. If other data about the subjects are available this may help in identifying relevant characteristics of the subgroups obtained, which in turn may lead to hypotheses about the mechanisms implied, to be tested in new investigations. These, however, should preferably follow other research designs, involving different values on relevant personality dimensions instead of persons as categories of classification. When there is a theoretical basis for hypothesis formulation, moreover, the empirical research may well start directly with the latter type of studies, avoiding the detour via a person by situation (etc.) study.

Another indication of the atheoretical character of the present research para-digm — and this represents a danger, too — is that there is a certain tendency in the research articles to treat the variance percentages as self-contained quantities

---

section of this chapter also apply to generalizability coefficients in this context and the use of such coefficients does not permit an adequate test of the three theoretical positions at issue. (The readers may ask themselves the question: What generalizability coefficients are to be expected for the different positions?)

existing independently of the context in which the data have been collected. The main concern often seems to be a comparison of the percentage values obtained in different investigations, and there is a corresponding neglect of the nature and conditions of the studies from which the percentages have been derived. As an example, it may be pointed out that the question of the "validity" of what is being studied seems to have attracted very little attention; in the case of inventory data, for instance, there has been hardly any discussion at all of the possible effects of response sets (see also Olweus, 1974).

An additional risk associated with this research paradigm is the possibility that a fairly sophisticated statistical treatment may contribute to the use of rather rigid and unrealistic empirical procedures, in particular in the case of three-way analyses. In these analyses the researcher as a rule tries to work with completely crossed designs (in which all possible combinations of levels of the factors occur) in order to obtain estimates of all the components of variance involved, usually with the exception of the error component. It should be obvious, however, that such designs may contain vary peculiar combinations of factor levels, a circumstance that certainly affects the relative size of the variance components and also the general trustworthiness of the results.

The preceding considerations point to the fact that the typical research paradigm used in these contexts may not be very well suited for finding answers to the basic question "how?" In addition, studies aimed at elucidating the person–situation issue often seem to be characterized by a certain degree of artificiality, and they have seldom focused on naturally occurring environments in which people have lived together for longer periods of time. This circumstance very likely has contributed to the rather low degree of consistency across situations often reported in empirical investigations ("personality coefficients," Mischel, 1968). The picture may be quite different when natural social settings are studied.

Within the aggressive motive area, for instance, I have obtained data indicating a considerable degree of consistency across situations, within a particular data source (such as peer ratings) and, more importantly, across different sources of data (e.g., inventory data versus peer ratings of overt aggressive behavior, see Olweus, 1974, 1975b). Very likely, the substantial degree of "cross-situational" consistency obtained was, in part at least, a consequence of the fact that the subjects, 13-year-old school boys, had known each other for several years and could judge each other's behavior with high accuracy. Similarly, in another investigation with a comparable sample of subjects (Olweus, in press) results were obtained indicating a high degree of stability of overt aggressive behavior over a period of one year, manifested in an average correlation of .76 (eight classes, a total N of 76). Results such as these and previous considerations suggest that the often reported lack of consistency in behavior, across situations and over time, may represent a considerable underestimation of the consistency found in "real life"[6] — a point that has been stressed by other authors as well (Block, Chapter 2 of this volume; Bowers, 1973; Wachtel, 1973a).

Acknowledgments

The author's research reported in this chapter has been supported by grants from the Norwegian Research Council for Science and the Humanities and the Swedish Council for Social Research. Preparation of this manuscript was aided by a grant from the Norwegian Research Council for Science and the Humanities.

[6] To avoid misunderstanding, this statement should not be taken to imply that I want to support a simple trait position in the aggressive area; see Olweus (1974, 1973a).

18

Interaction versus Main Effects as Goals of Personality Research

Richard E. Nisbett

The University of Michigan

It would seem safe to say that a conference on person—situation interactions would not have been organized, nor enthusiastically attended, unless there were a belief on the part of both organizers and attendees that such interactions were widespread and important. I share this belief, but I do not share, and wish to argue against, its corollary, which states that a chief goal of personality researchers should be to seek for person—situation interactions.

I have a suspicion that a good many personality psychologists regard the interaction road as an escape route from Mishel's (1968) attack on the notion that there are broad trait dimensions. Moreover, I further suspect that this conference is an attempt to develop a road map for this proposed escale route. My contribution to this cartographic undertaking is to point to what I believe are dangers on the way — intellectual equivalents of soft shoulders, falling rock zones, and narrow bridges. I argue that:

a. Few of the most important and productive studies in psychology generally, and in the field of personality in particular, have been reports of interactions.

b. Few of the important and viable person—situation interaction hypotheses current came about as a result of seeking for interactions in the first instance. These hypotheses were instead built on the wreckage of main effect hypotheses.

c. There are serious inherent disadvantages to interaction hypotheses, notably the difficulty of disconfirming them, their illusory aura of precision, and the disadvantages of complex designs employed to test them.

In this assessment of the prospects for person–situation research, it should be borne in mind that I am addressing myself to the traditional form of this research, that is, to the case in which persons are assessed on some dimension and then tested in various situations. I am not addressing myself to the quite different case discussed by Bowers (1973). In the research Bowers describes, there is no prior assessment of individuals; there is simply the finding that people behave consistently within particular types of situations designed to tap a particular individual difference construct, but that there is no consistency across types of situations designed to tap the construct. For example, Bill reliably behaves in a hostile way in situations of Type A, but not in ones of Type B. Tom reliably behaves in a hostile way in situations of Types B and C but in a decidedly nonhostile way in situations of Type A. Therefore, the fact that people get similar summed scores on hostility obscures the fact that there are reliable individual differences in their behavior.

I should like to express the opinion that Bowers' position is not an answer to Mischel's attack but a capitulation to it. The position throws in the towel on the question of the existence of broad trait dimensions, admitting that people cannot be characterized in trait terms, and holds out only for the highly circumscribed position that people are at least consistent about the situations in which they manifest behavior of a type that used to be regarded as a manifestation of a trait in the old days.

I personally welcome further research in the mode described by Bowers. It is possible that the consistencies may turn out to be broader than the minimal, situational-reliability type of consistency found to date. Behavior in one set of situations may turn out to be related to behavior in other, perhaps unexpected, sets of situations. I agree with both Mischel and Bowers that we are not likely ever to get back up to the level of generality implied by most trait theorists, but we may well find some interesting cross-situational consistences supporting a modified trait position.

It is the traditional interaction approach, where there is assessment or manipulation of at least two independent variables, that I wish to evaluate critically. I wish to contrast it with the simpler approach of working with one independent variable at a time.

DEVELOPMENTAL LEVEL OF THE SCIENCE OF PSYCHOLOGY

I have asked a score of psychologists to tell me what their favorite studies in psychology are. Two striking facts have emerged from my informal poll. First, there is more overlap in the nominations than may be expected. Studies by Asch (1956) on conformity, Harlow (1958) on monkey mother love, Milgram (1963) on obedience, Festinger and Carlsmith (1959) on the effects of insufficient justification of behavior, and several other studies all received a large number of votes. There is more uniformity of opinion about what constitutes important research, therefore, than a pessimist may assume.

The second striking fact, for me, is that most of the nominations have been of studies that are, conceptually at least, if not in actual experimental design, reports of main effects or simple, one-condition demonstrations. Few of the studies are reports of interactions.

It therefore appears that the most important research has been of the simple, main effect variety. I argue that it is likely to continue to be that way because the science of psychology is not yet, and is not likely to become in the near future, the mature sort of science to which we all aspire. Simply put, it makes no sense to go looking for interactions until you are rather sure of at least some main effects. It is pointless to search for intricacies in the absence of firmly fixed braod principles. I argue that we are at a stage in psychology comparable to preclassical physics. The sum total of issues that a Freudian, a Skinnerian, and a Piagetian could be expected to agree upon is very small. The structure of opinion in the field is therefore much more nearly like the division of thinkers prior to the Newtonian revolution in physics than to the relatively unified state of opinion following it. If this is true, then it is premature to search for interactions, as premature as it would have been to argue in 1400 that one should look for the interaction between gravity and levity. The former concept, as it later developed, had been grossly misapprehended, and the latter, of course, referred to nothing in nature at all.

Because the field of personality is even less mature than other branches of psychology, it follows that a search for main effects is even more likely to be the appropriate level of complexity for those of us engaged in personality research.

THE ORIGIN OF INTERACTION HYPOTHESES

My second argument against the search for interactions is also a quasi-empirical one. The person—situation interaction hypotheses with whose histories I am familiar have been resorted to, in the face of inconsistent main effects, rather than sought out in the first instance. This applies to:

1. McGuire's (1967) hypothesis that self-esteem interacts with the comprehensibility of persuasive communications such that low self-esteem people are relatively more persuaded by easily comprehensible messages, whereas high self-esteem people are relatively more persuaded by less easily comprehensible messages.

2. Schachter and Rodin's (Schachter, 1971; Schachter & Rodin, 1974) hypothesis that the obese respond more strongly to a broad range of external stimuli of high intensity than do normal weight individuals and respond less strongly to low-intensity external stimuli.

3. Fiedler's (Chapter 9) hypothesis that leader effectiveness is a joint function of leader characteristics and group and task constraints.

This generalization also applies to two other interaction hypotheses with implications for personality research:

1. Zajonc's (1965) hypothesis that the presence of others interacts with the prepotency of the response to be performed such that the lower the prepotency of the response, the more likely is the presence of others to produce a performance decrement, whereas the higher the prepotency the more likely is the presence of others to produce a performance increment.

2. The Miller and Campbell (1959) proposal that primacy effects in serial learning and persuasion studies are more likely if there is interpolated activity between exposure and testing, whereas recency effects are obtained when there is no interpolated activity.

Each of these hypotheses was resorted to after a mass of main effect studies had built up. The main effects were inconsistent and contradictory, and the interaction hypothesis was proposed so as to impose some order on the chaos. Therefore, the existence of these viable and useful interaction hypotheses cannot be called on to justify a search for interactions in the early stages of research. Moreover, a strong argument can be made that unless the investigator is lucky enough to guess exactly which variables are going to interact, and in what way, the prematurely complex interaction hypothesis is likely to obscure, rather than reveal, any underlying orderliness.

McGuire (1968) has argued that "if the universe to be described involves complexity, so must our theories and descriptions if they are to be valid" (p. 1170). It is not possible to quarrel with this, except insofar as it may be taken as a justification for complex theorizing in advance of data collection. McGuire himself was not arguing for such premature complexity, and it would be unfortunate if his observation, and similar observations by other investigators in the context of justifying their interaction hypotheses, were taken as a license for such a strategy.

DISADVANTAGES OF INTERACTION HYPOTHESES

Even when interaction hypotheses are empirically based, they suffer from many disadvantages vis à vis main effect hypotheses. Therefore, even when they satisfactorily explain existing data, they should be viewed askance and resorted to only with reluctance.

Difficulty of Refutation

One of the chief disadvantages of interaction hypotheses is that they are much harder to disprove than are main effect hypotheses. The half-life of an incorrect interaction hypothesis is much longer than the half-life of an incorrect main effect hypothesis. To demonstrate this point, I shall deal with two interaction hypotheses that I have worked on personality: (1) McGuire's (McGuire, 1968; Nisbett & Gordon, 1967) hypothesis that self-esteem interacts with message comprehensibility, and (2) Schachter and Rodin's (Schachter, 1971; Schachter & Rodin, 1974) hypothesis that the obese respond more strongly to intense external stimuli than do normal weight individuals and less strongly to weak external stimuli.

Each of these hypotheses has a reasonable, scientific sound to it, but I argue that each has, in practice, a kind of near immunity to disproof. A psychologist is not to be expected to roll over and play dead when confronted with data that contradict his hypothesis. Instead, he is likely to criticize the conflicting data. The more complicated the hypothesis being defended, moreover, the more grounds there are for criticism of conflicting data. For example, if a theorist holds that low self-esteem individuals are relatively more persuaded by easily comprehensible messages whereas high self-esteem individuals are relatively more persuaded by less comprehensible messages, he is not likely to fold his tents when confronted by a study showing only the main effect finding that low self-esteem individuals are more influenced by all of a variety of messages differing in comprehensibility. Moreover, why should he? He has a good many perfectly respectable sounding objections he may voice: (a) The messages did not in fact differ sufficiently in comprehensibility, (b) the nature of the issue employed was such that arguments concerning it were intrinsically highly comprehensible, (c) the subject population was perhaps unusually lacking in people genuinely very high (or low) in self-esteem, and (d) although perhaps differing sufficiently in self-esteem, the population was unusually intelligent (or unintelligent), so that comprehensibility differences could not exert their usual sway. The theorist does not usually have to resort to accusations of artifact or name calling. He may simply politely point to insufficient variation in one or another of the independent variables, or to the presence of another variable that precludes an adequate test of his hypothesis.

False Precision

If one proposes a literal crossover interaction, such as that of Schachter and Rodin concerning weight and stimulus intensity, there is a feeling of very great precision that is actually illusory. This is because support is generated for the hypothesis by any interaction of the general type specified. If normal and obese subjects are found not to differ in their response to low-intensity stimuli whereas obese subjects respond more intensely than normal subjects to a high-intensity stimulus, then a victory for the hypothesis is of course claimed. Similarly, if the obese are less responsive to a low-intensity stimulus and do not differ from normals in responsiveness to a high-intensity stimulus, then victory is again claimed. So the precision is merely apparent; the actual hypothesis in such cases is usually much looser than is implied in its formal statement. Once again, the theorists are not likely to throw up their hands when confronted with the finding that, say, obese individuals respond more intensely to both weak and strong stimuli. All of the armamentarium described above can be wheeled into action: both stimuli, the "weak" and "strong," are actually rather intense; the stimulus dimension is by its nature above the minimum reaction threshold for the obese, etc.

Cannot these arguments be used by the defenders of main effect hypotheses? Yes, of course they can, and they are all the time. It is just that an interaction hypothesis can survive a siege of inconsistent results much longer than can a main effect hypothesis. In fact, it is not at all uncommon for the interactionist to present main effect data as positive evidence for an interactionist theory. This is done with a sweetly reasonable explanation to the effect that, had more extreme values been employed on one or both independent variables, it is likely that the interaction could have manifested itself. In contrast, for a simple hypothesis of the form "A increases with B" no data except those showing that A increases with B would ever be adduced as supporting evidence. Although disconfirmatory data can be and often are explained away, moreover, there is only so much explaining away that a main effect theorist can do and be able to count on his fellow scientists continuing to listen.

It is my suspicion that some interaction theorists feel that their hypotheses should get extra points because they are more complex and "precise" than simple main effect theories. As has been pointed out, part of this precision is illusory, because a wider range of findings is usually accepted as supportive than is implied by the formal statement of the hypothesis. Beyond this, it should be noted that the greater complexity of the interaction hypothesis is not associated with any greater difficulty of obtaining a finding supporting the hypothesis, given that the hypothesis is false. In a space composed of $i \times j$ points, a roughly equal proportion of possible data patterns support main effect hypotheses and interaction hypotheses. In other words, one is no more likely to obtain by chance a data pattern supporting the main effect hypothesis "A increases as a function of B" than a data pattern supporting the interaction hypothesis "A increases as a function of B more strongly under Condition 1 than under Condition 2." Although interaction hypotheses are more complex, data patterns describing interactions are no less likely than data patterns describing main effects.

The Inherent Disadvantages of Complex Designs

Difficulty of refutation is not the only cost incurred by complexity. Interaction hypotheses require complex designs, and interactions involving several levels on two or more independent variables can be difficult even to describe verbally, let alone to fully comprehend. A finding that is literally not grasped intellectually goes nowhere − it cannot be used to generalize to the real world or even to interpret other research. It is partly this fact that is behind the opposition of many psychologists to the analysis of variance design, which is the necessary design for most person–situation interaction hypotheses. These psychologists are aware of the fact that the number of effect terms in a ANOVA table is equal to $2^n - 1$, where n = the number of independent variables. It is far from uncommon to discover that the results of a $2 \times 3 \times 2 \times 4$ design are virtually uninterpretable, because statements about main effects or simple interactions must be hedged around and constantly modified, in thought and in communication, by qualifications necessitated by the presence of higher order interactions. It is even more common to see in the literature misstatements and distortions resulting from failure to so qualify. The defender of the complex ANOVA design often asserts that these consequences are the necessary evils accompanying the attempt to go beyond oversimplified generalization. Usually, however, these evils were welcomed on board because the design incorporated one or more independent variables the proved importance of which was much too low to justify the confusion they engendered. It is easier to add possibly relevant independent variables than to think long, hard thoughts about the phenomenon under investigation.

Another reason for opposition to the ANOVA design is that there is frequent conflict, in practice, between the complexity of experimental designs and the likelihood of attaining ecological validity. In an experiment that is well thought out, every cell of the design presents to the subject materials that are plausible and that have some interest and meaning. The greater the complexity of the design, other things equal, the more difficult it is to meet these standards. It is not uncommon to read reports of research where subjects are asked, in some conditions of a complex design, to believe six impossible things before breakfast. The investigator, in these cases, has simply not been up to the task of thinking through the plausibility of the materials in every cell of the design.

Because the advantages of generalizability, disprovability, comprehensibility, and, in practice, ecological validity, all lie on the side of main effects, there is little justification for seeking, in the first instance, for interaction effects and good reason to resort to interaction hypotheses only with reluctance.

ACKNOWLEDGMENTS

The author was supported by NSF grant GS4008 while preparing this paper. He is indebted to Eugene Borgida, Timothy Wilson, and Robert Zajonc for a critical reading of an earlier draft.

19
Beyond ANOVA Psychology in the Study of Person— Situation Interactions

Henry A. Alker

Cornell University

The topic of person—situation interaction has received so much attention recently that the questions being raised have changed almost as quickly as possible answers to those questions have been proposed. For that reason this chapter commences with a brief review and analysis of some controversies in the literature that have been or may be resolved. From this reanalysis newer issues emerge that are the main import of this contribution. These newer issues concern the severe limitations of available parametric studies of person—situation interactions as reviewed, for instance, by Bowers (1973) and Ekehammar (1974). These limitations arise not only because there are practical reasons why such studies are not likely to be decisive but because, and perhaps most important, the logically independent specification of person variables and situation variables, which is required in the correct use of ANOVA analysis of variance designs, cannot and should not take place in certain cases of person—situation interaction. Finally, reciprocal causal interchange is not effectively modeled by ANOVA designs. Throughout this chapter I will use the phrase "person—situation interaction" broadly. It refers here to psychological phenomena in which characteristics of both persons and situations must be considered conjointly for purposes of adequate explanation. Other senses of the term "interaction," as identified by Olweus (Chapter 17) are indicated where appropriate.

THE DECLINE OF SITUATIONISM
AND THE EMERGENCE OF INTERACTIONISM

In an earlier paper (Alker, 1972) I emphasized the logical and empirical importance of person—situation interactions as part of a critique of Mischel's searching, if selective, critique. To draw a basic distinction between rational and irrational action the study of person—situation interaction is logically required. Brunswick (1955) made a related point some time ago. Identifying purposive behavior in any organism required the study of situations in which means—ends contingencies were reversed. The psychologist must determine whether the organism foregoes a previously favored response and prefers a previously disfavored response if that response now has the higher probability of obtaining the same goal. In Tolman's words, purposive behavior is *docile* behavior.

Harré and Secord (1973) have developed an important refinement of this argument. Their argument applied specifically to the intentional behaviors of people, a subclass of their purposive behaviors. It is claimed that the effects of situational variables on behavior can never be convincingly explained unless the research design also includes relevant variation of the individual differences. In particular, individual differences in attributing meaning to the experimental situation must be considered. From what Harré and Secord call the anthropomorphic point of view, the subject's point of view about the varying situation always remains a plausible alternative interpretation of the situation's purported simple or main effects. In order to attain convincing explanations, therefore, one must study person—situation interaction.

Bem's Reply and Reformulation

Bem (1972) replied to my paper with a defense of Mischel and some thoughts of his own on constructing cross-situational consistencies of behavior. His defense of Mischel included the point that some of the technical improvements in predicting personality over time that I had emphasized, for example, the uses of multiple regression, moderator analyses, and correction for attenuation, were mentioned by Mischel and therefore not neglected as I had claimed. My reply is simply that these techniques were not seriously considered by Mischel as providing counterarguments to his arguments about the miniscule amount of variance accounted for by person variance. Bem also claimed that there was negligible evidence, to date, of personality consistency over time.

The literature available at the time of my 1972 paper provided some additional examples that Bem could have considered. Stern, Stein, and Bloom (1956) have given what, by now, is a classical examplification of how larger correlations may be obtained through intensive, time-consuming, and costly analysis of the settings in which the criterion behaviors as well as the criteria themselves are observed. Hall and MacKinnon (1963), for example, report cross-validated concurrent multiple regression predictions of creativity in architects using various inventories that include .4 and .5 multiple correlations. Jack Block (Chapter 2) provides much more documentation of my claim that technically sophisticated studies with personality variables can yield larger correlations than .30. Bem himself (Bem & Allen, 1974) has more recently provided additional examples of successful moderator analyses yielding correlations of .5.

In this last report the moderator variable used by Bem is the subject's own report of how much he varies from situation to situation with regard to a particular trait in question, say, friendliness. Those responding that they do behave with little variation across situations are retained for (successful) behavioral prediction; those responding negatively are discarded from the sample. The moderator variable receiving special attention in my 1972 paper was membership in two more broadly defined populations, *viz.*, seriously disturbed versus "normal" individuals. It is worth comparing our approaches. It should be point out on the outset that my formulations are more general. Individuals who behave repetitively across situations and those who are more situationally specific are both included in my formulation.

Bem's and my moderator variables may overlap. Individuals who are high on measures of both anxiety and defensiveness (and so are seriously disturbed) were found by Kogan and Wallach (1964) to covary less from situation to situation with regard to the trait of riskiness. It seems that these motivationally disturbed or irrational risktakers are more concerned with creating favorable impressions than they are consistently cautious or consistently daring. Individuals low on defensiveness and anxiety, in contrast, define their performance in risk-taking situations differently. They chose their level of preferred risk in a task-oriented fashion that is more variable from situation to situation. The peculiarities of the task itself apparently make more of a difference. Is it a task, for instance, that required luck or skill to succeed? In Bem's terms these two types of individuals create different equivalence classes for defining the consistency of their behavior.

There are still differences berween Bem's recent formulation and my own. His new espousal of an idiographic perspective, although gratifying, does not go quite far enough. It is worth considering, as Bem now does, that individuals create different "equivalence classes" over which they interpret the variability of their behavior. Individuals differ both from each other and from the formulations of many psychological researchers when they construct these equivalence classes. However, a further question must be raised from the idiographic point of view. What does it mean when an individual reports that his or her behavior varies little or a lot from situation to situation with respect to a given trait? Creating equivalence classes may involve different processes for different individuals, especially those who are affectively preoccupied as compared with those who are more cognitively oriented.

Actually Bem and Allen (1974) use two different moderator variables, both of which deal with intraindividual variability in their research. The first moderator variable is the self-report described above. The second moderator variable is an "ipsatized variance index" constructed from the subject's report of what he would do in a variety of situations deemed relevant by the experimenter to a particular trait. This variance is compared with the subjects variability on other items deemed by the experimenter not to be relevant to that particular trait. The first moderator variable was used in their study of conscientiousness. The apparent reason for this shift is that the subject's self-rating on conscientiousness correlated less well (.62) with Bem and Allen's set of specific situations deemed to measure conscientiousness than the comparable self-report for friendliness did with a set of relevant behaviors in specific situations deemed to measure friendliness (.84). We are not presented with the correlations between these two different indices of the moderator variable for these two traits. Neither do we know whether the cross-situational prediction for low-variability individuals is equally successful for both measures of the moderator variable for both traits. It is curious that this point has not been clarified because one of Bem's (1972) criticisms of my earlier paper is that an example I provide of improved cross-situational predictability using ipsative measurement techniques fails to replicate in a further (at that time unpublished) study. Perhaps Bem's results are comparable.

The point here is that we need to know why different people regard themselves as varying a great deal or a little across situations before we can have full confidence in any index of this important moderator variable. Which type of individual is likely to be discarded from Bem's samples using either of his operational definitions for his moderator variable? Rational risk takers, for instance, can be expected, at least for the trait of riskiness, to acknowledge their cross-situational variability. More disturbed individuals, highly concerned with winning positive evaluations, might emphasis their cross-situational consistency. These orientations, of course, could interact with the particular trait in focus. Conscientiousness is more directly related to moral evaluation whereas friendliness probably is a more salient concern to persons worried about their popularity.

These arguments, which await empirical determination, offer a more idiographic interpretation of Bem and Allen's (1974) findings. Simply attributing the differences between friendliness predictability and conscientiousness predictability to the experimenter's failure to comprehend adequately the equivalence classes of subjects regarding the latter trait is too nomothetic an interpretation.

Bem and Allen (1974) assert:

> The basic point here is simply that there is no inherent conflict between an idiographic approach to assessment and nomothetic science of personality, whether one opts for a psychoanalytic orientation, a social learning viewpoint, or a systematization of everyman's trait theory. (p. 511)

There are genuine psychological questions why different subjects have different equivalence classes from psychologists studying their behavior. Resolving those questions may require reinvigorating the creative tension between idiographic personology and a nomothetic personality theory that regards the notion of equivalence class as theoretically primitive.

Endler's Reply

This reply (Endler, 1973) puzzled me because it contained data that supported many of the arguments that I had made. First, there appears to be a misunderstanding about my use of the term "pseudo-question." Following the use of this term in the work of ordinary language philosophers, I meant to convey that arguments about the relative amount of variance from situations versus the amount of variance from persons were pointless. Such arguments overlooked the variance from interactions. Consequently, for both logical reasons and empirical reasons such arguments were somewhat pointless to pursue. A major class of constructs in personality theory (and, I argue, many ordinary language traits) cannot be operationalized logically without studying person–situation interactions.

Nevertheless, I did pursue the argument for a few pages because it invited the application of Allport's radical idiographic perspective in an intriguing manner. The nomothetic claim that persons exhibited minimal amounts of cross-situational consistency in their behavior, it was argued, depended on *whom* one was discussing. The argument depended, furthermore, on what cross-situational consistency was considered to be. In terms of repeating behaviors in different situations, for example, smoking in bed, smoking in the shower, smoking in church, smoking in gas stations, and smoking at professional meetings, I argued that persons labeled irrational or highly disturbed were more likely to exhibit each consistency. Persons who would be considered more rational, "normal," or more cognitively self-controlled would exhibit less of this consistency. Consistency of behavior across varying situations in a difference sense of the term "consistency" might not involve such silly behavioral repetitiveness. Indeed, changing one's behavior over time in such varying situations might be precisely what a psychodynamic theory would predict. These theories focus on change and the sequential organization of behavior as well as on stability.

Endler (1973) presents data that dramatically confirms my argument about the relative size of person variance and situation variance being a function of how psychologically disturbed the sample is. For the normals in his Table 2 (1973, p. 292) ratio of variance explained favors situations over persons in impressive magnitudes from 6:1 to 18:1. For Endler's neurotic and psychotic samples, in contrast, this ratio reverses itself and now becomes 2 or 3 to 1 in favor of persons over situations. Mischel (1968, p. 81) explicitly argues about such ratios. Endler's new data, as well as those I already had cited, explicitly supported my argument about Mischel's position. This level appears to exist also for Golding's (1975) reanalysis of the data for at least one of his generalizability coefficients. The consistency in the data on this point is also recognized by Bowers (1973, p. 321). He notes that increased person variance tends to be sound in disturbed samples. This consistency suggests that not all moderator findings need be plagued by unreliability as some writers have implied.

Endler's (1973) claim that person variance is not more important for normals than disturbed populations is most puzzling. His reason is that it is equally unimportant for both. Consider his fascinating finding that in a psychotic sample person variance is 18.78%, the largest single source of variance other than residual in that study. Is that unimportant? The linear trend in Endler's data as one compares normals, neurotics, and psychotics suggests that a rather general empirical finding has emerged as a welcome but unanticipated by product of this controversy. Takala (Chapter 6, this volume) extends this generalization by showing that especially competent as compared with ordinary individuals give less evidence of cross-situational consistency for a psychomotor response style. Again we have another topic inviting future empirical and theoretical research. The subject requires theoretical articulations far beyond that provided by Mischel's (Chapter 25, this volume) concepts of generalization and discrimination. The intrapsychic organization of personality is at issue.

Endler's additional finding that combining normal and disturbed samples increased the amount of variance from persons speaks to another of my contentions. Restrictions of range in many samples cause underestimation of person variance. The combined sample yields person variance at 9.66%, which compares favorably with percentage figures of .93, 3.65, and 4.20 reported for person variance in normal samples in Endler's own data. This increase may not be as large in absolute terms as I should like, but it often suffices in samples of the sizes usually investigated to determine that person variance is not merely random. Such an outcome is a modest but nontrivial accomplishment.

Wallach and Leggett (1972), besides expounding on the problem of unreliable moderators, add a new point that merits more sustained discussion. They claim that the search for personality consistency should proceed by taking a leaf from the behaviorist's notebook without necessarily buying the rest of the manuscript, advocacy of situational specificity. That leaf explains and advocates the use of behavioral sampling instead of traditional or trait approaches to assessment.

This point merits further consideration than can be provided here because there has been in the literature to date no sustained rebuttal to the claim that behavioral sampling succeeds where more traditional approaches fail in finding personality consistency across situations. It is worth pointing out that not all consistencies have been discovered through behavioral sampling techniques. Gough (1964, 1968) reports several large sample cross-validations of predictions in the achievement domain using a standard personality test, the California Psychological Inventory (CPI). The first study (1964) reports a cross-validated multiple of .56 for predicting the high school grades. The second study (1968) reports cross-validated predictions of college attendance for high school students with point biserials of .51 for males and .52 for females. This issue, however, remains open. For reasons of space, it is discussed elsewhere (Alker & Owen, 1975).

This selective review of previous controversies suggests that the major unanswered substantive question concerns the importance of the person—situation interaction data that have become more focal as the debate develops. What do these data accomplish besides embarrassing crude forms of a trait or situationist position? To that question attention is now devoted. To preview my argument, the answer to that question is "not much."

LIMITATIONS OF AVAILABLE PERSON—SITUATION INTERACTIONS STUDIES

Bowers (1973) has vigorously and eloquently argued for certain implications of the prevalence of person—situation interactions. Reliance on manipulative experiments has biased our perspective in favor of situation—produced variability. Reliance on correlational designs has overemphasized the importance of person variance, at least as compared with interaction variance. I enthusiastically agree with most of his conclusions. Aside from the one qualification that personality theories are not always posthoc in their discussions of situation and interaction variance (cf. Greenstein, 1969; Stern, Stein, & Bloom, 1957), I find little difficulty in accepting the theoretical primacy of an interactionist position. I see such a position as complementing rather than replacing an emphasis on personality.

The argument that I wish to develop here seeks to articulate several promising versions of an interactionist position. In the course of developing this analysis, it becomes evident that the parametric studies of variance estimation that Bowers uses to motivate his arguments are seriously limited. These parametric studies employ ANOVA designs that may impoverish instead of enrich an interactionist perspective. Furthermore, the trichotomization of theory (e.g., Ekehammer, 1974) based on such designs into trait theories, interaction theories, and situationist theories itself must be considered suspect. The idiographic perspective has usefully counteracted nomothetic psychology's tendency to create straw people. What is needed now is a corrective for the creation of straw theories.

Limitations in Spatial—Temporal Frame of Reference

Virtually all of the studies reviewed by Bowers (1973) cover relatively short periods of time and space. Often, captive populations are used for reasons of convenience, and data collection usually takes a few hours or at best weeks. The actual time behavior is observed, if it is observed at all, for any particular subject is, typically spread over a few hours. Metaphorically speaking, I call such studies microscopic. It is my contention that this restriction in the available ANOVA studies of person–situation interaction (Olweus' second type of interaction, see Chapter 17) seriously biases evidence against personality theory in the psycho-dynamic and personological tradition. Consider the evidence on Maslow's theory of motivational maturation.

Questionnaire studies in particular experimental settings (e.g., Lawler & Suttle, 1972) and elsewhere have provided little strong evidence for the basic premise of the theory that sustained gratification of safety and security motives leads to the enhanced saliency of more "mature" motives, such as love and self-esteem. What if the phenomena described and putatively explained by this theory simply are far too macroscopic to be observed over short periods of time? Aronoff (1967), in a field study on a Carribean island, discovered support from developmental evidence that covered 10- to 20-year time spans. Specifically, individuals who experience sustained departures from their home of either siblings or parents while growing up are less likely to have progressed as adults beyond a security orientation. They are preoccupied with the predictability of need gratification. Individuals without such early disruptions, in contrast, develop more concern for love and even self-esteem needs.

Tan (1974) found additional dramatic confirmation of a Maslovian viewpoint with independent variables that were much more highly aggregated in their spatial–temporal definition. His study, done in the Phillipines, concerned fami-lies that varied in upward mobility. The first group included fathers and sons who were both peasants. The second group contained peasant fathers with sons in college. The final group contained fathers who had risen from being peasants and assumed middle-class occupational roles; their sons were also in college. The first of these groups was most concerned with security in both this world (family security, national security) and the next (salvation). The last group was more concerned with values suggestive of self-actualization (inner harmony, wisdom, mature love, a world of beauty). Again Maslow's theory of motivational salience receives confirmation. If we study individuals using constructs referring to microminiaturized renditions of personality variables, we have as a hidden cost an increased irrelevancy of such research to the major concepts of personality psychology in the personological tradition. That tradition studies lives.

In such macroscopic studies it is virtually impossible for practical and ethical reasons to unconfound the variance from persons, situations, and their inter-action. This unconfounding is made difficult, as well, for logical and other reasons.

People Characterize Situations

In making the assertion that people characterize situations I am proposing that the kind of people in a given situation help make and define that situation. In everyday life where people may seek out and select situations in which they participate, we should expect to find confounding of these two sources of variation. Introverts are less likely than extroverts to be found at cocktail parties, conventions, and other group activities. Extroverts are less likely to be found buried in the stacks of large libraries, day after day, week after week, year after year. This confounding of person variables with situations occurs not only because certain kinds of people are differentially attracted to different situations. People initially varying in personality characteristics may be expected, if confined for one reason or another, to those situations, to develop characteristics that are adaptive in those situations, and thus they become more homogeneous. Kohn and Schooler (1973) have demonstrated this effect with vocational settings. The application of an ANOVA design to such phenomena requires logically independent classification of person variables and situation variables. Unlike the paintings of de Chirico, which portray solitary individual confronting a world empty of fellow human beings, most situations are filled with people. Our characterization of the context in which a person finds her- or himself may be logically connected to our characterization of the person as well.

Possibly the most obvious way in which the kind of person one generally finds in a given situation produces effects is through aggregation. We could not detect such effects in a typical person–situation ANOVA study. Professor William Lambert at Cornell has been kind enough to give me some unpublished data on aggression that illustrate the point. Lambert's data involve correlations between father absence during infancy and proportion of emitted behaviors that are aggressive behaviors. The first variable is trichotomized: a score of 1 means no father absence, 2 means some father absence, and 3 means that the father died and so was permanently absent. Significant periods of one's personal history, that is, macroscopic rather than microscopic variation, are obviously involved in this variable.

The correlation in question was calculated first within each of six different cultures. Here the typical pattern emerges. On occasion the correlation is significant but more often it is not. The mean correlation is .156. This pattern is precisely what advocates of situational specificity may expect. Findings are hard to replicate and not very large. If the context changes, the correlation changes and often disappears. If we take a greater range, as advocated elsewhere (Alker, 1972), a somewhat stronger relation emerges. For the total sample of 134 individuals from all six cultures, the correlation is $.36, p < .01$. If we entertain a hypothesis concerning aggregation and correlate group means across six cultures, however, a much larger value results, $r = .90, p < .01$.

It can be argued, of course, that we are no longer talking about individuals when we are talking about group means. That is true from the perspective of a typical ANOVA design. My point is, however, that we are still talking about characteristics of people and characteristics of situations. Moreover, we are talking about both at the same time. In a larger sense of the phrase, then we are still talking about person–situation interactions.[1] If you prefer, we could call

[1] Olweus' third sense of interaction (Chapter 17).

these person–people interactions. From the standpoint of any individual in a particular setting one feature of that setting is the kind of behaviors other individuals in that setting are generally emitting. Even though there may be no discernible relation in that setting between father absence and proportion of aggressive behaviors at the individual level, it is false for that individual to conclude that these two variables are unrelated. A more adequate sampling of settings and an aggregated focus on the variables in question may show that these variables are powerfully related.

There has been a good deal of speculation about why naive individuals persist in the deluded belief that personality variables are substantially important when we purportedly sophisticated students of ANOVA research know that they are not. Peculiarities of the attribution process, ignorance of base rates in prediction, psychodynamically biased acceptance of psychodynamic concepts can all be assigned responsibility for this supposed delusion. No doubt such factors play some role. However, it should not be assumed that trait psychology is always comparably naive. One of the advantages of talking about traits in addition to talking about persons is that evidence of such relations in aggregated data become relevant.

A proper name for this point is in order. Most psychologists are familiar with the ecological fallacy. This fallacy occurs when one makes gratuitous inference from relations apparent between populations to relations of the same variables within populations. I propose the term *arboreal fallacy* for the converse of this mistaken inference. Drawing conclusions about the relations between variables by observing their relations only within populations does not allow us to draw conclusions about their relations when observed across populations. This point can be applied to both people and situations. "Arboreal" in the phrase "arboreal fallacy" is intended to remind people that sometimes psychologists study only individual trees in individual forests. Studying many trees in many forests is equally legitimate. Such a perspective, moreover, might contribute more to the eventual integration of the other social sciences with psychology.

Aggregations of the sort indicated above do not always occur. We do not as yet know why. Cross-cultural data that may help clarify this problem are difficult and expensive to obtain. Practitioners of personality psychology, however, can turn elsewhere for manifestations of their theoretical concepts at more aggregated levels. Sales' (1973) work is among the best recent examples involving this line of research. He has operationalized the concept of the authoritarian personality by studying the relevant cultural practices. Authoritarian inclinations are indexed by aggressive comicstrip heroes, by the registration of attack dogs, and the duration of prison sentences given for certain crimes. These indices proved responsive to variation in economic and cultural disruptions over the twentieth century in America. Comparable within-culture and between-culture studies for other personality constructs, such as fate control, machiavellianism, and empathy, are sadly lacking. I hope they are soon to be forthcoming. Aggregation, of course, is not the only fashion in which person variables and situation variables conjointly and nonindependently affect behavior.

Differing Persons Characterize Situations

This assertion deals with another aspect of the way different people behave in different situations. In this case the kind of person in the situation also constitutes and helps define what kind of a situation is at hand. In this case, however, the key feature of the situation is the diversity of individual differences in a given situation. Situations contain differing individuals among many obvious demographic dimensions. Some situations are heterogeneous with respect to age, sex, nationality, political belief, and ethnic group. Other situations are not. The development of the point to be made here concerns differences in personality, conventionally assessed, which demonstrably affect the way individuals respond to different situations. Here again ANOVA designs of the sort reviewed by Bowers (1973), Argyle and Little (1972), and Alker (1972) do not apply. The characterization of these differing situations is not logically independent of the characterization of the persons in these situations.

Some empirical examples of this point come from the study of social situations in which more than one person is essentially involved. One such situation is marriage. In connection with an investigation of family planning, Gough (1973) studies the personality characteristics of husbands who have undergone vasectomies. This decision requires a brief surgical intervention that irreversibly renders the male sterile without otherwise interfering with normal sexual functioning.

Gough (1973) reports that a certain combination of one personality characteristic in the husband, highsocialization (willingness to conform to socially identified values), in combination with low feminity in the wife is strongly associated with this decision. The way the husband responds to this interpersonally defined situation obviously is influenced by the significant other person in this situation.

A third way people characterize situations is with respect to their variability to one and the same trait. A particular selection may be characterized, for instance, by the extraordinary homogeneity or heterogeneity on a given characteristics present in that situation. Alker, Straub, and Leary (1973), for example, report in a study of sports officiating that variance differences instead of mean differences on various traits characterize difficult levels of competition. Individuals performing in the most demanding and competitive circumstances were characterized by the most homogeneity on relevant personality variables. This state of affairs apparently helps produce greater consistency in the making of officiating judgements on what are rather arbitrary matters.

No doubt there are many other such effects that can be detected, especially outside the framework of the transitory social situations with strangers that most frequently are studied in psychology laboratories. Of course, these effects will not occur on many other occasions. It depends on the personality characteristics involved, the social definition of the situation, and the response that is observed. Some kinds of responses, say in the political realm, may reflect effects of much larger groups than dyads. In families, moreover, the characteristic of both parents and offspring no doubt sometimes come into play in this manner. These examples, although somewhat rare given our current knowledge, are meaningful in the broader context of the development of personality psychology over the last several decades. Ever since the neo-Freudian critiques arrived on the intellectual scene — some call it the sociologizing of Freud — it has been increasingly recognized how the actions people take are usually social as well as personal in nature. It is time our simple ANOVA studies of persons and independently classified situations caught up with this reality. Of course, many person variables may be involved in such effects, not just one or two.

Beyond ANOVA Designs to Where?

These comments about the limitations in practice and in principle of simple ANOVA designs for the study of person—situation interactions suggest that we need constructive alternatives. One such alternative has already been identified, albeit implicitly. Traits construed as constructs in personality theory can be and have been used to summarize and aggregate patterns of interactions of persons with situations. This comment applies particularly to concepts dealing with purposively organized behaviors. Henry Murray talks about themes (Murray, 1959). Others (e.g., Tyler, 1965) have talked about strategies. Even Gordon Allport, according to Brewster Smith,[2] meant to include person—situation interactions as referents for trait concepts. Virtually every theorist of personality and culture, e.g., Erikson, Fromm, Horney, H. S. Sullivan, and their intellectual progeny, uses theoretical constructs that can be interpreted in such a fashion. Their concepts are macroscopic rather than microscopic. When one construes these theories as employing constructs at a higher level of aggregation, moreover, it is not simply aggregations over main effects created by persons in person—situation ANOVA designs.

A more novel approach to this problem needs, however, to be developed. New multivariate methods are required. One such method, borrowed from econometrics, is the two stage least-squares technique for estimating strengths of relation when it is assumed that two variables reciprocally interact (Blalock, 1971). Unlike ANOVA or even ordinary multiple regression techniques, this procedure does not estimate interactions *after* estimating main effects. If we wish to reformulate Bower's assertion of the primacy of an interactionist

[2] Remark made at symposium on the future of social psychology, American Psychological Association convention, Honolulu, Hawaii, August 1972.

position in ways that are not tied to simple ANOVA designs, this technique seems very much in order. In terms of the debate about persons and situations, this technique assumes that person variables affect situation variables and, in turn, are reciprocally affected by them (Olweus' last sense of interaction). The question of primary interest, then, becomes which direction of causation is more influential?

Kohn and Schooler (1973) have applied this technique to a particular problem, that of the interaction of the intellectual flexibility of a person and the substantive complexity of the job in which he is employed. They report a consistent pattern of results showing that the substantive complexity of one's occupation has stronger effects on one's psychological functioning than vice versa. This conclusion applies not only to one's intellectual flexibility but also to other personality variables, such as self-esteem and authoritarian conservatism.

This technique requires in its application a broad assessment of many different variables other than those particularly in focus, such as education, race, national background, region of origin, etc. These "exogenous" variables are used to estimate in the first-stage least-squares analysis what one's personality and occupational situation may have been without the effects of the interacting variables of particular interest. In the second stage these reciprocal effects for each of the two causal directions (person on situation and vice versa) are then estimated and compared. Without going into the mathematical details, it should be apparent that many macroscopic variables are being used. Contrary to the point argued by Bowers (1973), moreover, the use of a correlational technique does not appear to bias the outcome of a comparison of the relative effects of persons as compared with situations in favor of persons.

CONCLUSION

The ANOVA studies discussed here have bloomed in the controversy that has developed over the importance of persons versus situations. Possibly, they have had so much appeal because researchers have hoped to find some crucial experiments that can resolve competition between the various scientific viewpoints involved. This hope is naive. A paradigm clash that precludes the possibility of there being decisive crucial experiments is underway (Alker, 1976). Evidence helps in such arguments. A frequent role it seems to play is as a basis for falsifying a misrepresentation of what proponents of a different viewpoint assert. Mystification ensues. Interactionism, like any other "-ism," invites such a necessary process. An interactional perspective need not be impoverished by exclusive reliance on narrow parametric ANOVA studies. The positive contribution of interactionism in stimulating well-formulated research that identifies person and situation variables, as in the work of Fiedler and Spielberger in this volume, should not be obscured. Expansion of this perspective into new areas is also welcome. Attribution theory, for example, neglects the importance of person–situation interaction in its representations of person perception. Beyond that, however, ANOVA studies cannot carry the additional theoretical weight assigned them by Ekehammer (1974) and Bowers (1973). These ANOVA studies are, like the situation manipulation studies they have succeeded, solutions searching for a problem. That is the problem.

Part V

STRATEGIES FOR STUDYING PERSON BY SITUATION INTERACTIONS

Part V contains ten chapters (Chapters 20–29) that are organized around the theme of strategies for studying person by situation interactions. Whereas Part IV dealt primarily with criticizing existing strategies (and only secondarily with proposing alternatives), the present part focuses primarily on suggesting new directions for future research on interactionism.

Sarason (Chapter 20) suggests that personal and situational factors jointly influence behavior and that the personality versus situation issue is a pseudo-issue (see Endler, 1973). He bolsters his contentions with research data from test anxiety studies. Sarason proposes that interactional psychology can progress if future research investigates the effects of three types of variables: characteristics of situations, covert events, and behavior. He suggests that we need to invent better methods for assessing personal attributes and cognitive styles and research aimed at defining promising constructs. We should examine variability of behavior within situations and study the selection of situations by persons.

Fiske (Chapter 21) states that, unfortunately, person by environment interactions have been investigated at levels of abstraction that are far removed from the continuous moment to moment interchange that occurs between persons. We usually make abstractions on the basis of complex perceptions and cognitions of observations occurring over long periods of time instead of on the basis of single acts. He discusses three levels of analysis and the relationships among them: (1) societal problems, essentially a value-based approach; (2) attributions and how they are made, an intermediate level between 1 and 3; and (3) objective time-related observations of behavior, observations of specified microbehaviors within ongoing interactions. Fiske suggests that we start investigating behavior at a low microlevel, for example, "moment to moment interactions" between persons and their environment, in order to produce the fundaments of a more scientific psychology.

Raush (Chapter 22) points out that one seems inevitably to arrive at an interactional position as soon as one is concerned with molar human social behavior. He concludes that current approaches to person by situation interactions yield semantic, temporal, and contextual paradoxes. Raush favors a systems approach for investigating interactions and is concerned with the dynamic ongoing interaction process. He proposes analyses of sequences of interaction events represented by finite Markov chains (see also Bowers, Chapter 3; Fiske, Chapter 21; and Wachtel, Chapter 24 in this volume). The separation of independent and dependent variables is not very useful; instead the basic unit of analysis should be the interaction process. One important aspect of person—situation interaction is the person by person or interpersonal interaction (see also Chapter 23 by Peterson, and Chapter 29 by Golding).

Peterson (Chapter 23), like Raush, emphasizes recurrent interaction sequences. He is concerned with a restricted but essential class of person by situation interactions, namely those in which the situation is dominated by other persons (i.e., person by person interactions). Peterson proposes a functional paradigm for investigating interpersonal behavior in terms of recurrent interaction sequences. He focuses on constructual rules, strategies, tactics, and outcomes of interactions as important constructs for interaction psychology (see Mischel, Chapter 25, and Argyle, Chapter 26). Peterson proposes a multitrait—multimethod methodology for investigating social interaction.

Wachtel (Chapter 24) emphasizes clinical and naturalistic observations of feedback cycles inherent in interactions. He suggests that it is insufficient to merely proclaim that behavior is jointly determined by person variables and environmental events. Wachtel believes that our units of analysis have been too narrow and restrictive. By examining self-perpetuating cycles of interaction we can discern coherence and lawfulness in behavior (see Block, Chapter 2; Bowers, Chapter 3). We should examine the interaction of unconscious processes and the perception of current environmental events, in influencing behavior.

Mischel (Chapter 25) examines some of the problems and issues relevant to the "consistency" issue in personality, and provides a conceptualization of person by situation interactions. Mischel pays special attention to cognitive individual differences, e.g., strategies (see also Peterson, Chapter 23, and Argyle, Chapter 26), and emphasizes the interaction between cognitive variables (e.g., construction competence, encoding strategies, selfregulatory systems, etc.) and psychological situations in effecting behavior (see also Mischel, 1973a). Mischel believes that because behavior is always determined by many variables it may be impossible to achieve broad sweeping generalizations. Like Cronbach (1975), Mischel believes that many qualifiers need to be appended to our laws, and we should respect the complexity of human behavior. Therefore, he proposes no overall methods but suggests that we be alert to the pitfalls and dangers of oversimplifying the nature and causes of human behavior.

Argyle (Chapter 26) suggests that it is necessary to predict and explain behavior in terms of the properties of persons and of the properties of situations. He is primarily interested in social behavior. Argyle compares and contrasts predictive and generative models of behavior. Some aspects of behavior are measureable and common to all situations (e.g., amount of talk, gaze, proximity). These follow the predictive model of behavior. However, other aspects of behavior (what people say, what they do at a party, which moves they make at chess) have to be treated differently. Argyle suggests that a "generative rules" strategy, analogous to that used in linguistics, is most appropriate when we deal with discrete entities of behavior situations and possible persons. Argyle develops his "generative rules" approach in his paper (see also Fiske, Chapter 2; Raush, Chapter 22; Peterson, Chapter 23; and Mischel, Chapter 25).

Pervin (Chapter 27) emphasizes the need of representative designs (see Brunswik, 1956) in research on person by situation interactions. One should attempt to sample situations, ecologically in terms of natural habitats. Pervin defines personality in terms of the person's pattern of stability and change (coherence) in relation to defined situational characteristics. He examines free responses of subjects in terms of the subject's perceptions and affective and behavioral responses to the (selected and required) situations they encounter in their daily lives. He uses factor analytic techniques to analyze his data. Pervin (like Alker, see Chapter 19) indicates that it may not be possible to separate the person from the situation in the interaction process, and therefore one should focus on the person–situation sequence as the basic unit of analysis. Previously, Pervin (1968), who is concerned with dynamic interactions, has suggested that the term "interaction" be reserved for undirectional causality, and the term "transaction" for reciprocal (or multidirection) causation. In Chapter 27 he suggests that we focus on the total pattern of stability and variability of the person's feelings and behavior, in relationship to *specific* groups of situations, instead of focusing on transsituational stability of traits or situation-specific behavior.

Zlotowicz (Chapter 28) proposes that neither persons nor situations determine a specific behavior. Behavior is an inseparable aspect of situations and is a way of describing and classifying situations. Interactionism and situationism are seen by Zlotowicz as two types of what he called "responsism." Personality is a particular aspect of situations in which individuals differ. Because situations are constructed by persons, there is little to be gained by discussing person by situation interactions. The aim of psychology should be a comparative approach to situations where one describes, classifies, and interprets situations in terms of what they mean to people.

Golding (Chapter 29), in the last chapter in Part V and in this book, discusses construal styles in interpersonal stimulus situations. Like Peterson (Chapter 23), Golding is concerned with person by person interactions within the context of person by situation interactions. He examines interpersonal attributions as a function of individual differences by means of multidimensional scaling of attributions and correlations of "points of view." He suggests that situational forces may reside primarily within the individual. Individuals to a great extent create the situations to which they respond (see Stagner, 1975; also Magnusson and Endler, Chapter 1; Bowers, Chapter 3; Mischel, Chapter 25, Pervin, Chapter 27; and Zlotowicz, Chapter 28).

20
The Growth of Interactional Psychology

Irwin G. Sarason

University of Washington

Seemingly out of the blue the question of the primacy of personality characteristics, traits, and disposition has again become an issue in the field of personality. Although the phrasing of the question has varied, its major dimensions have to do with the roles played by personality attributes and situational factors in the determination of behavior. Mischel, Jeffery, and Patterson (1974) have recently characterized the issue this way:

> ... Advocates of trait theory seek to discover underlying, generalized dispositions that characterize persons relatively stably over time and across many situations, and search for behaviors that may serve as "signs" of such dispositions. Behaviorally oriented psychologists, on the other hand, focus on behavior directly, treating it as a sample from a wider repertoire rather than as a sign of generalized inner attributes. Unlike trait psychologists, behavioral psychologists see behavior as highly dependent on the situation in which it occurs and therefore do not assume broad generalization across diverse situations. . . . (p. 231)

The view expressed in this chapter is that this personality versus situation issue is pseudoissue. It is reasonable only if one ignores the role of covert influences over behavior and the burgeoning interactional psychology literature. I shall try to show why an interactional approach to behavior requires references to both individual difference variables and situational constraints.

An intriguing aspect of this issue to pseudo-issue concerns the reasons for its present controversial status. Among the determinants, two seem especially important. One has to do with advances in the experimental analysis of behavior, and the other with perceived stagnation in the field of personality assessment. The major influence in the former, of course, has been B. F. Skinner, who has emphasized the need for great specificity in the definition of behavior and the environmental events that activate it. Behavioral analyses of a wide variety of situations have been reported with both animals and humans. At the human level, deft use of environmental contingencies has been shown to exert a salutary influence on persons suffering from diverse behavioral inadequacies. The successes of the operant approach have served to reinforce some psychologists' attention to directly observable stimuli and responses, while stimulating others to search out the cognitive processes that mediate the effects of environmental contingencies.

Personality assessors have sought to identify attributes of individuals that are predictive of behavioral events. The approaches taken include projective techniques, true—false inventories, rating scales, and other devices. Some of these devices (for example, the Rorschach) grew out of theoretical positions, whereas others were created to accomplish as practically as possible certain tasks, such as diagnosing schizophrenics with the MMPI or identifying with the same instrument persons likely to be involved in hunting accidents. Whether justifiable or not, a pervasive pessimism has been evident in the field of personality assessment for a number of years. Contributing to the pessimism have been frequent failures to relate traits and attributes inferred from measuring instruments in a meaningful and consistent way to significant types of behavior.

In a vague sort of way, then, the current controversy over trait and behavioral approachs seems an understandable product of certain S^Ds (frequent demonstrations that reinforcement "works") and S^Δs (frequent failures to demonstrate that inferred personality characteristics "work"). Is the current controversy over the relative importance of personality and situational factors but a prelude to abandonment of major portions of the field of personality assessment? If one were writing a play on this topic, the first act might concern the flourishing of traditional personality traits and attributes and the second might describe the awakening giant of behavioral analysis which is used to assess the response repertory of the individual with an eye to revising the repertory. Perhaps in the third act the old order would give way to the new. This may seem to be a workable, if not dramatically compelling, scenario; yet, as I see it, it is not the way things are likely to develop. This chapter presents some thoughts concerning a third act, which I think may be more in accord with reality than the one just outlined. The sketch to be presented foresees major reforms within the field of personality assessment as a result of which the content of assessment instruments will change and the ties between inferred personality characteristics and behavior will be strengthened, not weakened. Before I provide the details of this happy conclusion, I should like to analyze some issues important in shaping the current controversy over personality and the situational determinants of behavior. In doing so, it will be possible to lay the groundwork for an optimistic and, I think, realistic ending.

THE PERSON AND THE SITUATION:
REAL AND ILLUSORY ISSUES

The reality of persons and situations is that they exist — but never in isolation. Personal characteristics of an individual, even if their reliability over time is high, interact with each other and with changing conditions of life. As a consequence, it seems somewhat simplistic to demand transitional validity of particular measures of a personality characteristic without having given thoughtful consideration to the gamut of transituational events and the variables that influence them.

Consider the characteristic or trait of gregariousness and the realities involved in elucidating its relationship to behavior. Let us assume that the construct of gregariousness does have transituational validity. What are the impediments to demonstrating this fact? These are some of them:

1. The way in which the construct has been defined may be inaccurate or too vague in certain respects.
2. The measure of the construct may not be completely appropriate to the task of assessing gregariousness.
3. Gregariousness may be related to behavior in different ways depending on the potency of other individual differences.
4. Gregariousness may be related to behavior only under certain circumstances.
5. The situations used in research investigations may not accurately mirror these circumstances.

There is nothing "new" about these impediments to testing in convenient neat ways an hypothesis that interests us. Cronbach and Meehl in 1955 and, now 20 years later, Cronbach (1975), have reminded us of the complexities of construct validation. Perhaps more emphasis has been given to imperfections in the technology of assessment than to the uncontrolled variables that characterize psychological experiments. Yet the latter may prove to be even greater stumbling blocks to progress than the former. The problems that beset the experimental approach range from failure to take account of experimenter effects, to the need for replication, to the lack of correspondence between the hypothesis to be tested and the methods employed in a particular investigation. On top of these problems are those pertaining to the populations to which generalizations can be drawn based on research findings. This is, in part, the perennial problem of trying to draw universal conclusions on the basis of an experiment that studied 40 male students 18–19 years of age at a college in Mississippi.

The restriction of scientific endeavors simply to the study of functional relationships between environmental variables and behavior seems at first glance to be consistent with the physical sciences paradigm after which many psychologists strive to model their science; but is it really? Eysenck has succinctly answered this question:

> No physicist would dream of assessing the electric conductivity, or the magnetic proper-
> ties, or the heat-resisting qualities of matter, of "stuff-in-general" . . . Much energy was
> spent on the construction of Mendeleev's tables of the elements precisely because one
> element does not behave like another. Some conduct electricity, others do not, or do so
> only poorly; we do not throw all these differences into some gigantic error term, and
> deal only with the average of all substances. But this is what experimental psychologists
> do, in the cause of imitiating physics! It may be suggested that the root of many of the
> difficulties and disappointments found in psychological research, as well as well-known
> difficulties in duplicating results from one study to another, may lie in the neglect of
> individual differences. (Eysenck, 1967, p. 5)

Awareness of the complexities involved in studying human behavior cannot help but result in caution when one is interpreting research results and assigning blame for results that seem either uninterpretable or not in accord with expectations and hypotheses. Thoughtful consideration of the multidimensional nature of persons and situations should restrain one from phrasing controversies in either—or terms, such as the person—situation or trait—behavioral issues. A broad perspective is especially needed in analyzing the results of research on personality. It is almost self-evident that the impacts of personal characteristics, covert events, and environmental stimulation interact with each other. A red light is a powerful stimulus, and usually is a dominant influence on our automobile driving. However, there are exceptions. Being upset or inebriated can drastically alter the stereotyped response to a red light. Some psychotics seem virtually oblivious to external stimulation, failing to respond to questions, requests, and social advances. Yet they come to the dining hall promptly and seem almost conventional in certain aspects of their interactions with others. *The reality of human behavior is that it is modified by both environmental stimulation and stimulation the individual supplies for himself in the form of preoccupations, expectations, and interpretations of what is going on in the environment.*

Failure to take account of this reality can have profound and unfortunate consequences for the outcomes of research studies. This was pretty much what Sarason, Smith, and Diener (1975) found when they reviewed experimental studies of personality. These investigators examined the percentages of variance accounted for by situational, personality, demographic, and interactions among these variables. Their investigation involved studies permitting estimation of components of variance reported during 1971 and 1972 in three journals: the *Journal of Personality and Social Psychology,* the *Journal of Personality,* and the *Journal of Consulting and Clinical Psychology.* Low percentages of variance were accounted for by all the variables investigated. One set of comparisons revealed 35% of situational main effects accounted for more than 10% of the variance, compared with 29% of the personality main effects, and 11% of Situation X

Personality interactions. The median proportion of variance accounted for was in no case greater than 5%.

Although these results seem representative of the personality literature during the early 1970s, it must be recognized that the percentages of variance accounted for vary widely depending on the situational manipulations and individual difference variable studied. An obvious, often crucial, yet neglected favor in research concerning interactional psychology is the range of individual difference measures and the levels of experimentally manipulated variables in Dispositional X Situation experimental designs. One would generally expect an individual difference variable to account for more variance if very different groups, such as schizophrenics and normals, were compared than if normal groups differing in locus of control were studied. One is not likely to win a distinguished scientist aware by accounting for 98% of the variance while demonstrating that clinical acrophobics experience more anxiety atop the Eifel Tower than do paratroopers. Similarly, the results of comparing the problem-solving performance of groups who have taken either knockout doses of Valium or a hefty amount of amphetamine is unlikely to overly impress us.

An important and neglected fact is that most current interaction studies have been designed to explore relatively subtle psychological phenomena. The results of surveys such as the one mentioned are not as discouraging as they may otherwise appear to be. All three sources of variance — situations, personal characteristics, and their interactions involve complexities. If a researcher's construct has been imperfectly defined, if his assessment of a characteristic central to the construct is not completely appropriate, if the situation in which groups differing in the characteristic interacts with other unassessed characteristics, and if assorted other problems, such as experimenter bias and unusual task characteristics arise, is it surprising that all three sources of variance turn out to be low?

It seems completely reasonable that the relative potencies of individual difference and situational variables vary from type of situation to type of situation and among individual difference variables. As a consequence, determining the transituational nature of a particular disposition may be far from a straightforward task. There are probably many reliable personality dispositions. However, the manner in which these dispositions influence overt behavior depends on the circumstances in which the behavior occurs.

The points made here about the challenge confronting interactional studies (the pitfalls may, of course, be even greater in unidimensional studies that ignore relevant interactions) are equally applicable to clinical situations. Psychotherapy, behavior therapy, and biophysical therapies often vary in their effectiveness depending on the characteristics of the client, his or her immediate life situation, the type of therapy employed, and the behavior of the therapist. Research has shown that different rehabilitation approaches are needed in the treatment of juvenile delinquents who differ in levels of social maturity and anxiety (Palmer,

1968; Sarason, 1976). Most of us who have on occasion been asked to recommend a psychotherapist to a troubled individual probably rely more on our admittedly imprecise assessment of the clinician as someone who can be interpersonally effective than on his or her training. Whereas clinician effects play a role in behavior change when shock therapy is employed with depressives, however, the role seems less central than in psychotherapy.

DIRECTIONS FOR THE STUDY
OF INTERACTIONAL PSYCHOLOGY

The most tantalizing illusion that must be ignored by students of behavior is that persons and situations simply represent alternative, almost competing causative agents whose validities can be conveniently determined. Although the variance accounted for by these factors can be determined, it is necessary that their interactions be determined. Because these effects are not constants over populations, greater efforts must be made to achieve some degree of representative design in psychological research. Doing so will require an increase in the complexity of research designs. In Act 3 this growth toward an interactional psychology takes place.

An example of this growth is provided by a study I am presently conducting that concerns subjective judgments of quality of life. The impetus for the study came from the need to assess persons' perceptions of the quality of life in their community. Because the initial phases of the project were concerned primarily with constructing a measurement instrument, I originally felt that a sample of Seattle residents would be adequate. Fortunately it became possible to obtain quality of life judgments from residents of eight other cities in the United States differing significantly in known ways, such as crime rate, level of health care, and adequacy of housing. Preliminary evidence suggests that a measuring instrument devised in a community with a favorable ecological environment differs in noticeable ways from one devised in an unfavorable community setting. Other examples of this point abound in the literature. Just to mention one, there is reason to believe that a measure of life stress developed with highly education subjects may be much less appropriate for use with less well-educated subjects. Sample appropriateness is an important factor in many types of research and failures to compare systematically Person X Situation interactions in different populations has no doubt contributed to some of the pseudo-issues, controversies, and failures at replication in psychology.

Development of a truly interactional psychology requires a broadening of the scope of research investigations so as to encompass the effects of three classes of variables. These are:

1. Situations.
2. Covert events.
3. Behavior.

Situations

The unfortunately typical definition of the situation in psychological research has been the stimulus conditions in which the researcher is particularly interested. Research on demand characteristics, experimenter bias, and differential motivating instructions have served to highlight the fact that the agenda of experimental situations often includes uncontrolled elements of which the researcher may be unaware. At the present time, the whole matter of the definition of elements of situation is shrouded in clouds and smoke.

Two types of data are sorely needed. One type grows out of studies of behavior as a function of objectively defined situational variables, such as preperformance instructions. Many situational variables, because they seem theoretically irrelevant, are almost totally ignored (room characteristics, temperature, and humidity). Other variables (sex and age of experimenter) are recognized as being at least potentially important but are not studied systematically because they are not central to the hypothesis under study. The second type relates to personal reactions to situations in the form of subjective judgments. Magnusson and Ekehammar's work illustrates this approach, one outcome of which is quantitative estimates of the similarity of meaning in different situations to persons (Ekehammar & Magnusson, 1973; Magnusson & Ekehammar, 1973).

Covert Events

A number of writers have emphasized the usefulness of an information-processing approach to behavior. Bowers (1973) and Mischel (1973a) have made convincing cases for developing ways to assess cognitive processes, such as those involved in encoding and categorizing of information. I have proposed that anxiety be conceptualized as part of the individual's information-processing system (Sarason, 1975). Rotter's stress on the important roles played by expectancies and subjective reinforcement values anticipated much of the current effort to integrate cognitive and learning orientations to behavior. As Carlson (1975) has pointed out, the study of cognitive styles has added to knowledge of "how" persons think and feel in contrast to "what" they think about and feel.

Covert events may be viewed as inputs in the information-processing system that shape the *psychological situation* to which the person responds (Wachtel, 1973a). The promise of this idea is the suggestion that new approaches to assessment may lead to more successful efforts at construct validation than have been characteristic of the field during recent decades. Two directions for research that seem especially necessary are the invention of new methods of assessment, and the definition of promising constructs. Behavioral assessment has proved appealing because it does not require inferences about covert events. Research on the assessment of covert processes has not led to any empirical breakthroughs on a broad front. On the content side, the list of cognitive events and processes that require assessment grows larger and larger. The list includes a variety of factors related to the way in which the individual perceives, interprets, and responds to the world about him:

Self-preoccupations, self-statements, and daydreams.
Ambivalences and conflicts.
Attributions, labeling habits, and appraisals.
Expectations and assumptions.
Problem-solving strategies.
Cognitive rehearsal skills.
Self-observations and introspections.
Awareness of alternative response possibilities.

Advances in the cognitive approach to personality seem to require means of identifying and quantifying individual differences in human information-processing systems.

Behavior

One of the major contributions of psychology has been the development of reliable ways of describing and measuring the strengths of overt responses. Less progress is evident in the study of determinants of overt behavior. Although I have stressed the need to relate (1) obvious and not so obvious situational factors and (2) covert events to the dependent variables (behavior) of psychological research, I am really talking to the wrong group. Researchers who study personality are much more aware of the interactional aspects of experimental situations than are most other groups within psychology.

ACT THREE

So where is the happy ending? The happy ending begins with the realization that glib phrases, such as "the trait versus situation issue," do not solve problems. Instead of tilting at this sort of windmill, we must face the fact that there is no substitute for creativity and inventiveness. This is true particularly in the study and assessment of covert processes. The ancient Greeks explained overt behavior by using the will of the gods as a prime construct. Freud introduced a number of constructs, including primal repression, which has proved to be completely untestable. At the present time we seen to be afflicted by a high percentage of tired complicated constructs. Partly for that reason the cognitive constructs suggested by Mischel seem refreshing and promising. However, we need reliable ways to infer covert events such as self-preoccupations, daydreams of particular types, and cognitive rehearsal skills and then relate them to behavior in a theoretically coherent manner. How can we do this?

In some ways, psychology has gone through a series of profound traumas in the evolution of its theory. With strong convictions that behavior is not a product of struggles between Poseidon and Athena, psychological theorists have managed to create their own entities, ranging from the dozens of vague interacting constructs suggested by Freud to Hull's alphabet soup. As one examines psychological theory, it seems evident that it has become more limited and conservative. It seems somewhat unrealistic to think that Hull's V, K, H, and D can be conveniently assessed and related in terms of main effects and interactions to behavior. What Hull gave us was a general orientation in terms of which one might examine problems of learning, but he often left us flat when it came to explicating the ways in which these constructs interacted with each other. Perhaps theoretical orientations — as contrasted with well-explicated theories, such as those in physics — are as much as we can hope for at the present time in the study of behavior.

One way of moving from theoretical orientations to theories may be by focusing on behavior in relatively circumscribed situations. One might think of individual differences among researchers in terms of the content of their work, the situations they study. A significant step in the history of the experimental analysis of behavior was Skinner's preoccupation with what rats did in that little box with a bar. Each of us remembers the sense of awe during the 1950s that often accompanied the application of operant methods to particular types of persons and situations (children, mental hospital patients). We have seen that ideas developed to account for knowledge that accrues concerning these applications often can be extended to situations that seem phenotypically to be different.

Test Anxiety: A Subplot

Perhaps I can illustrate this point with a situation that has preoccupied me for a long time, text anxiety. Everyone experiences evaluations and there are wide differences in response to being evaluated. Because evaluated performance has person, social, and vocational consequences, there seem to be good reasons for investigating its determinants. Because of the wide individual differences in reactions to tests and evaluations, it seems reasonable at an early point to attempt quantification of them. A number of investigators have been especially drawn to the problem of test anxiety, which may be viewed as the disposition to respond with worry and self-preoccupation (Sarason, 1972, 1975b).

Measuring this disposition in a variety of ways, researchers have compared groups differing in test anxiety in situations that pose degrees of evaluational threat. The available evidence suggests that differences in performance between groups differing in assessed test anxiety are reliable and not caused by differences in intelligence. In situations that emphasize evaluation of the subject's performance, high-test anxious groups tend to perform more poorly on general ability tests, verbal learning, and other task than do low test-anxious groups. When the evaluational component is not emphasized, these differences are either much reduced or nonexistent. When performance has been studied as a function of anxiety and situational factors, the results have usually been clearer when a test anxiety instead of a general anxiety individual differences measure has been used. There is evidence that the disposition to be test anxious is, at least in part, learned. The available evidence is consistent with the interpretation that in performance situations an interaction exists between demand and personal characteristics. Demand characteristics are not absolutes. They are perceived and, as we know, personal needs influence our perceptions.

Given the results I have mentioned just briefly, it is not surprising that efforts to interpret them have stirred up a good bit of interest. The interpretation I have placed on them is that evaluational cues can evoke a variety of covert reactions, one of which is to become self-preoccupied. The highly test-anxious individual seems prone to emit such cognitions as "What will happen if I fail?" It seems reasonable that saying such things to oneself during a test may interfere considerably with the task at hand. Therefore, test anxiety can be viewed in part as a cognitive mediator of overt behavior.

The individual preoccupied with anxiety is engrossed in thought. Can their interfering effects be reduced? If one views test anxiety as a defect in the individual's information-processing system, two courses of action merit exploration. High test anxiety might be reduced through a situational manipulation, reducing the preperformance emphasis on evaluation of the subject's performance. Another approach is more cognitive and is aimed at increasing the individual's ability to cope with evaluational stress. One way of accomplishing this may be through exposing the highly anxious individual to a model who demonstrates adaptive coping skills. Another way might be through use of an anxiety reduction program, such as a systematic desensitization program. Both modeling and desensitization have been shown to lower test anxiety and to strengthen skills needed in coping with evaluational stress.

Let me go back to the origins of research in test anxiety. They were primarily the intriguing puzzle of worry over evaluation when engaged in performing intellective tasks. For a number of years, the research performed dealt with the effects of evaluation stress on groups differing in assessed test anxiety. During this early phase of research, the main focus was on laboratory studies in which evaluational stress was experimentally manipulated. In a later phase, the developmental antecedents of test anxiety were explored. More recently the focus has shifted to training and therapeutic programs for reducing the undesirable effects of test anxiety. A number of valuable components of these programs have been identified. They include:

1. *Information* provided to individuals about themselves, others, their jobs and responsibilities, and reasonable expectations about performance

2. *Observational learning* opportunities in which the individual observes an adaptive model
3. *Self-monitoring and self-control* skills in monitoring and controlling thoughts and behavior
4. *Attentional training* in skills needed for focusing attention on task-relevant activities
5. *Relaxation and desensitization training* directed toward fostering adaptive coping responses useful in frightening situations
6. *Practice and reinforcement* in applying stress coping skills

What I have been describing may be viewed as an expansion of the nomological network described by Cronbach and Meehl (1955). As this expansion continues and new relationships are uncovered, it is likely that labeling test anxiety as a circumscribed area of study may seem somewhat inaccurate. For example, there may not seem to be a compelling reason for relating test anxiety to juvenile delinquency, yet recent evidence suggests that highly test-anxious juvenile delinquents are more responsive than are delinquents low in anxiety to observational learning in which adolescents are exposed to models who demonstrate prosocial solutions to interpersonal problems (Sarason, 1972; Sarason & Ganzer, 1973). This suggests the need to relate anxiety over evaluations of one's intellective skills to social behavior.

The study of test anxiety may also contribute to understanding the relationship between school performance and juvenile delinquency. One popular view of this relationship is that delinquency often increases when adolescents leave school prematurely (that is, earlier than is customary). Presumably this is because the adolescent becomes bored after dropping out of school, susceptible to peer pressure from other dropouts, and commits crimes in order to get material goods and excitement. The chain of events may really be quite different, however (Elliott & Voss, 1974). Delinquency does not increase appreciably among dropouts. Two factors seem especially important in determining whether dropouts commit crime: one is the availability of a job and the other is the existence of a marital partner. Crime among young people is negatively correlated with working and being married.

If dropping out of school and committing crime are not related in as strong a manner as has been thought, perhaps poor school performance and delinquency are positively related. Adolescents who are afraid of school and find it frustrating comprise a disproportionately large share of juvenile delinquents. If these youngsters leave school and get married they do not represent significant crime risks. A crucial question is: Why do dropouts have such frustrating school experiences? The answer to this question no doubt has many complexities, but it seems likely that one important factor is anxiety over failure, potential failure, and performance in academic situations that pose an evaluational threat. Therefore, test anxiety may be an important factor in two social problems, delinquency and dropping out of school, as well as in the personal lives of students.

Test anxiety is but one of the many difference variables which in interaction with situational factors influence behavior. As with the other individual difference variables, there are varying interpretations of the empirical findings. Although these interpretations may not be especially relevant to all students of interactional psychology, the empirical findings very nicely illustrate the close linkage that exists between personal attributes brought by individuals to situations and the characteristics of those situations. The performance of high, middle, and low test-anxiety groups may or may not differ depending on the way in which the situation is structured to the individual. Research on test anxiety reinforces the need to know as much as possible about *both* individuals and the situations they confront.

CONCLUSIONS

Individual differences are among the most obvious aspects of behavior. These differences can be defined in various ways giving different weights to overt and covert responding. In any event, experience plays a potent role in shaping individual differences. Three tasks that challenge us are how to define the variables along which people differ, how to assess them, and how to relate assessed characteristics to behavior. Who believes that these characteristics alone can explain behavior? I do not know very many students of behavior who believe uncompromisingly in either the pure trait or the pure situationist approaches.

The person versus situation controversy is a pseudo-issue. We should be concerned with human behavior and its determinants and empirical inquiry into their relationship. It may be that Skinner is right about covert events being like the snow on a television set. If so, fine — but I think he is wrong. The important point is that the burden of proving our theoretical orientations and hypotheses is on us. Some of us may begin our inquiries because of curiosity about individual differences; others may begin with certain types of intriguing situations. It seems inevitable that the paths of these two groups will cross.

Curtain.

Acknowledgements

I am indebted to Ronald E. Smith and Karen Lindner, who read an earlier draft of the manuscript and provided me with their valuable criticisms and suggestions.

21
Personologies, Abstractions, and Interactions

Donald W. Fiske

University of Chicago

A good friend and colleague likes to needle me from time to time by asking me what major advances have occurred in personality research and theory in the last decade or two. Each time, I am a bit annoyed because he forces me to consider the recent history of the field and to recognize that it is not advancing as a science ordinarily does. We have seen no revolution, such as the recent one in geology. Although each of us can nominate a few significant ideas or findings from the last couple of decades, ideas and findings that were exciting in 1965 seem ordinary in 1975. We have had no change in paradigms, in Kuhn's terms (Kuhn, 1970). In fact, we do not agree on any general paradigm and hence do not have what Kuhn calls a science. Within the field of personality, there is very little on which there is consensus.

The existence of this conference seems to reflect implicit recognition of this state of affairs. Realizing the gross inadequacies in our present theories and techniques, many of us are turning away from old models and exploring new strategies for investigating the phenomena subsumed under the rubric "personality." The fascinating but unproductive study of the person is being replaced by investigation of the interactions between persons and situations. We may, however, not be going far enough: We may be simply shifting our emphasis to the study of whole persons as they interact and to the study of total situations as people react to them, when we should be analyzing immediate, direct interactions between people.

The emphasis on interacting is a promising one because it enables us to consider the function of the interactive process. I see that function as adapting. If we emphasize adapting, we will be sharing the guiding orientation of biology and of those cultural anthropologists who seek to determine the adaptive value of the standard behaviors observed in each culture.

LEVELS OF ANALYSIS

Interactions have been studied at many levels of analysis. For the purposes of this chapter, let us consider four specific studies that suggest the range of levels which have been investigated within the personality domain. (Even more abstract levels of analysis are found in such fields as anthropology and sociology.) In each illustrative study, we shall consider only one of the relationships that have been analyzed.

Length of Psychotherapy

The first study asked whether the length of the counseling treatment was related to outcome (Fiske, Cartwright, & Kirtner, 1964). In broader terms, is adapting to and utilizing the psychotherapeutic situation greater for longer periods of treatment? The interaction here is that between the counselor and the client during treatment. That is, the interactive event is the total treatment, best viewed as a long person–situation interaction, of which length was the aspect measured in this single analysis. In addition to that variable, there are the judgments of the therapist and of the client about the degree of success of the treatment, and several gain scores.

Agreement Between Observers of Situation Tests

Magnusson and his associates (Magnusson, Gerzén, & Nyman, 1968) have studied adapting to the task and the setting for situation tests, as reflected in observer ratings of leadership and two other traits. The interactive event was the total behavior of the subject during a test, a person–situation interaction. One group of subjects was observed in two situations where the tasks were similar and the peer group was identical. Another group was observed in two situations where the tasks and the peer group were different. Each situation was observed by a different set of four raters. One analysis concerned the agreement between sets of raters.

Hostile Actions Sent and Received

Studies of social interaction, involving adapting to the behavior of peers, have been conducted by Raush and his colleagues (Raush, Farbman, & Llewellyn, 1960). They observed hyperaggressive boys in a residential treatment center. In one analysis, they report the frequency of hostile acts "sent" by these boys and the frequency "received" from other boys. For each of several designated settings, each boy was watched by an observer for several minutes; the observer then left and wrote down a verbal description, which was later coded. The interactive event to which the summary data refer is the total interaction among the boys for the 2-week period during which the observations were made of numerous brief person–person interactions. Note, however, that these summaries were the relative frequencies of specific actions observed, recorded, and then coded as hostile. For these statistics, the counts were summarized over two observations in each of six settings and over six boys.

Signals for Yielding the Speaking Turn

The last example comes from the work of my colleague, Starkey Duncan (Duncan, 1972). He was studying adapting to the acts of another in a conversation. He uncovered six cues based on acts of speakers in the last couple of seconds before they stopped talking. The interactive event here is the end of one speaking turn and the beginning of a turn by the other person, a phase in the ongoing person–person interaction. The particular analysis concerns smooth exchanges of speaking turns as contrasted with simultaneous talking, that is, interrupting, the other person starting before the first speaker stops. Each exchange of speaking turns was classified on that variable and also on presence of one or more cues versus absence of any cue. The videotapes of conversations, both natural ones and some unstructured conversations between strangers for research purposes, were carefully observed several times to determine whether there was simultaneous talking and whether each cue was given.

Common Sense Psychology

The first three examples are quite readily understood by a layman. They involve no technical terms, only everyday words with somewhat restricted definitions, if they are defined at all. These analyses parallel questions that are asked in everyday life: Did this person get better adjusted from his psychotherapy? Is this person a good leader? When a boy is hostile toward others, are they hostile toward him?

Over the four examples, the central concepts vary in degree of abstraction. Adjustment or change in adjustment is highly abstract and encompasses a large number of separate aspects. Leadership is a fairly broad term, covering varying styles and varying requirements. Hostility at a moment in time is somewhat less abstract. The concepts in Duncan's work, such as gesture and speaking versus not speaking, seem relatively concrete.

The four illustrations also indicate the range of meanings for the term "interaction." It can be applied to the total series of interviews in a patient's psychotherapy, to the entire activity during a situation test, and also to a sequence in which one person's act follows an act of another person. In spite of their wide range, each of these temporal durations has been used as a unit of analysis in an empirical study. More generally, interaction is often used to refer to person–situation interactions. In this instance, the referent should be the way the person perceives and construes the situation on entering it, the reactive set which is maintained more or less throughout the given encounter. Within that more enduring framework, there are person—person interactions on a moment to moment basis (and also person—thing interactions). The researcher can attribute general qualities characterizing the person's behavior within the situation or he can study the continuing interaction process at a more molecular level.

In each of the first three illustrative studies, the attribution summarizes behavior over a period of time. This summarizing is just like the way we describe friends, or students for whom we are writing recommendations. Each score is derived from a larger number of very brief interactions. For example, in the Raush work, there were several brief interactions in each observation period and 12 observation periods. In this instance, the final statistic, frequency of hostile acts, was obtained by simple arithmetic. In the other instances, the score is a judgmental average, a measure of central tendency that ignores the variation of the distribution of observations.

More critical is the nature of the relationship being analyzed. In the Raush instance, total hostility shown was compared to total hostility by others. Of more importance would be the question: When a boy performed a hostile act at breakfast, was it followed by a hostile act from another boy? Similarly, when a peer made a hostile act, did the subject act in a hostile way? The number of instances of such sequences of hostile acts could have been counted, along with instances of other sequences where a hostile act was not reciprocated. (Later analyses by Raush were of this kind.) We should look for relationships between specific acts, for example, for sequences of two acts. A study of the acts preceding each hostile act tells more about how hyperaggressive boys interact than does a comparison of summary values.

What I am saying is undoubtedly fairly obvious. What may not be so obvious is the way we slip from one level of analysis to another very easily and almost without recognizing it. We move easily from "Joe's hostile gesture followed Tom's hostile remark" to "Joe is hostile because Tom is hostile," then to "Hostility begets hostility," and back to the prediction that "Tom made a threatening gesture; therefore Joe is likely to do a hostile act." As noted by Wiggins (1974), we make statements about actions, persons, and future occurrences. When the same label is used for each kind of statement, we blur the distinctions between the usages: an attribute of an act is not a disposition attributed to a person, and an attributed disposition is not a prediction that a specific response will occur under given circumstances. We are prone to assign a concept to a person without explicating the process by which we make that inference from sequences of actions between that person and others.

THE NATURE OF OUR DATA

When we interpret a person's behavior or attribute a disposition to him or her, we are not simply observing and we are not just a recording instrument; instead, we are processing in a complex manner our perceptions of his or her behavior and of him or her. We are functioning as operators, rather than transducers. Following Barker (1965), an observer is a transducer when he or she scans psychological phenomena and transforms them into data in accordance with rules for categorizing. For example, the coder may search for the occurrence of gestures and note the time at which each begins and ends.

Modifying Barker's usage somewhat, an observer is an operator when he or she interacts with the input and thereby affects the output. Almost all data in the personality domain are produced by operators. A person observes behavior and processes it in a highly complex way to produce a personality judgment or rating. In most instances, the operator stores a series of impressions and then operates on them to form a judgment. The raters of leadership were therefore operators.

In Duncan's work, the coders were essentially transducers. They watched the entire videorecording for instances of one cue, and again later for each of the other variables. That coding could not be done by a device — it did require a decision as to whether the speaker was gesturing and when the gesturing ended. Human transducers and operators both receive sensory input and perceive and construe it. They can be said to be making judgments. In one instance, however, the judgment is relatively simple and is based on a brief physical act; in the other, a somewhat longer action or an extended series of actions are judged as an entity.

(In considering the temporal extent of the behavior being coded, we must, of course, distinguish between that behavior and the judge's behavior. The judge's act of making a judgment is ordinarily a very rapid one, taking a few seconds at most. In contrast, the behavior being judged may be of any duration, from almost instantaneous to many years.)

Interobserver Agreement

The degree of agreement between observers is closely related to the transducer–operator distinction. Psychologists have known for decades that interobserver agreement is good on ratings of specific, manifest acts, fair on ratings of traits, and poor on judgments concerning diagnosis and psychodynamics. The more inferential the rating, the lower the agreement. Some of the empirical evidence has been compiled by Mischel (1968). Although the evidence has been accumulating over the decades, the obtained levels of agreement have stayed essentially the same. We are not progressing in this respect.

Although both the degrees of agreement and their variation over the observer's task are well known, psychologists seem unconcerned. Perhaps they feel there is nothing that can be done about it, and they are probably right. Yet it is also clear that the crucial feature of a science is intersubjective agreement (cf. Popper, 1959). An advanced science has agreement on theory, constructs, and laws. This agreement is based on agreement on the separate observations that are analyzed to obtain the relationships supporting the laws. The data of a science

278 DONALD W. FISKE

must not be specific to the particular observer. There must be such close congruence between the observations by different observers that the observers are essentially interchangeable.

High reliability by summing over large numbers of item responses or raters is not at all the same thing as high reliability for each separate observation. The coding of discrete acts from videorecordings can be done with very close agreement between coders.

TIME: A NEGLECTED
BUT FUNDAMENTAL CONTINUUM

In addition to procuring high interobserver agreement, the study of discrete acts has the advantage of permitting the analysis of actions in their temporal sequence. These actions make up the ongoing, constantly changing interaction between a person and his immediate environment. As Piaget (1971) puts it, "Behavior is at the mercy of every possible disequilibrating factor, since it is always dependent on an environment which has no fixed limits and is constantly fluctuating" (p. 37). To adapt to the ever-changing situation presented by the actions of the other person in a conversation, a person produces a series of actions, each related to acts of the other and to his own preceding acts. Each act of the other changes the situation and the person acts to adapt to the new situation.

Most personality research treats time only in gross terms or neglects it. To understand behavior, we must identify and understand the strong temporal regularities discernible at this level of sequential molecular acts. These regularities are probabilistic. At the one extreme, there are conventions that are violated at one's own risk. If a friend meets you, sees that you are looking toward her or him, and greets you, you must return the greeting. At the other extreme, there are optional actions. It is not necessary to reply to a conventional "How are you?" by telling the inquirer how you actually feel or even by the conventional "Fine, thanks, how are you?"

The conventions and rules often provide alternatives. Duncan's finding of six alternative cues for ending a speaking turn is particularly interesting because the empirical data indicate that any one of these cues serves the same purpose as any other. The demonstration of alternatives opens up a whole new area of individual differences: Does a person use one or two of these cues more than most people do? Does he or she use certain cues when the other person has manifested particular acts earlier but use other cues in the absence of such preceding acts? Does his or her relative use of these cues depend on the specification of the kind of interactive situation as determined empirically from earlier sequences of acts involving both persons? Duncan and I intend to explore these questions in the months ahead (cf. Duncan & Fiske, 1977).

Temporal Aspects of an Act

An act can be analyzed into three temporal features: moment of onset, moment of offset or termination, and period when it is occurring. Turning the head toward the auditor exemplifies an onset; mentioned above was termination of a gesture as a cue for ending a speaking turn; a continuing gesture illustrates an act that is important while it is occurring (e.g., it can serve to indicate that the speaker will continue to keep the speaking turn).

The Pace of Interaction

Interaction is often on a moment to moment basis. The person–situation interaction in driving a car in traffic provides a familiar example. The rapid pace of adapting in a conversation, a person–person interaction, was mentioned earlier. The turn-ending cues in Duncan's work occur in the last couple of seconds before the speaker stops. They help us to understand why most exchanges of speaking turns, even between strangers, are smooth, without simultaneous talking. The exchange occurs rapidly. Perhaps because the new speaker has been alerted by the cues, the average temporal interval between one speaker stopping and the other beginning can be very short, even less than a second (Jaffe & Feldstein, 1970). The speed of interacting in a natural conversation can get close to the speed of complex, discriminative reaction time. The systematic study of moment to moment interactions at that pace requires painstaking efforts. Such analysis can be done well only from recordings, which can be played back as many times as is necessary to code the action sequences precisely. For example, at the initiation of a conversation, there may be several alternating movements and glances between two people, the whole sequence taking less than a second (Cary, 1974). At times, the playback must be slowed or done on a frame by frame basis.

Absolute timing is not the central issue. The critical matter is temporal order. The onset and offset of each act must be located on a temporal continuum so that relationships can be examined between these aspects of an act and aspects of another act by the other person.

The Fundamental Role of Time in Science

The framework provided by time is crucial to the study of interaction. We can appreciate it better if we step back and look at the role of time in other sciences. Its position in modern physics is obvious, especially in Einstein's contributions. Evolutionary and developmental concepts in biology involve large orders of magnitude for time, whereas the processes in physiology and neurology have shorter temporal ranges. Time is a key component in economic theory and especially in econometrics. It is also central in those areas of psychology that seem to have established some firm facts and general propositions, for example, conditioning, learning, perception.

PERSONOLOGIES FOR THE FUTURE

The preceding discussion has considered several reasons that personality as a discipline is progressing so poorly (additional reasons are given in Fiske, 1974). However, what can be done? I propose that we identify several fields of study; they may even be separate disciplines, although they should interact. The important matter is the sharp and explicit identification of each field, each personology, so that it is not confused with any other. The investigator in each of these types of research must be continually aware of the specifications of his or her area and of the clearly defined limits to which his or her findings apply. The most important specification is the source of the problem; others are the kind of data used, the kind of concepts involved, and the type of relationship being studied. The following classification is proposed tentatively; it is not exhaustive.

Society as the Source of Problems

There are now and there will continue to be many psychologists who will study interactions as found in problems that society presents to us. By a societal problem, I mean one that laymen and psychologists consider important to human welfare. There are many of these problems: The alleviation of the psychological distress experienced in interpersonal encounters; the fitting of persons to vocations so that society obtains maximal use of a person's capabilities while at the same time that person obtains appropriate satisfaction from the sustained interaction with his or her vocational environment; the evaluation of social programs.

Society not only sets the problem but also decides when the problem has been solved. The employer tells us whether he or she is satisfied with our selection procedures and the employee tells us whether he or she is satisfied with his or her job.

In a societal problem, the major concepts are those of the everyday world: productivity, satisfaction, maladjustment, distress. Most of these concepts can be measured only by using human observers as operators. The patient is the primary source for reports of personal distress. Maladjustment is judged by the patient or by those who interact with him or her. Satisfaction with a job or with an employee is someone's judgment as reported to us. Although productivity on some jobs can be measured objectively, the employer makes the decision as to what products are to be counted and, when more than one product is involved, how the counts are to be combined. So societal problems study human judgments and society provides the criteria to be maximized.

Even the diagnosis of psychopathology is essentially judgmental, and the agreement between such judgments is well know to be distressingly limited. The day may come when pathological groups may be identified on highly objective measures, such as the presence of poor visual tracking of a swinging pendulum (cf. Holzman, Proctor, Levy, Yasillo, Meltzer, & Hurt, 1974). Note that this kind of data involves the moment to moment interaction between the patient and a part of the physical environment.

The data used in investigating societal problems are largely if not wholly judgmental; the observers being operators, there is always a degree of softness or looseness (what is sometimes called error of measurement) in such research. More critical than the "random error" is the systematic bias contributed by the individual observer.

Exact replication of findings will be rare in investigations of societal problems. One major step toward progress is to reduce the discrepancies from differences in measurement methods by agreeing on a standard set of procedures for representing each concept: Different procedures can give different estimates of the relationships between concepts in this domain (Fiske, 1973).

The relationships investigated in societal problems are those between society's concepts. As the earlier illustration indicates, however, the observed relationship between outcome and length of psychotherapy depends on the source (operator) which assesses outcome and the method by which that assessment is made.

There are many other kinds of societal problems besides those mentioned. One is the study of attitudes and values. Another is relationships between ethnic groups. A major problem is education, the total interaction between student and school. Although we can measure acquisition of information and of some techniques, we do not have any consensus on the goals of education and we still assess the outcome of educational experiences primarily by judgments.

The Several Interactions Involved in Studies of Societal Problems

In this kind of personology, there are several kinds of interaction that are, of course, conceptually separate. One is the general interaction between the subject and his or her environment: The environment here may include all the settings to which he or she must adapt (as in research on adjustment) or may be a particular setting, such as that in which he or she works. This interaction involves all the behavioral phenomena at which research is aimed.

Another interaction is that between the subject and the observer providing the observations. This continuing interaction produces the perceptions, cognitions, and impressions that the observer has about the subject. Although it can be viewed as a segment of the more inclusive interaction described above, it is that segment as construed by the observer who sees the subject from a particular perspective and who knows the subject primarily in terms of the specific interaction between them. (In this chapter, the particular case of self-report data has been omitted to simplify the exposition. The extension of the argument to such data seems straightforward.)

The third interaction is that between the observer and the measuring procedure. It occurs when the observer is producing his judgments for research purposes. The observer interacts with the experimenter and reacts to the task set for him and to the content of the instrument used to collect the judgments.

Research within the framework of the personology for societal problems is severely handicapped by the complexity of each of these kinds of interaction. The complexity of the first kind of interaction needs no comment. The problems associated with the interaction between the observer and the subject stem from the individuality of the observer. Much methodological research has been done on the interaction between the observer and the process of measurement. We know that the obtained judgment data can be affected by the experimenter, by the type of task he sets, and by the particular content of the instrument (cf. Fiske, 1971). Because the findings of any one investigation may be influenced by these specific components of its overall plan, the difficulties in establishing general propositions for this personology are enormous.

Comparison with Current Applied Research

Although the purposes of this proposed personology would be much the same as those for current research on these problems, the orientation of the investigator in the new personology would be quite different. He or she would realize that the topic was the perceptions and evaluative judgments of particular executives, clinicans, patients, or others, and not crude estimates of some underlying reality. He or she would recognize the fact that the manifest content of the protocols involved laymen's common sense terms, laymen's dimensions of evaluating and construing people, and that the only scientific constructs involved would be those the investigator applied to aspects of these individually flavored construals. For example, the investigator might study what components of psychotherapeutic treatment were associated with patient reports of relief from distress and what components were associated with diagnostic judgments of improvement, all within one treatment center. At a later time, he or she could determine whether the findings were the same for the patients and diagnosticians at other treatment centers.

The Investigator as the Source of Problems

The other main kind of personology should be one in which the investigator determines the problem to be studied. That wording was chosen to emphasize the need for problem finding, for coming at phenomena with a discovery orientation (cf. Getzels, 1964). We should look at person—situation interactions from fresh perspectives. We should try to see what is there, instead of trying to find what we expect to find. I grant that researchers always have some expectations and cannot look at any set of phenomena without some a priori notions. We can, however, do our best to let the phenomena speak to us. The need for taking a fresh look is particularly great in the domain of personality phenomena, to which we bring so many preconceptions that have been reinforced by the greater or lesser success with which we have adapted to the world of people.

My prime illustration is the work of Duncan (Duncan, 1972; Duncan & Niederehe, 1974). He videotaped two conversations and laboriously transcribed them, coding a large number of variables for speech intonation, paralanguage (pauses, nonspeech sounds, etc.), and body motion. Reviewing the transcriptions, he began to see regularities: a number of the recurring behaviors clustered together, appearing simultaneously or within a few seconds of each other, especially toward the end of a speaking turn. Hence he decided to make the exchange of speaking turns the focus of his attention in these exploratory studies. Much later, he looked at the point between linguistic units. He found that the timing of auditor back channels, feedback responses relative to that linguistic point, was related to whether the speaker subsequently signaled that he or she was continuing to speak (Duncan, 1974). Duncan had the great advantage of looking at phenomena about which there was little everyday folklore. In fact, most of these acts are peripheral to the attention of both speaker and auditor. We do not have verbal labels for many of the behavioral distinctions Duncan has made because we do not talk about them or think about them. The important point, however, is the illustration of aspects of interaction that remain to be explored.

The concepts can be specified closely in this personology. The lowest level of concepts includes those referring to the several kinds of acts. The next level of conceptualization can build directly on these, with explicit connections to those at the lower level. Concepts will have to be created as needed, just as in the natural sciences. They will be fresh constructs, not encrusted by effects of corrosion; i.e., they will have few connotations other than those stemming from the theoretical context in which they are placed.

Most crucial is the kind of relationship involved. The empirical data are used to identify action sequences with a specific temporal order: A precedes B. The strength of such successive occurrences, considered in the light of the behavioral context surrounding them, can be determined quite objectively. The behavioral context for each interactive sequence includes other acts occurring at the same time and preceding acts by each of the two participants. The whole stream of actions occurs, of course, within a larger setting, both physical and psychological. The interaction between a person and the total situation may affect the observed frequencies of some acts without affecting their interrelationships.

This kind of personology is not restricted to face to face conversations. One can listen to the exchange of speaking turns in telephone conversations which do not have visual cues. Cary (1974) has studied the visual interaction prior to the opening of a conversation. Some human ethologists are working within this personology.

This type of research is part of a trend toward studying interactions and behavior in natural or quasi-natural settings where the observer records but does not insert experimental stimuli into the ongoing flow of behavior. Other instances are Hess's return from the imprinting laboratory to electronic recording of phenomena in duck nests in the field (Hess, 1973) and the observations by Csikszentmihalyi and Getzels (1971) on the actual production of a stilllife sketch, in their study of creativity.

The Production and Utilization of Attributive Judgments

A third kind of personology can be identified between these other two. Because judgments about other people, especially evaluative judgments, play a central role in the various interactions falling within the personology for societal problems, we need to know more about how such judgments are formed and used (cf. the individual construal styles in Golding, Chapter 29, this volume). One hypothesis is that we do not ordinarily construe and label the behavior of another person while we are interacting with him or her but do so when we think about a previous period of interaction or when we want to describe that person to someone else (as in writing a recommendation for a student). More generally, we need the help of cognitive psychology in learning how a person processes the information provided by the behavior of another person (cf. Chapter 25 by Mischel).

It seems likely that this personology can contribute to our understanding of societal problems in the first personology and may be related to the objective, fine-grained analyses in the second personology. For example, a pilot study by my student, Patrick Shrout, suggests that the amount of many nonverbal acts in a conversation is related positively to favorable attributions and negatively to unfavorable labels, the attributing being done by observers of the videotaped conversation.

That kind of study has for me the undesirable feature of using experimental subjects under the unnatural conditions of a psychology laboratory. Research on the attributive process awaits some creative methodology allowing us to work under highly naturalistic conditions. Although the extensive investigations of attribution in the laboratory (e.g., many reviewed in Jones, Kanouse, Kelley, Nisbett, Valins, & Weiner, 1971) have produced a number of intriguing findings, it seems dangerous to generalize from stimuli that are brief, contrived verbal descriptions to the complex input received in natural interactions, and from subjects who are conforming to task requirements to people in everyday interacting.

Meaning and Content.

The personology in which the investigator discovers the research problem in objective observations of interactive sequences of acts may strike many psychologists as excluding the rich phenomena associated with the content of verbal interactions; after all, it is the content to which people attend when talking to others. Insofar as meaning and content are involved in societal problems, they should be investigated within that framework.

The meaning attributed to a person's actions is a judgmental matter, depending largely on the individual (operator) ascribing the meaning. We have not learned how to reach such high degrees of consensus on the categorizing of content that the coders are interchangeable, and it does not seem likely that we ever can. The units of observation that are used in the psychological interpretation of the content of a person's speech are highly arbitrary. The basic data seem inevitably judgmental. Hence the study of meaning belongs within the third personology. It is essentially the investigation of the content of people's judgments about others.

The Eventual Integration of the Three Personologies

Societal problems are being attacked today in ways as rigorous as the topics permit. Fairly sophisticated methodology is employed in current research: Both multivariate statistical analysis and test theory are brought to bear on the problems. What is lacking is the basic scientific foundation. Much of the work is pragmatic; it searches for empirical relationships. Although it should be a kind of engineering in which basic theory is applied to practical problems, it is not like engineering in the physical sciences or like the practice of medicine with its base in biology because the basic psychological theory and knowledge are simply not available today.

At some future time, the personology in which the investigator identifies the research problems should provide a firm grounding for the other personologies. The investigation of moment to moment interactions between the person and his or her environment, both human and inanimate, should produce a store of fundamental knowledge that can enable us to understand more adequately how people form judgments about other people, especially evaluative judgments about adjustment and functioning in the context of work and in other contexts. It should also provide a foundation for the study of the helping interactions between patient and psychotherapist (cf. Fiske, in press).

CONCLUSIONS

Interactions between a person and his or her environment have been studied at levels of abstraction far removed from the moment to moment interchange continually occurring between a person and others. In most research, the data are judgments abstracting from complex perceptions and cognitions, judgments referring to observations over sustained periods of time instead of to single acts.

Psychologists should do what they can do to study such societal problems as human distress and its treatment, as judged at the more abstractive levels of analysis. Psychologists should also pursue an alternative personology that uses objective observations of the physical acts of each participant, relating each act to other acts of that person or the other person. Concepts and propositions at higher levels can be explicitly linked to those at the level below and the level above. These steps can lead to a developing science for the interactive phenomena comprising the personality domain.

22

Paradox, Levels, and Junctures in Person—Situation Systems

Harold L. Raush

University of Massachusetts

Many years ago I had the opportunity to follow the interactions of a small group of very disturbed children with each other and with surrounding adults in a variety of daily life settings and over some of the course of a rather extended residential treatment program. I was later able to supplement these studies with studies of "matched" socially adequate children in similar settings. More recently, I have worked with couples and families — clinically with troubled marriages and family groups, and in more formal research mostly with young married "normal" couples studied in a variety of conflict situations over a period of about 2 years.

In the course of all this, and in the course of trying to integrate my colleagues' and my work with that of others, I have learned a few things. I also have become more confused about some things. The main body of this chapter comes from my confusions. First, however, let me summarize briefly some things I think I learned.

SITUATIONS, PERSONS, AND THEIR INTERACTIONS

Situations

One thing I have learned has been consistently emphasized by those with a behavioral and social learning orientation. That is the importance of situations and situational cues for everyday behavior. From my own starting point of a personalistic "depth" theory bias the fact that the specific situation was a major determinant of behavior came as a surprise, but the findings — my own and that of others — have been consistent.

Situations, I learned, are more than specific stimuli. They not only constrain the probabilities that certain behaviors occur and others do not, they also organize the patterning of behavioral sequences (Raush, 1965). Whereas in situation X behavior a is likely to lead to behavior b, in situation Y the same behavior a might very well lead to behavior c. Except to researchers, the point is an obvious one: The joke that gets a big laugh at a party is likely to produce hard, unfriendly stares if told at a funeral. Situations act as contextual frames not only for influencing events but also for influencing what leads to what.

Persons

People also differ from one another and, like situational differences, individual differences affect not only the probabilities of certain behaviors as compared to others but also the patterning of behavioral sequences — the "what leads to what" (Raush, 1965). For example, among hyperaggressive children an act coded as friendly by observers is far more likely to lead to a hostile response than is the case with socially adequate children. Similarly, adults who report getting on well with their marital partners are far less apt to engage in negative tit for tat responses to negatively affective acts by the partner than are couples who report getting along badly (Raush, Barry, Hertel, & Swain, 1974). As with situations, individuals can be thought of as contextual frames influencing not only the distribution of events but also the interrelations between successive events.

The Interaction: Person-in-Situation

Even in terms of persons and situations as independent systems we find some consistency: persons are *somewhat* consistent over a range of situations and situations are *somewhat* consistent in their effects over a range of persons. Were this not so we could not give specific names to either persons or situations. As has become more and more apparent from research (see also Cronbach, 1975), however, we cannot generalize about persons without implicit or explicit reference to the situations for which the generalizations are presumably valid, and we cannot generalize about situations without implicit or explicit reference to the persons for whom the generalizations are presumably valid. There is no such thing as a nonsituation — we are always embedded in one situation or another; similarly, for psychology, situations exist only with respect to persons. As both Wachtel (1973a) and Mischel (1973a) recognize, despite their differences, we can describe or select situations that maximize or minimize person variance; we can also describe or select persons that maximize or minimize situational variance.

When both person and situation variables are made explicit their embeddedness in one another becomes apparent (Argyle & Little, 1972; Bowers, 1973). Consistency increases when we specify person-in-siutation. For example, Tom may be consistently disruptive when faced with situations lacking in structure, rather than being disruptive in all situations, whereas Mary may become consistently disruptive when faced with highly structured situations, rather than being disruptive in all situations. So too — although far less noted — with situations. A competitive group game may lead consistently to disruptive behavior with children made anxious by competition, although not with all children, whereas an unstructured social situation may lead to disruptive behavior by children made anxious by lack of external control (Raush, Dittmann & Taylor, 1959b; Raush, Farbman, & Llewellyn, 1960). Somewhat paradoxically, consistency is more apt to emerge if we avoid two fallacies: (a) the "personologist fallacy" that a characterological label is consistently relevant across all stimuli, and (b) the "experimentalist fallacy" that the investigator's definition of the stimulus is consistently relevant across all subjects.

As has been noted (Mischel, 1973a), the specificity of person-in-siutation descriptions has indisputable practical advantages over generic labels. Although behavioral methods have in theory emphasized environmental cues, in practice, as Mischel (1973a) notes, the cues have been recognized as varying with individual experience; in work with people both stimulus and reinforcing cues are geared to individual experience. Although psychoanalytic methods have in theory emphasized individual historical development (not traits — as Wachtel, 1973a, points out), in practice, psychoanalysis has been directed toward investigating and modifying the meanings of environmental cues for the individual so as to enable more adequate differentiations among situations (cf. Dittmann & Raush, 1954).

Despite regressions to the argument, there is agreement in recent literature that the question of which is more important, person or situation, is unanswerable. It is not only unanswerable in general; it is unanswerable in specifics. This is not only because we lack a metric enabling comparison, or because total representativeness is pragmatically inachievable, but because the question is logically unanswerable. To quote Bowers (1973): " . . . situations are as much a function of the person as the person's behavior is a function of the situation" (p. 327). To ask the question is equivalent to asking "Which is more important (or which contributes more to physiological functions), the circulatory or the respiratory system?" "The more sensible question," as Endler (1973) puts it, "is '*how* [his italics] do individual differences and situations interact in evoking behavior?' " (p. 289). Although each system may be described somewhat independently, the description must be in the context of other systems. As early as 1953, Sullivan stated this conjunction in his definition of personality as "the relatively enduring pattern of recurrent interpersonal situations which characterize a human life."

PARADOX AND LEVELS OF ANALYSIS

Semantic Boundaries

Semantic issues contribute to our difficulties in trying to answer the question of how persons and situations interact. For example, it is not entirely clear what we mean by "person." The boundaries between what is "me" and what is "not-me" are somewhat elastic rather than wholly fixed. Phenomenologically, the glasses I wear are an object apart from me; yet I am not quite me without them; my beard is even more borderline between me and not-me; a pimple, a pain, a cold are "not-me." Are they then situations? No doubt there are rules that determine these attributions (cf. Kelley, 1973); my point is only that the boundaries are vaguer than we sometimes think. This is not only true of physical aspects but of psychological ones as well. Consider a dream: It is my dream, yet it is a situation for me to respond to. So too an idea, a thought, a feeling, an action, although mine, become stimuli, to which I react. If one speaks of them as internal stimuli that already implies an ambiguity between person and situation. Moreover, and again phenomenologically speaking, I can find myself in behavior that feels false or embarrassing or right to myself – as though a part of self becomes a situation seen as concordant or discordant with another part or with a whole.

Traits are similarly ambiguous. My guess is that ordinarily we think rather rarely of either ourselves or others in terms of traits. When we do, it is with an implicit delimited range of situations in mind (cf. Bem & Allen, 1974). That is, if we think of someone as dependent or aggressive we are most often implicitly excluding situations in which the person is reading a book, watching a movie, taking a bath; if we speak of someone as efficient we are most often not referring to behavior at a cocktail party or response to a joke. This is not a matter of either consistency or inconsistency. It is that different traits are relevant to different situations, and traits "belong" as much to situations as they do to persons. Even for such presumably stable internal aspects as capacities, environmental modification, whether in skis, typewriters, or institutional arrangements, can have massive effects on performance. Although we may prefer – as a matter of common semantic perspective – to locate capacities in the person, capacities "refer to" situations, and can be as logically located in situations as in persons. To quote Bateson (1972):

> ... adjectives ... which purport to describe individual character are really not strictly applicable to the individual but rather describe *transactions* [italics Bateson's] between

the individual and his material and human environment. No man is 'resourceful' or 'dependent' or 'fatalistic' in a vacuum. His characteristic, whatever it be, is not his but is rather a characteristic of what goes on between him and something (or somebody else). [p. 298][1]

The boundaries of situations can also be fluid. They can be clear enough in, say, a baseball game or a supermarket [although even here, as Barker (1968) notes, persons are required to fill positions]. However, some "situations" are more perplexing. Is friendship or marriage a personal or situational attribute? A major source of variance in the behavior of "normal" young couples in experimentally induced conflict situations (Raush, Barry, Hertel, & Swain, 1974) is the couple as a unit. Couples differ from other couples and each is at least somewhat consistent in its ways of handling interpersonal conflict over a variety of situations. Moreover, a couple's patterns of managing conflict are surprisingly consistent over the first 2 years of marriage. Most astonishing — and one sees this dramatically in couples and families who seek therapy — is the intermeshing of individuals to form consistent response patterns to situations. Yet how do we "locate" the couple or family within a person or situation conceptual framework? From the personal point of view of a particular member the couple or family seems to be a situation in which many other situations are embedded; from the situational point of view an individual member plays out a conjointly assigned part in which other members collude. In such continuing relationships the attribution of events to either persons or situations is arbitrary. In clinical work with couple or family units a major therapeutic task is moving beyond such attributions.

Temporal Frameworks

Furthermore, when one studies or works with temporal sequences involving interchanges among two or more persons, our concepts undergo even greater strain. As Bateson (1972, p. 288) notes, in any interchange involving more than one step — i.e., A acts, B responds, A responds to B — any act can be either a stimulus for the following act, a response to a prior act, or a reinforcement for a prior response. So too at a broader level Person B represents a situation for Person A, a person for whom A himself presents a situation, and a source for either pleasure or displeasure.

Unlike the typical experiment, most of our experiences involve extended and often reiterated (instead of one shot) exchanges with persons and situations. We can and do organize our experiences into different temporal levels of analysis. Failure to explicate the temporal framework of reference is a source for

---

[1] Because these transactions change we can expect traits to change. We seldom refer to people these days in such terms as reverent, pious, obedient, sinful, prideful. New traits emerge — self-aware, liberated, actualized.

interpersonal misunderstanding. It is also a major source for conceptual confusions and research misdirections, particularly in examining person–situation relations.

Take the matter of traits and trait labels. On the basis of a probabilistic contingency model, even with no learning involved, behavior can (under defined circumstances) be expected to change radically over a series of interchanges (Raush, 1972). Partner A may over a sequence of interactions shift from predominantly dominating to predominantly submissive behavior while Partner B shifts from submission to dominance. Trait description of Partner A as dominant would be consistent with observations at the beginning of interchange but wholly discrepant with observations at later stages (and vice versa for Partner B). Yet the model involves no essential change in either person; each maintains in this hypothetical example a completely stable contingency matrix. Whereas the behavior shifts markedly, each person is wholly consistent and each individual matrix or any part of it may legitimately be given a trait label if one so wishes.[2]

Empirically, we have seen such behavioral shifts in the interactions of couples who by self-report were getting along badly with one another (Raush, Barry, Hertel, & Swain, 1974). In the first two of four conflict situations presented in the study the wives in such couples employed tactics of coercion and attack with their husbands, and the latter responded rather docilely. Were we to observe these scenes only, we would label the women in these discordant couples as "coercive," the men as "docile." In the following two scenes, however, there is a systematic reversal. The male lambs become tigers and it is the wives who are now docile. The fixed sequence of presented scenes disallows any inference that it is always the wives who are the first to attack. However, the *pattern* is identifiable: grievance collection with eventual eruption. The pattern is visible only over time. A pattern may be wholly consistent and observations may be completely reliable; yet data at one point in time can differ sharply from data at another point.

The temporal level of analysis has also major implication for notions of reinforcement. Consider Partner A's response to Partner B's coercive acts. If A responds with a conciliatory act, a simple reinforcement view based on the temporal frame of the single act would suggest that B, reinforced for coercion, would continue to act coercively. In fact that seems to happen with the couples who are having trouble with one another. With most couples, however, a conciliatory response by A will shift B's subsequent response from coercion to a positively toned reaction (most often a reciprocal conciliatory act). Were this not true it is hard to see how we could escape from statically maintained or

[2] From this theoretical perspective, however, the label must represent an "if–then" (or person in relation to situation) statement at a time perspective broader than acts located at one segment of a sequence.

escalating conflicts. A major difference in the interpersonal behavior of disturbed and socially adequate preadolescent children was in the ability of the latter to avoid the escalation of aggression — typical among disturbed hyperaggressive children — by foreseeing future consequences and by putting their own and others' behaviors in a broader time frame than immediate response (Raush, 1965; Raush & Sweet, 1961). Within the context of a continuing relationship, and when intense emotional states do not disrupt ordinary capacities, reinforcement must be considered in a broader temporal context than the single act. Temporally defined situations, not single stimuli, may be the predominant reinforcers for our most salient behaviors.

If in this preceding discussion temporal organization has been considered primarily from the aspect of persons, we should not thereby neglect the fact that situations are organized in time. Our inferences as to situational consistency will be profoundly affected by our understanding and selection of situational unit. A single baseball inning differs from a whole baseball game and that differs from a baseball season. Weekday behavior is likely to differ from weekend behavior; summer behavior may differ from winter behavior; and the primary issues of one stage of life may differ from the issues of another stage. Findings on situational consistency will depend, as with persons, on the temporal frame chosen for analysis.

Contextual Levels

In addition to problems of temporal frame and what has been called "punctuation" (Bateson, 1972; Watzlawick, Beavin, & Jackson, 1967) a confounding of contextual levels plagues analytic efforts. Take, for example, the case of dominance. A child (and the same seems true for monkeys and rats) who displays a dominating act is *most* apt to evoke from the recipient a complementary submissive response; however, a dominating act also has some, although lesser, likelihood of getting a symmetrical dominating response — a struggle for dominance. A submissive (as compared to a dominant) presentation is much more likely to evoke a complementary act (dominance) and much less likely to evoke a symmetrical act (submission). In this sense submission controls the other's actions more than does dominance. A seeming paradox results from failure to recognize a shift in level.

Such seeming paradoxes are not uncommon in everyday interactions. One sees them often in the clinic, but also elsewhere: the mother who tells her child to be less dependent on her — so that his or her independent behavior becomes an illustration of dependence; the wife who insists that her husband be more dominating — so that his dominating behavior becomes submissive compliance. In some modern "liberated" couples (Fishbane, 1974) one sees the paradox of the husband taking the "traditional" male dominant role by instructing the wife — although the lesson is in "how to be more liberated"; a further paradox appears in the "liberated" wife's demand that her husband take the dominant role of instructor.

Who then is dominant and who submissive?; who is dependent and who independent? Trait terms appropriate at one conceptual level are inappropriate at another level. So too with situational terms. A baseball game will, as S. B. Sarason (1974) notes, differ according to whether the situation is described from the orientation of a particular game position, or from structural arrangements involving all players, or from the physical environment or from the business and social factors that determine what games are played and where.

Transformations

As Wachtel (1973a) emphasizes and as indeed Bowers (1973) and Mischel (1973b) agree, people do more than react passively but actively seek out and create situations. One need not confine this to neurotic so-called repetition compulsions. Given the options, we all choose our intimates, our social occasions, our work situations, our living arrangements.[3] Alker (1972), Bowers (1973), and Wachtel (1973a) all suggest that the selection, engendering, and creation of consistent situations and environments may legitimately be thought of as reflecting personality characteristics. The power of persons to transform situations is strongly evident in observations of couples (Raush, Barry, Hertel, & Swain, 1974). For some couples a simple decisional conflict over a specific issue becomes converted to a seeming life and death, win or lose struggle over power and the maintenance of personal integrity. Conversely, other couples are able to transform a "hot" relational conflict to specific issues and to use conflict as an opportunity for interpersonal exploration and mutual development.

The "activity" of situations is less often noted. That is, although the power of situations to influence behavior is recognized, we seldom note that just as persons select situations so do situations select persons — the "who" that is to behave. Teachers and others who work with groups of children are often keenly aware of this: the situational variations that shift specific children to the forefront or background. One can, as another example, hardly imagine Hitler coming to power in other than a situation of profound crisis.

Situations not only "select" but they may also transform persons. Biographies and novels often speak to the power of situations to effect transformations of character. It is possible to think of such transformations as the emergence of latent traits. Such an interpretation is, I believe, both unnecessary and unwarranted. As a small personal example I find that working as a therapist with families brings out in me a previously unsuspected flair for drama (something that can be useful but about which I also must be careful). I cannot believe that

---

[3] The choices are not necessarily toward maximum comfort or certainty. Preferences vary as to degrees of risk and uncertainty (cf. Munsinger & Kessen, 1964).

until I began such work a trait for "acting" lay buried in a hidden corner of my brain — like a potato at the bottom of a basket. It seems more reasonable to consider that a new situation may from existing possibilities create a new structure.

The relation between persons and situations is a continuous conjoint interchange process. It is the source of change. We enter into and create situations so as to effect personal and situational modifications. Few would engage in an argument, a political struggle, a new job, a field of research, a relationship without hoping to induce personal or situational transformations.

Consistency as a Problem of Level

Postulating continuous open interchange between persons and situations provides another view of consistency. Given stable probabilistic transition matrices, there can be total consistency in a person's response to situations and total consistency in a situation's response to persons; yet in continuous interaction over time the "behaviors" of both persons and situations may change radically in appearance. Theoretically, we need assume no learning and no essential change — the "rules," "laws," or "forces" can be entirely fixed and the process entirely predictable (Raush, 1972). Moreover, although we assume a person to be fully consistent in his or her probabilities of response, his or her interactions with different situations, i.e., with situations that respond to him or her differently, can produce different behavioral probabilities and different behavioral outcomes; conversely, although we assume a situation to be fully consistent in its probabilities for change, its interactions with different persons, i.e., with persons who respond to the situation differently, will similarly produce different behavioral probabilities and outcomes. At a subsystem level we have then (hypothetically) total consistency; the interaction between two fully consistent subsystems constitutes a new system producing predictable change; the subsystems remain stable, but the products are altered.

There is nothing magical about this. The preceding paragraph describes the process of a simple finite Markov chain yielding systematic change over time as a result of fixed intrinsic relations. The seeming paradox is simply in whether we refer to subsystem, the total system, or the behavioral outcomes.[4] Such questions as are persons consistent, are situations consistent, are answerable only in a particular immediate practical sense. We may, for example, ask: Will Johnny continue to be aggressive toward his peers in his classroom, or will a classroom situation continue to be apathetic? Such questions, whether directed from interest in persons or in situations always contain, it should be noted, an implied reference to the other subsystem.

---

[4] Neither is any of these meant to imply that learning cannot or does not occur in ordinary relations between persons and situations. Some examples given above suggest learning and reorganization.

Although practical specific questions about consistency may be answered, answers to more general questions depend on semantic, temporal, and contextual levels of analysis. Such general questions are similar to asking "Is the weather consistent?" I cannot predict with any certainty what tomorrow's or next week's weather is going to be; however, I fully expect summer to consistently be warmer than winter and annual rainfall to be reasonably predictable. As to persons and situations, they are phenomenologically consistent enough so that we can more or less live with one another in our environments and pattern our lives around some expectations, and they are phenomenologically sufficiently changeable so as to call on our capacities for new learnings and so as to spare us total redundancy and boredom.

AN INTERACTIONAL STRUCTURAL VIEW

In our attempts to answer the question of how persons and situations interact to evoke behavior, it is easier to indicate where we are and to infer why we are there than to suggest where we should go. Nonetheless, some directions do emerge.

Persons and Situations as Quasi-Independent Structured Subsystems

Persons and situations can be conceived of as bounded systems. In the sense that each system can be described in terms of its own structures and its internal relations it can be thought of as independent. In such conceptions interrelations between systems remain implicit. For example, one can explicate circulatory and respiratory structures and internal laws — such as relations among heart rate, blood volume, and pressure — independently. Similarly, one may describe the structure of a baseball game, its subdivision into parts, teams, player positions and its rules with only implicit reference to actual players; or one may describe the cognitive, physical, and emotional capacities, or the schemata that guide the conduct of a particular player, with only implicit reference to the game itself.

When, however, they are viewed from the standpoint of a unit that encompasses them, systems often can no longer be conceptualized as independent. That is, when the reference unit becomes, for example, the functioning of the total organism, circulatory and respiratory systems become interdependent; oxygen and waste products exchange require permeability in the boundaries of what were formerly thought of as independent systems. Contextually, we have shifted to a level of analysis in which circulatory and respiratory systems (as well as other systems) become subsystems of a larger system. At this broader level, where the functioning of the organism depends on boundary relations among subsystems, our reference to the boundary relations must become explicit. At a still broader contextual level, the organism as a whole must be conceived of in relation to its environment, and it is *those* boundary relations which become the primary focus.

From the point of view of psychological function persons and situations are *quasi-independent* rather than independent systems. As with circulatory and respiratory systems they are embedded in broader contextual structures — individual life patterns and social institutions. Most often, data on statistical interaction suggest that boundary relations at the conjunction between person and situation constitute new transformed systems.

Such abstract notions of systems, boundaries, levels of analysis, and transformations have specific implications. They suggest that, except in the few limiting cases in which persons and situations function as independent dimensions, traditional notions of independent and dependent variables and of experimental control may no longer be tenable. A concrete instance illustrative of the fragility of these common methodological conceptions was in observations made for the purpose of comparing interaction of hyperaggressive and socially adequate preadolescent boys (Raush, Farbman, & Llewellyn, 1960). Our aims were to establish as precise controls as were possible under practical limitations. Children were matched in age, social class background, IQ, and the social composition of the groups. Furthermore, they were studied in matched settings. Finally, because we had the same adults supervising the activities of each of the two groups, the social environments of the children were, we assumed, established as similar. Only limited observation was required to show the absurdity of this latter assumption. Adults behaved very differently toward the two groups. The groups differed in behavior toward adults and adults responded differently. To have failed to respond differentially would have been absurd — equivalent to reacting undifferentially to a greeting and a kick. Moreover, not only were our ideas of control over variables put in doubt; conceptions of independent and dependent variables and of simple cause and effect became similarly suspect. For example, the adults' behavior toward them affected the childrens' subsequent responses which in turn affected the following adult responses, and so on.

We can, of course, create experimental conditions in which environments are unresponsive and unchanging. However, few would wish to confine generalization to the psychology of the unresponsive environment. To go beyond such a psychology requires a reorientation that recognizes the boundaries between person and situation as fluid and permeable; that focuses on behavior as the emergent of boundary relations; that considers persons and situations as quasi-independent systems from the conjunctions of which new systems may consolidate; and that takes *change* as fundamental, deriving consistency and stability as temporal and conceptual abstractions from the flux of changing events.

Person—Situation Isomorphisms

Behavior as an emergent will be related to the degree of isomorphism between person and situation. The isomorphism may be a given or may be part of an evolving process. The reorientation puts behavior into a somewhat different context and suggests some alternative directions of research and analysis. Consider two examples, wine tasting and mother–infant communication.

In wine tasting we have a relatively stable person–situation transaction. The expert is capable of multiple discriminations of the characteristics of a wine. For such discriminations to emerge, however, the wine itself must match his or her capacities – a cheap ordinary wine cannot call forth a range of discrimination. The novice, in contrast, when faced with a complex wine, lacks the skills to enable more than crude discrimination; given a poor wine, however, the behaviors of expert and novice may be very similar. From the point of view of personality (in this case, the discriminative capacities of the tasters) inferences can only be made through situations (i.e., wines) isomorphic with these capacities; from the viewpoint of situation (in this case characteristics and quality of a wine) inferences can only be made through persons (tasters) whose capacities are isomorphic with the discriminatory possibilities of the situation. The description of the wine – the behaviors – are neither in person nor situation, but in the *interface* between the two. The abilities of the taster may be more differentiated than the wine; the wine may be more differentiated than the abilities of the taster. *At any given moment,* however, *the judgment can be based on no more than the maximum overlapping isomorphic structures at the interface.*

Communication between mother and infant involves a similar matching issue, but as part of an evolving process. Adult structures for encoding experience and for behavior are far more differentiated than those of young infants. To the extent that infant structures are minimally differentiated – for example, pleasure and displeasure – the behavior of mother, as a situation, can be encoded only into these minimal terms. Unlike the bottle of wine, the mother can accomodate to the primitive differentiations as they appear in the infant's behavior, assimilate these encodings to her own more differentiated substructures, and act so as to maintain or alter the infant's state. With maturation and experience the infant comes to develop substructures that mesh with those of his or her environment as defined by significant others. *In the interpersonal framework, in which each person is situation for the other, behavior is still a function of isomorphism in substructures but the process is a continuing and developing one.*

Conjunction and Disjunction

When the substructures of person and situation are wholly conjunctive – the qualities of the wine matching the connoisseur's expertise – the person-in-situation system is by definition wholly redundant. One can predict one from knowing the other. High degrees of conjunctiveness may occur in some realms of activity, in some places, and at some times. Reports from observers in modern

China, for example (Kessen, Bronfenbrenner, Stevenson, Caldwell, Yarrow, & Maccoby, 1974), suggest an astonishing – to Western eyes – conjunctiveness among personal attitudes, familial behaviors, and institutional structure of schools and factories.

Disjunctions between persons and situations seem more common to Western societies of our own era. Personal differentiations are often unmatched by situational opportunities; situational differentiations – as in bureaucracy – may overburden personal capacities for differentiation. When substructures between persons and situations fail to mesh, several outcomes are possible. If substructural boundaries of persons and/or situations are flexible, then either person or situation will change. As noted earlier such modifications, whereby personal learning takes place or situations are redefined, occur for some couples faced with interpersonal discrepancies. A literature on cognitive dissonance describes other alterations in personal perceptions or situational attributions. Where boundaries are rigid, however, behavioral outcomes are likely to be either alienation or fragmented superficial conformity. One sees such outcomes where institutional arrangements (as in schools) fail to provide the differentiations (in roles, positions, physical loci) that mesh with the individual subsystems of the person—participants who are bound to the institutions.

Change

From the above orientation the questions for research become less those of relative proportions of person or situation variance or of predictions of behavior under fixed circumstances; the more salient issues concern *points of entry* into an exchange process and the effectuation and maintenance of structural change. From the point of view of person and situation as interrelated systems, change can theoretically be initiated at any point of overlap. Among factors determining the point of entry would be the number and kinds of differentiated substructures, the permeability of the substructure boundaries, the flexibility or rigidity of the substructures, the number of connections between a particular substructure and other substructures, the channels of communication among substructures, and the potential for isomorphic changes in each subsystem.

Specifically, structural changes may be induced by modifications in either person or situation. It may be easier to effect a change, for example, in the teacher (or a change of teacher) instead of in the student who is having the ostensible problem; or it may be easier to effect a change in the student than in the institutional arrangements of the school. Moreover, depending on the interconnections, a change in social behavior (whether approached from the side of person or situation) may, for example, ramify to a broader network of other change – as in performance or anxiety level – than a change in performance or anxiety level, per se; or the reverse may be true. In a close network of interrelated persons, a change in Person C, for example, may influence the system more than change in Person A, who is seen as the focus of a problem.

The requirement of potential isomorphism cannot be neglected. A personal change, as for example in psychotherapy, is likely to be dissipated and assimilated to former situational structures unless it can be matched with situations isomorphic to that change; psychotherapy may be effective in *inducing* personal change but may fail when situations for *maintaining* the changes are lacking – a matter too often ignored by psychotherapists and by evaluative research. Similarly, situational and institutional modifications may in themselves effect change but fail to mesh sufficiently with personal structures so that in long-term outcomes the changes are assimilated to former structures. Institutional changes by social planners – in schools, mental hospitals, prisons, etc. – have often been vitiated by failure to induce or maintain required parallel changes in personal values and attitudes.[5]

Recent movements in psychotherapy (Boszormenyi-Nagy, 1965; Bowen, 1971; Haley, 1963; Minuchin, 1974; Speck & Attneave, 1974; Watzlawick, Weakland, & Fisch, 1974) suggest a growing consciousness of person and situation as quasi-independent systems. In these approaches the context of psychotherapy shifts to emphasize conjoint systems instead of either person or situation. From this focus the initiation of change is a matter of optimal point of entry required to induce structural modification in the systems relation. New situations may be prescribed, coalitions and alliances may be altered, relations among events may be cognitively reframed. Couples, families, critical social networks are worked with – as primary loci of recurrent significant person–situation intermeshings. The point of entry, however, may even be a single specific person. For example, Bowen sometimes chooses to work solely with the single individual who is most differentiated, postulating that the person in the system who is most open to change is likely through further differentiation to be most capable of inducing effective parallel changes in his/her network of significant others.[6] One may even consider psychoanalysis from this structural perspective (cf. Levenson, 1972).

Such views, it should be clear, are not a new eclecticism, nor are they simply technological refinements of practice. They represent a different orientation and a different set of questions. Within this orientation much remains unknown. For

[5] Events in the Chinese cultural revolution can be interpreted as indicating conscious recognition of the requirement of isomorphism between person and situation in the induction and maintenance of change. The general fragility and limits of transformations within a particular socioeconomic context are suggested by Gadlin (1974).

[6] Montalvo and Haley (1973) somewhat similarly reframe traditional child guidance practices that focus on treatment of the "problem" child. We should note, too, that an abandonment of the notion of the "autonomous" person leads to serious ethical issues that are not considered in this chapter.

example, although any point of entry into person–situation interrelations is hypothetically possible in effecting change, the determinants of optimal points are theoretically (as well as practically) all too obscure. Furthermore, the power of former structures to reconstitute themselves is indeed well known to all who work with change; the conditions for maintenance of altered structures, although some suggestions are noted above, are similarly all too obscure.

The intermesh between persons and situations can evolve to new meanings. Given that structures are sufficiently flexible, disjunctions between persons and situations may result in the transmutation of previous schemata or the emergence of new schemata whereby the relations between events are altered. The process can have a constructive or destructive outcome and the sets of events affected can be limited as in specific metaphors, acts of humor, or solutions to specific problems — or they can be widespread — as in a religious conversion or change in life philosophy. Such transmutations suggest that, beyond simply conjunction or disjunction, persons and situations may interact in an amplificatory fashion, shifting systems relations to new levels (cf. Hoffman, 1971), whereby a new person–situation isomorphism can be effected.

The Interpersonal Framework and the Myth

From new meanings new concepts emerge, particularly as they are shared interpersonally. To the extent that persons participate in a common culture and time era and are faced with identical social institutions, person–situation disjunctions tend toward homogeneity. The emergence of new schemata therefore tends to become interpersonal, interrelational, and interactional.

Moreover, because persons present situations for one another, the sharing of an emergent meaning involves a problem of isomorphism among persons. To test this isomorphism what is preconscious must become conscious, what is implicit must become explicit and what is private must become public. In that process of communication through which a private schema is transformed to a shared (or partially shared) conceptualization, language evolves. Conjoint participation in conceptualization can, however, imply far more than mere words or altered connotations of old words and can concern far more than cognitive processes.

I have called such shared schemata *myths*:

> By myth I mean the juncture of social and personal modes which selects and codes ongoing events. *Relationship* is a myth which codes a major part of our interactions with some others; *social justice, knowledge, morality, the right behavior at the right time, love relations between parents and children, relations between young and old, maleness and femaleness and the relations between these, self-actualization,* these are myths. Some historic myths no longer preoccupy most of us: *the nature of obedience to God, the presence or absence of the Messiah, the nature of Trinity, the code of chivalry, the divinity of monarchs,* though they once served to code the experience of our ancestors and people once lived, died, accepted and renounced, destroyed, plundered and killed

by these myths. They are more than cognitive concepts; they are affectively loaded and they are loaded for action. . . .

. . . The myth is no less real than our buildings, which we create, furnish and modify and which, in turn, create our lifestyles, our sense of relationships, our notions of public and private, dyadic and familial, work and home. The creation of the myth is a continuing and reciprocal process. The myth is selected, created, enlivened and modified by personal and institutional events; it also selects, organizes and interprets, and modifies personal and social events. (Raush, 1974)

In its monitoring power the myth represents a situation that is *between* (or among) persons. For example, couples who are identified by their community as being especially close to one another refer to "working at their relationship" in resolving interpersonal issues (Strauss, 1974); it is as though "the relationship" achieves a status that is quasi-independent from the individual participants. So too, among couples involved in feminist movements actions are monitored less in terms of individual rewards or sanctions and more in terms of conjunctiveness or disjunctiveness with the feminist ideology (Fishbane, 1974). Similarly, the ideology of communal living alters relations among a multiplicity of events, leading to new probabilistic behavioral contingencies that seem counter at times to individual reinforcement histories and simple reinforcement principles (Kanter, Jaffe, & Weisberg, 1975).

As has been suggested earlier, our custom of thinking of persons and situations as independent physical entities becomes disjunctive when we consider inter-àctive phenomena between (or among) persons in continuing relationships. The disjunction increases when myths enter as third parties. An approach to these complexities requires change in the kinds of data we gather and in ways of looking at these data. For example, the analyses above suggest that learning and reinforcement are not always of specific behaviors. A set of probability relationships involving a complex of person–situation–behavior networks may at times undergo transformation or transmutation. Reinforcement may at times be at a level of feedback directed toward maintaining the structural consistency of a system. A myth – whether of self, other, or world – can be reinforced – whether by self, other, or world – by actions "true" to (or isomorphic with) that myth. The process by which interpersonal constructions are achieved and maintained becomes a primary subject for inquiry.

Furthermore, our own status as investigators cannot be divorced from these considerations. The psychological study is an interactive phenomenon. Investigator and subject – or therapist and client – are interpersonal roles played by rules that define the investigative situation. Neither are the roles independent; subject must play subject if investigator is to play investigator and vice versa. The mythology of the situation – the importance of research, its subject matter, investigator–subject status relations – may be shared (or unshared) in varying degrees. Both investigator and subject are part of their mutually (if asymmetrically) created context. The myths – from which our data arise – can be tested only through our continuing search for alternative points of entry: and from disjunctions new isomorphic transformations may emerge.[7]

CONCLUSIONS

Notions of persons and situations as independent variables have been rejected. Concepts of experimental control and of simple cause—effect connections have been questioned in relation to their salience for most person—situation transactions, particularly as these concern interaction with others. Consistency and stability have been seen as primarily contextual problems.

What has been suggested is an orientation to persons and situations as more or less differentiated quasi-independent subsystems forming a system at person—situation junctures. Behavior is seen as deriving from substructural boundary relations. Such boundary relations will be affected by subsystem differentiations and by permeability and flexibility in substructures. The system at the juncture of persons and situation is then seldom a fixed entity but most often involves continuing substructural interchange and modification in relation to the potential isomorphism among its parts. Persons and situations may therefore be studied in terms of conjunctions, disjunctions, and openness to structural change. Instead of trying to predict toward fixed states or conditions, we need to examine change processes, ranging from those which derive from stable probability contingencies to those which suggest genuine transmutations of sets of probability relations. From this context *point of entry* questions supersede questions of independent—dependent variable relations both analytically and as sources of data; meaning is seen as emergent and as continually evolving from person—situation relations; and learning is set in a broader context of system organization. The interpersonal is given special emphasis, and the myth is suggested as the conjoint behavior created from the interpersonal person—situation complex.

Interactionism, as Ekehammar (1974) suggests, has a distinguished history of appeal. It is a position that one seems to arrive at inevitably if one is concerned with molar human social behavior. Yet the appeal has not been matched with method. The approach has been too vague and general; and current technology — the experiment as primary data-gathering source, the overly general questionnaire, common statistical methods in psychology — all premised on fixed stable relations, has not favored its development. Structural systems concepts are yet too abstract, but they have the potential for concreteness. A conception of change as fundamental, with stability as conceptually and temporally derived,

---

[7] For example, one can conceive of "experimenters" and "subjects" transformed to "coinvestigators."

suggests the need for analytic methods other than our traditional ones. The extension of an interactional view into the interpersonal realm emphasizes this orientation toward process. It also places a social emphasis on the development of meaning, and — in conjunction with what seems to be a growing trend toward phenomenological exploration of meaning as an interactionist method — suggests the study of conjoint meanings.

Acknowledgments

I want to thank Jeffrey Baker, Howard Gadlin, George Levinger, and Ester Shapiro for their critiques of an earlier version of this chapter.

23

A Functional Approach to the Study of Person—Person Interactions

Donald R. Peterson

Rutgers University

During the first half of the twentieth century, the study of personality was almost exclusively devoted to intrapersonal phenomena. Despite the presence of situational concepts in the formulations of Lewin, Murray, and a few others, the main body of research and theory over those years did not in fact deal with environmental influences. It was limited almost entirely to the study of persons. Dynamic conceptions and trait theories flourished. Personality tests abounded. The conceptions and methods required for serious investigation of situational influences on behavior were nowhere to be seen.

This imbalance was corrected in the sixties, when Sells (1963a), Endler, Hunt, and Rosenstein (1962), Endler and Hunt (1966), Mischel (1968), Peterson (1968), and others insisted on the incorporation of situational factors in any comprehensive approach to the study of behavior. Some of the arguments, especially Mischel's, were frequently interpreted to imply a neglect of person variables, and this led several critics (e.g., Bowers, 1973; Wachtel, 1973a) to propose more evenly balanced interactionist views, in which persons, situations, and the relationships among personal and situational variables were all brought into the compass of theory and research. Some of the earlier formations (e.g., by Endler & Hunt, 1966; Peterson, 1968) were thoroughly interactionist from the start. Once the necessity for examining person—situation interactions was established, further argument about the relative importance of one set of variables or another lost all profit and attention could be directed to more productive questions. How can person—situation interactions be most powerfully conceived? Above all, how can they be investigated so that knowledge about personal characteristics, environmental influences, and the relations among these are systematically and usefully developed?

The statement to follow deals with a restricted but particularly interesting set of person–situation interactions, namely those in which the situation is dominated by one or more other persons. A general paradigm for the study of interpersonal behavior will be outlined by designating a unit of analysis, proposing a conceptual framework, and suggesting procedures for the conduct of inquiry and the organization of knowledge about interactions among persons. Following this, research in progress on the development of methods for examining a prototypic class of social interactions, namely those in marital relationships, will be summarized.

We have focused attention on interpersonal relationships for several reasons. The main one is the strong but not easily defended belief that interpersonal behavior is more important than practically anything else one may examine in the entire domain of human existence. Among all possible person–situation interactions, we expect those in which other persons are dominant to be more important than those involving nonhuman objects, not only in the determination of human distress and malfunction but in the more general processes of human living. Furthermore, it seems that any knowledge gained by studying interpersonal behavior is likely to bear on issues in the more general field of person–situation interactions. In fact, close analysis of person–person interactions may place the more general issues in sharper relief than any diffuse attempt to study all possible human behavior in reference to all possible situational influences has any chance of doing.

THE INTERACTION SEQUENCE AS UNIT OF INQUIRY

Our approach to the study of interpersonal relationships begins with the idea that the relationship between any two people can be defined through reference to the recurrent interaction sequences which take place between those people. The essential qualities of interpersonal relationships are abstracted from the facts of transactional behavior sequences.

> There is no way to divine directly the nature of the relationship between two people. One must examine by any means at his disposal what people do to each other in the give-and-take sequences of daily living. That is where the relationships are. That is where the contracts are broken or fulfilled. That is where the meaning of interactive social behavior resides. The phenomena of social interbehavior can be distinguished from the phenomena of individual action, but both must be behaviorally defined. (Peterson, 1968, p. 90)

Two people meet for the first time. They do things to and with each other. They speak, they gesture, they may touch. In the process, each forms a conception of the other, and of self in relation to the other. Mutual feelings arise. Each affects the other in some way. The interactive process continues to an outcome. Consummatory acts of some kind are exchanged and the interaction is at an end.

The two meet again, and this time there is some variation from the previous pattern of interbehavior. Perhaps the conditions for the encounter are different, and different outcomes occur. New information is added and the conceptions of each about the other may be changed. Different feelings may be aroused, and the relationship has taken on a richer meaning. However, then this encounter ends also and becomes part of the interbehavioral history out of which the relationship is forming. Eventually, some of the interaction sequences stabilize and in long-standing, well-developed relationships may become regular to the point of rigidity. The behavior of each party to the relationships, including the thoughts and feelings that are part of that behavior, depends on the behavior of the other. The role of each in relation to the other may often be crudely characterized by a pair of summary terms, parent—child, lover—lover, student—teacher, but in highly evolved, complex relationships these terms seldom do justice to the full richness and subtle varieties the relationship may entail. For comprehension of these, return to the original events defining the relationship is required. To understand a relationship, one must know what the people do to and with each other over time. For me, the patterned totality of these recurrent interaction sequences is the relationship.

The notion of defining relationships through the examination of recurrent interaction sequences is of course not original with us. Sullivan's concept of characteristic patterns of living in reference to significant others represent the same idea. The concept is very familiar to readers of books on transactional analysis by such writers as Eric Berne (1964) and T. A. Harris (1967), the communications analyses of Bateson, Jackson, Satir, Watzlawick, Haley, and others (e.g., Watzlawick, Beavin, & Jackson, 1967), as well as the theoretical statements of Thibaut and Kelley (1959), Homans (1961), Raush (1965), and Carson (1969),[1] to name only a few of the people who have approached the study of social behavior in this way.

It is the choice of the interaction sequence as a fundamental unit of inquiry, more than any other feature, that sets the present approach apart from state—trait conceptions and establishes the foundation for its distinctive paradigmatic quality. For example, we study a quarrel between a man and his wife as reported in an interaction record. They are driving with friends to a party and the husband invites his wife to sit beside him. She is already seated elsewhere and says "I'm fine here." He is hurt by this, feels rejected and angry, but says nothing until they arrive at the party. There he begins to drink more heavily than usual, which he knows will irritate his wife, and at one point lights a cigarette, even though he and his wife have mutually agreed to stop smoking.

---

[1] See also Paul Wachtel (Chapter 24) on self-perpetuating interaction cycles in this volume.

She sees him do this, watches him put the cigarette in an ashtray for a moment, strides across the room and puts out the cigarette. He turns to see her complete this act, becomes enraged, and hisses an obscenity at her. She glares at him contemptuously, says, "Don't be such a child," and stalks out of the room. Later interaction records, along with interview reports and other data, reveal a recurrent pattern in which the husband makes an untimely affectionate overture toward his wife, the wife rebuffs him, he is hurt and angry, retaliates non-verbally, and his wife at once punishes and defeats him by calling him childish or immature.

In studying sequences of this kind, we are concerned with the functional relationships among the covert and overt behavioral acts of the participants as they occur in the process of interaction over time. Of course we are concerned with the states of the people involved, but only in reference to the conditions, both internal and external, which arouse and maintain those states. Once we have examined the couple by several related methods over relatively long periods of time, we may arrive at certain traitlike assertions about some aspect of a class of interactions between them. Maybe the husband is generally oversensitive to criticism from his wife. Maybe the wife does not like her husband much. These generalizations are inductively derived from multimodal observations of ongoing behavior as it occurs in the process of living, however, not from single observations of behavior at any one point in time. Furthermore, the behavior of each participant is described in functional relationship to the behavior of the other. In these regards the functional approach we are pursuing is fundamentally different from traditional state—trait conceptions of personality and situation. Close analysis of each individual case (in this case each dyad) is required. If generalizations develop over sets of cases, well and good, but regularities of an idiographic kind are sought first and are sufficient to many practical and scientific aims. The laws to be developed relate antecedent to consequent events in the rapidly flowing process of human interaction, as opposed to static relationships between situational and personal characteristics, however sophisticated evaluations of the latter qualities may be. Above all, the functional paradigm offers a basis for systematic change (e.g., if significant acts of one participant are modified, functionally related acts of the other should change reciprocally), which is far more direct than any provided by present state—trait views of person—situation interactions.

The concept of recurrent interaction sequence is familiar, but studying those sequences effectively is not at all simple. One set of problems is theoretical. Somehow or other, the most important aspects of interactions must be identified. Other problems are procedural. Methods for examining interaction must be devised. Still other problems are analytical. Most traditional statistical methods are useless for the study of time-ordered events, and appropriate models for the analyses of sequential processes need to be developed. Unfortunately, all these issues are interdependent. It is the sorry plight of anyone who seeks to develop practically useful. scientifically acceptable methods for studying interpersonal behavior that the theoretical, procedural, and statistical issues must all be dealt with at once.

CONCEPTIONS OF INTERACTION PROCESS

If we can agree that interpersonal relationships can be defined through reference to recurrent interaction sequences, the next task is a conceptual one, that is to define the aspects of interaction most worth examining. In this task, we are confronted immediately by a bandwidth–fidelity dilemma. We seek reliability, but we also seek comprehensiveness and, given finite investigative resources, any gain in scope is accompanied by a loss in precision. In our work at Illinois, we have been trying to develop clinically useful means for studying interpersonal behavior. This at once sets a direction and imposes a demand on the selection of pertinent concepts. Unlike pure scientists, we cannot afford to neglect features of the relationship that exert important influences on the lives of the people we are trying to understand and help. All we can do is accept the inevitable inaccuracies which must arise from that condition.

In our decisions to examine some aspects of interactive behavior rather than others we have been guided largely by pragmatic concerns. We have chosen concepts that seem important in determining difficulties in interpersonal relationships and which also seem vulnerable to systematic change. We want to look at those aspects of interbehavior that are most likely to go wrong in the lives of people in our society, and that when improved are most likely to help people lead better lives together.

We began our effort toward conceptualization with an extensive literature search. Unfortunately, Clifford Swensen's excellent review of theory and research in interpersonal relations (Swensen, 1973) was not available at the time our work began, but we examined most of the same material. It seemed to us that the formulations that offered the greatest promise for clinically useful analyses of interpersonal relationships fell into three main groups. First were the behavioral conceptions, concerned mainly with patterns of reciprocal reinforcement, stimulus control, and the contractual rules governing interbehavioral exchange. The formulations of Stuart (1969), Liberman (1970), Azrin, Nester, and Jones (1973), and the Oregon group (e.g., Weiss, Hops, & Patterson, 1973) exemplify this view.

Many of the most important phenomena in interpersonal relationships, however, involve cognitive–affective processes, particularly those of construal and attribution, and strictly behavioral conceptions do not deal easily with covert events. It is not clear, for example, how a behaviorist is to examine a prayerful interaction between a devout Catholic and the Virgin Mary, or even the silent ruminations of a wife who sits alone drinking, broods over the frequent absences of her husband, concludes that he must be meeting another woman, and decides to leave him. The behaviorists, of course, have a perfect right to ignore human experience, but we think there may be advantages in studying such processes, and in fact the second major group of formulations that has emerged from our literature search deals with scarcely anything else. These are the phenomenological viewpoints of such people as Carl Rogers and R. D. Laing.

The third group of clinically pertinent formulations includes both behavioral and experiential elements and extends as well to relations among these in the process of interpersonal communication. Bateson, Jackson, Haley, Satir, Watzlawick, and others working originally at the Mental Research Institute in Palo Alto are the foremost proponents of this prospective, although without serious distortion the transactional analytic approaches of Berne (1964) and Harris (1967) can also be brought within its bounds.

Actually, after reading all that literature, my own view of essential features of interaction sequence did not change much. I had believed for some time (Peterson, 1968) that a suitably comprehensive formulation would have to deal with explicit behavior, covert process, and the communicational exchanges by which patterns of interpersonal relationship were developed and modified. For that matter, I did not find a single useful idea in all the contemporary literature that had not been anticipated in some form by Sullivan. Sullivan's concepts were frequently abstruse and difficult to comprehend, however, and the language of modern social psychology should be helpful in the more precise descriptions needed for systematic development of knowledge about interpersonal behavior. Shortly before we began our work, Robert Carson (1969) had integrated Sullivanian concepts, social exchange theory, and his own viewpoints in a particularly thoughtful statement about interaction concepts of personality. The conceptual framework for our work was influenced by his and closely related to it.

We centered our initial inquiries about five main features of social interaction. These were the *setting conditions* under which interactions took place, the *interpersonal contracts* or normative rules governing relationships, the *interpersonal strategies* people develop as they aim to attain satisfactory outcomes, the *interpersonal tactics* they employ as they proceed through the exchange, and the *interpersonal outcomes* themselves, the reward–cost consequences that accrue from the interactions and presumably influence the regularities which interpersonal relationships assume over time.

In examining setting conditions, we supposed that the same kind of situationan dependency which characterized individual behavior might also hold for interactional behavior, and particularly that such environmental influences as the presence of other people might have significant influences on the course of an interaction. In examining contracts, we were especially interested in the implicit rules of governing the rights and obligations of participants in the interaction. Almost by definition, dissatisfaction with a relationship involves some discrepancy between what somebody is doing and what another thinks he or she ought to be doing. We saw the identification and clarification of those rules as an important goal for clinical inquiry. In examining interpersonal strategies, we were concerned with the plans of participants for attainment of desired interpersonal aims. We assumed that the most interesting of these would be ulterior, the hidden agendas of human transaction, and therefore not only unacknowledged but often cognitively inaccessible to the participants. Still, we thought the concept of strategy might help guide the search for important aims. In studying the tactics of interbehavior we intended to deal with the interpersonal messages, the reports, suggestions, and commands through which participants communicated with each other. In studying outcomes, we were concerned with the reward–cost consequences of the exchange, as well as with any changes in construal and subsequent plan that might have come about through the interaction.

That is about as far as we went in our preliminary formulation of important aspects of social interaction. We identified parameters but deliberately stopped short of specifying relations among them. Whether one typically changes a construal by changing explicit behavior or the other way around, for example, is for us an open question. Commitment to a strong theoretical position on such issues can be misleading, and in our present state of knowledge commitment is both premature and unnecessary.

PROCEDURES FOR STUDYING INTERPERSONAL BEHAVIOR

Now we come to still more difficult questions. How can we study all those phenomena at once? How can we translate the concepts we have just identified into a useful methodology for studying interpersonal behavior? In trying to develop answers to those questions we spent a good deal of time surveying the literature on the assessment of interpersonal relationships. There is no shortage of techniques. Murray Straus' (1969) compendium of family measurement techniques describes 319 instruments for measuring some aspect or other of family life. Glick and Haley's (1971) annotated bibliography on *Family therapy and research* contains over 2,000 references. For the most part, however, the psychometric qualities of these methods have been only very casually examined, relations among diverse methods are rarely studied, and the techniques tend to relate to such global, static traits as marital satisfaction or parental attitudes instead of to the processes of interbehavior with which our inquiries are concerned. The methods we are developing are not completely unrelated to previous work in assessing interpersonal behavior. The structured interview methods of the communications analysts, the family task procedures of researchers at UCLA and elsewhere, the self-report methods of Lorr, Laing, and others have furnished useful guides for our work. To a considerable extent, however, we have had to construct our own methods and we are now in the process of trying these out. In line with my earlier statement about procedures for studying social behavior (Peterson, 1968), we are attempting to exploit the basic methodology of behavioral science in developing clinically useful assessment operations. This gives us verbal inquiry or interview, systematic observation and records of behavior in natural settings; systematic elicitation of behavior by means of tests and experimental analogs; and the experimental management or functional analysis of behavior as the basic classes of methods requiring development. To us, functional analysis is the same as treatment, and we are deferring development of those procedures for a later state, after means for determining base rates and analyzing the complex processes of interpersonal behavior have been defined. Our methods at this point are therefore restricted to interviews, observations, records, and the systematic elicitation of behavior.

The interview methods we have developed take the form of guided inquiries, in which the information to be sought is specified at the outset and lead questions are stated for beginning to elicit that information but the strategies of further inquiry are left to the interviewers. We have tried several questionnaires over the course of the research. The battery we are using now includes two devices designed specifically to elicit reports about the marital relationship (The Marital Precounseling Inventory, Stuart, 1973; and the Marital Role Questionnaire, Tharp, 1963), two designed to get at more general features of interpersonal relationship (The Interpersonal Checklist, LaForge & Suczek, 1955, and the Relationship Inventory, Barrett-Lennard, 1962) and one general personality questionnaire (The Personality Research Form, Jackson, 1967). Our procedures have included several situations designed to elicit interactive behavior analogous to that which occurs outside the laboratory or clinic. Other investigators have used a wide range of such methods, such as conjoint projective inquiries, family tasks, games, and role playing methods. Our choice of previous methods was dictated largely by frequence of use. Among all such methods, some version of a revealed differences task (Strodtbeck, 1951) has been used more often than any other, and we have employed a variant of the method with our couples. In order to get individually pertinent information, we have introduced another procedure. This is a simulated problem interaction task somewhat like the analog procedure of the UCLA group (Goldstein, Judd, Rodnick, Alkire, & Gould, 1968). In our version we ask participants to select a recent, important problem interaction they have had and to reenact it as authentically as possible while we record the behavior on videotape. Later, we take them back to the control room for a replay and an inquiry. In this, the tape is stopped at critical points and questions are asked about affective reactions and construals (How did you feel then? What were you thinking?) as the interaction proceeds. The final set of procedures is made up of observations and interaction records. Our assistants go into the homes of participants bearing portable video cameras and record whatever goes on during the time they are there. The information gained so far from these observations, however, has been disappointing. Behavior in the presence of an observer with a camera tends to be stilted, and the most significant encounters between the pair are unlikely to occur in the short time the observers are around. We do not see any obvious way to avoid these problems in direct observations but we have tried to get the closest possible account of significant relational events by means of interaction records. During the week between the first session and the second, participants are asked to record any particularly troublesome exchanges or especially enjoyable ones that go on between them. Forms are provided to describe where and when the interaction has taken place, the course of the interaction (who did and said what to whom, how the participants felt, and what they thought during the exchange) and how it came out. These are the kinds of facts we need to know if the setting conditions, rules, strategies, tactics, and outcomes of interaction sequences are to be described.

PROBLEMS OF ANALYSIS

The clinical assessment of interpersonal behavior in the natural environment poses some issues for the analysis of data that do not arise under the artificial conditions of laboratory research or standard psychometric evaluation. The first of these has to do with the *punctuation* of ongoing streams of behavior and, through appropriate punctuation, the identification of units of exchange. In laboratory research or psychometric testing, the problem is solved by brute force. One simply initiates the sequence by displaying one set of determining stimuli and terminates it with another. In natural settings, however, interaction sequences are made up of action—reaction chains that vary greatly in length and complexity, and the problem of segmenting interbehavior into meaningful units is more difficult.

The most promising work we have seen on the definition of interaction sequences has been done by Harold Raush and his colleagues (Raush, Dittman, & Taylor, 1959a; Raush, 1972). Following Raush, we mark the beginning of an interaction sequence by any action on the part of one person that is followed by a reaction on the part of another. The end of the sequence is more difficult to define but we have decided to retain the concept of consummatory exchange to designate end points and intend to examine how reliably judgments about these can be made.

The second problem in oraganizing data on clinically important interaction sequences is one of *combination.* Definition of "recurrent interaction sequences" requires decisions about class membership over a set of interactions. Rules must be defined for deciding whether any two interactions are the same or different. We have not solved this problem in detail. As far as we know no one else has either, but the general principle to be followed seems clear enough. The elements to be included in any class of recurrent sequences are defined by their occurrence together and in order over a series of observations. Once such a sequence begins the events to follow are predictable. Transition to a different sequence is marked by a loss of serial dependency such that actions at the end of one sequence do not allow prediction of the actions to follow and these then become part of another sequence.

Studying the psychometric properties of assessment methods gives rise to some more familiar problems. The first of these is a problem of *dependability*. We need to determine whether two people employing our guided interview methods develop the same formulations about the interpersonal behavior of the participants, whether multiple observers can agree on their characterizations of behavior in the home, whether the problem-solving strategies and metacommunicational messages observed in the analog situations can be reliably deciphered.

Provided decent intramethod dependabilities can be established, we are next concerned with question of intermethod *convergence*. Most research on interpersonal relationships is based on a single operation. Investigators use a revealed difference method, or the prisoner's dilemma game, or a test of some kind, and base all their generalizations on this one procedure. This is a very risky practice, as I have said in my earlier book and as has been shown again, recently and forcefully, in research on method correspondence in the study of interpersonal behavior. For example, Olson and Rabunsky (1972) compared four verbal report measures of family power with each other and with an observationally derived measure of "outcome power." Relationships among the verbal report measures were negligible and none of those was related to the observational measure. These kinds of results concern me, and I think they should concern others.

We intend to study convergences among methods by the general logic of the multitrait—multimethod matrix that Campbell and Fiske (1959) defined several years ago. For some of our codes, the use of this model seems straightforward. One way or another, by each of our methods, we are almost sure to wind up attributing some patterns of affection and dominance to the participants, and studies of correspondence among these descriptions over all methods should be of some interest. For the units and parameters of greater concern to us however, the problem appears more difficult. These are the sequential patterns of interactive behavior and the multiple aspects of behavior displayed over those sequences which constitute the dominant theoretical and practical focus of our research. We expect to be able to develop some way, however, of defining recurrent interaction sequences and of expressing significant facts about the main features of those interactions so that we can communicate our findings to others. We may then begin to see whether the essential features of interactive behavior over time look the same from one procedural perspective as they do from another.

We expect some degree of convergence to prevail among methods. If there is no convergence we need to know it, qualify our reports accordingly, and attempt to develop some useful complementarities among methods. That is, even if interactional patterns as construed from a questionnaire do not look the same as when examined through observation or in an interview, perhaps each method can provide elements of useful data in forming a treatment strategy or studying different aspects of developmental process. If so, ways of integrating data from different procedures, not merely intercorrelation them, need to be worked out more carefully than they ever have been before. In some of these analyses we will be concerned with the *utility* of separate data components (interviews, questionnaires, home observations, analogs, etc.) in approximating consensus formations by multiple judges using all available data.

Two other problems in appraising the quality of our methods are those of *stability* and *generalizability*. Questions of stability are of obvious importance for any procedures that may be used to evaluate change, but our research so far has not approached this issue. We can gain information about a kind of generalizability through the analyses of intermethod convergence discussed above, but we freely acknowledge that our efforts to evaluate patterns of interaction in the natural lives of participants are still based mainly on observations in a research center. There is no way to evaluate generalizability properly except to observe behavior over long periods of time in the settings where it naturally occurs and our preliminary study is not geared to do this.

In later work, we hope to examine various methods for modifying interpersonal behavior and to study the natural development of interpersonal relationships over such periods of rapid change as adolescence and early marriage. Issues of method, however, have a logical priority over the others. If we can learn to study interpersonal relationships effectively, questions about natural development and planned change may be approached with hopes of significant discovery and dependable knowledge that our present methodology does not justify.

Acknowledgments

Several faculty members and students at the University of Illinois and at Rutgers University participated in this work. Stephen Golding and I have been most persistently involved. The research has been supported by grants from the University of Illinois Research Board, the National Institute of Mental Health, and The Grant Foundation.

24

Interaction Cycles, Unconscious Processes, and the Person—Situation Issue

Paul L. Wachtel

City College of the City University of New York

Few modern personality researchers, theorists, or clinicians are likely to disagree that behavior is jointly determined by environmental events and person variables. Yet, beyond agreement on this broad, almost platitudinous level, there is considerable ambiguity and disagreement regarding precisely *how* person variables and situational variables jointly bring about the events that psychologists study. To evaluate the contributions from various theoretical perspectives, or even to determine where they differ in substance and where only in semantics or in allegiance to different men and different historical traditions, is no easy matter.

In this chapter I take the position that much of the current debate in personality theory derives from the utilization — by theorists of a variety of persuasions — of conceptual strategies and units of observation which have been too narrow or restricted. It is my contention that it is possible to discern a level of orderliness in how people live their lives that can encompass the seemingly contradictory views and findings of psychoanalytic observers and of researchers guided by social learning theory. On this level of coherence — the self-perpetuating cycle of interaction — it is possible to integrate the roles played by unconscious processes and by perception of current environmental events and, importantly, to gain some understanding of how these interact. The rejection by social learning theorists of conceptions of unconscious motivation and conflict and by psychoanalytic thinkers of efforts at direct intervention into troubling life patterns is thereby put in a new light.

SELF-PERPETUATING INTERACTION CYCLES

Let me at this point indicate very concretely what I have in mind when I suggest that the self-perpetuating cycle is an extremely useful unit for the study of personality. Consider a man who may be described by a psychoanalyst as evidencing reaction formations against intense and frightening rage. We may notice that he frequently acts in an excessively and inappropriately[1] meek, helpful, or cooperative manner. We would probably see some ways in which he suffers from this pattern of behavior, either directly or indirectly (e.g., depression, low self-esteem, psychosomatic symptoms). Moreover, we would be likely to see some evidence that very angry, destructive behavior is being actively held back (perhaps in his dreams, in slips of the tongue, in "accidental" or "unintended" consequences of his actions, in the degree to which his excessive niceness is greatest when anger or assertion would seem most likely, etc.). Patterns such as this have been understood, with some justification, as reflecting the persisting influence of intraphysic conflict.

However, let us step back and examine such a life with a wider lens. We might then be struck by some other aspects of this man's excessive meekness and niceness. Looking at how others react to the social cues embodied in his behavior, we would be likely to find that this pattern of behavior leads to a variety of ways in which he gets taken advantage of, dismissed, deprived, and frustrated.

Living that way is likely to be infuriating. Yet fury, indeed even annoyance, is not part of his self-image nor of the pattern of behavior he finds permissible. His social adaptation and sense of being acceptable has emphasized being "nice" to an extreme, and arousal of anger is frightening; so he tries even harder to inhibit the feelings and incipient behaviors aroused and emphasizes again cooperative, mild-mannered habits of thought and action. Instead of solving his dilemma, however, this (far from completely conscious) strategy again leads to experiences that generate angry feelings and hence (given his particular adaptive strategy) the need to defend against them. Thus, although his defensive behavior may be understood as in response to conflict over angry impulses, the impulses themselves can be seen as a function of the defense against them: Were he not acting in such a way that he constantly stifled himself and invited others to do so, he would not be so full of rage. On the other hand, were he not so full of rage, so ready to do very hostile and destructive things, he would not be so afraid of giving up the desperate defensive efforts. Impulse leads to defense, defense leads to impulse, and the cycle keeps maintaining itself.

---

[1] It is important to recognize that not *any* nonaggressive behavior can be taken as evidence for a defense against aggressive tendencies. As discussed below, the rules for making such inferences are not as explicit as we may hope, but they are far from as arbitrary as is sometimes implied.

Let me give a second brief example and then elaborate how I think the cyclical view differs from the traditional psychoanalytic one. Suppose one sees in a particular patient evidence for strong Oedipal conflict — longing for sexual union with the pure, chaste, care-giving mother, and anxiety as a result of such forbidden longing. Suppose also, as is commonly the case, one sees difficultues in the patient's sex life (whether gross, as in impotence or acute inability to make advances to the opposite sex, or more subtle, as in being able to feel lustful only with women he does not like, or functioning as a sexual athlete but not really being able to make an emotional commitment to the partner.) One *could* understand his sexual problem as a function of his Oedipal conflict, and this would, I believe, often be justified. It is only part of the story, however.

Again expanding our view, we can see how the signals the patient gives off as a result of his conflict — that is, his actual overt (although sometimes subtle) interpersonal actions and messages — lead to consequences that feed back in such a way as to intensify his longing for a fantasied figure who is pure, all-giving, all-protecting, nurturant, and larger than life. (Here it is important to recognize that the figure longed for *is* a fantasy. The word "mother" obscures. He does not long for the *real* mother. Alexander Portnoy does not long for the Sophie he describes to us in such repulsively accurate terms. He longs for a *fantasy* figure, who has become enmeshed with his concept of "mother.")

Now, in traditional psychoanalytic accounts, such fantasy figures, as well as the various conflicted impulses the patient is struggling with (e.g., the rage in the first example, the desire to wallow in mess or disorder in an obsessive, etc.) tend to be viewed as *preservations of the past,* as fantasies and wishes from *childhood,* which have remained unchanged since then. The processes of defense are viewed as creating a split of psychological functioning that renders certain psychological processes and events not susceptible to the influence of new perceptions of reality or newer, more sophisticated cognitive developments that alter the person's understanding of how the world works. In the language of ego psychology, perception and organization are characteristic of the ego, and the id, which is split off from it, is not influenced very much by perceptual processes and does not show the kind of organization or pressures toward logic and consistency that are seen in ego processes.

This model stresses that the surprising wishes and fantasies which become evident in the course of psychoanalytic exploration have been preserved in their original form, essentially uninfluenced by what has come later (i.e., we want childish things and maintain childish fantasies *in spite of* our adult reality). To return to our hypothetical Oedipally conflicted individual, for example, he is seen as suffering from a piece of his childhood which influences his present without being influenced by it, and the persistence of which has to do with an intrapsychic state of affairs (the defenses which keep it "id" instead of allowing it to be integrated into the ego and hence made reasonable). The cyclical view, in contrast, sees his Oedipal longings not as a direct preservation of childhood, and not as persisting in spite of how he currently lives, but as a result of precisely how he is currently living and what feedback he is currently receiving. In this view, early childhood fantasies and fears play an important role in *starting* the patient on a life course in which restrictions and inhibitions are characteristic of his sexual encounters. Once the pattern is started, however, both self-initiated restrictions and the disturbing or disappointing response of partners to anxious, constricted, or insensitive actions by the patient begin to have effects on the process, confirming his apprehension and conflict about sexual experiences and hence leading him to again approach sex fearfully and once more induce the experiences that confirm his anxieties still again. The early fantasies that have been so major in initiating his repeated pattern are also likely to be maintained by the feedback that is generated: If one already has a tendency to long for the figure who once nurtured, soothed, and caressed one's body without the performance demands of adult sexuality, such a tendency is likely to be strengthened by repeated experiences of unsatisfying sex in adulthood, even as it arouses anxiety which helps to keep those adult experiences unsatisfying.

CYCLICAL PSYCHODYNAMICS AND
SOCIAL LEARNING THEORY

The cyclical view described here shares much with the Freudian model but differs in important ways. Both, for example, emphasize the importance of unconscious processes and suggest that early experiences are likely to have a major role in shaping later personality. In the cyclical view, however, seemingly irrational and anachronistic wishes and fantasies are not just remnants of the past but are understood in terms of the kind of experiences the person continues to have (largely because of the influence and consequences of those very wishes and fantasies); and the critical role of childhood is understood in terms of the way in which the particular patterns of behavior one develops skew the kinds of later experiences one is likely to encounter and hence create an idiosyncratic environment of a sort likely to maintain the very pattern which produced that kind of environment in the first place.

Perhaps most importantly, the two models differ in their implications for how personality changes. Elsewhere, in a more extended presentation (Wachtel, 1977), I have tried to show how the cyclical psychodynamic model lends itself to an integration of psychodynamic methods with those of behavior therapy and have argued for the value of such an integration both in clinical practice and in personality theory.

To many proponents of social learning theory, such an integration seems unlikely, if not impossible. It has been claimed that psychodynamic and social learning approaches are "fundamentally different" (A. A. Lazarus, 1973; Mischel, 1971). In its current state, social learning theory does seem to differ rather substantially in some respects from psychodynamic approaches. Perhaps most crucially, writers in the social learning tradition have tended to more or less explicitly disavow any interest in conflict, as well as the necessity for inferring motives and expectancies of which the individual is not aware. Mischel (1971) asserts that "social behavior assessments do not . . . infer [the individual's] conflicts and motives" (p. 77). Bandura's (1969) large and influential volume does not have a single reference to conflict in its 27-page index. Brody (1972), moreover, whose text is strongly in the camp of social learning theory, explicitly acknowledges that such findings as those of Epstein and Fenz, which are based on a conflict model, "do not appear to be amenable to an analysis in social learning terms" (p. 333) (although he then goes on to endorse social learning theory with no further mention of Epstein and Fenz's work, adding that social learning theory may be fruitfully integrated with Eysenck's theory because it shares such "ideological presuppositions" as being "antipsychoanalytic").

Brody's statement in particular reveals that the disavowal of interest in conflict and unconscious processes (which Dollard and Miller showed long ago can be readily conceptualized in learning theory terms) is not a logical necessity but an ideological commitment. Instead of being viewed as an *alternative* to the concepts of social learning theory, psychodynamic concepts can readily be seen as complementary concepts that, among other things, fill in some of the details in the open-ended, content-free skeleton provided by social learning theory (cf. Pepitone, 1974).

The importance of reinforcement per se is not being questioned, for example, if one looks for possible reinforcers of individuals' behavior of which they are not aware and which they may even vehemently deny are in fact reinforcing their behavior (nor, in such instances, if one understands further that their denial of the role of such reinforcers is itself reinforced by reduction of the anxiety generated by thoughts such as "I enjoy hurting my mother" or "I feel better when I can get someone else to take care of me"). Similarly, the concept of expectancy is extended but certainly not challenged by considering that individuals may anticipate outcomes to certain actions that are quite idiosyncratic and that, again, they do not recognize as the expectancy which guides their behavior (i.e., "unconscious fantasies").

Part of the opposition to concepts of unconscious motivation, conflict, or fantasy seems to derive from insufficient knowledge and understanding of recent trends in psychodynamic thought. Formulations in terms of energies, libidinal cathexes, etc., are indeed problematic, but these problems have been recognized by a number of psychodynamic thinkers as well, and it has been clearly demonstrated that such formulations are not at all essential to the main points of psychoanalysis (e.g., Klein, 1967; Loevinger, 1966b; Schafer, 1972, 1973; Wachtel, 1969). In particular, Klein's effort to recast psychoanalytic thinking in feedback terms, and Schafer's development of an "action language" for psychoanalysis, in which all thinglike entities are eliminated and the full range of psychoanalytic ideas is expressed in terms of what the person is doing, go far toward reducing the gap between psychoanalytic thought and academic psychology and are "must" reading for anyone who purports to understand the potential contribution of psychoanalysis. Schafer's approach in particular is strikingly congruent with Mischel's (1973b) emphasis on considering what a person *does* rather than what he or she *has*.

Mischel's (1973a) contention that "[t]he psychodynamic approach [sic] ... shares with the trait approach a disinterest in behaviors except as they serve as signs — albeit more indirect signs — of generalized dispositions" (p. 254) lumps all psychodynamic approaches together. It should be clear that the cyclical psychodynamic view described here is in fact crucially concerned with the person's behavior — indeed even the persistence of unconscious motives and fantasies is understood in terms of the consequences of what the person actually does in his daily life. However, if not *exclusively* concerned with behavior as providing clues to cognitive and motivational processes, this approach certainly does view behavior in this way as well. The data with which one is confronted in doing intensive psychotherapy seem to many to require inferring motivational tendencies and cognitive constructions which are influential in the person's life, although not readily accessible to awareness.

Social learning theory has been derived primarily from a data base of experimental research, and accounting for the data they encounter, social learning theorists have not seen a need to make such inferences. The experimental method is, of course, an enormously important tool of scientific investigation, but as a rather exclusive data base for theorizing about personality, experiments can be limiting and can lead to misleading conclusions regarding what kinds of concepts are necessary. I have previously discussed, for example (Wachtel, 1973a), how experiments frequently fail to address the way in which we generate the stimuli we encounter, and thereby lead to overlooking an important way in which consistency characterizes a human life, even if in principle behavior may vary considerably when the situation is different.

Even more importantly, perhaps, experiments frequently fail to examine the *kinds* of behaviors and situations in which the concepts of psychodynamic theories seem necessary. The need for standardization, among other things, has led to the investigation of a restricted range of behaviors in response to a restricted range of situations. Not only are independent variables chosen that can be presented in a preprogrammed way, but both independent and dependent variables tend to be chosen that can be identified, labeled, or categorized quickly and with high reliability. The advantages of such a choice are obvious; the difficulties both in conducting and in interpreting research not so designed are drummed into every graduate student very early in his or her career.

What is less frequently noted, however, is the price that is paid for these gifts that the wry god of methodology has bestowed upon us. To gain the advantages just noted, investigators are often required to investigate the phenomena of interest, to them only by approximation or analogy. The assumption, and the hope, is that the variables are the same in the laboratory situations and those of everyday life. However, there is good reason to be skeptical that this is indeed the case. Particularly with regard to the role of unconscious motives, fantasies, and conflicts, such experiments may be misleading. In having chosen stimuli and responses of minimal ambiguity, many studies are set up in precisely the way that most effectively minimizes the role of unconscious organizing processes, and theories primarily derived from such studies indeed find little need for conceptualizing such processes. In the kinds of situations investigated in the laboratory, behavior seems to vary smoothly with changes in stimulation with no need to conceptualize more complicated mediators that require a good deal of inference (see Wachtel, 1973a, b for a fuller discussion of the issue of ambiguity and unconscious processes).

The Relevance of Behavior Therapy

It may be objected, with some justification, that social learning theory has not been limited in its concerns exclusively to the results of experiments, and that in some respects its most important source of support is the success of the therapeutic efforts with real-life problems that have derived from this point of view. Here several considerations are relevant. First of all, as social learning writers themselves frequently point out, the success of therapeutic efforts is by no means a clear indication of the correctness of the theory that underlies them. The factors that account for the efficacy of systematic desensitization, for example, are by no means clearly established, and explanations of this therapeutic method have stressed psychodynamic, Hullian, Guthrian, cognitive, operant, and other concepts (cf., Davison & Wilson, 1973; Feather & Rhoads, 1972a, b; Goldfried, 1971; Leitenberg, et al., 1969; Wachtel, 1977, Chapter 8; Weitzman, 1967; Wilkins, 1971; Wilson & Davison, 1971; Wolpe, 1958).

Second, it may be noted that the interaction between social learning theory and clinical practice has not been bidirectional, as has been the case in psychoanalysis. Psychoanalytic theory has not only been the theoretical foundation for particular kinds of clinical practices but has also been extensively influenced in turn by the observations deriving from these practices. Freud revised his conceptions extensively on a number of occasions as a result of what he observed in his clinical work. There are few comparable instances in which social learning theory has been similarly influenced by observations in the clinic. The concepts one sees represented in the texts on social learning theory are almost exclusively derived from laboratory experiments. The creative innovations and clinical observations reported by behavioral practitioners have had little impact on how social learning writers tell students to conceive of personality. Their role in the textbooks has been almost exclusively to demonstrate the sufficiency of these laboratory-derived concepts. (The recent increase of interest by social learning theorists in "self-control" seems to be a noteworthy exception, and a very positive sign.)

It must also be noted that the effectiveness of behavior therapy with the broad range of problems people bring to the clinic has by no means been clearly established, nor has its superiority over traditional psychotherapeutic approaches. The clearest demonstrations of efficacy have been in reducing a number of quite specific fears and in instituting a number of basic social behaviors, such as minimal language or orderly ward behavior in autistic, retarded, and schizophrenic individuals. These demonstrations are not unimpressive, especially where they have established behavior that others have felt was impossible to institute, and they are bolstered by a large number of case studies which provide more or less impressive circumstantial evidence for the efficacy of these principles with more complex and subtle problems of human intimacy, despair, identity, and self-fulfilment. In these latter realms, however, the evidence for behavior therapy is on very much the same footing as that for psychodynamic therapies, which can also present case studies with more or less impressive documentation. It is simply not the case that therapeutic efforts which have eschewed the notion of unconscious motives, thoughts, and conflicts have been proved clearly superior to those which do utilize such concepts. (For a fuller discussion of the relative evidence for the two approaches to therapy, see Wachtel, 1977, Chapter 8).

Furthermore, in practice, the behavior therapists I have observed do seem to infer motives and conflicts that the patient does not report, although they do not do so as frequently as dynamically oriented therapists. Published case reports and writings on theory by behaviorally oriented psychologists, however, tend to explicitly rule out the role of such events. This has the effect of making an important part of clinical practice an "underground" which, because it is inexplicit and hidden, cannot be fully developed or examined. It also leads to unnecessary restrictions in theory. Much of what goes on in behavior therapy is consistent with the laws of learning in the same sense it is consistent with the laws of physics. It does not contradict these laws, but those laws alone hardly account for what goes on or give the therapist much guidance as to what to do next.

Evidence, Experimental and Not

In evaluating statements about the evidential status of psychodynamic concepts, it is important to recognize how frequently the question of whether there is sufficient evidence is treated as equivalent to whether there is *experimental* evidence, as if other contexts for observation have no relevance. Much of the evidence for psychodynamic concepts involves discerning coherences in complex events that bring some order to what otherwise may appear to be a bewildering collage of unrelated occurrences. As an increasing number of sophisticated psychoanalytic thinkers have begun to recognize, the rules of evidence and logic of inquiry relevant here are in many respects more akin to those of such disciplines as history or literary criticism than to those of laboratory science. Psychodynamic hypotheses tend to be formulated from and verified by a network of converging observations that are capable of confirming or disconfirming hypotheses, or leading to their alteration or refinement.

Unfortunately, the rules for evaluating these converging observations tend to be implicit rather than explicit, and to be taught primarily via an oral tradition rather than through a literature accessible to all. It is frequently suggested by critics who seem unfamiliar with the actual interpretive activities of good clinicians that analysts view occurrences that are the opposite of what they expected as evidence equally confirmatory of their hypotheses, and therefore that their formulations are impervious to empirical disconfirmation. Students who find themselves in the hands of skilled supervisors, however, soon find they cannot get away with such nonsense. If the student is to support his or her formulation by the patient's denial of it, the denial must be shown to have rather special properties. The denial, or the manifestation of opposite behavior, might be extremely, perhaps inappropriately, intense; or the opposite behavior might be evident particularly when its antonym would be strongly expected; or the consequences of the one kind of behavior might quite regularly, and "surprisingly," turn out to be those one would expect from the trend the therapist postulates. In instances where several of these sorts of considerations converge with what is occurring in the patient's dreams, his or her slips of the tongue, and the experiences gained with similar kinds of patients, *then* the confirmation by opposites begins to look more substantial.

The explication of the rules of evidence and inference in psychodynamic thought is a major need, long overdue. There are rich lodes of insight here, which have directed observers to notice things that the laboratory investigator would never have thought to see or connect. However, there is also much fool's gold, for which a high price has been paid. Combined with the utilization of tape recordings of therapeutic sessions and other interactions to replace the recollections that have had to suffice as data in the psychoanalytic literature heretofore, such explication can be of major importance. Inquiry into the logic of psychoanalytic inference and the development of ways of investigating coherences in recorded psychoanalytic data (e.g., Luborsky & Auerbach, 1969; Dahl, 1972) should help to clarify and solidify the kinds of evidence and inferences that have played such a major role in psychodynamic thought and may help to establish such "converging network" kind of evidence as an accepted complement to the yes–no hypothesis testing of the laboratory.

Experimental Evidence

My argument for the legitimacy of nonexperimental evidence for such concepts as unconscious conflict or defense should not be taken to imply that the experimental evidence is all negative. In fact, there is some rather strong support for these concepts from experimental research. In a previous review of the research on "perceptual defense," for example, (Wolitzky & Wachtel, 1973), I have indicated how this research is more consistent with psychodynamic conceptions than most recent discussions of it have acknowledged. The work of Silverman and his colleagues (e.g., Silverman, 1971, 1972) provides particularly striking experimental evidence for the importance of conceptualizing unconscious processes. In a large number of studies, some of which have been independently replicated, Silverman has found that stimuli presented tachistoscopically, of which the subject has been unaware, have increased or reduced particular psychopathological reactions in ways consistent with predictions from psychoanalytic theory, and that these effects have *not* been manifested when the subject has perceived the same stimuli at speeds where they can be registered consciously. Space precludes detailing here the variety of striking findings reported by Silverman or indicating why experimenter bias explanations or earlier criticisms of tachistoscopic studies, such as those of Eriksen, do not seem relevant to Silverman's studies.

It is perhaps understandable that this work has been largely ignored so far by antipsychoanalytic writers (Silverman's findings are startling and in some respects puzzling even to a psychodynamically inclined psychologist, such as myself, and are reported in a matter of fact way as if they are perfectly expectable), but they can no longer be responsibly ignored by writers who claim no role for unconscious processes. This is hardly the only evidence in experimental work that supports psychodynamic assumptions, but it is perhaps the most dramatic, and it represents a strong challenge to theorists who exclude concepts of unconscious processes. Particular studies in the series, or particular details, can be seen as vulnerable, but the entire body of findings has achieved a critical mass that requires a response.

UNCONSCIOUS PROCESSES
AND PERSON—SITUATION INTERACTIONS

The question of whether it is necessary to conceptualize unconscious processes and emphasize multiple and conflicting motivations is the kind of issue that is very much at the heart of the current ferment in the study of personality regarding the person—situation issue. For the real debate among proponents of differing views is not over whether behavior varies from situation to situation or whether stable individual differences can be identified — almost everyone can agree that both are true — but rather over *how much* of the variance is attributable to persons, to situations, and to their interactions and, more importantly, over *how* the variability and stability occur, that is, over the *processes* that are necessary to conceptualize in order to account for what is observed and to intervene effectively.

Much of the work that Ekehammar (1974), in his review of interactional psychology, labels as interactionist is concerned with the first of these two issues. That is, it is concerned with *statistical* interaction and emphasizes that in analysis of variance designs the interaction between person and situation variables tends to account for more of the variance than does either of the main effects. Some of the limitations of this approach have been concisely stated by Ekehammar (1974, p. 1041). I should like to elaborate briefly on a few in terms of their relation to what has been presented in this chapter and to try to clarify thereby in what respect the present approach is an interactional one.

For one thing, as Ekehammar notes, "the relative magnitude of the main components can be manipulated in a favored direction through a selective sampling of persons and situations" (p. 1041). Ekehammar (1974) gives relatively little weight to this consideration, for he feels that in the studies he has reviewed "there seems to be no reason to believe that the selection of persons and situations has been biased in order to sustain a certain hypothesis" (p. 1041). The discussion of methodological issues in traditional research noted earlier in this chapter (see also Wachtel, 1973a, b) suggests, however, that there may be more skewing than has been recognized; for not only is the selection of a particular sample of people or contexts of concern, so too is the sample of *behaviors.* One may get quite a different picture if one asks children whether they prefer bad food now or terrible food later, or tallies the frequency of talking or smoking or drinking, than if one is concerned with the determinants of genuinely intimate sharing of feelings, the experience of a coherent identity, or the maintenance of a feeling of ease in conversation with a shy partner. The latter kinds of behaviors are harder to study and to reliably categorize, but certainly no less important.

Additionally, toting up variance components tells us little about how or why things happen as they do, only what factors seem to be weighty. An understanding of the *process* can lead to a refining of our model so that we ask better questions, which may yield quite a different set of numbers.[2]

The conceptualization of self-perpetuating cycles discussed here represents one way of trying to address person—situation interactions in terms of process. Like many other psychologists whose views have been shaped by experiences doing psychotherapy, I have felt a need to include as part of the process some conception of unconscious motivation and fantasy and of conflict. Perhaps because of this emphasis on unconscious processes, Ekehammar (1974) has categorized my position as one of "personologism," depicted as "advocating stable intraorganismic constructs . . . as the main determinants of behavioral variation" and implicitly treated my position as deemphasizing the role of environmental events. As I have tried to show in this chapter, (see Wachtel, 1977, for a more detailed presentation), however, there is a substantial difference between psychodynamic views which postulate that many of the most

---

[2] A similar point has been made by Holt (1970) in a different context, in a paper which also confronts and challenges the oft-voiced conclusion that clinical modes of personality assessment have been shown to be without value.

important processes influencing our current personality are sealed off from influence by current environmental input and those psychodynamic views, such as that presented here, which treat the unconscious processes as part of a set of interlocking events in which what is currently going on plays a very crucial role.

The perspective presented here seems to me a more thoroughly interactional one than many that are so labeled. In the present view, persons and situations can in fact hardly be separated, for it is stressed that in some of the most important aspects of our lives the situations we encounter depend on who we are, as who we are depends on what we encounter. Unconscious motives and fantasies, in this view, are not structures or properties carried around by a person but ways of coming to terms with continuing experiences in daily living, even as they influence those very experiences and help shape and select them.

SELF-PERPETUATING CYCLES AND TRUNCATED RESEARCH

From the perspective of the cyclical view presented here, a great many lines of research, from a variety of theoretical viewpoints, may be seen as truncated, in the sense of providing a picture of only a portion of the cyclical processes that determine (or constitute) behavior. When explicitly recognized as such, studies of this sort can be of considerable value in providing a detailed picture of one aspect of the network of influences and outcomes in psychological phenomena: It is hard to study everything at once. However, when there is not explicit recognition of truncation, misleading or unproductive research is likely.

I have recently, for example, discussed in some detail the problems and limitations of cognitive style research as it is typically conducted (Wachtel, 1972a; Wolitzky & Wachtel, 1973). One problem with this work is that it seems to promise something very exciting and glamorous – picking up real "personality" characteristics with just a few simple, objective laboratory tests – yet in fact in most cases it is directly assessing only abilities, which may or may not form the basis for a particular personal style, depending on a host of other variables. The relation between scores on such tests as the rod and frame or embedded figures and the matters that have traditionally fascinated students of personality are far more complicated and indirect than the literature in this area tends to suggest. This confusion is caused in substantial measure by an empirical and conceptual strategy that implicitly treats people as static things or structures[3] instead of viewing man as dynamically interacting with and responsive to

---

[3] The literature on field dependence does, of course, discuss change in amount of field dependence with increasing age, and even how different kinds of child rearing make the amount of increase and final level achieved greater or lesser. It should be clear, however, that this has not been discussed in fully interactional terms (although it can be) and has been treated primarily in terms of factors that influence the parameters of the structure.

events. Environmental stimulation, in most cognitive style research, is primarily of interest as a way of revealing what structure the person carries around with him or her.

The conception that originally sparked much of the research on cognitive style (e.g., Klein, 1958) was potentially a much more integrative and useful one. It could have led to examination of how particular modes of organizing thought and perceptual input led to actions and adaptations that eventually fed back to stabilize and perpetuate those very modes (at least in a particular class of perceived situations). Shapiro (1965) did do this to some extent, treating cognition as much more part of a sequence of adaptive efforts than was true in most of the cognitive style work, although presenting an excessively and un-necessarily typological picture. In most of the laboratory research on cognitive style, however, a rather static approach has been employed, which instead of viewing cognition as part of a sequence of adaptional efforts and perceived consequences, studies the cognitive activity just in itself or for purposes of categorizing the individual (see Wachtel, 1972b).

This kind of problem — treating a cognitive product as an end point instead of as a part of a process that leads to further events which feed back and influence subsequent (although instantaneous, in the sense of an integral calculus) cogni-tions — is apparent as well in the tachistoscopic research on perceptual defense mentioned earlier and is one of the main reasons I have suggested that such research is more relevant to students of microscopic perceptual processes than to personality theorists (Wolitzky & Wachtel, 1973). It is similarly apparent in much of the research — still potentially of considerable importance — relating aspects of attention deployment to personality and psychopathology. In re-examining recently one of my own contributions in this area (Wachtel, 1967), I became aware of ways in which the implications of the *actions* that flow from cognitions, and their perceived consequences, had not been fully considered. That paper had been concerned with clarifying the variety of ways in which concepts of breadth and narrowness of attention have been used to elucidate phenomena related to cognitive style, arousal, anxiety, and schizophrenia. Al-though the paper still seemed to me in retrospect to contribute toward eluci-dating how variations in cognitive activity mediated personality phenomena, I was equally impressed by what I had left out. In reviewing my discussion, for example, of the various ways in which anxiety influences the deployment of attention, it seemed to me that I did not consider sufficiently how focus on a restricted range of cues, or inability to synthesize and coordinate enough stimulation, can hamper adaptation, leading to further anxiety, still further restriction, etc. I would now highlight such momentum-generating sequences to a far greater degree and would be dissatisfied with any formulation that did not include a focus broad enough to encompass such a cyclical process and/or describe how the cycle came to an equilibrium or was interrupted or reversed. (There has not been very much emphasis in this chapter on this latter, and crucial, aspect of a cyclical psychology – why cycles do not repeat themselves indefinitely. The issue, which is particularly crucial in devising strategies and conceptions of psychotherapy, is discussed in various ways in Wachtel, 1977.)

Many more considerations are obvious implications of the views presented here but must await future communications to be spelled out. For one thing, we obviously need far more observational research on meaningful interpersonal behavior in ecologically relevant contexts. Far too large a proportion of psychology's research activity has been concerned with laboratory analogs. It should be clear that the conception stressed here points particularly to the importance of naturalistic observation.

Second, the conception presented here has obvious implications for the notion of "stimulus control" of behavior and suggests that there are empirical as well as philosophical problems with conceiving of stimulus control as the basic reality behind an illusory sense that the person her- or himself is responsible for what he or she does. I have presented arguments elsewhere (Wachtel, 1969) for the view that conceiving of behavior as determined is no more or less sensible or useful than conceiving of it as genuinely chosen. The considerations presented here point to observations and perspectives that further highlight the stimulus control conception as but one way of organizing the data, which if relied on exclusively can have serious distorting effects (see also de Charms, 1968; Wheelis, 1973).

Finally, the views presented here clearly imply that a far more complex view of motivation is required than is typically found in nondynamic theories. I have shown that psychodynamic theorizing about unconscious motives need not be characterized by a depiction of thinglike entities possessed by a person and locked into him early in childhood; a dynamic view can be wholly consistent with all we know about environmental influences. In fact, the model presented here seems to me to be one of the few genuinely interactional accounts of motivation of which I am aware. Far from being viewed as structured residues of childhood, motivational processes are depicted here as very much a function of how the person is currently leading his or her life and what happens to him or her, both as a result of his or her own actions and as a result of more extrinsic factors; yet the organizing effects of motivational variables are treated as real and powerful, leading to particular behavioral choices in response to stimulus conditions, to selectivity in what stimulus conditions are encountered, and to particular ways of construing what is encountered so that the very term "stimulus" begins to look vague or anachronistic.

In the laboratory, it is (relatively) safe to assume that certain common and obvious motives are operative, or to define motivational variables in terms of simple, discrete operations of deprivation or stimulation. In most real social situations this is simply not the case. It *is* necessary to "infer conflicts and motives," and the choice is between doing so naively and/or through the eyes of the society's normative expectations, versus doing so in a way that utilizes the guidelines for observations and inference which have accured from decades of clinical focus on motivational variables in particular (see Wachtel, 1977, Chapter 6 and 7, for a much fuller discussion of this issue and of the importance of motivational conflicts).

There have been, to be sure, enormous difficulties with psychodynamic methodology and theorizing. But one can be nourished by a body of work without swallowing it whole. Perhaps what is needed is a concerted effort by dynamic and nondynamic observers to examine the same (real-life) material and to determine what concepts and inferences each seems to need and what each leaves out that the other insists on noticing. If this chapter should kindle interest in such a collaborative research effort, its purpose will have been achieved.

25

The Interaction of Person and Situation[1]

Walter Mischel

Stanford University

In this chapter I want to look again at some of the enduring problems and issues relevant to the "consistency" issue in personality and to consider once more the conceptualization of person—situation interactions.

THE DATA ON CONSISTENCY

Jack Block (Chapter 2) has reviewed an impressive body of data, drawing extensively on his own voluminous work (1971), attesting the coherence and continuity of personality. For me, the surprising part of his scholarly survey is that he seems to assume I disagree with his assessment of the state of the data on the consistency issue. Although our emphasis and language differ, however, Block's appraisal of the data appears basically congruent with mine in 1968 and now. We do differ, however in the implications we draw from those data. First, let us consider the data themselves.

Block concludes, first, that appreciable continuity over long periods of time is found in well-done studies using R data (personality ratings by observers) and S data (self-ratings); moreover, these two types of data may be (and often are) significantly related. I agree. Temporal consistency and agreement among judges in personality ratings – by self and by others – is not and has not been in dispute.

Block stresses that the patterns for R data and also for S data, and their links, demonstrate that continuity and consistency reside within the individuals being studied. Here our emphasis differs, but perhaps not crucially. I prefer to stress the active cognitive *constructions* that underlie complex social perceptions, not

Portions of this paper are based on Mischel (1973).

to belittle the "reality" of personality but to underline its complexity. I am not dismissing perceived consistencies in human qualities as artifacts or fictions by emphasizing their cognitive, constructive nature any more than an emphasis on the constructive nature of "perceived constancies" in the perception of stable size and shape implies an unreal physical world. Cognitive psychologists tell us (e.g., Lindsay & Norman, 1972; Neisser, 1967) that even as simple an act as recognizing the letter "A" involves an active cognitive construction (not a mere reading of what is "really there"). Then surely the far more complicated perception of personal consistency in ourselves and others also requires an active imposition of order – a jump beyond the information given to construct the essential underlying gist of meaning from the host of behavioral fragments we observe. Human information processing – whether in the recognition of a best friends' enduring "warmth" or of the word "warmth" on the printed page – involves continuous interactions between what is "out there" in the world of "stimuli" and what is "in here" in the head of the perceiver.

Consequently, it may not be possible to assign the residence of dispositions exclusively either to the actor or to the perceiver; we may have to settle for a continuous interaction between observed and observer, for a reality that is constructed and cognitively created but not fictitious. In such a construction process, semantic networks are likely to figure heavily (e.g., D'Andrade, 1970, 1973; Shweder, 1975), and "prototypes" or "schemata" may be generated that permit a wide range of distortions and transformations in specific instances and still yield consistent agreement among observers about the underlying gist. Research by Posner and Keele (1968) and others (e.g., Shaw & Wilson, 1974) seems highly suggestive here. Their work indicates that subjects readily and reliably learn the "central tendency" and variability of a given pattern, abstracting information about the basic schema from the specific stored instances with great efficiency. Such research on the genesis of abstract ideas ultimately should prove highly relevant for understanding the perception of personality. When we understand how people recognize the basic prototype underlying numerous transformations of a physical pattern, presumably we will also be well on the way to understanding how diverse behaviors may be judged as instances of the same basic disposition (e.g., Cantor & Mischel, 1977).

I want to assert once again that arguments about the existence of coherence and basic continuity in personality strike me as gratuitous at this point: I know no one who seriously doubts that lives have coherence and that we perceive ourselves and others as relatively stable individuals that have substantial identity and continuity over time, even when our specific actions change. However, this recognition of continuity exists side by side with the equally compelling evidence that complex human behavior is regulated by interactions that depend intimately on situational conditions (stimulus variables) as well as on dispositions. Humans are capable of great differentiation in their behavior, and they show extraordinary adaptiveness and discrimination as they cope with a continuously changing environment. It is this behavioral discriminativeness, in my view, that accounts for the difficulty in demonstrating impressive cross-situational consistency when ongoing behavior is studied objectively, that is, in the domain of so-called "T data," instead of by trait ratings. Indeed, Block himself concludes that T data (based on standardized, objective, specific measures of ongoing behavior) tend to provide "extremely erratic" consistency evidence and are related to R data and S data in "uneven" ways. Again I agree.

I suspect that Block sees these limitations of T data as reflecting the triviality and artificiality of most objective measures of ongoing behavior. But for me the implications are very different. The discriminativeness (specificity) of behavior as it unfolds in diverse situations *in vivo* merits serious attention at least as much as the consistencies we construct from it over time. An important test — although surely not the only one — of the utility of constructs about personality dispositions remains their ability to predict the individual's behavior in specific situations. Unless R and S data predict T data appreciably, the links between trait impressions and specific behavior in situations remain tenuous. Although traditional trait ratings may serve as summaries in everyday language of the gist of our impressions of each other, they do not capture the interactions between person and conditions as the ongoing behavior is generated; and they certainly do not illuminate the causes of behavior. As Wiggins (1974) colorfully puts it, traits are "lost causes": they require, rather than provide, scientific explanation.

In sum, a recognition of the continuity and coherence of perceived personality attributes must coexist with the finding of "specificity" at the behavioral level. The latter may be viewed as reflecting man's discriminative facility, not merely the biases of faulty measurement (Mischel, 1968, 1973). To me, the term "discriminative facility" (responsivity to changing conditions) seems preferable to "specificity" because it avoids the negative meanings implied by the "specificity" of behavior (e.g., the implications of inconsistency, fickleness, and unreliability in human nature).

Whereas discriminative facility is highly adaptive (E. J. Gibson, 1969), a reduced sensitivity to changing consequences (i.e., indiscriminate responding) may be characteristic of an organism adapting poorly. In fact, indiscriminate responding (i.e., "consistent" behavior situations) often may be shown more by maladaptive, severely disturbed, or less mature persons than by well-functioning ones (Moos, 1968). For example, studies of hyperaggressive children undergoing therapeutic treatment have suggested that " . . . there appears to be a trend for social behavior to become more related to situational influences with ego development . . . the children seem to have gained in the ability to discriminate between different situations" (Raush, Dittman, & Taylor, 1959a, p. 368). Whereas relatively more indiscriminate behavior tends to be found in more immature and/or disturbed individuals, its extent should not be exaggerated. Even extremely disturbed behavior, for example, may turn out to be highly discriminative when it is examined in detail (e.g., Lovaas, Freitag, Gold, & Karrorla, 1965).

CONSISTENCY IN SOME OF THE PEOPLE SOME OF THE TIME

Fully recognizing the discriminativeness that people so often display, Bem and Allen (1974) proposed that consistency may characterize some people at least in some areas of behavior. They began by noting that traditional personality research on traits had erroneously assumed that all traits would characterize all people. Bem and Allen suggest, instead, that whereas some people may be consistent on some traits, practically nobody is consistent on all traits; indeed, many traits that are studied by investigators may be completely irrelvant for many of the people who are studied. To get beyond this problem, Bem and Allen suggested looking only for those people who would be consistent on particular traits. Specifically, they tried to identify (preselect) those college students who would be consistent and those who would not be consistent on the traits of friendliness and conscientiousness. Their hypothesis was simply this: "Individuals who identify themselves as consistent on a particular trait dimension will in fact be more consistent cross-situationally than those who identify themselves as highly variable" (Bem & Allen, 1974, p. 512). The results, on the whole, supported the hypothesis; for example, students who described themselves as consistent in their level of friendliness tended to show a relatively consistent level of friendliness across a number of measures (such as ratings by their mothers, fathers, and peers, as well as direct observations of their friendliness in a small group discussion and in a waiting room). In contrast, those who described themselves as variable in their friendliness in fact tended to be less consistent.

The Bem and Allen study nicely demonstrated the point that individuals may (and do) display some consistency in some behavior patterns but not in others. For example, one person may show relatively consistent friendliness, another consistent dependency, and a third consistent honesty, but no one is likely to be consistent with regard to all of these dimensions. Consequently, when an investigator tries to compare many people on any given dimension, only some may be found consistent with regard to it but for most the dimension is one on which their behavior is highly discriminative. In many cases the dimension may even be entirely irrelevant. Therefore efforts to find cross-situational consistency in randomly selected samples of people are bound to yield poor results. It may be possible to demonstrate consistency but, as Bem and Allen put it, only for "some of the people some of the time." Interestingly, it was the people themselves who predicted their own consistency, again providing support for the notion that each person knows his or her own behavior best (Mischel, 1972).

The Study of Environments

While some of us have been searching for cross-situationally consistent people, others have been focusing more and more on the social and psychological environments in which people live and function. The dramatic increase of interest in the environment as it relates to man is documented easily; from 1968 to 1972 more books appeared on the topic of man–environment relations from an ecological perspective than had been published in the prior three decades (Jordan, 1972).

As is true in most new fields, a first concern in the study of environments has been to try to classify them into a taxonomy. Environments, like all other events, of course can be classified in many ways, depending mainly on the purposes and imagination of the classifiers. One typical effort to describe some of the almost infinite dimensions of environments, proposed by Moos (1973, 1974), calls attention to the complex nature of environments and to the many variables that can characterize them. These variables include the weather, the buildings and settings, the perceived social climates, and the reinforcements obtained for behaviors in that situation — to list just a few.

The classification alerts us to a fact that has been slighted by traditional trait-oriented approaches to personality: Much human behavior depends on environmental considerations, such as the setting (e.g., Barker, 1968), and even on such specific physical and psychosocial variables as how hot and crowded the setting is, or how the room and furniture is arranged, or how the people in the setting are organized (e.g., Krasner & Ullmann, 1973; Moos & Insel, 1974). Many links between characteristics of the environment and behavior have been demonstrated. For example, measures of population density (such as the number of people in each room) may be related to certain forms of aggression (even when social class and ethnicity are controlled; Galle, Gove, & McPhersen, 1972). Likewise, interpersonal attraction and mood are negatively affected by extremely hot, crowded conditions (Griffitt & Veitch, 1971).

Some psychologists have tried to classify situations with characteristics ranging from gravity and the physical terrain to social norms (Sells, 1973). Others (studying business executives and work situations) have grouped situations as similar if they elicited similar behaviors (Frederiksen, 1972). Focusing on the *perceptions* of observers, there also have been efforts to classify situations on the basis of their perceived similarity, emerging with such traitlike characterizations of situations as "positive," "negative," "passive," "social," and "active" (e.g., Magnusson & Ekehammar, 1973). Similarly, Moos (1973, 1974) and his associates have obtained ratings of the "perceived social climate" in such institutions as psychiatric wards, prisons, and schools.

Depending on one's purpose, many different classifications are possible and useful. To seek any single "basic" taxonomy of situations may be as futile as searching for a final or ultimate taxonomy of traits; we can label situations in at least as many different ways as we can label people. It is important to avoid emerging simply with a trait psychology of situations, in which events and settings, rather than people, are merely given different labels. The task of naming situations cannot substitute for the job of analyzing *how* conditions and environments interact with the people in them.

The Charge of "Situationism": Where Is the Person in Personality Psychology?

Many of my colleagues feel that in recent years there has been an overemphasis on the importance of the environment and the situation at the risk of under-emphasizing, or even "losing," the person (e.g., Bowers, 1973; Carlson, 1971). This is a serious charge; losing the person in personality psychology is as bizarre as losing matter in physics or the elements in chemistry.

The criticism of "situationism" (advanced by Bowers, 1973, p. 307) attacks a "situationism" that emphasizes situations as the causes of behavior while "being inattentive to the importance of the person." Situationism is defined as an explanatory bias that tends "either to ignore organismic factors or to regard them as ... subsidiary to the primary impact of the external stimulus" (Harré & Secord, 1972, p. 27).

Closely paralleling the charge of "situationism" is the humanistic protest to the behavioral approach in general. The essence of the humanistic protest is that behaviorally oriented psychologists (i.e., "situationists") treat and manipulate people as if they were externally controlled rather than free, self-determining beings who are responsible for their own actions and growth. Some of these criticism and charges seem justified objections against the pure environmentalism of B. F. Skinner's (1974) radical behaviorism. The characteristics of the environment interact with the people in it, and it is foolish to ignore either side of this interaction.

The recognition that the environment is important for human behavior is a welcome insight for most personality psychologists. (Although Kurt Lewin told us about the environment's role long ago, his impact seems to have been more on textbooks and social psychologists than on personality theorists.) But a psychological approach requires that we move from descriptions of the environment — of the climate, buildings, social settings, etc., in which we live — to the psychological processes through which environmental conditions and people influence each other reciprocally. For this purpose, it is necessary to consider how the environment influences behavior and how behavior and the people who generate it in turn shape the environment in an endless interaction. To understand the interaction of person and environment we must consider person variables as well an environmental variables, and we must analyze the nature of person–situation interactions psychologically.

An Example of Interaction

Let me give an example of such interaction from my own research. Consider the question: What influences selective attention to positive versus negative information about oneself? We have found that when people succeed they process information about their own assets and liabilities quite differently than when they fail (Mischel, Ebbesen, & Zeiss, 1973, 1976). Specifically, success (and probably other positive affects) increases attention to personal assets and decreases attention to personal liabilities. Thus the "situation" (i.e., the affective success–failure manipulation) influences the subsequent information and situations to which individuals attend and to which they expose themselves selectively. The impact is not only on the person's performance, but also on the way he or she subsequently structures and chooses his or her own psychological environment. The successful person selects different information from the environment and goes to different parts of it physically than does the unsuccessful one. Moreover, even if exposure to assets and liabilities is made to occur for the same amount of time, success leads to differential memory for the two types of information: People who expect to succeed remember their personality liabilities relatively less well than their assets. The total data illustrate how "situations" change people (including what they know and remember) just as people change their situations, in a continuous interaction.

It is noteworthy that the patterns of selective attention also depend on the individual's personal qualities. Specifically, "sensitizers" (on Byrne's Repression–Sensitization Scale) were more likely to attend to their liabilities, and repressors to their assets. In other words, people who tend to focus on assets rather than liabilities (as inferred from R–S scores) also tended to do so when given a chance *in vivo* to get one or the other type of information about themselves. As expected, the effects of these individual differences were strongest in the control conditions and were nullified when treatment effects were powerful, i.e., in the success condition.

In these studies we also found that the influence of the "situation" on subsequent behavior and information processing seemed to depend primarily on how it altered the person's relevant future expectations (Mischel, Ebbesen, & Zeiss, 1976). That is, the effects of success–failure expectancy overshadowed those of experience when the two were pitted against each other, indicating that the situation influenced the person mainly by changing what he or she expected would happen next, instead of by "stamping in" a particular reinforcement history.

The Limits of Interaction Studies

As noted before (Mischel, 1973a), although there is little doubt that a comprehensive approach to personality must take full account of person–situation interactions, many of the interaction studies using the strategy of Endler and Hunt cannot help us answer the crucial question: After an individuals' idiosyncratic pattern has been identified, can it be used accurately to predict consistencies in his or her subsequent behavior? The interaction studies have shown there are extensive Person X Situation interactions, but they have not yet demonstrated that useful predictions can be made in advance about individual consistencies across a set of specified conditions. Such demonstrations seem essential in light of the frequent failures to achieve replications in this domain (e.g., Averill, Olbrich, & Lazarus, 1972; Wallach & Leggett, 1972, pp. 313–314). My concerns about the limitations of the interaction studies are even greater in light of Golding's (1975a) recent analysis documenting their methodological limitations. He rightly emphasizes the need to demonstrate that such interactions are meaningful and replicable. Moreover, the interaction studies have not explained the nature of the obtained interactions.

Some researchers hoped that studies of person, environments, and their interaction would answer the question "Are persons or situations more important in efforts to predict behavior?" As I and others have noted often before, however, the question "Is information about situations more (or less) important than information about individuals?" serves mostly to stimulate futile debates. The answer must always depend on the particular situations and persons sampled; studies can be set up to show almost any outcome. The question of whether individual differences or situations are more important is an empty one that has no general answer (e.g., Moos, 1968, 1969).

Moreover, in current debates on this topic, "situations" are often treated like entities that supposedly exert either major or only minor control over behavior, without specifying what, psychologically, they are or how they function (Alker, 1972; Bowers, 1973; Wallach & Leggett, 1972). But while some situations may be powerful determinants of behavior, others are trivial. The relative importance of individual differences and situations will depend on the situation selected, the type of behavior assessed, the particular individual differences sampled, and the purpose of the assessment.

CONCEPTUALIZING THE PERSON

It has been easier to demonstrate the existence of extensive person–situation interactions than to explain them. It is now necessary to analyze the psychological bases for "interaction"; without such an analysis, an emphasis on interaction is in danger of being little more than the announcement of the obvious. Granted that both "environments" and individual differences are important and interact, how can the impact of situations be conceptualized in *psychological* terms? When people respond to the environment they are confronted with a potential flood of stimuli; how are these stimuli selected, perceived, processed, interpreted, and used by the individual?

To answer these questions requires the development of more adequate conceptualizations of individual differences or "person variables." In recent years a great deal of personality research has focused on the processes through which social behaviors are acquired, evoked, maintained, and modified. Much less attention has been given to the psychological products within the individual of cognitive development and social learning experiences. A focus on processes — on the psychological conditions that influence behavior — is an important advance in a field that traditionally has dwelt on the stable attributes of persons with little attention to how conditions affect what people think and feel and do. However, a comprehensive psychology of personality also must attend to person variables that are the products of each individual's total history and that, in turn, regulate how new experiences affect him or her. Even if one grants that many traditional dimensions of individual differences have limited usefulness, personality psychology cannot exist without person variables.

The person variables to be discussed next were proposed to provide a synthesis of seemingly promising constructs about persons developed in the areas of cognition and social learning (Mischel, 1973a); hence they are called "cognitive social learning person variables." The selections should be seen as suggestive and constantly open to progressive revision. These variables were not expected to provide ways to accurately predict broadly cross-situational behavioral differences between persons; the discriminativeness of behavior and its unique organization within each person are facts of nature, not limitations unique to particular theories. But these variables should suggest useful ways of conceptualizing and studying specifically how the qualities of the person influence the impact of stimuli (environments, situations, treatments) and how each person generates distinctive complex behavior patterns in interaction with the conditions of his or her life.

First, one must deal with the individual's *competencies* to construct (generate) diverse behaviors under appropriate conditions. Next, one must consider the individual's *encoding* and categorization of situations. A comprehensive analysis of the behaviors a person performs in particular situations also requires attention to his or her *expectancies* about outcomes, the *subjective values* of such outcomes, and his or her *self-regulatory systems and plans*. Although these variables obviously overlap and interact, each may provide distinctive information about the individual and each may be measured objectively and studied systematically (Mischel, 1973a).

Cognitive and Behavioral Construction Competencies

As a result of observing events and attending to the behavior of live and symbolic models (through direct and film-mediated observation, reading, instruction) in the course of cognitive development the perceiver becomes able to generate a vast range of behavior patterns. Although the prevalence and importance of such observational learning has been demonstrated convincingly, it is less clear how to conceptualize just what gets learned. The phenomena to be covered must include such products of learning as sexual identity, the rehearsal strategies of the observer, the social rules and conventions that guide conduct, and the personal constructs generated about self and others (e.g., Mischel, 1971).

The concept of *cognitive and behavioral construction competencies* alerts us to our *cognitive activities* – the operations and transformations that each of us performs on information – as opposed to a store of static cognitions and responses that we "have" in some mechanical storehouse. Each individual acquires the capacity to actively construct a multitude of potential behaviors. Great differences between persons exist in the range and quality of the cognitive and behavioral patterns that they can generate, as becomes obvious from even casual comparison of the different competencies, for example, of a professional weight lifter, a distinguished chemist, a retardate, an opera star, or a convicted forger.

Encoding Strategies and Personal Constructs

For personality psychology, an especially important part of information processing concerns the ways we encode and group information from stimulus inputs. The "environment," the " situation," the "stimulus" are perceived, coded, and categorized by each person and these cognitive operations influence the impact that they have.

As I have discussed elsewhere, people can readily perform *cognitive transformations* on stimuli (Mischel & Moore, 1973), focusing on selected aspects of the objective stimulus (e.g., the taste versus the shape of a food object): such selective attention, interpretation, and categorization changes the impact the stimulus exerts on behavior (Geer, Davison, & Gatchel, 1970; Holmes & Houston, 1974; Schacter, 1964). How we encode and selectively attend to observed behavioral sequences also greatly influences what we learn and subsequently can do (Bandura, 1971a, b). Clearly, different persons may group and encode the same events and behaviors in different ways (e.g., Argyle & Little, 1972; Kelly, 1955) and selectively attend to different kinds of information (Mischel, Ebbesen, & Zeiss, 1973). The same "hot weather" that upsets one person may be a joy for another who views it as a chance to go to the beach. A stimulus perceived as "dangerous" or "threatening" by one person may be seen as "challenging" or "thrilling" by the one next to him.

Even if we focus on "behavior" we cannot avoid the fact that the definition and selection of a behavior unit for study requires grouping and categorizing. In personality research, it is the psychologists who do the categorizing; they include and exclude events in the units they study, depending on their interests and objectives. They choose a category — "anxiety," "masculinity–femininity," or "delay of gratification," for example — and study its behavioral referents. In personality assessment, however, it soon becomes evident that "subjects" (like psychologists) also group events into categories and organize them actively into meaningful units. Lay people usually do not describe their experiences objectively; each person groups events in terms of his or her own categories and perceptions (Kelly, 1955) and these may or may not overlap with those of psychologists or of other individuals. For example, what is "conscientiousness" for one person may have an entirely different meaning for another (Bem & Allen, 1974); a trait category that fits me may be quite irrelevant for you.

So far the person variables considered deal with what individuals *can* do and how they categorize (code) events. But we also must move from what we know and how we perceive (categorize) events to what we *do,* from potential behaviors to actual performance in specific situations. This move requires attention to the determinants of *performance.* For this purpose, the person variables of greatest interest are the individual's expectancies. It often helps to know what individuals can do, and how they construe events and themselves, but to predict specific behavior in a particular situation it is essential to consider their specific expectancies about the consequences of different behavioral possibilities in that situation. These expectancies guide peoples' selections (choices) of behaviors from among the many which they are capable of constructing within any situation. We generate behavior in light of our expectancies even when they are not in line with the objective conditions in the situation. If you expect to be attacked you act vigilantly or defensively even if your fears later turn out to have been unjustified.

One type of expectancy concerns *behavior outcome relations.* These *behavior-outcome expectancies* (hypotheses, contingency rules) represent the "if ___, then ___" relations between behavioral alternatives and expected probable outcomes in particular situations. In any given situation, we generate the response pattern that we expect is most likely to lead to the most subjectively valuable outcomes (consequences) in that situation (e.g., Mischel, 1973a; Rotter, 1954). In the absence of new information about the behavior–outcome expectancies in any situation, one's performance will depend on one's previous behavior–outcome expectancies in similar situations. This point is illustrated in a study which showed that presituational expectancies significantly affect choice behavior in the absence of situational information concerning probable performance–outcome relationships (Mischel & Staub, 1965). But the same study also showed that new information about behavior–outcome relations in the particular situation may quickly overcome the effects of presituational expectancies, so that highly specific situational expectancies become the dominant influences on performance.

Adaptive performance requires the recognition and appreciation of new contingencies. To cope with the environment effectively, we must identify new contingencies as quickly as possible and reorganize behavior in the light of the new expectancies. Strongly established behavior–outcome expectancies may handicap our ability to adapt to changes in contingencies. Indeed, "defensive reactions" may be seen in part as a failure to adapt to new contingencies because one is still behaving in response to old contingencies that are no longer valid (Mischel, 1971). For example, if on the basis of past experiences a man overgeneralizes and becomes convinced that people will take advantage of him unless he is hostile toward everyone, his own suspicious, aggressive behavior may prevent him from ever being able to disconfirm his belief. The "maladaptive" individual is behaving in accord with expectancies that do not adequately represent the actual behavior–outcome rules in his current life situation.

A closely related second type of expectancy concerns *stimulus–outcome relations*. The outcomes we expect depend on a multitude of stimulus conditions. These stimuli (signs) essentially "predict" for us other events that are likely to occur. More precisely, each of us learns (through direct and observational experiences) that certain events (cues, stimuli) predict certain other events. Outside the artificial restrictions of the laboratory, in the human interactions of life, the "stimuli" that predict outcomes often are the social behaviors of others in particular contexts. The meanings attributed to those stimuli hinge on learned associations between behavioral signs and outcomes.

For example, through learning, "shifty eyes," "tight lips," "lean and hungry looks," obese body build, age, sex, eye contact, posture, and many even subtler behavioral cues (e.g., regarding the status and power of others) come to predict for us other behaviors correlated with them. Some of these stimulus–outcome associations presumably reflect the perceiver's idiosyncratic (unique) learning history, and his or her own evolving personal rules about stimulus meanings. Many of these associations, however, are likely to be widely shared by members of the same culture who have a common language (D'Andrade, 1970; Shweder, 1971, 1972). We also learn a shared nonverbal "sign language" that presumably underlies much of the nonverbal communication among people (Ekman, Friesen, & Ellsworth, 1972).

Subjective Stimulus Values

Two individuals who have similar expectancies nevertheless may act differently because the outcomes they expect have different values for them (e.g., Rotter, 1954, 1972). For example, if everyone in a group expects that approval from a teacher depends on certain verbalizations, there may be differences in the frequency of such statements resulting from differences in the perceived value of obtaining the teacher's approval. Praise from the teacher may be important for one person (e.g., a middle-class youngster striving for grades) but inconsequential for another (e.g., a rebellious "delinquent"). Such differences reflect the degree to which different individuals value the same expected outcome. What delights one person may repel his neighbor. Therefore it is necessary to consider still another variable: the subjective (perceived) value for individuals of particular classes of events, that is, their stimulus preferences and aversions, their likes and dislikes, their positive and negative values (Mischel, 1973a).

Self-Regulatory Systems and Plans

Although behavior depends to a considerable extent on externally administered consequences for actions, everyone also regulates his own behavior by self-imposed goals (standards) and self-produced consequences. Even in the absence of external constraints and social monitors, we set performance goals for ourselves and react with self-criticism or self-satisfaction to our behavior depending on how well it matches our expectations and standards. The expert sprinter who falls below his past record may condemn himself bitterly, while the same performance by a less experienced runner who has lower standards may produce self-congratulation and joy.

Another feature of self-regulatory systems is the person's adoption of *contigency rules* and *plans* that guide behavior in the absence of, and sometimes in spite of, immediate external situational pressures. Such rules specify the kinds of behavior appropriate (expected) under particular conditions, the performance levels (standards, goals) that the behavior must achieve, and the consequences (positive and negative) of attaining or failing to reach those standards. Plans also specify the sequence and organization of behavior patterns (e.g., Miller, Gallanter, & Pribram, 1960). Individuals differ with respect to each of the components of self-regulation depending on their unique earlier histories or on more recently varied instructions or other situational information.

Self-regulation provides a route through which we can influence our environment substantially, overcoming "stimulus control" (the power of the situation). We can actively *select* (choose) the situations to which we expose ourselves, in a sense creating our own environment, entering some settings but not others, making decisions about what to do and what not to do. Such active choice, rather than automatic responding, may be facilitated by thinking and planning and by rearranging the environment itself to make it more favorable for one's objectives (e.g., Thoresen & Mahoney, 1974). Even when the environment cannot be changed physically (by rearranging it or by leaving it altogether and entering another setting), it may be possible to *transform* it psychologically by self-instructions and ideation (Mischel, 1973a, 1974).

Summary of Person Variables

To summarize, individual differences in behavior may be caused by differences in each of the discussed person variables. First, individuals differ in their *construction competencies,* that is, in their competence or ability to generate a desired response pattern. For example, because of differences in skill and earlier learning, individual differences may arise in cognitive–intellective achievements. Differences in behavior also may reflect differences in how individuals *categorize* a particular situation. That is, people differ in how they encode, group, and label events and in how they construe themselves and others. Performance differences in any situation depend on differences in *expectancies* and specifically on differences in the expected outcomes associated with particular responses, patterns, and stimuli. Differences in performance also may be influenced by differences in the subjective *values* of the expected outcomes in the situation. Finally, individual differences may reflect differences in the *self-regulatory systems and plans* that each individual brings to the situation.

It would be both easy and inappropriate to transform these person variables into generalized traitlike dispositions by endowing them with broad cross-situational consistency or removing them from the context of the specific conditions on which they depended. Consider, for example, the variable of "generalized expectancies." In fact, "generalized expectancies" tend to be generalized only within relatively narrow, restricted limits (e.g., Mischel, Ebbesen, & Zeiss, 1973; Mischel & Staub, 1965). The generality of "locus of control," for instance, is limited, with distinct, unrelated expectancies found for different kinds of outcomes (Mischel, Zeiss, & Zeiss, 1974). If the above person variables are converted into global traitlike dispositions and removed from their close interaction with situational conditions they are likely to have limited usefulness.

CONCEPTUALIZING INTERACTION

Let us now consider more concretely how the interaction of persons and situations may work.

When Do Individual Differences Make a Difference?

The conditions or "situational variables" of the psychological environment may be conceptualized as providing the individual with information; this information influences person variables, thereby affecting how the individual thinks and acts under those conditions. "Situations" (environments) thus influence our behavior by affecting such person variables as how we encode the situation, the outcomes we expect, their subjective value for us, and our ability to generate response patterns.

Recognizing that the question" Are persons or situations more important?" is misleading and unanswerable, one can now turn to the more interesting issue: When are situations most likely to exert powerful effects and, conversely, when are person variables likely to be most influential?

Psychological "situations" (stimuli, treatment) are powerful to the degree that they lead everyone to construe the particular events the same way, induce *uniform* expectancies regarding the most appropriate response pattern, provide adequate incentives for the performance of that response pattern and require skills that everyone has to the same extent. A good example of a powerful stimulus is a red traffic light; it exerts powerful effects on the behavior of most motorists because they all know what it means, are motivated to obey it, and are capable of stopping when they see it. Therefore it would be easier to predict drivers' behavior at stop lights from knowing the color of the light than from making inferences about the "conformity," "cautiousness," or other traits of the drivers.

Conversely, situations are weak to the degree that they are not uniformly encoded, do not generate uniform expectancies concerning the desired behavior, do not offer sufficient incentives for its performance, or fail to provide the learning conditions required for successful genesis of the behavior. An example of such a weak stimulus is the blank card on the TAT projective test with the instructions to create a story about what might be happening; clearly the answers depend more on the storytellers than on the card.

In sum, individual differences can determine behavior in a given situation most strongly when the situation is ambiguously structured (as in projective testing) so that people are uncertain about how to categorize it, have to structure it in their own terms, and have no clear expectations about the behaviors most likely to be appropriate (normative, reinforced) in that situation. To the degree that the situation is "unstructured" and each person expects that virtually any response is equally likely to be equally appropriate (i.e., will lead to similar consequences), the significance of individual differences will be greatest. Conversely, when everyone expects that only one response is appropriate (e.g., only one "right" answer on an achievement test, only one correct response for the driver when the traffic light turns red) and that no other responses are equally good, and all people are motivated and capable of making the appropriate response, then individual differences become minimal and situational effects prepotent. To the degree that people are exposed to powerful treatments, the role of the individual differences among them are minimized. Conversely, when treatments are weak, ambiguous, or trivial, individual differences in person variables should have the most significant effects.

So far we have considered such "treatments" as those in laboratory studies or therapy programs. But the complex social settings of everyday life also vary in the degree to which they prescribe and limit the range of expected and acceptable behavior for persons in particular roles and settings and hence permit the expression of individual differences (e.g., Barker, 1968; Price, 1974). In some settings the rules and prescriptions for enacting specific role behaviors greatly limit the range of possible behaviors (e.g., in church, at school, in a theater, at a conference), whereas in others the range of possible behaviors is broad and often the individual can select, structure, and reorganize situations with few external constraints. Because in particular settings certain response patterns are rewarded and others are not, different settings become the occasion for particular behaviors in different degrees.

Behavioral Appropriateness and Situational Constraints

Situations can be classified according to the range and type of behaviors considered appropriate within them. In one study, college students were asked to rate the appropriateness of 15 behaviors in 15 situations (Price & Bouffard, 1974). Examples of the behaviors are *run, belch, hiss, write, eat;* examples of the situations are *in class, on a date, on a bus, at a family dinner, in a restroom.* The average appropriateness ratings were calculated for each of the many combinations of behaviors and situations. These ratings could range from 0 (the behavior is extremely inappropriate in this situation) to 9 (the behavior is extremely appropriate in this situation).

Analyses of this kind applied to a wide range of behaviors and situations can provide useful information. High values for a behavior indicate that it is considered appropriate in many situations, low values suggest that it is generally inappropriate. Likewise, the degree of *situational constraint* for a particular situation can be indexed simply by averaging the appropriateness ratings of the behaviors in that situation. The results of follow-up research also indicated that situations that have high constraint also tend to be seen as potentially embarrassing, as requiring more careful self-monitoring of one's behavior, and as demanding certain behaviors rather than others (Price & Bouffard, 1974).

It would be especially interesting to examine the degree of *variation* among individuals (not just the average level) found for particular behaviors in particular situations. The most "powerful" situations would be those that usually allowed little variation; the "weakest" situations would be those in which variation among people was typically high. Individual differences would be expected to exert the greatest influence in the weak (high-variation) situations and to have the smallest effect in the powerful (low-variation) ones.

Predicting from Situations and/or Persons

Person—condition interactions are never static, but environmental stabilities can be identified that help to account for continuities in behavior and permit useful predictions. Although the psychology of personality cannot ignore the person, it is also true that behavior sometimes may be predicted and influenced simply from knowledge about relevant stimulus conditions, especially when those conditions are powerful (Mischel, 1968). The potency of predictions based on knowldge of stimulus conditions is seen, for example, in studies that try to predict the posthospital adjustment of mental patients. Such research has shown that the type, as well as the severity, of psychiatric symptoms depends importantly on environmental conditions, with little consistency in behavior across changing situations (Ellsworth, Foster, Childers, Gilberg & Kroeker, 1968). Accurate predictions of posthospital adjustment require knowledge of the environment in which the expatient is living in the community — such as the availability of jobs and family support — rather than on any measured person variables or in-hospital behavior (e.g., Fairweather, 1967; Fairweather, Sanders, Cressler, & Maynard, 1969).

In another domain, to predict intellectual achievement it also helps to take account of the degree to which the child's environment supports (models and reinforces) intellectual development (Wolf, 1966). Finally, when powerful treatments are developed — such as modeling and desensitization therapies for phobias — predictions about outcomes are best when based on knowing the treatment to which the individual is assigned (e.g., Bandura, Blanchard, & Ritter, 1969).

The significance of the psychological situation was vividly demonstrated in a simulated prison study (Haney, Banks, & Zimbardo, 1973). College student volunteers were carefully selected, on the basis of extensive interviewing and diagnostic testing, to have exemplary backgrounds and no antisocial tendencies. Nevertheless, less than one week after they had been exposed to what the authors referred to as the inherently pathological characteristics of the realistically simulated prison situation itself, all subjects assigned to the role of "guards" were exhibiting extreme antisocial behavior. The authors concluded that few of the "guards" reactions could be attributed to individual differences on generalized dimensions (e.g., empathy, rigid adherence to conventional values, Machiavellianism) existing before the subjects began to play their assigned roles. The potency of the situation undoubtedly left some lasting effects, particularly in beliefs, as evidenced by the subjects' postexperimental statements (e.g., "I learned that people can easily forget that others are human" (p. 88). But it was also most likely that once the prison experiment was over, the "guards" gave up their newly characteristic aggressive and harassing behavior and all exsubjects soon started to respond in terms of the current context of their lives.

Although situations can be extremely potent, when relevant situational information is absent or minimal, when predictions are needed about individual differences in response to the same conditions, or when situational variables are weak, information about person variables becomes essential. As we have seen in earlier sections, moreover, such predictions may be possible at least for "some of the people some of the time," as Bem and Allen (1974) have suggested.

Specific Interactions Between Person and Conditions

Traditionally, trait-oriented personality research has studied individual differences in response to the "same" situation. However, some of the most striking differences between persons may be found not by studying their responses to the same situation but by analyzing their *selection* and construction of stimulus conditions. In the conditions of life outside the laboratory the psychological "stimuli" that people encounter are neither questionnaire items, nor experimental instructions, nor inanimate events, but involve people and reciprocal relationships (e.g., with spouse, with boss, with children). We continuously influence the "situations" of our lives as well as being affected by them in a mutual, organic interaction (e.g., Raush, Barry, Hertel, & Swain, 1974). Such interactions reflect not only our reactions to conditions but also our active selection and modification of conditions through our own choices, cognitions, and actions (Wachtel, 1973a). Different people select different settings for themselves; conversely, the settings that people select to be in may provide clues about their personal qualities (Eddy & Sinnett, 1973; Mischel, Ebbesen, & Zeiss, 1973).

The mutual interaction between person and conditions (so easily overlooked when one searches for generalized traits on paper and pencil tests) cannot be ignored when behavior is studied in the interpersonal contexts in which it is evoked, maintained, and modified. The analysis of complex social interactions (e.g., Patterson & Cobb, 1971a) vividly illustrates how people continuously select, change, and generate conditions just as much as they are affected by them.

If you change your behavior toward another person he or she generally shows reciprocal changes in behavior toward you (Raush, Dittman & Taylor, 1959a). In Raush's (1965) studies of naturalistic interactions, for example, "the major determinant of an act was the immediately preceding act. Thus if you want to know what child B will do, the best single predictor is what child A did to B the moment before" (p. 492). Construed from the viewpoint of Child A, this means that A's own behavior determines B's reactions to him or her; if A provokes B, B will reciprocate aggressively. In that sense, the person is generating his or her own conditions.

The other side of the interaction is the fact that B's behavior is always constrained by what A has done the moment before. Studies of the interactions among husbands and wives illustrate this point (Raush, Barry, Hertel, & Swain, 1974). In these studies, husband—wife interactions were observed as the couples coped with such conflicts as how to celebrate their first wedding anniversary when each had made different plans. For example, Bob has arranged and paid in advance for dinner at a restaurant but Sue has spent half the day preparing for a special dinner at home. As the couple realizes their conflict and tries to resolve it, their interactions continuously reveal that each antecedent act (what Sue has just said to Bob) constrains each consequent act (how Bob responds).

The meaning and impact of each act also depends on such additional considerations as the total context and situation in which it occurs as well as on the relationship and "style" that each couple develops. " . . . Situations thus 'inform' persons, selecting segments of personal experience; persons also inform situations, selecting segments to respond to" (Raush, Barry, Hertel, & Swain, 1974, p. 212). Such variables as the person's constructs, expectancies, self-regulatory rules, and plans presumably guide the situations that he selects and generates, and how he interprets them; they influence the responses that he emits and that in turn shape his environment as much as he is shaped by it.

The Specificity of Situations

Given the multiplicity and complexity of the determinants of behavior, it should not be a surprise that situations (or "treatments" in experimental and clinical contexts) tend to produce specific rather than generalized effects and that the effects are often weak (e.g., Sarason, Smith, & Diener, 1975). As Bowers (1973) put it, "Although it is undoubtedly true that behavior is more situation specific than trait theory acknowledged, . . . situations are more person specific than is commonly recognized," (p. 307). That is, the impact of particular situations or treatments depends on the particular people in them.

There is a growing belief throughout psychology and the social sciences that "treatments" may not have broad, highly generalized, stable effects. Specificity may occur because of the large range of different ways that different people may react to the "same" treatments and reinterpret them (e.g., Cronbach, 1975; Neisser, 1974) and because the impact of most situations usually can be changed easily by other coexiting conditions (Mischel, 1974). Even a relatively simple "stimulus" or "situation," therefore, may produce a variety of often unpredictable specific (and weak) effects depending on a large number of moderating variables and the many different ways in which the particular "subjects" may view them. (Consider, for example, the many variables that may determine whether or not one chooses to delay gratification, discussed in Mischel, 1974.) Situational specificity is the other side of the coin of behavioral specificity.

The recognition that behavior is always determined by many variables and that a focus on any one of them must lead to limited predictions and generalizations is not confined to the area of personality psychology. This conclusion has been reached for "treatments" as diverse as interview styles in psychotherapy, teaching practices and classroom arrangements in education, and instructions to aid recall in memory experiments. For example, after a survey of research on memory Jenkins (1974) cautions us that: " . . . What is remembered in a given situation depends on the physical and psychological context in which the event was experienced, the knowledge and skills that the subject brings to the context, the situation in which we ask for evidence for remembering and the relation of what the subject remembers to what the experimenter demands" (p. 793). The same conclusions probably apply as well to the subject matter studied in any other subarea of psychology.

As a consequence, it may become more difficult to achieve broad, sweeping generalizations about human behavior; many qualifiers (moderators) must be appended to our "laws" about cause and effect relations — almost without exception and perhaps with no exceptions at all (Cronbach, 1975). On the other hand, although the need to qualify generalizations about human behavior complicates life for the social scientist, it does not prevent one from studying human affairs scientifically; it only dictates a respect for the complexity of the enterprise and alerts one to the dangers of oversimplifying the nature and causes of human behavior. That danger is equally great whether one is searching for generalized (global) person-free situational effects or for generalized (global) situation-free personality variables.

26
Predictive and Generative Rules Models of P x S Interaction

Michael Argyle

Department of Experimental Psychology, Oxford

Our problem is to predict and explain behavior in terms of the properties of persons and of the properties of situations. I am particularly concerned with the prediction and explanation of social behavior. I should like to present here two rather different approaches to this problem, because different principles seem to be involved for different aspects of social behavior.

Certain aspects of behavior are measurable and common to all situations, for example, amount of talk, gaze, proximity. These can be predicted from equations in the tradition of Newtonian mechanics and the gas laws. There are other aspects of behavior, however, such as what people say, which moves they make at chess, and what they do at a party, that have to be treated somewhat differently. I shall argue that a "generative rules" approach, as used in linguistics, is more appropriate and that we have to deal with discrete entities (of behavior, situations, and perhaps persons), rather like the discrete structural units in genetics or chemistry.

THE PREDICTIVE P X S MODEL: $B = f(P,S)$

This is the simplest conceptual model of personality–situation interaction, and one that has been implicitly assumed by a number of investigators. Our concern here is with the prediction of individual behavior, and this involves completing the details of the Lewinian equation. How can the equation be made to work?

B. As Lewin intended it, B referred to the choice of one action from a range of possibilities (Lewin, 1935). However, I shall use B to refer to the quantity of specified dimensions of behavior, e.g., percentage of gaze. These are all aspects of behavior that can be used over a variety of situations. Moreover, we shall take it to mean behavior as measured by the investigator.

P. We need a conceptualization of P in a form that enables a wide range of predictions in different situations to be made. Lewin himself thought of P in structural terms — individual goals, barriers, etc. — but his concepts have fallen into disuse. We know now that surface traits, defined in terms of behavior, do not lead to good predictions. The approach I suggest is in terms of measures of stable, underlying aspects of personality that are not dependent on particular situations, for example, cognitive or physiological aspects of personality. We shall consider later what these core properties of personality are.

S. Very little research has been carried out on situations, compared with the volume of work on personality. It is only during recent years that environmental psychology has produced systematic research in this area (e.g., Proshanksy, Ittelson, & Rivlin, 1970) and research workers have tried to identify the dimensions of situations. In order to apply our formula it is not enough to show that behavior is different in different situations; behavior must be shown to be a function of some measurable or scalable property of situations, when other aspects are held constant. These may be aspects of situations that can be measured by the investigator, for example, physical properties, or properties involved from a consensus of subjective ratings.

f. In order to discover the functional relationship involved it is necessary to carry out investigations in which both P and S are varied systematically. In experimental psychology there are many studies showing, for example, how learning curves differ for subjects of different intelligence or extraversion, how anxiety is a function of trait anxiety and the stressfulness of situations, and so on. Preferably, there should be at least three levels of P and S, so that curvilinear relations can be shown, but this has rarely been done. Unfortunately, there is a difficulty with this design in the field of social behavior, as we shall explain below. Nevertheless it has been done, and we can illustrate this approach by considering research on gaze, i.e., where B is the percentage of the subject's gaze or the percentage of mutual gaze between two persons.

A considerable number of studies have been carried out showing the effects of P, S, and P X S interaction on gaze. Detailed references to this research are not given, because this research is reviewed by Argyle and Cook (1976).

P Variables Affecting Gaze

Demographic factors

  Age. Gaze falls from childhood to adolescence, then increases.

  Sex. Gaze and mutual gaze greater for females.

Culture. Arabs and south eastern Europeans high: some American Indians low.

Physiological.

Extraversion. Extraverts gaze more.

Motivation.

Affiliative. Interaction only, no main effect (see below)

Cognitive structures.

Internal-external control. Interaction only (see below)

Field dependence. Field dependents gaze more.

Mental Health, classification.

Autism. Very low gaze.

Schizophrenics. Reduced gaze; short glances. (when interviewed by psychologists)

Depressives. Reduced gaze; look down (when interviewed by psychologists)

S Variables Affecting Gaze

Physical properties of situations

Distance. More gaze at greater distance.

Density. Less gaze with more density.

Conditions of visibility. More gaze through one-way screen or dark glasses.

Dimensions obtained from subjective ratings

Cooperation—competitive. Interaction only, no main effect.

Difficulty of task. Less gaze for difficult topics.

Intimacy of topic. Less gaze for intimate topics.

Friendly—hostile relations. More gaze for friendly relations.

Same—equal status. More gaze at higher status person.

P X S Interactions Affecting Gaze

A number of studies have found P X S interactions:

1. Dominance—dependence and high—low reinforcement for gaze: Exline and Messick (1967) found no main effects for a P X S interaction: dependent Ss looked more under *low* reinforcement for gaze, dominant Ss vice versa.

2. Internal—external control and high—low gaze by other: Lefcourt and Wine (1969) found no main effects, but an interaction; inner controllers looked more at a gaze-avoiding interviewer, and vice versa.

3. Need for affiliation, sex, and cooperative—competitive situations: Exline (1963) found that need for affiliation interacted with cooperative—competitive situations, as shown in Figure 26.1. It can be seen that there are no main effects of P or S, apart from a sex difference, that there is a strong P X S interaction, and that sex also acts as moderator variables.

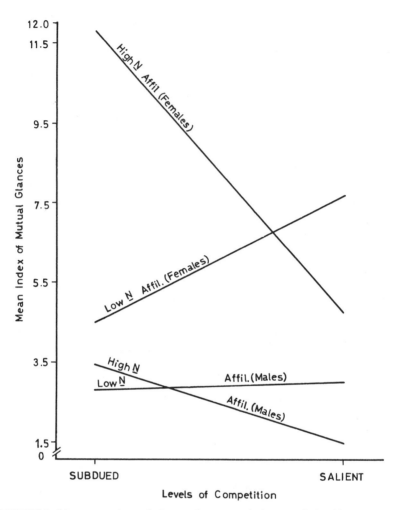

FIGURE 26.1 Mean percentage of time each sex spends in mutual visual interaction for each of two levels of N affiliation at two levels of competition.

Limitations of the Predictive P X S Model

A's behavior depends on the situation, the situation includes the behavior of B, and others; B's behavior depends on A's. One way of predicting A's and B's behavior is by taking their relative scores on stable personality measures. For example Carment, Miles, and Cervin (1965) found that the more extraverted member of an otherwise homogeneous dyad spoke first in 26 out of 33 pairs, spoke more in 24 out of 33 pairs, and persuaded the other to change their minds in 39 out of 43 pairs. The effects of differential intelligence were slightly greater.

Meltzer, Hayes, and Schillenberg (1967) found little consistency between individuals in measures of their amount and loudness of talking, between different groups. However, measures of relative amplitude, talking time, and interruptions in the group correlated with similar measures for other groups at over .50. Similar considerations apply to the prediction of leadership in informal groups; it is the person with the highest level of abilities needed by the group in their main task who is likely to lead.

Another approach is to assess the compatibility of two people. Schutz (1958) was able to create incompatible groups by having more than one person keen to dominate, or by having some group members with strong affiliative needs and others with weak ones. In fact nearly all combinations of two or more people are incompatible to some degree, in the sense that their preferred styles of behavior do not easily fit together. Some mutual accommodation is necessary, and this is done by a kind of nonverbal group problem solving. A does not say "I want to talk most of the time"; instead he makes use of nonverbal synchronizing cues that enable him to do so (Argyle, 1969). The prediction of interpersonal attraction depends very much on the similarity of two people, and perhaps on their complementarity. Whether or not A likes B is more a P X P interaction than a function of P alone.

A problem of a different kind for students of P X S interaction for social behavior is that people normally choose their situations, these choices reflecting their personalities (Bowers, 1973). Experimental designs in which people are allocated to situations miss this important aspect of P functioning, as well as perhaps placing them in unfamiliar settings. One example of persons choosing situations is the way in which people choose jobs that fit their pattern of interests, as measured, for example, by the SVIB. Another is the way people choose social atmospheres that suit them: In the United States it has been found that authoritarians often join military academies instead of universities (Stern, Stein, & Bloom, 1956). There is considerable evidence for the general hypothesis that people seek out and are most satisfied by environments that "fit" their personalities (Pervin, 1968).

Wachtel (1973a) points out that people often produce certain responses in others — bad temper, intimidation, or shyness, for example, It is possible to "define situations" in different ways, and special signals are sent suggesting possible definitions. Symbolic interactionists have emphasized the importance of such moves in social interaction; ethnomethodologists have argued that the way to analyze what happened is to elicit verbal accounts from the participants (Harré & Secord, 1972). We should not exaggerate the power individuals have to change situations; some people have very little effect and some situations cannot be changed much. This should perhaps be rephrased to say that one way in which P contributes to behavior is by changing the behavior of others, and the way the situation is defined. In the changed state of affairs P may feel that he or she is confronted by an objective situation.

We shall argue below that the aspects of behavior that are most relevant in, for example, a game of hockey, a Scottish ball, and a psychology seminar are quite different, so that there is no common aspect of B to be predicted. This can be partly met by the use of wider, more abstract categories of behavior. Therefore, "gives information," one of the Bales categories, could include feed-back at a T-group and giving a sermon in church. Likewise, both could be assessed for the lengths of the utterance involved. Either analysis, however, would miss the most important aspects of the behavior in question.

To conclude, the $B = f(P,S)$ model does have a certain application to broad categories of behavior and to measureable aspects of situations. It also fails to deal with the facts that persons both choose and modify situations.

A GENERATIVE RULES APPROACH
TO P X S INTERACTION

Before I introduce this model, I should like to discuss some conceptual models that have been put forward to deal with the sequence of events in social behavior.

S—R Model

This model assumes that a social response is only affected by the last move by the other interactor:

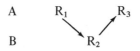

Social behavior is thus an example of a Markov chain. Examples are imitation and response matching, reciprocity, the reactive sequences found by Bales (1951), and the principles built into conversational computer programs (e.g., Weizenbaum, 1967). More elaborate S—R models take account of more than one preceding response: a familiar example is the effect of reinforcement. Clarke (1975) found that fifth-order artificial dialogs (i.e., where four preceding utterances are given) were indistinguishable from real dialog. The main objections to S—R models are (a) they do not allow enough weight to proactive plans by individuals, linking $R_1-R_3-R_5$, etc., and (b) they do not allow for embedding or other aspects of phrase structure.

The Social Skill Model

This model draws an analogy between social performance and the performance of motor skills (Argyle & Kendon, 1967). It is shown in Figure 26.2. This model

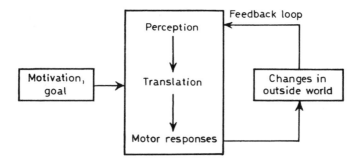

FIGURE 26.2   Motor skill model. (from Argyle, 1969.)

has been heuristically important in pointing to the importance of feedback, and hence to gaze phenomena, in suggesting several different ways in which social performance may fail, and in suggesting methods of training in social skills (Argyle, 1969). Its main weaknesses are that (a) as it stands it is schematic and only capable of rather general predictions of the kind just mentioned; (b) it does not take seriously the independent activity and plans of other interactors; and (c) it does not include the shared rules of social situations.

Integration of the S—R and Social Skills Models

A's second move, R_3, is a joint product of x, A's proactive plans, and y, the S—R and the rule-following links between R_2 and R_3:

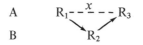

R_3 is therefore a piece of creative problem solving, integrating these different influences. How do interactors perform this constant, high-speed creativity? It is done partly through A having only a limited repertoire of responses, but more importantly through A and B keeping to the agreed rules of particular situations.

The Rules of Language and of Games

There is an almost infinite variety in the contents of what people may say. Partly for this reason in linguistics there is no attempt to predict what anyone will actually say. The goal is to arrive at a finite set of rules that can demarcate the (infinite) set of acceptable utterances in a language from the set of unacceptable ones (Chomsky, 1957). This is a less ambitious goal so far as prediction is concerned, but it does lead to understanding the structure of language and enables others to be taught these principles. There is a second reason for abandoning the goal of complete prediction – the possibility that human behavior is in part unpredictable.

As a model of other forms of social behavior, language has several interesting properties, that appear to be shared by social behavior.

1. Small units (phonemes), which are themselves meaningless, combine to produce larger units (morphemes), which are meaningful; these in turn combine to form sentences, which communicate information. Birdwhistell (1971) produced a list of 60 "kinemes," the gestural equivalents of phonemes; however, there is no evidence that these units are used as the basis of meaningful behavior elements. Closer equivalents of phonemes are perhaps shifts of gaze, proximity, posture, etc. (Argyle, 1975).

2. There are paradigmatic rules about which word may occur at a given point in sequence, and syntagmatic rules about the sequence of words.

3. The rules of sequence are nonstochastic; the ordering of words follows complex rules of syntax.

4. Words can have arbitrary meaning.

5. Words can have complex meanings in terms of other words and concepts.

6. The meaning of a word depends on its position in a sentence.

7. In addition to the syntactical rules of combination and sequence, there is also a semantic system determining the meaning of a sequence of words.

8. Speakers of a language cannot usually state these rules but can recognize whether they have been followed or broken (competence) and to some extent can follow the rules themselves (performance).

9. The same sentences can have more than one meaning; it requires elucidation of the "deep structure" to indicate which is intended.

The model has an obvious application to the study of games; the approach would be to discover the rules of, say, cricket, not to predict who would win, etc. The discovery of such rules requires new research methods, such as deliberate rule breaking, interviewing the socially mobile, and consulting rule books. Garfinkel (1963) was the first person to use rule breaking as a research procedure. In one of his experiments subjects played noughts and crosses; at one point the experimenter placed his mark on one of the lines, instead of between them, and the reactions of subjects were studied.

If two or more people want to play a game they must decide what game it is to be and then agree to keep the rules. Otherwise there is chaos. Social episodes appear to be introduced by a series of negotiating signals by means of which the definition of the situation is agreed. In games there appear to be two kinds of rules, those which are fundamental to the game (putting 0's in the squares at noughts and crosses), and social conventions, such as wearing white clothes to play cricket.

Similar considerations apply to social situations. I have found, for example, that interviewers report that they would be unable to cope with interviewees who speak the wrong language, tell lies, or ask all the questions, but are not worried about interviewees' appearance or posture.

However, there are also intermediate cases of rule breaking that fall short of total disruption; moreover, there is rarely a total collapse of social interaction, but there are attempts to restore it (Goffman, 1971). It is sometimes possible for two people to play slightly different social games, e.g., A is receiving a tutorial, B is having an affair. However, the point remains that there has to be a sufficient degree of cooperation in keeping to the same set of intrinsic rules for social interaction to take place.

The Classification of Situations

The structural approach was developed to understand the rules governing the sequence of social acts in particular situations. However, it has an immediate application to the classification of situations.

The method of studying this problem that has been most commonly used is multidimensional scaling or principle components analysis of ratings (Argyle & Little, 1972; Magnusson, 1971). Joseph Forgas (1976) at Oxford has recently carried out a survey of the classification of situations by Oxford students and housewives. He found the 25 most common situations for each group and subjected them to multidimensional scaling, followed by regression analysis. The dimensions that discriminated best between situations for these subjects are given in Table 26.1. The three dimensions for the students are shown in Figure 26.3. It can be seen that there are a number of tight clusters of situations. However, closer inspection reveals that the cluster 3–7–23 consists of the situations "Discussing an essay during a tutorial," "Acting as a subject in a psychology experiment," and "Attending a wedding ceremony" – three situations that are totally different in objective respects and in the behavior required.

1. In the first place each situation defines certain social acts as relevant and meaningful. The signals used at auction sales would be ignored in church; the moves at Scottish dancing would be regarded as insane at a dinner party.

TABLE 26.1

Housewives	Students
I. Intimacy, degree of involvement	Involvement, intimacy
II. Self-confidence, know how to behave	Evaluative, pleasant, friendly
III. Pleasant-unpleasant	Self-confident, how how to behave

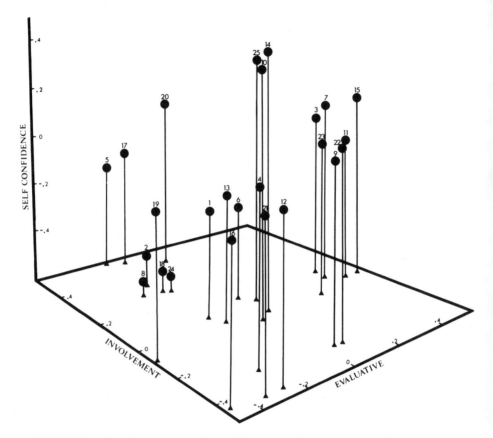

FIGURE 26.3   Multidimensional scaling of 25 situations (from Forgas, unpublished, 1976.)

Although amounts of speech and gaze, etc., are universal to all situations, their meaning and relevance is not; and social acts are often specific to situations.

2. Although people can classify situations or place them on seven-point scales, this taps only a very small part of their knowledge about these situations. Dinner parties may be felt to be more friendly than seminars, but participants have to know a great deal more than this in order to take part in such social situations. What we need are new research methods capable of exploring subjective knowledge and conceptualization of situations.

I suggest that social situations are akin to the chemical compounds, in being discrete, not continuous entities. Each situation, e.g., a dinner party or auction sale, like cricket and hide and seek, is a structured system of interdependent parts. The situation "cricket" cannot be dimensionalized by removing, for example, the ball or by adding some more or larger balls. If situations are

TABLE 26.2
Work situations

	Informal	Intermediate	Formal (rituals)
Work situation	Coffee Research Discussion College lunch	Lectures Seminars Tutorials Interviews Examinations (dentist, doctor, bank, shopping, i.e., work for others)	Degree ceremonies College functions

discontinuous, like chemical compounds (or elements) but unlike length and temperature, it follows that intermediate cases cannot be found. Clearly there is no continuous set of games intermediate between chess and cricket, but are there situations continuously intermediate between church services and psychology conferences? Almost certainly there are not, although there are mixed cases, and there are dimensional variations in the size of conferences, for example.

It follows that each person consists of a set of discrete states and patterns of behavior, manifested in different situations — his or her performance at psychology conferences, at home, as a psychotherapist, etc. It is not possible to generalize across these situations to traits, because totally different aspects of behavior are involved in each case.

It may be necessary to use dimensions in addition to discrete situations or groups of situations. One such dimension is informal—formal. Situations that are primarily work oriented, for example, vary along this dimension. Mine are given in Table 26.2.

Another approach to the analysis of situations is feature analysis. For example, games could be classified for the presence or absence of (1) a ball, (2) bats, (3) teams, etc. Osgood (1970) carried out such an analysis for interpersonal verbs, in terms of (1) active—passive, (2) deliberate—impulsive, etc. In other spheres of structural analysis, use is made of both elements and relations between them. I am working toward such an analysis for social situations but can only provide notes toward a solution as yet.

The Components of Situations

In order to take part in a game of cricket or a tutorial, to visit the riding stables, or to attend College guest night, the interactors must master the basic components of these situations. These include the following.

Special moves. Each situation defines certain moves as relevant and important: e.g., making love—various types of bodily contact; tutorial—read part of essay; dinner party—pass food, pour wine; shopping—try on trousers; interview—ask personal questions. Some aspects of behavior are found in a range of different situations.

Goals. This is probably the best starting point for situational analysis. The following list, or something like it, classifies situations by the goals of interactors:

Primarily social/cooperative, including most family life, play, eating together.
Male—female sexual activity.
Competitive games.
Aggressive conflict.
Negotiation, buying and selling.
Joint work, with cooperation and supervision.
Joint discussion, problem solving, decision taking.
Teaching, therapy.
Lectures and other public performances.
Interview, interrogation.
Religious and other rituals.

(After Krause, 1970; Harré & Secord, 1972; and others.)

Structural/motivational themes. The list above envisages pure, elementary, paradigmatic types. However in any particular situation a number of different motivational themes may be present and constitute the underlying structure of that situation. For example, a dinner party involves the following:

Social/cooperative.
Male—female relations.
Joint work (for hosts only).
Self-presentation.
Eating.

It does not involve buying and selling, therapy, etc.

Rules. It would be possible to define situations entirely in terms of rules of different kinds, but I have chosen to use other ideas as well. Rules specify what should and should not happen, including who may be present, what should be worn, and appropriate sequences of behavior. In the case of rituals the rules specify what is to happen in some detail. Competitive games can be subdivided on the basis of their rules, as can different kinds of rituals and interviews. A dinner party has rules about time, order of courses, dress, topics of conversation, seating, etc.

Roles. Most situations generate social roles. Dinner parties have hosts, guests, and sometimes servants, as well as male/female roles and senior/less senior guests.

Pieces. Most situations involve special environmental settings or props. Cricket needs bat, ball, stumps, etc.; a seminar requires blackboard, slides, projector, and lecture notes. There are rules governing the use of such pieces, each of which has a special social meaning and implications for interaction.

Concepts. To take part in Scottish dancing one must know the significance of "second corner," "the ladies' side," etc; to play cricket one must know what an "innings" and an "over" is. We suggest later that more expert and experienced performers use more elaborate concepts, e.g., in Scottish dancing "rondel," "reel of three"; in chess "fork," "discovered check," "open game," "Sicilian defence," etc.; or the terms used in different schools of psychotherapy to describe the state of the patient or the therapy — "resistance," "negative transference," etc.

Generative Rules and the Prediction of Ongoing Behavior

In order to predict the next move a player is going to make at chess we have to understand the game and know the present state of play. There are degrees of prediction: (1) Only moves within the rules are possible — a pawn cannot move like a knight; (2) a whole range of moves are very unlikely because they are to the player's obvious disadvantage; (3) prediction within the remaining moves is more difficult and depends on the player's skill and the strategies he or she has learned.

It may be suggested that the more formal a situation is, the greater the S variance, and the more predictable behavior is from the situation. There has been a lot of interest in greetings, because greetings have a clear sequence of behavior, with four distinct phases (distant salutation — approach — close phase — admission to changed relationship) (Goffman, 1971; Kendon & Ferber, 1973). If we consider a more ritualised situation, such as Scottish dancing, the sequence of a particular dance is predictable from beginning to end, apart from mistakes and overlooking variations in style and skill. The number of steps involved is of the order of 400.

Prediction can be made at several levels. In speech there is a higher degree of predictability of words within phrases than between them. However, whole utterances can also be predicted from the preceding series of utterances (Clarke, 1975). A simple and universal example is the question—answer sequence. A more elaborate one, including nonverbal components, is often used by school teachers: teacher asks question — children hold up hands — teacher points at one child — he or she answers — teacher comments or asks further questions. Systematic work in discourse analysis will probably lead to general rules for the sequence of utterances. David Clarke's research at Oxford has shown already that subjects have sufficient implicit knowledge of such rules to reconstruct the original order of a set of utterances that have been shuffled into random order, with a very much above chance degree of accuracy.

There are some rules that operate across all situations. For example, the rules of grammar apply in all situations involving speech. There are probably universal rules for nonverbal aspects of behavior too, for example "An act by A should be responded to by an act by B appropriately in terms of time relations, i.e., without a period of nonresponse and without interruption" (Argyle, 1975, p. 381). The precise time relations vary between situations and cultures.

Personality and Situation

How do persons fit into situations as characterized above? It would be convenient if persons fell into discrete structural types — as Freud and Lewin supposed. We could then proceed as in chemistry and predict the effects of combining P and S as discrete structured entities. To some extent persons are discrete — males and females, schizophrenics, depressives, etc., and different age groups. However there is little doubt that persons also vary along continuous dimensions. We therefore have to deal with both principles here.

The structural approach to situations establishes the limits of individual variation. The percentages of variance from P and S can be studied for those aspects of behavior that are universal — amount of talk, anxiety, etc. This cannot be done, however, for aspects of behavior that are unique to situations, e.g., strategy of bidding at an auction sale, style and skill of play at cricket, manner of procedure as a psychotherapist, and so on.

Choice of situations.   There are individual differences in the range of situations chosen. Some people spend a great deal of time making speeches, others chatting, others watching TV. The systematic analysis of range of situations is potentially a most interesting aspect of individual differences.

Grouping of situations.   As I shall show below there are differences in the ways in which situations are subjectively grouped, and presumably in the behavior produced in them (Figure 26.4), e.g., the level of skill, the anxiety produced.

It is possible to use the predictive $B = f(P, S)$ approach within structural groupings to predict the behavior defined as relevant from those aspects of persons most relevant for this prediction, which fall into several categories.

Motivation.   There is a certain degree of variation in the forms of motivation that are relevant to each situation. In informal social situations there can be variations in needs to affiliate, dominate, or engage in self-presentation and sexual behavior; in games there is variation in the desire to win, in Scottish dancing to do it perfectly, or flamboyantly.

Ability. Variations in ability at nonsocial activities can be relevant, e.g., in determining leadership of working groups. Variations in social skills are found in all situations; These affect the performance of the individuals in question and the whole course of interaction. These effects are probably least in rituals, where variation is only in the manner of performance.

Knowledge of rules and concepts. If a person does not know the rules, he or she is not likely to obey them. If he has learned a somewhat different set of rules for a situation, he may be an unwitting rule breaker. This is one of the main sources of trouble in intercultural encounters, including interclass and interage interaction. If a person has not mastered the concepts, he is also in difficulty. Bannister and Salmon (1966) have obtained evidence to show that one trouble with schizophrenics is that they do not have adequate concepts for persons. Just as gardeners need a concept of "weed" and Scottish dancers a concept of "second corner," so do participants in all social situations need concepts for persons and social performance.

Several kinds of research are in hand, using the generative rules model:

1. Research is in progress to discover the "conceptual schemas" that people use in different situations and to compare the skilled and unskilled and people from different cultures in this respect. More skilled performers are expected to have longer term plans and to possess more complex concepts, enabling them to pursue more complex strategies. There are clearly such differences between expert and inexpert players at cricket and chess, and it seems very likely that the same is true of social performance too.

2. Situational analysis appears to be an essential step in the study of interaction sequences: It is impossible to make any predictions about moves at chess before studying the rules and pieces.

3. If situations are discontinuous, there are also likely to be internal forces, maintaining each situation as a functioning system. If a change is induced in some aspect of a situation by external forces, several other aspects of the situation are also likely to change.

With these notes toward an analysis of the role of persons in situations three conclusions emerge: (1) the aspects of persons that are needed are different from those considered previously; (2) some of these person properties are themselves specific to situations; and (3) the effects of P are different in each kind of situation.

If a dimensional approach to situations is abandoned in favor of discrete structures, P X S variance research is made impossible and $B = f(P, S)$ equations cannot be found — except for rather limited, universal aspects of behavior, such as amount of gaze, and equally limited emic dimensions of situations. However, more exact prediction of individual performance in specific situations can be achieved by studying the contribution of relevant aspects of P to relevant aspects of B in a particular S.

Although the approach holds out the promise of universal principles of behavior, predictable from structural features of situations and some features of persons, little progress has been made so far in this direction.

APPLICATION OF THE TWO P X S MODELS

Treatment of Mental Patients with Social Behavior Difficulties

For some years we have been treating patients with neurosis and behavior disorders who have social anxieties or are inadequate in social situations, by means of role playing with videotape playback and related methods (Argyle, Trower & Bryant, 1974; Argyle, Bryant, & Trower, 1974). Some of the research from this project can be interpreted in terms of the two P X S models presented in this chapter.

The predictive model.   Bryant and Trower (1974) surveyed 223 Oxford students, asking them to report how much anxiety or difficulty they experienced in 30 everyday situations. A principal components analysis yielded a first component of general social difficulty; a second component distinguished between situations involving making initial contacts with strangers, and situations involving more intimate relationships. This information is of some limited use in directing the treatment of individual patients.

When a patient reports difficulty with a specific situation, it is useful to be able to form some idea of how far this reflects general P tendencies and how far P X S interaction, that is, an abnormal reaction to this situation. In the second case one possibility is for him or her to avoid the situation, where possible, and otherwise to concentrate social skills training on this situation alone.

It is also useful to know how an individual groups situations, in terms of his or her reported feelings and behavior. Argyle and Little (1972) carried out a principal components analyses for a number of individuals who reported their behavior with 12 target persons on 18 scales. An example of the results for one subject, an apprentice, are shown in Figure 26.4. Sometimes these groupings are highly idiosyncratic. For example, an assistant professor of nursing grouped her mother with her subordinates at work as far as her social behavior was concerned.

In this connection should be mentioned the very interesting finding by Moos (1968) and Endler (1973) that S variance is lower for mental patients. This can be set alongside the finding that patients are higher on external control than normals (Minton, 1967). Patients are more consistent across situations because they are unable to react constructively to situations in a way that enables them to control events.

Generative rules model.   When a patient reports difficulty with a particular situation, the treatment includes instructions in the structure, goals, rules, etc.,

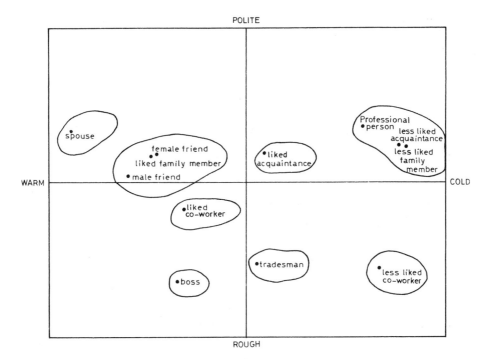

FIGURE 26.4 Graphic representation of 12 stimulus figures on the first two principal components for a single subject's grid (from Argyle & Little, 1972.)

of that situation. A common example is parties — one of the most difficult situations for young people. They do not understand the conventions and rules, for example, about how to initiate and terminate encounters at parties. The training, like teaching tennis, involves learning the goals and rules as well as the actual skills involved. We are planning to carry out an experimental trial to study the effectiveness of this form of situational training.

Racial Prejudice, Intercultural Communication

Predictive model. Certain aspects of intercultural communication can be tackled by this model. Where it is found that there are differences of proximity, gaze, orientation, etc., between two cultures, culture can be regarded as a systematic source of P variance. Collett (1971) succeeded in training Englishmen to deal with Arabs on this basis.

However the variance from P and S may also vary between cultures. Ruth Benedict (1946) observed that the Japanese were more affected by situations than were Americans or Europeans. Argyle, Shimoda, and Little (unpublished, 1976) carried out a study of variance attributed to P and S replicated in England and Japan and found that, for most of the dimensions of reported behavior studied, variance attributed to S was significantly higher and that attributed to P lower for the Japanese.

Generative rules model.   Many difficulties in intercultural contact arise out of different rules for situations, e.g., eating, buying and selling, dealing with women, which in turn are related to different concepts and goals. The system of buying and selling in an Arab market is totally different from that in a European or American department store, In the Illinois Culture Assimilator, instruction is given on understanding behavior in 50—100 types of situations or encounters, found to be troublesome in critical incident surveys (Fiedler, Mitchell, & Triandis, 1971).

Acknowledgments

I am indebted to Dr. Dávid Clarke, Dr. Peter Collett, and Rom Harré for some of the ideas in this chapter, and to the SSRC and the Oxford Regional Hospital Board for supporting the research reported.

27

The Representative Design
of Person—Situation Research

Lawrence A. Pervin

Livingston College,
Rutgers University

There was an interesting article in *The New York Times* a while ago which seemed to capture many of the issues inherent in person—situation research. The heart of the matter is expressed in the following statement: "I am exactly the *same person* I was before, but my situation in life is different and I behave as differently as if I were another person" (Krim, 1974).

Because the brief article serves to illustrate some of the points I wish to make, let me give some more of the details. The author, Mr. Seymour Krim, tells us that from 1961 to 1965 he was an editor and generally was cool, rational, reassuring, and smiled compassionately at the temperament of his writers. In this own terms, he disciplined his own needs for approval because they were irrelevant. However, there was "another self that lived a separate life," which came out when Mr. Krim himself became an author. Now Mr. Krim says that he is aggressive and anxious about the acceptance of his writing, finds it hard to relax, is blunt and demanding instead of diplomatic, and is less able to be objective or take an impersonal view. His confusion and insight are expressed as follows:

> What does it all mean?" I often ask myself with some wonder, as if I were a stranger to myself. I am the same man, I smoke the same foolish cigarettes, wear approximately the same clothes, respond to the same music and movies. It means, I'm afraid, that situation is more crucial than personality; at least that is so, or seems to be so, in my case. *The situation you're in determines who you are....* And yet, I tell you frankly that in my heart I'm exactly the same man who used to be reasonable, detached, smilingly helpful to those raw egos so aggravated by their unfulfilled position in life and so much less fortunate than myself! (Krim, *The New York Times*, November 18, 1974)

371

Mr. Krim's confusion is, I believe, similar to that of most of us in personality research and probably has the same basis. He recognizes both stability and change in his behavior in relation to situations and seeks to account for such stability and change in terms of himself or the situation. He concludes, with some hesitance, that the situation determines who you are and yet he feels that he is the same man regardless of the idiosyncratic nature of the situation. Must we choose between one and the other? Should we conclude that behavior is situationally determined and that it is only we as observers who attribute stability in behavior to the person (Jones & Nisbett, 1971) or can we accept our confusion as in fact a clear statement of the problem and a description of the phenomenon? Within the latter context we accept both stability and change, person and situation, and seek to understand the relationship between the two. Personality is now seen to express both stability and change, and such questions as the following are asked:

1. Do individuals differ in the general extent to which their behavior is stable or varying across situations (Fiske & Rice, 1955)?

2. Do individuals differ in the range of behaviors (behavioral repertoire) they express in different situations? In trait terms, do some traits apply primarily to some people and minimally, if at all, to others?

3. Do individuals exhibiting the same kinds of responses (behavioral repertoire) differ in the variability with which these responses are exhibited? In trait terms, do people who can be characterized as possessing the same traits differ in how variable they are in relation to each trait (Bem & Allen, 1974)?

4. Can we understand people in terms of their differing patterns of stability and change (i.e., kind and degree) in relation to different situations? In other words, can we define personality as the individual's pattern of stability and change in relation to defined situational characteristics?[1]

In this definition of personality we not only emphasize what is stable and what changes, but the *pattern* of ways in which the person responds the same or differently to various situations. It is this pattern of stability and change in relation to defined situations that now becomes the focus of our search. Understanding this pattern becomes the task of personality research. Mr. Krim is neither the objective and compassionate editor nor the aggressive and anxious author, nor is it true that he is determined by the situation. He is not more his self in one situation than in another, although he may feel this way. Neither is he without a self, although he also may at times feel this way. Instead, he has a self, he is a person, and this self (personality) consists, among other things,

[1] This statement appears to be similar to the following statement by Magnusson (1974b): "They [studies] show that the effects of situations on behavior are different for different individuals. It is the pattern of behavior, over situations with varying properties, that characterizes an individual" (p. 124).

of his varying behavior in situations where he is editor or author and his stable behavior in choosing clothes, cigarettes, music, and movies.

CURRENT PERSON–SITUATION RESEARCH AND BRUNSWIK'S REPRESENTATIVE DESIGN

Within the context of person–situation research defined above, the views of Egon Brunswik (1950, 1956; Hammond, 1966; Postman & Tolman, 1959) appear to have important implications. Brunswik was primarily interested in perception, but he also attempted to develop a systematic approach to psychology generally. In his book *Perception and the Representative Design of Psychological Experiments,* Brunswik (1956) emphasized the study of molar forms of behavior, a dynamic analysis of the interaction between organism and environment, and the representative design of research. Representative design was contrasted with systematic design. In systematic design, modeled after the procedures of physics, one (or a few) variable(s) is chosen for study, generally in the context of the laboratory setting. The problem with systematic design research is that decisions concerning the variables to be studied and the setting of investigation are arbitrary and unrepresentative of the organism in its natural habitat. Therefore, systematic design is to be replaced by representative design in which there is a representative sampling of situations from the organism's ecology. The results of systematic design are of questionable ecological generalizability. To improve on this, Brunswik suggests that we sample broadly the conditions (situations) under which the organism has to function. For Brunswik the sampling of situations could be considered more critical than the sampling of persons, permitting thereby the study of the adaptive functioning of an individual across a wide variety of settings.

In attempting to handle the full complexity of behavior, Brunswik spoke of distal, proximal, and central events. Distal events are those with which the organism is not in immediate contact. A distinction is made between overt distal variables, such as size and shape, and covert distal variables, such as the perception of a social trait in a person. Perceptual achievement (i.e., valid judgment) is more difficult with covert distal variables than with overt distal variables. Proximal events are those which exist at the boundary or skin surface of the organism (e.g., the representation of the situation on the retina). Finally, central events are events within the organism of mediating processes between what is registered on the surface and the perceptual response. On the output side one may also speak of proximal reactions, or molecular response behavior, and distal reactions, or molar behavioral achievements in the organism's adaptation to the environment. Perceptual responses and associated behavioral acts may serve as feedback information, beginning the process of perceptual achievement and adaptation anew. Within this model, the task of psychological research is to understand the adjustment of the organism to an uncertain environment. This is done through representative design research or the study of organismic adaptation in situations encountered in the course of daily living. Whereas Brunswik's emphasis was on distal—distal relationships, or between objective characteristics of situations and independently measured objective characteristics of the responding organism, it was understood that different schools in psychology typically focus on different aspects of the relationship between ecological environment and organismic response.

Now what are the implications of Brunswik's views for person—situation research? First, it is suggested that we sample a broad range of situations. Second, it is suggested that we study persons in situations that are as nearly representative of their daily living as possible. A problem with many questionnaire efforts to assess person—situation interactions is that the situations described and responses provided may have limited applicability from the standpoint of the individual responding to them (Ekehammar & Magnusson, 1973; Endler & Hunt, 1968; Magnusson & Ekehammar, 1975b). An analogy may be drawn here to the person perception literature where responses of subjects have been found to vary according to whether the persons judged are known to them and whether the traits used are familiar to them (Koltuv, 1962). Unless situations and behaviors are representative our results can have but limited ecological generalizability.

A third implication has to do with the sampling of subjects. In some of Brunswik's work on the validity of size judgments, only one subject was used. He felt that through the sampling of situations with one person, as opposed to the sampling of persons in one situation, one could grasp the essentials of functional achievement.[2] To generalize across individuals it is necessary to obtain a representative sample of subjects, each subject, however, responding to a representative sampling of situations from his or her own environment. Therefore, the third implication from Brunswik's work is that we should consider studying one or a few subjects and sample broadly for each over situations.

The fourth and final implication is that a full understanding of person—situation interaction involves an appreciation of the many steps and processes involved in the ecological environment—organism—ecological environment arc (Barker, 1968). In particular, we want to be aware of the possible differences in cue utilization in social judgments (i.e., covert distal variables) as opposed to physical judgments (i.e., overt distal variables). As Leeper (1966) has noted in relation to Brunswik's work, most situations that are important to people are

---

[2] Note here that Brunswik's consideration of the sampling of situations as opposed to the sampling of persons and his comparison of systematic design and representative design bear some similarity to Cronbach's (1957, 1975) discussion of the two disciplines of scientific psychology.

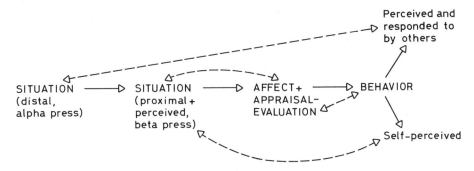

FIGURE 27.1   Descriptive analysis of the process of person—situation interaction.

ambiguous. In such situations different individuals may use quite different cues and make quite different cognitive responses in what is otherwise the same objective (distal) situation. This may require greater attention to central mediating processes than is the case with judgments of physical objects or perceptual attainment in size constancy.[3]

Drawing upon and extending Brunswik's views, we may consider the model in Figure 27.1 for any one instance of person—situation interaction. The model suggests that the basic considerations are an objectively defined situation, a perceived situation, an affective or emotional response and evaluation of the potential consequences of various responses (Price & Bouffard, 1974; Rotter, 1955), and a behavioral response. The broken arrows suggest the interdependent nature of the parts. For example, ordinarily perception of the situation is associated with an affective response and an evaluation of situational constraints prior to behavior. However, it is possible for a situation to trigger a behavioral response that leads to an affective response. Likewise, the perception of a situation may quickly trigger an affective response that colors the further perception of the situation. Therefore, the linkages among the parts are complex and not always unidirectional. The value of the model may be that it calls attention to relevant considerations (e.g., relationships among cognitive, affective, and behavioral variables) and it allows us to evaluate whether an investigator is studying the entire process of person—situation interaction or a part of it. In terms of representative design, we want to sample a broad range of situations that are as close as possible to those faced by the individual in his daily living. It is hoped that such sampling can permit valid ecological generalizations concerning person—situation interaction.

---

[3] A number of studies have demonstrated that cognitive structuring of persons may differ from the cognitive structuring of nations (Scott, 1974; Signell, 1966). The former domain tends to be much more influenced by affective factors.

INDIVIDUAL PERCEPTIONS OF SITUATIONS,
AFFECTS, AND BEHAVIOR

The overall aim of the research to be presented is the development of a conceptual scheme and a methodology to answer the following question: "In what ways, and why, do people remain stable (consistent) in their behavior and in what ways do they vary, according to which situational characteristics?" In terms of conceptual approach, the goal is a differentiated understanding of the transactions between people and situations as opposed to an emphasis purely on persons, purely on situations, or on a global Person X Situation interaction effect.[4] In terms of methodological approach, the effort is to adapt some of the techniques of person perception (implicit personality theory) research toward the specific goal of understanding person–situation interactions. In particular, an emphasis is placed on the development of free-response methods, as opposed to checklists or questionnaires, to study an individual's perception of situations in his or her life and his or her perceived pattern of behavior in relation to these situations. Such techniques permit one to study situations and responses that are meaningful for the individual while still providing for systematic data analysis (Rosenberg & Sedlak, 1972).

In this research considerable data are gathered on each subject and the subjects are immediately informed of the goals of the enterprise: "We are interested in the situations in your current life, how you perceive them, and how you are the same or different in these situations." Each subject is asked to do the following:

1. List the situations in his or her current life. A situation is described as involving a specific place, in most cases involving specific people, a specific time, and specific activities. The "current life" is left to include the past 6 months. The subject reviews his or her daily life and lists the situations that occur and are of some importance. For example, situations noted include the following: presenting my ideas before a class, arguing with my mother, studying alone, being at a big party, alone with a good friend, etc. Each situation represents a concrete situation for that subject. Because the subject generates his or her list of situations, he or she is free to list situations that are relevant to him or her and to survey a broad range of situations over which his or her feelings and behaviors may remain stable or vary.

2. Describe (adjectives, traits, phrases) each situation. This generates a list of situation traits.

3. Describe how he or she feels in each situation. This generates a list of feelings which, again, are relevant for the individual.

---

[4] The term "transactions" is used here to suggest that the individual, through his or her perceptions and his or her behaviors, shapes and defines situations as well as being shaped and defined by them.

4. Describe his or her behavior in each situation. This generates a list of behaviors in situations.

5. The result of the first four steps is a list of situations, a list of situation traits, a list of feelings in situations, and a list of behaviors in situations. The fifth step involves the subject indicating the applicability (2 = very applicable, 1 = somewhat applicable, 0 = not at all applicable) of each situation trait, feeling, and behavior to each situation. In other words, for each situation we have how the subject perceives it and how he or she perceives feeling and behaving in it. The procedure described is analogous to the procedure used by Rosenberg (Rosenberg & Sedlak, 1972) in his research on implicit personality theory. However, whereas Rosenberg asks subjects to list people, traits of people, and feelings elicited by people, our research asks subjects to list situations, characteristics of situations, and feelings and behaviors in situations.

What kind of data are generated by such an approach? Let us take one subject, Jennifer, and study her in detail and then contrast her with another subject. Jennifer is a junior college student. When I first met her she seemed to me to be a bright, conscientious student, highly motivated, able to pursue her studies independently, and friendly in a slightly timid, shy way. In the course of being a subject she seemed to relax and to be able to joke at times. As with each of the other subjects, she found the research to be of considerable interest and enjoyed the opportunity to examine her life in a reasonably systematic, relatively nonthreatening way.

Jennifer began by listing the environments in her life (home, school, work, friends, crowd). She then listed 23 situations that she felt covered the situations of significance in her current or recent past life. In relation to these situations she listed 64 situation traits, 62 feelings, and 59 behaviors. The nature of these characterizations will become clear as we consider the factor analyses of her ratings.

The ratings of situations, feelings in situations, and behaviors in situations can each be treated separately or, because the situations are constant throughout, the data can be analyzed across the separate groups of ratings. In general, the same situations tend to cluster together, or load on the same factor, in each of the analyses. However, there may also be some variation and this variation often is of considerable interest. For example, it is of interest if the person reports behaving in the same way in situations that are perceived very differently or experienced very differently. Conversely, it is of interest if the person reports behaving very differently in situations that are perceived and experienced similarly. Factor analyses were completed for Jennifer's ratings of situations, feelings, and behaviors, and across all ratings for the twenty-three situations. Illustrative results of the factor analysis across all ratings are presented in Table 27.1.

The first factor clearly has to do with unpleasant home situations. The factor is

TABLE 27.1

Illustrative Results from the Factor Analysis of Jennifer's Ratings of Situation Characteristics ($N = 64$), Feelings ($N = 62$), and Behaviors ($N = 59$) for 23 Situations

Factor	Illustrative situations	Situation traits	Feelings	Behaviors
Home—volatile	Mother blows up at me. Honest with parents about leaving. Mother refuses gift. Someone else comes home upset.	Emotional, angry, volatile, excitable	Angry, pressured, involved, insecure, unhappy	Sensitive, concerned, caring, suppressed, confused, not compulsive
School work — pressure to perform	Have to participate in class. Have to perform at work. Do the job wrong at work. In a strange place.	Demanding, threatening, pressuring, awkward, challenging, embarrassing, unconcerned	Self-conscious, challenged, vulnerable, awkward, pressured, anxious	Self-conscious, controlled, ambitious, determined, compulsive, cool, responsible, diligent, nonrebellious
Friends, alone	With friend – no problem. With friend – problem. Alone.	Emotional, gentle, friendly, generous	Caring, concerned, comfortable, melancholy, sad	Concerned, caring, emotional, involved, insightful, responsive
Uncertain	Come home from Philadelphia. In a crowd. Taking the bus to class. Want to leave to go to Philadelphia. In a strange place.	Ambiguous, nondefined, uncertain, unconcerned, ignoring	Bottled up, melancholy, sad, lonely, frustrated, confused	Preoccupied, detached, quiet, self-conscious, controlled, cool, introverted

predominantly defined by the situations being emotional, volatile, hostile and her feeling frustrated, depressed, tense, rejected, and victimized in them. Whereas certain behaviors are common to the situations in the group, the factor analysis of behavior ratings indicates that there are some important differences. When she is directly in conflict with her parents and feels strongly about the issue (e.g., honest with my parents about wanting to leave home), she tends to be aggressive, emotional, uncontrolled, angry, and rebellious. These behaviors do not tend to be characteristic of her in volatile home situations where others are upset (e.g., mother refuses father's gift, someone else comes home upset). In these situations she tends to be the peacemaker, supportive, loving, controlled, selfless, insightful, loyal, and patient. There is a group of situations with shared perceived characteristics, feelings, and behaviors, therefore, that can be subdivided into two groups in terms of additional distinguishing behaviors.

The second factor is pretty consistent throughout. It contains situations at school and on the job where she feels that she has to perform and do well. In these situations she feels challenged, vulnerable, and pressured and behaves in a controlled, determined, compulsive, and responsible way. What is interesting is that she tends to behave this way despite large differences in feelings. For example, doing the job wrong at work and being praised for doing well are associated with the same behaviors although they are associated with very different feelings. Whereas in situations at home similar feelings are associated with different behaviors, in situations at work different feelings are associated with similar behaviors. The relationships among situation characteristics, feelings, and behaviors are indeed complex!

The third factor primarily concerns being with female friends, although being alone is associated with some of the same characteristics. These are involving, gentle, friendly situations in which she feels concerned and important and tends to be caring and responsive. Although they are associated at times with some pressure and sadness, they stand in contrast with situations of nonsupport, such as being in a crowd, and situations of criticism and shame, such as being caught not working. Finally, the fourth factor contains situations that are perceived to be ambiguous and nonsupportive. The factor is primarily defined by the common situational characteristics (i.e., ambiguous, uncertain, unconcerned) and the common feelings experienced in them (i.e., bottled up, sad, confused). Although there are some shared behavioral characteristics, two subgroups of situations can be defined. In uncertain home situations Jennifer tends to be jocular and sharp witted. However, in uncertain impersonal situations (e.g., in a crowd, on the bus to class), she is very detached, cool, introverted.

The more detailed analyses of Jennifer's data bring out some interesting characteristics. First, there is the relative absence of positive situations of love, relaxation, interest, and excitement. Second, there are feelings of self-consciousness and anxiety that enter into a whole range of situations and that are associated with a wide range of behaviors. Third, there are interesting and suggestive common loadings of situations on factors. For example, being honest with her parents about leaving and her mother blowing up at her are seen to have common characteristics and suggest a concern about loss and separation. Fourth, in the factor analysis of behaviors being loyal, suppressed, and the peacemaker correlated negatively with being aggressive, honest, confident, and expressive. Therefore, one wonders about "the price" that she pays for being the loyal peacemaker. Finally, one can note that at times the distinctions among situation traits, feelings, and behaviors are blurred. In fact, this is common to all of the subjects that have been tested. What is striking is how the same word can be applied to the situation, to the self experiencing the situation, and to the self behaving in the situation. This is particularly true with affectively toned words and may be suggestive of the important role of affects in influencing how we organize and perceive situations as well as how we behave in them (Plutchik, 1974; Tomkins, 1962).[5]

To return to Jennifer in the context of person–situation interaction, we can consider the situations in her life, how she perceives and organizes them, and, accepting her report as accurate, how she is the same and different in different kinds of situations. Jennifer would appear to almost always be sensitive, vulnerable, and insightful. She also is friendly, warm, and accepting except for when she is in some volatile home situations, at which times she is uniquely irritable, angry, upset, depressed, uncontrolled, and rebellious. Note that these situations are in contrast with situations when she is behaving as the peacemaker. She is generally moody and somewhat preoccupied except for situations in which she has to perform (e.g., school, work) in which cases she is assertive, compulsive, diligent, responsible, determined, confident, and outgoing but also quiet, controlled, and cool. The contrast here I believe relates back to the awkwardness, vulnerability, and pressure she feels in these situations. These feelings would also account for her being flustered and self-conscious while behaving in a confident, assertive way.[6] Jennifer is generally anxious, except for when she is with friends, where she is particularly honest, expressive, enthusiastic, and outgoing. Finally, she generally is involved and caring except for when she is in uncertain situations, where she is detached, preoccupied, introverted, controlled, and cool.

One can focus on the ways in which Jennifer is the same in all situations and say that her behavior is person determined, or one can focus on the behavior that is different in each situation and say that her behavior is situationally determined. However, neither of these statements really makes sense. She is some ways in all situations, some ways in most situations with some exceptions, and some ways only in a few specific situations. She may seem like a chameleon in her behavior in two extremely different situations, but there are some

---

[5] Plutchik (1974) has observed a relationship among personality traits, emotions, and interpersonal behavior.

[6] It is interesting to note here my comment that at school she seemed friendly, although in a timid, shy way.

common threads that hold the fiber together and there is a pattern to the weave. It is these characteristics that the dynamically oriented psychologists have tried to capture, correctly emphasizing the important role of affects and the goal-directed nature of behavior. However, dynamically oriented psychologists have considered an encapsulated man and have failed to appreciate the importance of situational contexts, which help to shape behavior and which play a role in defining the person.

The pattern of transactions between self and situations obviously can vary considerably. In the few subjects tested to date there are clear differences in the number and kinds of situations listed, the organization or grouping of these situations, in the traits (situation, feeling, behavior) used, in the organization of traits in relation to situations, and in the stability of groupings of situations as one moves from feelings to behavior. In all cases there is an intelligible pattern of person—situation interaction, but the pattern of interaction may be different in any two cases. It would seem, then, that the task ahead of us is the definition of the kinds of situation—feeling—behavior patterns that are possible and an understanding of the basis for the alternative patterns.

INDIVIDUAL PERCEPTIONS OF SITUATIONS, FEELINGS, AND BEHAVIOR: WHAT THEY SUGGEST AND THEIR IMPLICATIONS FOR THE REPRESENTATIVE DESIGN OF PERSON—SITUATION RESEARCH

A number of observations can be commented upon on the basis of the few subjects studied to date.

Environments

The number of environments or general contexts within which situations occur seems to be small and relatively standard across subjects (e.g., home, work, school, friends, recreation).

Situations

There is variability in the number of situations listed and the kinds of situations listed. In the five subjects studied to date, the range in number of situations was 23—56. Even at the maximum, the number of situations necessary to describe the movement of persons through their current and recent past lives does not seem inordinately large. Furthermore, the number of factors necessary to account for the variation in perception of situations, feelings, and behaviors does not seem inordinately large. The results to date suggest that approximately five factors can account for 60% of the variance. The range of factors observed to date is four to nine. One is reminded here of Miller's (1956) article on the magical number seven (plus or minus two) in which he suggested that there is a limited number of dimensions along which people can perceive and judge phenomena.

One is struck with the interindividual variation with which similar situations are perceived and experienced. At the same time, these varying descriptions seem to fall along some common dimensions (i.e., warm, supportive — cold, rejecting; tense, threatening — relaxed, calm; interesting, stimulating — dull, boring; constraining — free). The first three dimensions bear an obvious similarity to Osgood's evaluative, potency, and activity dimensions and correspond to Mehrabian and Russell's (1974) emphasis on evaluative, activity, and potency dimensions in relation to experiencing the physical environment. The dimensions also are similar to the categories noted by Insel and Moos (1974) to characterize environments: relationship, personal development, system maintenance, and system change.

In terms of individual differences, one can learn a great deal about the individual in terms of the number and kinds of situations listed, the kinds of situations not listed, and the ways in which situations are grouped together on the basis of common traits. The ways in which perceived situational characteristics stand in correspondence to one another or in opposition to one another can be quite informative about the life of the individual and his or her construct system.

Situations, Affects, Behaviors

The data suggest considerable variation in the ways situations are perceived and experienced, and how individuals behave in them. Furthermore, the linkages between affects and behaviors are quite complex. The same feelings may lead to different behaviors in different situations and different feelings may lead to the same behaviors in different situations. We saw this in Jennifer. In another subject, feelings of warmth and support with friends and feelings of anxiety with authority figures both were associated with friendly, sociable behavior. In the same subject, feelings of anger led to attack in some situations and withdrawal in other situations. The relationship of perceptions of situations, to feelings in them, to behaviors in them seems to be a quite informative aspect of the functioning of the individual.

In general, subjects have a hard time describing behaviors that can be measured objectively by an observer and which communicate what is going on in the situation. Because it seems desirable to be able to check the subjects' perceptions of their own behavior against their actual behavior, there is a need to develop a list of behavioral attributes which can be reliably measured and which meaningfully communicate what is going on. The work of the ethologists is suggestive here (Blurton-Jones, 1972; Hinde, 1974). To the extent that individual reports of their behavior are matched by independent observations, we are basing our work on a solid foundation. To the extent that these reports are not matched by independent observation and only appear to be expressive of the constructions of the individual, we are dealing with what Livesley and Bromley (1973) have called "behavior perception" — the construction of relationships between situation factors and individual action. This may still be an important area of investigation.

The Role of Affects in Organizing Phenomena and Channeling Behavior

Within the context of this research, affects have emerged as an important basis for the organization of situations and as a contributor to behavior. What is striking is the extent to which situations are described in terms of affects (e.g., threatening, warm, interesting, dull, tense, calm, rejecting) and organized in terms of the similarity of affects aroused in them. In other words, we may organize situations not so much in terms of cognitively perceived similar attributes but in terms of bodily experiences associated with them. It is interesting to consider this phenomenon developmentally. When the infant is becoming aware of situations, it is primarily in terms of differences in feelings created by them. The infant feels good in some situations and bad in others, aroused in some and quiescent in others, tense in some and calm in others. Situations appear to be distinguished much more in terms of feelings aroused by them than in terms of some cognitively perceived set of attributes. For example, Lewis and Freedle (1973) have observed that situations alter the pattern of infant vocalizations as early as 12 weeks of age and an important aspect of these situations appears to be whether they are restrictive—constraining or nonrestrictive. These early, affectively toned groupings of situations may serve as the basis for later groupings of situations. Such categorizations, *primarily* based on affective factors, may be contrasted with categorizations *primarily* based on cognitive factors. This possibility seems all the more important in terms of the relationships also observed between emotions and terms used to describe interpersonal behavior (Lewis, 1974; Plutchik, 1974).

Along with their possible role as organizers of perceptions of situations, affects may serve as the intervening link between situations and behavior. A similar view has been expressed by Mehrabian and Russell (1974) in relation to their studies of environment and behavior. One possibility, for example, is that behavior in a situation reflects the individual's efforts to express certain affects within the context of the perception of certain rewards and punishments for alternative behaviors. Feeling inhibited, or the sense of acting a façade, would then be expressive of the sense of acting in accord with the receipt of rewards or avoidance of punishments instead of acting in accord with one's affects. Feeling uninhibited and "one's self" would be expressive of the situation where one is free to disregard the rewards and punishments in the situation because they are minimal or because they are perceived to be compatible with expressions of feelings.

CONCLUSION

Let us return now to the representative design of person—situation research. The research presented on individual perceptions moves in the direction of Brunswik's representative design in terms of the sampling of a wide range of situations that are relevant to the individual being studied. The emphasis here has been on the perception of molar behavior in relation to a representative sampling of situations. For each individual studied the sampling of behaviors and situations was allowed to vary so as to be representative for that individual. At the same time, the research has departed from Brunswik's emphasis on distal—distal relationships and this suggests a further direction for this research. While studying individual perceptions of situations. feelings in situations, and behaviors in situations, we also need to look at the relationship between objectively defined characteristics of situations (distal situation) and perceptions of situations, and the relationship between objective descriptions of behavior (distal response) and perceptions of one's own behavior. Regardless of the part of the environment—organism—environment arc studied, however, it is desirable that our studies of person—situation interaction include a representative sampling of situations. Similarly, in describing someone's personality, it is desirable that we focus on the pattern of stability and change that is characteristic of their functioning in the many situations they encounter in their natural habitat.

Acknowledgments

This paper was prepared while the author was a Visting Research Fellow at Educational Testing Service. The support of ETS and my colleagues in the Division of Psychological Studies is gratefully acknowledged. The research reported was also supported in part by a grant from the Rutgers University Research Council. My appreciation is expressed to Floyd Turner who assisted in the analysis of the data.

28

Situations, Interactions, and Comparative Psychology

Michel Zlotowicz (deceased)

Laboratoire de Psycho-Biologie de l'Enfant, (E. P. H. E.) France

Psychology lacks neither ideas nor facts. What it now seems to need most is the means of making a choice among ideas and then of relating them to facts.

I am not an experimentalist. I would rather view myself as an "investigator." This, of course, implies a preference for data collected in "natural" conditions, that is, conditions distorted as little as possible by the investigator's activities, such as field observations. Interview techniques may make an effective contribution to data collecting (even though they imply active intervention), insofar as they leave the subject free to express her- or himself. As to experimentation, it is a method of checking and criticizing data, that is, of treating as well as collecting them.

The psychologist lives in a world of unceasingly renewed facts and has quite a number of ideas. Among these ideas he or she probably wishes to select those which enable him or her to orient him or herself on what Paul Valery has called "the infinite Ocean of facts." At this point, the two principal dangers are fear and lack of patience, which result in an anxious quest for proof and verification. Hence the widely noted greater interest in data analyzing techniques instead of in conditions under which data are collected.

Therefore, a particular field of psychology may be treated in different ways, according to varying requirements as to accuracy and validity. The results, often obtained at the price of considerable technical refinements, may not be interpreted outside their original frame. This generates problems in the comparison of results, the more so in that their solution requires knowledge of the initial data. One would like to start all over again, in order to determine the extent to which the data might have been distorted to fit the selected pattern of analysis. In other words, results in psychology too often appear to reflect the chosen method instead of being an intelligble manifestation of reality.

Now, in our branch there is by no means universal agreement about even the most general formulas, in particular those which contain such terms as "situation," "response," and "behavior." Even agreement on words tends to be deceptive, moreover, as shown in the many different uses of the same word. This is, for instance, the case with the universal use of "stimulus": Gibson (1960) has listed a large number of different meanings of this word used simultaneously by one author or authors belonging to the same trend.

In the project for an "interactional psychology" one can discern a disillusion with the methods used to date in the study of personality and social behavior. The discredit cast on the search for personality traits or types by the development of the "social learning" theory (Mischel, 1973a) is nevertheless accompanied by a certain distrust of the neobehaviorist shades of this so-called "situationist" trend.

For my part, I value the renewal brought to psychology by the neobehaviorist trend as well as by the influence of animal ethology. I see this primarily as a reversion to what is concrete, as a new wish for a careful study of the individual before generalizations are made. From this angle two events seem particularly significant and promising as to the new orientation of psychology. The first is the transition of confirmed experimentalists from the laboratory to clinical psychology (Ferster, 1967), following the development of behavior therapy. One important consequence of this is the interest invested in individual interactions within home and social environments (Patterson, 1973, 1974) as with the "token economies" (Krasner & Krasner, 1973).

The other event is most tangible in the field of developmental psychology. Here one may quote the vast synthesis achieved by Bowlby (1969, 1973) as well as the contributions of Blurton-Jones (1972, 1974) and McGrew (1972). Here again we find an essential interest in the description of interaction among individuals.

In both instances there is a new call for a precise functional description, stressing issues of comparison and classification that until then had been somewhat neglected. Also, with these new developments, one of the future tasks of psychology will be to relate observed behavior to speech collected during the observation itself or by means of interview or questionnaire techniques. This implies a view of the object of psychology that places situations in the foreground. We shall therefore begin by discussing this issue of situations and examine the bearing both of criticisms of "situationism" and of defences of "interactionism." We shall then stress the importance of description and classification problems, within the framework of a psychology that to be general must essentially be comparative.

"SITUATIONISM" OR "RESPONSISM"?

Let us start from the concept of situations. Is there really a "situationism" as stated by Bowers (1973)? Can one cope with this by considering "interactions" of situations and persons?

The main objection to partisans of the S—R schema or "situationists" is that their formula does not allow for the variations that are introduced to responses not only by situations but also by the quite undeniable differences between individuals.

Nobody actually denies that any situation applies to individuals, as shown by the interpolation of a factor in the S—R schema: P (personality) or O (organism). However, O or P are usually put inside brackets and a number of research works tend to make S vary on the assumption that P is constant.

Let us note, nevertheless, that neobehaviorists are less open than it seems to such criticism. They have on many occasions plainly shown their interest in experimental case studies and their concern to adjust their procedures to each individual. It therefore seems that Skinner (1969) is fully entitled to consider himself as "beyond the S—R schema," and not merely from this standpoint but still more essentially, as we shall see, when he stresses the consequences of response quite as strongly as its antecedents.

In fact Bowers' criticism is mostly aimed at the diffuse but massive trend of experiments in which individual differences are drowned in group means and where the basic procedure is to compare experimental and control groups.

Interactional psychology is therefore a protest against bracketing the P factor in the S—R formula. The question of whether this intermediate term between S and R should be designated O or P is liable to interest interactionists. An S—O—R formula puts more stress on the variations of state that condition the efficiency of the situation in obtaining a response. In contrast, an S—P—R formula grants the organism several steady dispositions or "traits" that may modify the response, either independently of the situation or at least by affecting it.

As for us, we shall confine ourselves to noting that the "interactionist" position accepts the same basic entities as the S—R schema. The term *response* in particular is in no way disputed, and this is why "situationism" and "interactionism" may be described as two varieties of what should be called "responsism."

In fact, to follow Bowers (1973) would mean wholly admitting the response as the primary and unalienable data of psychological observation (or rather experimentation). Psychology can be termed as the science of responses, its objective being to explain them. The one remaining issue is whether the determinants of responses are to be found within situations or persons. The interactionism advocated by Bowers contains the assertion that these two types of factors must not be considered separately and that neither of them should be privileged. He states: "obviously, and to some considerable extent, the person and the situation are codeterminors of behavior, and they need to be specified simultaneously if predictive accuracy is desired" (p. 322).

We shall not make any distinction between the very strong assertion of a determinism in response (codeterminors) and the positivist mitigation of this assertion according to which it merely remains to predict (predictive accuracy). We shall stress instead the sequence where the response becomes the phenomenon to be explained, as well as the mistake that substitutes the word "behavior" for the word "response."

Behavior definitely is not response. The confusion between these two terms is an important aspect of the history of behaviorism. Much of the present uneasiness stems from this confusion rather than from other aspects of "situationism" that Bowers has criticized (i.e., the assimilation of the S–R schema to the experimental paradigm or the equating of the experimental paradigm to causality), and the primacy bestowed on environment. The quotation from Bowers shows how topical the dispute is, whereas the scope of its bearing is demonstrated by the history of behaviorism and its contemporary competitors (gestalt, symbolical interaction, psychoanalysis).

As noted by Tilquin (1950), in the subtitle of his remarkable book (*Le behaviorisme: Origine et développement de la psychologie de réaction en Amérique*), behaviorism is basically a psychology of reaction or response, not of siutation. In taking account of behavior, Watson and his first adepts accomplished an important revolution that was recognized and accepted even by a great number of their opponents. There was definite hope of a new science, based on the study of human and animal behavior, that would really be both general and comparative. In spite of Watson's reductionist tendencies, his contribution was valued by those who helped to launch this new psychology: gestaltists in Germany; Piéron and Janet in France, Mead and many others (the whole pragmatic trend) in the United States.

However, behaviorists narrowed their field and the bearing of their revolution: They too often reduced behavior to response, to cater to what was believed to be the requirements of experimentation. In becoming "responsists" they also created a caricature of "situationism." Behavior ceased to be an action and became a mere response at the same time as its correlative component, the situation, which could have been conceived as the subject's "construction," became the "constructor" of the response and was thus reduced to the stimulus. This, as has often been said, was to substitute the reflex arc for behavior. Within the S–R schema, the essentials of psychology were accordingly represented by the dash relating the two terms.

Such a position was just barely defensible in the field of classical conditioning. As soon as one left this field, it was constantly softened and disarticulated along with all the possible changes in meanings and substitution of terms. What remains is a persistent tendency to consider the response as the central data in psychology, and this appears very clearly in the interactionist model put forward by Bowers.

A major consequence of this unfortunate reduction of behaviorism to the S–R schema was the development, in the field of personality studies, of ideas and techniques that owed practically nothing to behaviorism *per se.* This trend, which may be described in general as "psychometrical," aimed at establishing an inventory of personality "traits" by analyzing individual differences and ordering them factorially. Enough has been said about the shortcomings of this trend, in particular by Peterson (as early as 1965) and Mischel. We can merely add that the criticism of it springs from a strong comeback by neobehaviorism, just as its rise was related to the responsist deficiencies of prior behaviorism.

And indeed, Skinner and his fellow neobehaviorists had only to reintroduce the subject's activity (as an "operant") as a parameter of their basic schema to give a violent jolt to a number of established positions in the field of psychology: The undeniable successes achieved by neobehaviorists in personality study, together with the practical extension to behavior therapy, have brought on a crisis in the fields where the old S–R schema has not been able to assert itself entirely. The present debate bears witness to such a crisis.

BEHAVIOR AND SITUATION

By restoring to the response one of its main characteristics, that of activity, neobehaviorists escape from some of the criticisms leveled against the S–R schema. Moreover, by adding the concept of consequence and relating it to the response by means of a contingency relationship (cf., for instance, Kanfer & Philipps, 1970, p. 54ff), they break up the order of succession between the terms of the S–R couple. This should avoid any oversimplified idea about causality, so that, finally, their formula frames a behavioral aspect (R) between two situational aspects (Sd and C).

The foremost issues therefore becomes that of the relationship to be established between behavior and situation. This relationship, as shown by the neobehaviorist formula, can be neither causal nor even mere succession.

We shall start from these two concepts and introduce the particular instances of stimulus and response later. We shall therefore be led to defend a certain type of situationism, very different from the one criticized by Bowers. As to the "interactions" we shall need to mention, they cannot be those between the situation and the person. More specifically, we are unable to accept the terms of a discussion that merely offer to reduce R, S, and P (and their interaction being known). Indeed, if we knew S and P, there would be no need whatever to analyze behavior.

If, like so many others, we accept the choice that compels the psychologist to study behavior instead of states of conscience, this to us remains a tactical choice: a means of approaching data rather than the definition of an object. Knowledge of others can only be achieved by observing behavior and translating the observations into situational terms.

Among specialized probers of conscience a professional collusion can arise, where from psychophysics was born. However, this could not happen without an ambiguity about man and animal, adult and child.[1] This we see as the basic, positive side of the "behaviorist revolution": the necessary link between animal and man could only be established by the study of animal behavior. In the same way, to understand a patient one had to follow the twists and turns of what Janet called "conducts," and to understand a child one could not remain centered on his "states of mind."

However, behavior cannot be reduced to a response determined by a stimulus; in itself it is just one aspect of the part of the world in which it generates and which is usually called situation. To reduce the whole represented by situation and behavior to the S–R schema is equivalent to substituting a new dualism for the Cartesian dualism of thought and space that is at the origin of the psychology of conscience. This new dualism is created between the body, the organism from which responses stem, and the world which produces stimulations. This may be true in laboratory conditions, if one bears in mind that the experimenter is an active participant, and that by handing out stimuli he or she substitutes her- or himself for the world. As Gibson (1960) puts it: "the secret of a good experiment is to discover the relevant stimuli before doing the experiment" (p. 702). This implies a wide investigation that constantly must be restarted: before one considers the world as a boundless laboratory, one should find out what the world is for animals as well as for human beings; and if not a laboratory, what else?

First of all, we shall retain the idea that the living being and its environment belong to the same nature, and that this environment is not essentially physical, but biological and significant: it is a world of *events*. Among observable events two types may be distinguished, that is, a living being and its observer. They can then be differentiated from the viewpoint of the observer: events–behaviors and events–situations.

The event–situation is at least what Peirce called an "interpretant," that is, a part of the natural world that is significant *from the standpoint of a receptor.* The event–behavior is likewise a significant part of the natural world, but one where *the receptor appears to the observer as an actor,* who is liable to modify the situation to the extent that this is apparent to the observer by means of behavior.

When refining his analysis, the observer should avoid making such perilous

---

[1] On this point there are some useful and accurate remarks in the book by Chein (1972), in particular his Chapter 6, "E. B. Titchener, the Behaviorist Revolution and the Qualities of Experience."

reductions of the S–R schema that the situation becomes the actor. We think it important instead to consider to what extent and how the situation is created for the observer by the behavior of the actor. Still, and first of all, how are the concepts of stimulus and response introduced into such a description? It is not a question of rejecting, only of limiting them. In our opinion, the only instance where the word "stimulus" may be used is when a natural event is reproduced or imitated in the laboratory. Moreover, in keeping with Skinner's concept of a differential stimulus, stimulus will be considered as a signal for the subject, not as a cause of the response.

The stimulus being a signal, the response will also be similar to natural behavior, created in the laboratory. The observer will use it as a criterion of the effectiveness of the stimulus, of its function as a signal. Finally, to avoid any temptation to establish a causal link between stimulus and response, let it be said that the stimulus may preceed or succeed the response. In the latter case it is called reinforcement.

There is no behavior outside situations, and the only situations are those manifested by behaviors. Stimulus and response are not given as such in nature but are obtained at the price of an abstraction oriented by the experimenter's needs. In fact, we very often have a construction instead of an abstraction. This means that stimuli are created by physical apparels and responses are delimited by instrumental constraints (of which the "shaping" technique is a sophisticated instance).

If stimulus and response are regarded as similar, in the laboratory, to situation and behavior in nature, it will help us toward a better understanding of the link between them, that is, of the dash in the S–R formula.

In a Skinner box, to manipulate a lever and obtain food as a result is the equivalent of a complex natural sequence of actions such as the search for food and its consummation. Any event preceding the lever pressing may acquire value as a signal of the possibility of obtaining food. The response is necessary merely insofar as it allows the animal to fulfill a vital function, and this function is natural. The craft of the experimenter partly consists of knowing this require-ment and in adjusting his device to it. The response is not determined by the stimulus or the reinforcement but by the whole experimental device, its instru-mental characteristics, and its adaptation to vital needs. Thus, the necessity arises in that the animal's need can only be satisfied in compliance with the experimenter's requirements.

There exists a vast and real psychological knowledge of the conditions that make an experimental device efficient. It does not appear in the statistical relationships established among stimuli, responses, and consequences. This is part of the so-called knowhow of the experimenter, and it is by this means that he or she wields power over the animal.

In this respect, experiments with animals are not unrelated to man's social life. This is why some aspects of the latter should be studied as S–R–C chains: in social life there is a multitude of situations of constraint or dependence, regarding beings, institutions, or technical devices. However, these situations have to be analyzed to understand why it appears as though stimuli determine response.

Therefore, in evaluating experiments, one must take account of their abstract and constructive nature and compare them carefully with what they seek to reproduce. Such a comparison is only possible if one requirement has been met: that studies occurring under natural conditions be replicated in the laboratory or, in the case where the laboratory results merely serve as a guide for the study of facts, in their ordinary setting. It is in connection with these settings that the concept of situation, in our opinion, shows its full worth. In its full meaning it appears liable to be used in any field of psychology and even be its true object. Here, we think, is the most valuable outcome of the behaviorist revolution. This has been rightly noticed by Mead, whom we shall quote more than once in the rest of this chapter.

SITUATION AND "EXPERIENCE"

Behaviorists rarely think in terms of reducing all stimuli to their physical conditions. Furthermore, "situations" was the word they used when feeling that it would be a mistake to talk about stimuli whenever events became too complex. (Hence also the use of such expressions as "stimulating situations" or the distinction between "molar" and "molecular" stimuli; cf. Gibson, 1960.) Watson was not unaware of the fact that events—situations, such as loss of support, constraint of caress, have no determined physical existence and are relative to the living organisms that undergo them, just as sudden noises are unexpected for the subject but not for the experimenter.

The followers of the organismic trends in psychology, including Kantor, who claims to be a behaviorist, have stressed the fact that any situation is relative to the organism and its behavior. The idea most worth considering, however, is probably von Uexküll's *Umwelt* (1934), particularly as it has strongly influenced animal ethology. It has been offered as an explanation for conducts that appear very elementary compared to those studied by behaviorists.

Instead of distinguishing characters pertaining either to environment (stimulus) or to the organism (response), von Uexküll (1934) prefers to assign a motor and a perceptual character to the functional relationship between the animal and physical environment. These characteristics are not considered as separately pertaining one to the organism and the other to environment, but as both belonging to the functional circle that links them, the *Umwelt*. The "inside world" of the subject is no longer conceived as a sort of space, internal to the organism, but as its relation to the object as receptor and effector.

Along the same lines as the *Umwelt* concept, we think it useful to assign to the situation a power of fixing and transmitting the "interior world" of the subjects.

This is what Mead, not becoming as involved with philosophy, calls "experience." Helped by some quotations from the work of Mead (1934), with further elicitation of some of the consequences, we shall confine "situationism" to that experience and subjectivity which is communicable, transposable, and analyzable by means of the situations that behaviors reveal.

This is the point at which we diverge from the neobehaviorists, who hold that the study of "private events" does not belong to science. On the contrary, and in the interests of a general and comparative psychology, one must assert that such events are an essential part of our field. One's very intention in analyzing situations is to make them "public," that is, communicable and mutually comparable.

First, let us state, with Mead (1934), why psychology must in a wide sense be behavioristic:

> Psychology is not something that deals with consciousness; psychology deals with the experience of the individual in its relation to the conditions under which the experience goes on. It is a social psychology where the conditions are social ones. It is behavioristic where the approach to experience is made through conduct. (pp. 40–41)

One cannot state more clearly that the study of behavior or conduct is a means and not the aim of psychology, which is to account for experience. This was also Janet's opinion (cf. Chein, 1972; Prévost, 1973).

Regarding the aim of psychology, Mead's formulations are sometimes contradictory. We shall adhere to those which appear most consistent: Psychology must be behavioristic "in that it states the experience of the individual as completely as it can in objective terms" (Mead, 1934, p. 35).

What are these "objective terms"? Mead's first proposition seems somewhat "responsist": "Psychology starts off with this problem of getting correlations between the experience of individuals and conditions under which it takes place, and undertakes to state this experience in terms of behavior" (Mead, 1934, p. 36). Under the influence of gestalt psychology, however, Mead arrives at a second formulation, which seems to us to be decisive.

He starts by stating profoundly the basic position that differentiates gestalt from Watsonian behaviorism: the assertion of an "element which is common to the experience of the individual and the world which determines the conditions under which that experience arises"; or, more accurately, "a certain structure that has to be recognized both in the experience of the individual and the conditioning world" (Mead, 1934, p. 35).

This leads him to the assertion that, in our opinion, constitutes the platform of "situationism," which is also interactionist: "We are trying to state the experience of the individual and situations in as common terms as we can, and it is this which gives the importance to what we call behavioristic psychology" (Mead, 1934, p. 39). As a matter of fact, such a psychology is a synthesis of behaviorism and gestalt; the study of behavior should make it possible to transpose experience into the situation. However, situation is considered as a structure common to the individual and the world, which is comparable to von Uexküll's *Umwelt*.

This general conception of psychology results in statements that should be stressed as being totally opposed to the S—R doctrine and to "responsism" which in our opinion is the latter's most typical aspect. "Organic processes or responses in a sense constitute the objects to which they are responses" and "the social process in a sense constitutes the objects to which it responds or to which it is an adjustment" (Mead, 1934, p. 77). This statement leads to a remarkable reversal of the relationships usually admitted to between stimulus and response: "the organized stimuli answer to the organized responses" (Mead, 1934, p. 131). Such a statement, however, although possibly shocking to followers of the traditional S—R schema, should in no way surprise neobehaviorists, used as they are to consider an "operant" as a response that procures a stimulus.

We do not propose to dwell on the underlying philosophical influence of these assertions: Hegelianism, pragmaticism (Peirce, James, and Dewey), phenomenology (through gestalt). Still, it should be noted that Mead as well as von Uexküll and many other thinkers of the 1930s are opposed to dualism and mechanism. This opposition still has a persistent influence, as shown by some recent trends. This also seems true of the aim of an interactional psychology.

For example, the concept of *intention,* not at all favored by behaviorists, is now reappearing in some fields of psychology. Taken by Brentano from medieval philosophy and transmitted to phenomenology, intention is considered to be one of the central concepts of the psychology of conscience. This is somewhat mistaken and unfair, insofar as *intentio,* at least for Ockham, in the sense of an intellectual tension, is a concept that far from implying the existence of conscience in fact stresses intellectual activity.

As to animal ethology, following Heinroth, it does not hesitate to admit "movements of intention" in the animal. These are outlines of responses, in infraliminar conditions of stimulation, at least according to the behavioristic definition offered by Tinbergen (1951). However, as often happens when definitions are too restricted, the term may be used in ethology in a much more liberal way. It seems more accurate to hold, with Hinde (1970), that movements of intention are the beginning of an act not followed by immediate fulfilment.

More recently Bruner (1974), when studying "the organization of early skilled action," admits the importance of the actions the young child *tries* to perform before possessing the necessary motor capacities to achieve them. However, having ascertained the possibility of defining intention from a neurophysiological point of view, he offers (Bruner, 1974, pp. 168—169) a much too wide behavioral description, which does not allow one to differentiate "intention" from "purpose." Still, let us note a remark insofar as it is critical of the S—R schema: "It is the nature of objects or states that arouse such intentionality that they operate like triggers or releasers, more like threshold phenomena than like reflexes in which stimulus magnitude determines response magnitude" (Bruner, 1974, p. 169).

In the same volume, Shotter (1974), more accurately in our opinion, stresses the original and perhaps fundamental content of intention. He recalls that for the phenomenologists "mental activity is directed upon an object" and adds "it is this, its intention, which distinguishes one act from another, not the temporal order of behavioral *events*" (Shotter, 1974, p. 220). Let us offer some comment, as Shotter uses the word *event* in the specific sense of a physical event exterior to the subject: We shall say that it is not so much what preceeds the act that allows us to characterize it, but the act or acts which succeed it. This is an idea Mead has often expressed.

Shotter, however, is anxious to state the originality of human behavior and believes in psychology "as a moral not a natural science." Hence he tends to neglect the general aspect of his definition: what is common to animal and man. Like Bruner, he also tends to assimilate "intention" and "purpose," for instance when he writes that "human behavior is to be explained by reference to an end" (Shotter, 1974, p. 221).

Intention is a psychological event that is observable in a number of animal species and not just in man. It is not a fact of conscience but an elementary, instantaneous act that potentially contains the equivalent of a sequence of acts. Still more accurately, intention is a mixed event, between behavior and situation; it is an action by means of which the "interior world" or "experience" becomes manifest. This is why it should be studied within the frame of a "situationism" that has nothing in common with the S–R schema, but, like the concept of role, with Mead's social behaviorism.

The acts of intention described by ethologists also possess the property of being perceived as such; that is, events are related to those that may follow them. Acts of intention therefore achieve the remarkable economy of action generally ascribed to thought and speech. Being perceived like messages, they belong to the category called "physiognomic perception" by Werner (1948), which, according to him, plays a major role in the primitive forms of representation observed in animal as well as in man.

Also, the great psychologist Wallon (1934) had paid particular attention to the study of events, such as attitudes and postures, which allow what would nowadays be called "nonverbal communication." These are all instances where it is particularly obvious that the organism appears to other organisms as a significant situation. They also illustrate the opinion we now have to defend: the most interesting interactions between person and situation need to be looked for in the situations themselves. They can be found if one admits that the latter are constructed and significant.

SITUATIONS, PERSON, AND INTERACTIONS

Before examining how the study of "interactions" is essentially part of the description of situations, a distinction must be introduced: on the one hand, there are concrete situations, which are those that present themselves to the person and the observer. On the other hand, there are typical or generic situations, which are worked out by the psychologist in his endeavours to determine which are the comparable and repeatable aspects of the concrete situations he studies. Stimuli and responses are typical elements of this kind, within the very specific conditions of experimental analysis, as already stressed.

To establish inventories of typical situations is precisely the main objective of comparative analysis, and we shall outline some of their means and purposes. Therefore, we shall admit the existence of generic situations (such as danger or frustration) that are valid for all or some animal species, or for some members only of a particular species. As to the human being, it is of course important to ascertain whether the situations he or she experiences has something in common with those known by members of other species. However, it is equally important to describe varieties of situations that are particular to certain individuals and as an extreme to one single individual. In our opinion, this is how one should state the issue of "interactions" between situation and person: one has to list a descriptive (and in particular in classifying) inventory of the situations in which the persons are involved.

If it is true that any living being can be distinguished from all others by its own form and its conditions of existence, its behaviors merely testify to the world of situations that is its own. We hold that the discovery of this particular world is precisely the object of personality psychology.

In such a view, differences in state appear as differences in actualization of situations for a particular individual. Organic conditions may play an important role here and the consistent differences that can be observed between individuals (dispositions or traits) are to be sought in their usual world of situations, chosen or inflicted.

Neither personality nor situation is a cause of behavior, but behavior is a means of describing and classifying situations and, therefore, individuals. One lists situations in which the person is involved and which he or she often has constructed; personality traits are not conceivable outside a situation; means of response for the individual are often aspects of the situation in which he or she finds her- or himself. Then one evaluates "interactions" between components that are themselves interactions. This is a task which the existence of a statistical technique does not by itself legitimate, even if it makes it possible. As shown by many criticisms, one cannot find causality in the S—R schema, and it seems more legitimate to consider the response as a "clue" to the stimulus instead of as an effect, and even more so if one admits that the "same" situation from the observer's viewpoint may be experienced differently by two distinct individuals. It would be more profitable to go back from the response (or rather from behavior) to the situation it witnesses and from there to the person.

In the form in which it has been undertaken by means of factorial analysis, the search for personality traits may, without any paradox, be considered as a study of typical situations valid for classes of individuals. In this field, few results are as reliable as those which have led to the description of an introversion—

extraversion factor. What does such a trait mean? Is it a factor that determines responses or behaviors? We would prefer to consider it as a moment in an inventory of situations: where one person chooses to stay at home and another to go to a party; where one enjoys outdoor sports and the other music. When somebody chooses to watch television, moreover, is this introversion or extraversion? It may be assumed that by means of such inventories one grasps types of responses; however, one should instead point out relationships between concrete situations experienced by individuals. One thus contributes to the discovery of generic situations which, being human, are most often social.

Should one say, for instance, that there is an "interaction" between introversion and the situation of going to the pictures if one discovers that "introvert" individuals do not go to see the same films as "extraverts"? Here, we would consider it more interesting to establish a typology of films rather than to evaluate this interaction.

The works of Ekehammar and Magnusson (1973), as well as Endler's (1975) comments appear to advance in this direction, in particular when their aim is an "analysis of situational dimensions" (Magnusson, 1971). When such an author as Endler (1975) states that "not enough attention has been paid to assessing the psychological significance of various types of situations" (in press) we consider him to be to a large extent in agreement with the "situationist" standpoint we have endeavoured to defend, and even more when he adds that "situations do not exist in a vacuum but have psychological meaning for people" (p. 15). Is it not somewhat contradictory however, to deprive situations of such a "significance" only to reinstate it later in the shape of an "interaction" with the person? Should one not rather consider situations significant from the start, in particular when the only knowledge we have of these situations is through verbal expression, and when they are constructed by the subjects through representation?

DESCRIPTION AND COMPARATIVE PSYCHOLOGY

The refinements of analysis authorized by statistical techniques (correlations, partition of variance, "moderator," factorial analysis and automatic classifications[2] must not lead us to forget that the fundamental issues remain those of description.

In psychological research, description is considered an unrewarding task and explanation the noble task par excellence. Up to now, what necessities have we really been able to establish? This eager yearning to explain, which causes so many research workers to rush toward the S–R schema in spite of its recognized

---

[2] The works of Benzecri (1973) constitute a "summa" of the new techniques of factor analysis and automatic classification.

weaknesses, periodically leads to discouraged confession and belated criticisms of the bearing of experiments without previous description.

In particular, it is somewhat illusory to aim at an explanation of behavior — even an interactionist one — while confessing how little one knows about what situations really are. However, it must be said to the credit of interactionists that they remind the narrowest among behaviorists of the fact that situations are not physical beings but events, always related to individuals. It is in no way contemptible to undertake a minute description of them, especially of situations as complex as those that are generally experienced by human beings.

As we have stressed, an accurate knowledge of situations, and their mutual relationships and significance, would tell us much about the persons involved. Such an approach has to be essentially descriptive, classifying and interpretative, that is, comparative. Patterson (1974), after a minute study of interactions between a child and the members of its family, offers a work project that seems valid for many instances: "one begins with field observation, including the collection of systematic data. Suggested functional relations are then subjected to laboratory (or field) manipulations to test the hypotheses originally generated by field data" (Patterson, 1974, p. 910). However, the intermediate stage between observation and experimental intervention, i.e., the analysis of collected data, deserves to be stressed more strongly. One may even assume that if such an analysis is sufficiently accurate, experimental intervention may be unnecessary. Whereas any premature intervention will, in the long run, make it necessary to start the descriptive study all over again. To describe is a difficult task, however, one that is scarcely undertaken because of the problem of finding answers in advance to three questions: what to describe, how to describe, and why describe at all? Here is some very succinct advice.

What To Describe.

Any psychological research implies a comparison between the observer's and the subject's viewpoints. This comparison is made through the situation the subject's behavior manifests to the observer. It is in this way — because of the necessities of biological adjustment or the usual arrangement of social contingencies — that many situations are common to different animal species or to human beings among themselves, and in particular to observers and subjects. Therefore, any investigator has a previous knowledge of situations, and the aim of the investigation is to specify or to improve this knowledge, which, in the field of observation and investigation, is the equivalent of hypotheses in the experimental field.

How to Describe.

The concrete situations presented for observation by behavior are dependent on the repertory of actions of the species or individuals under study. One of the major tasks of description, therefore, is to list these repertories. McGrew (1972) offers an inventory of actions in the preschool child, inspired by similar studies on nonhuman primates. Such inventories should lead to groups of activities correlated within functional systems (play, aggression, fear, etc.) and then to description of typical situations.

Such a description is comparative, insofar as it is functional and interpretative. Conducts are segmented into units of identical value (functional viewpoint), the value being characterized by the consequences of each elementary conduct. The conducts belonging to a same functional set have the same value, in the sense that they have the same consequences. The significance of these conducts (interpretative viewpoint) is given by the determination of the situations that are their context and by means of which they acquire a psychological content in the eyes of the observer.

Research inspired by animal ethology or neobehaviorist analysis of interactions in home or social environment are instances of functional and interpretative descriptions. With the study of subjects endowed with speech new issues appear, but also new means. Here is the realm of content analysis. We shall mention the existence of new procedures of description and interpretation, generated by Propp's (1928) analysis of fairy tales. These have been described by the French mathematician Regnier (1974). We have here, as in the ethological and neobehavioristic trends, a method of functional description: each unit in the text is classified and interpreted according to its context, and in particular to the next unit.

Why Describe?

In the different instances we have just mentioned, description consists of several processes: one has to determine units of analysis, to classify, and to interpret. The remarkable thing is that in spite of the enormous variety of the fields to which they may be applied, description methods still have common properties. They are all comparative, insofar as they search for both common and different characters among units of conduct or speech. Moreover, they all have the same aim: the inventory of typical situations constituting the *Umwelt* or significant universe of individuals or species.

The study of situations, using techniques of comparative description, should as such be inserted into the frame of a general psychology which itself is necessarily genetic and comparative.

First of all, we see how developmental psychology is wholly comparative because of its object: the child, during its development, passes through every field of psychology. First he or she is an animal, not knowing anything about her- or himself, a vegetative being not even making her- or himself or known by whole behaviors, but merely by elementary responses. To a certain extent, this could legitimate the S–R viewpoint. Still, one has to view these responses as outlines of behaviors due to appear in the later development of the child.

Child psychologists have to be incessantly in search of the elementary conducts observed in the animal, hoping to find a homologue in the infant. They must also make use of data collected in societies different from the one to which they belong and of documents concerning the history of their own culture. Specifically, if they are interested in the child's representations of the world and the children themselves, they have to confront the results with what people of other cultures or periods have thought about the world and themselves. They therefore must be conscious of the diversity of cultural contexts of development as well as of its biological necessities. They must compare their own observations of development with what has been described in other animal species as well as in other cultures.

This is why they expect the different fields of psychology to yield a unity of view, in which their own field is restricted. This unity of view does not imply a unity of methods: they are not going to give a minute study of what the child says on the plea that animals do not talk. They will be particularly interested, however, in the study of the animal, in the knowledge they may gain about vital situations in which the animal is involved: some situations in which the animal is involved are common to concrete or imaginary situations experienced by the child.

The necessity of comparison in developmental psychology has been recognized and stressed by some of the great masters in this field. The issue is often mentioned in the works of Piaget (1926), Wallon (1942), and Werner (1948). More recently, Bowlby (1969, 1973) has studied early development by comparing attachment and reactions to separation in the animal and the child. Starting from the works of Wallon and Bowlby, we have attempted to show how the symbolical expression of anxiety in the child can be analyzed and interpreted according to the acquired knowledge of its biological origins (Zlotowicz, 1974).

Personality psychology has set as its ultimate aim to determine what it is that singularizes each individual in his or her acts and appearances. We have suggested that such a determination calls for knowledge of the situations that are common to different individuals. In the case of adults, such knowledge may have the benefit of privileged means, such as interview and questionnaire, which enable one to list very complex and subtle inventories. Imaginary or represented situations may then be compared to those revealed by the study of behavior in adult, animal, or child.

Description and interpretation of situations is at least an objective that may be credited with being common to the different fields of psychology, even if within each of these it uses different techniques. Let us add that the disciplines more particularly concerned with humans, such as history, sociology, or anthropology, also deal with situations.

The explanation of human nature, which is the aim of psychologists, including those who specialize in the study of animals, undoubtedly requires knowledge of our biological nature. However, it also belongs to the series of "humanities" and requires the study of the specific situations the natures of which are historical, social, and cultural.

29
The Problem of Construal Styles in the Analysis of Person— Situation Interactions

Stephen L. Golding

University of Illinois
  Urbana-Champaign

As the nature of this volume clearly indicates, most theoreticians and researchers in the clinical—personality—social domain of psychology stress, to varying degrees, the importance of understanding person—situation interactions. This consensus breaks down, however, as soon as one moves to a more concrete level and begins to examine the meaning various theorists give to the term "interaction" and how they suppose that these interactions operate (Alker, 1975; Bowers, 1973; Ekehammar, 1974; Golding, 1975a, b, 1976; Olweus, Chapter 17; Mischel, 1973a). In my own work on the assessment and conceptualization of interpersonal behavior (Golding, 1975b; Golding & Knudson, 1975; Knudson & Golding, 1974) I have found that the lack of an adequate conceptualization of the "situation" component of person—situation interactions is perhaps the most troublesome aspect of this problem. In the brief space allowable in this volume, I will attempt to present an adumbrated outline of the nature and scope of this problem, and indicate the kinds of data that are supportive of the arguments presented. Readers wishing to pursue the arguments presented here in greater depth should consult Golding (1975b, c; 1976).

As is evident from a variety of sources (e.g., Magnusson, 1974b; Mischel, 1973a; Moos, 1974), there is an increased concern with the assessment of "situations." The basic problem in carrying out such an assessment program, however, has been a lack of attention to what is supposed to be meant by the term "situation." At the crudest level, investigators have assumed that different experimental manipulations, different time frames, or different behavioral contexts define different situations, and have then searched for, discovered, and proceeded to interpret the "meaning" of statistically significant person—

situation interaction terms. That this approach is conceptually and methodologically insufficient has been demonstrated by a variety of critics (Alker, 1975; Bowers, 1973; Golding, 1975a; Mischel, 1973a; Olweus, Chapter 17). The alternative approach, based conceptually on earlier work by Henry Murray, has been to measure the consensual environmental perceptions of a group of subjects. However, close inspection of the data that follow this approach (e.g., Moos, 1968) suggests the existence of strong individual differences (Alden-Wiggins, 1975; Ellsworth & Maroney, 1972; Golding, 1975a, b). For example, one discovers that approximately 25% of a typical environment perception scale's variance is attributable to between-environment differences, whereas approximately 75% is attributable to within-environment (i.e., individual) differences; moreover, environment perception scores are moderately related to a variety of personological and demographic characteristics (Alden-Wiggins, 1975; Ellsworth & Maroney, 1972). Given these data, it may be relatively meaningful to speak of *consensual* beta press, but it is surely just as meaningful to speak of *individual differences* in beta press.

The problem of unraveling and interpreting person–situation interactions therefore becomes one of estimating the extent to which such interactions are functionally related to individual differences in "situational perception." If one may make the reasonable assumption that interpersonal behavior in a given interaction is highly contingent on the individual's definition of the situation (or construal of the interpersonal field), then we need to direct our attention to the perception of interpersonal events, with particular reference to individual differences in the manner in which these events are construed. This emphasis owes considerable intellectual debt to much prior research and theorizing in psychology (Bowers, 1973; Kelly, 1955; Lewin, 1935; Raush, 1965, 1972; Sullivan, 1953), but we must now examine this issue far more throughly than has been done in the past (Golding, 1975c). More specifically we must investigate (a) the extent and magnitude of such individual differences in construal style, (b) the personological and social behavioral concommitants of such styles, (c) the temporal and contextual consistency of such styles, (d) the processes by which such styles are acquired and can be modified, and (e) how such styles link up with other psychological processes to influence overt behavior within and across situations of varying types.

Some illustrative data that bear on issues (a) and (b) can provide an empirical framework for subsequent discussion. A group of undergraduate subjects, predominently male, were asked to make attributional judgments of the interpersonal characteristics of same-age peers on the basis of brief descriptions of various interpersonal interactions. Twenty-nine brief descriptions (vignettes) that spanned the commonly reported two-dimensional (affiliation–disaffiliation; dominance–submission) circumplicial domain of interpersonal behavior were constructed on the basis of prior research (Golding & Knudson, 1975; Knudson & Golding, 1974). Each vignette described a brief interpersonal interaction in behaviorally specific terms. The undergraduate subjects were asked to make attributional judgments of the "responder" on eight semantic differential-like scales: dominant–submissive, sociable–unsociable, cooperative–uncooperative, friendly–hostile, honest–dishonest, frank–secretive, calm–anxious, and good natured–irritable. Additionally, the subjects completed a variety of self-report measures including scales from the Interpersonal Checklist (LaForge & Suczek, 1955), the Personality Research Form (Jackson, 1967), and the Machiavellianism scale (in Robinson & Shaver, 1970). The data (for each subject: eight attributional judgments for each of the 29 vignettes) were analyzed by means of Tucker and Messick's (1963) "points of view" technique in order to identify consistent individual viewpoints about stimulus (vignette–scale combinations) differences. Seven unrotated viewpoints (subject dimensions) were identified and reoriented using correlations between the unrotated dimensions and the personality measures as rotational criteria. In this manner, one can interpret various positions in the rotated viewpoint space in terms of outside correlates.

The most essential data from this study are presented in Tables 29.1 and 29.2. Table 29.1 presents the correlations between subjects' projections on four of the

TABLE 29.1
Correlations between Subject Projections on Rotated
Viewpoint Dimensions and Mean Scale Usage

Mean scale usage	Rotated viewpoint dimensions[a]			
	III[b]	IV[c]	V[d]	VII[e]
Dominance	−10	32	−32	35
Sociability	−18	23	−44	36
Cooperativeness	−09	26	−46	35
Friendliness	−08	30	−60	50
Honesty	−04	40	−64	50
Calmness	20	12	−61	51
Good Naturedness	−11	29	−57	44
Frankness	−20	23	−36	40

[a]Decimal points omitted. Correlations greater than or equal to an absolute value of .18 are significant, $p < .05$, two tailed. Rotated Viewpoint Dimensions I, II, and VI are omitted because of their high similarity to Dimensions VII, V, and III, respectively.

[b]Viewpoint III is associated with a PRF factor of desirable dominance, $r = .35$

[c]Viewpoint IV is associated with a PRF factor of cognitive structure, $r = .40$

[d]Viewpoint V is associated with Machiavellianism, $r = .34$

[e]Viewpoint VII is associated with a PRF factor of affiliativeness and/or ICL scales of affiliativeness, $r = .37$.

TABLE 29.2

Idealized Ratings for Selected Conceptual Individuals and Vignettes

Response type[a]	Vignette[b] number	Scale	Conceptual individuals				Consensual individual[c]
			III	IV	V	VII	
FD	16	DOM	1.90	2.31	2.09	1.61	1.50
		FRIEND	2.23	2.43	1.43	2.28	2.28
F	7	DOM	0.16	0.46	−1.74	−1.33	−0.74
		FRIEND	1.87	1.92	1.58	2.42	1.90
FS	6	DOM	0.65	−1.23	−3.00[d]	−0.83	−1.11
		FRIEND	2.39	1.59	0.99	3.00[d]	2.09
S	10	DOM	−2.29	−1.93	−2.42	−2.54	−2.46
		FRIEND	0.81	1.71	0.61	3.00[d]	0.85
HS	26	DOM	−1.64	−1.21	−2.48	−0.76	−0.54
		FRIEND	−1.03	0.50	−0.94	−0.12	−0.33
H	18	DOM	0.39	1.08	0.54	1.96	0.73
		FRIEND	−2.24	−1.70	−2.56	−2.17	−1.67
HD	3	DOM	0.63	1.26	0.56	2.55	1.61
		FRIEND	−2.39	−1.13	−1.31	−2.34	−1.71
D	1	DOM	0.78	1.25	1.28	1.28	1.14
		FRIEND	−0.64	1.31	−2.35	−0.33	0.04

[a]Refers to the perceived friendliness (F), hostility (H), dominance (D), or submissiveness (S) of responder based on a multidimensional scaling of vignettes (see Golding, 1975b).

[b]See Golding (1975b) for complete vignette descriptions.

[c]Values calculated as actual scale means across 123 real individuals.

[d]Idealized ratings for these values exceeded the original +3 to −3 scale. Of the 1,624 idealized ratings fewer than 2% exceeded the original scale bounds, typically by small magnitudes.

rotated viewpoint dimensions and their mean use of the eight attributional scales. Because each subject's mean on each scale is calculated as an average across 29 rather different vignettes, these values can best be interpreted as reflecting a *generalized* attributional tendency. The most immediate and obvious contrast is between viewpoint Dimensions VII and V. Subject projections on Dimension VII (associated with self-reported affiliativeness) correlate positively, and quite substantially, with the desirable pole of all attributional scales. Contrast this with the data for viewpoint Dimension V (associated with self-reported hostility and a Machiavellian world view). Here the generalized attributional tendency is toward seeing others as unfriendly, dishonest, hostile, and so forth. The discrepancy between the generalized world view of these opposing interpersonal viewpoints is quite pronounced. One can reasonably infer that the phenomenological experience of individuals who are differentiable along the personality dimensions related to these viewpoints are rather different. The point to remember, however, is that both types of individuals are reacting to the same given set of interpersonal situations.

The patterns of construal style associated with the rotated viewpoints can be examined in reference to particular "modal" types of interpersonal situations by means of the data presented in Table 29.2.

Table 29.2 presents the idealized ratings[1] associated with Conceptual Individuals III, IV, V, and VII, as well as the "Consensual Individual's" (see Footnote c, Table 2) ratings on the primary attributional scales of dominance—submission and friendliness—hostility for eight vignettes that span the interpersonal circle. With respect to attributions of dominance—submission, Conceptual Individual VII (associated with self-reported affiliativeness) shows a rather clear pattern, being in general agreement with the Consensual Individual, except for vignettes involving hostility and hostile dominance, in which case he attributes considerably more dominance. Conceptual Individual VII also tends to show a pattern of "overattributing" friendliness in friendly vignettes and hostility in hostile vignettes. Conceptual Individual III (associated with desirable or friendly dominance) attributes friendliness at levels in general agreement with the Consensual Individual for friendly interpersonal responses but tends to overestimate hostility for hostile responses. With respect to attributions of dominance—submission, Conceptual Individual III generally attributes more dominance to friendly responses and less dominance to hostile responses than does the Consensual Individual. Conceptual Individual V (associated with self-reported hostility and a Machiavellian world view) displays a generalized tendency to overattribute hostility or to underattribute friendliness for most vignettes. With some exceptions, there is also a general tendency to overattribute submissiveness or to underattribute dominance. Conceptual Individual IV (associated with self-reported "cognitive structure") does not appear to present any clearly interpretable pattern.

The major purpose of this study was to examine interpersonal attributions as a function of individual differences. In order to begin to unravel the basis of so-called person by situation interactions, it was argued that such interactions might occur because individuals reacting to putatively the same objective interpersonal situation construed the meaingfulness of situations differently and hence responded differently as a function of their style of construing. The results of this exploratory study of individual differences in interpersonal construal style can be summarized by means of four general conclusions. First, there do appear to be individual differences in construal style that are moderately related to the various personological measures used in this study. Second, if one

---

[1] These idealized ratings are calculated by mathematically estimating the ratings that would be given by a "conceptual" individual whose projection on the particular viewpoint dimension in question fell +3 standard deviations from the mean of all real subjects' projections. See Tucker and Messick (1963) for details.

broadly characterizes these construal styles in terms of the degree of affiliative-ness versus hostility implied by the personological measures with which they are associated, then one can conclude that individuals who describe themselves as affiliative tend to have a generalized positive attributional set toward others, whereas individuals who describe themselves as aggressive, hostile, or suspicious tend to have a generalized negative attributional set. Third, individuals who are strongly associated with particular construal styles tend to show differential usage of the primary interpersonal dimensions of dominance—submission and affiliation—hostility in their judgments of perceived similarity—dissimilarity be-tween various interpersonal responses occurring in reference to a variety of interpersonal stimuli.[2] In particular, whereas the Consensual Individual tends to weight differences in the affiliation—hostility of responses as more important than differences in dominance—submission, conceptual individuals associated with personologically meaningful construal styles weight these dimensions in a different fashion. For example, individuals who see the world as manipulative and hostile tend to use the dominance—submission dimension far more than the affiliation—hostility dimension; individuals who describe themselves primarily in affiliative terms tend to use these dimensions much in the same fashion as the consensual individual. Fourth, at the level of attributions with respect to individual vignettes, the results are suggestive of patterns as a function of both construal style and type of interpersonal response being construed. For example, whereas "affiliative" individuals tend to overattribute dominance to hostile responses, "friendly dominant" individuals see these same responses as more submissive (even more so than the Consensual Individual); moreover, whereas both "affiliative" and "friendly dominant" individuals tend to attribute more hostility to hostile responses than the Consensual Individual, they differ with respect to their attributions of friendliness to friendly responses.

Most current statements about the influence of situations on human behavior treat situations as psychological forces the existence of which is fundamentally independent of persons. The data from this study imply, however, that situa-tional forces may reside primarily within the individual. These data have impor-tant implications for our study of person by situation interactions. To the extent that situations exist as perceived, the phrase "the situation," implying a consen-sual ontological status across actors, is essentially meaningless. If person by situation interactions exist in our data as a function of the nonequivalence of situational perception across subjects (Bem & Allen, 1974; Bowers, 1973) and, furthermore, if subjects can be shown to be relatively consistent in their construal styles, then we will have come a long way toward understanding the nature of human behavior in context and building empirically based theories of such behavior. Somewhat paradoxically, our concern with the situational deter-

---

[2] This conclusion is based on a multidimensional scaling analysis reported in detail in Golding (1975b).

minants of human behavior may turn out to highlight the active role that individuals assume in creating the situations to which they believe themselves to be the responder. Although this conclusion may hardly be surprising to a sophisticated, interpersonally oriented theorist or clinician, it is necessary to provide additional constructive replications of the type of data uncovered in this study if such as assumption is to hold a central position in an empirically based psychology of interpersonal behavior.

References

Alden-Wiggins, L. Psychiatric ward atmosphere and patient behavior change. Unpublished doctoral dissertation, University of Illinois, Urbana-Champaign, June, 1975.

Alker, H. A. Is personality situationally specific or intrapsychically consistent? *Journal of Personality,* 1972, **40,** 1–16.

Alker, H. A. The incommensurability of humanistic and behavioristic approaches to personality change. In Wandersman, A., Poppen, P., & Ricks, D. (Eds.), *Humanistic and behavioristic approaches to personality change: A confrontation and a synthesis.* New York: Pergamon Press, 1976.

Alker, H. A., & Owen, D. Behavioral sampling vs. traditional assessment: the vanishing winner's circle. Unpublished manuscript, 1975.

Alker, H. A., Straub, W. F., & Leary, J. Achieving consistency: The psychology of basketball officiating. *Journal of Vocational Behavior,* 1973, **3,** 335–343.

Allport, G. W. *Personality: A psychological interpretation.* New York: Holt, Rinehart & Winston, 1937.

Allport, G. W. Traits revisited. *American Psychologist,* 1966, **21,** 1–10.

Allport, G. W., & Vernon, P. E. *Studies of expressive movements.* New York: Macmillan, 1933.

Alston, W. P. Dispositions and occurences. *Canadian Journal of Philosophy,* 1971, **1**(2), 125–155.

Anastasi, A. Heredity, environment and the question "How?". *Psychological Review,* 1958, **65,** 197–208.

Angyal, A. *Foundations for a Science of Personality.* Cambridge, Mass.: Harvard University Press, 1941.

Argyle, M. *Social interaction.* London: Methuen, New York: Aldine-Atherton, 1969.

Argyle, M. *Bodily communication.* London: Methuen, New York: International Universities Press, 1975.

Argyle, M., Bryant, B., & Trower, P. Social skills training and psychotherapy. *Psychological Medicine,* 1974, **4,** 435–443.

Argyle, M., & Cook, M. *Gaze and mutual gaze.* Cambridge, England: Cambridge University Press, 1976.

Argyle, M., & Kendon, A. The experimental analysis of social performance. *Advances in Experimental Social Psychology,* 1967, **3,** 55–98.

Argyle, M., & Little, B. R. Do personality traits apply to social behavior? *Journal for the Theory of Social Behavior,* 1972, **2,** 1–35.

Argyle, M., Trower, P., & Bryant, B. Explorations in the treatment of personality disorders and neuroses by social skills training. *British Journal of Medical Psychology,* 1974, **47,** 63–72.

Aronoff, J. *Psychological needs and cultural systems.* Princeton, N.J.: Van Nostrand, 1967.

Asch, S. E. Studies of independence and conformity: I. A minority of one against a unanimous majority. *Psychological Monographs,* 1956, **70,** Whole No. 416.

Ashton, H., Millman, J. E., Telford, R., & Thompson, J. W. The effect of coffeine, nitrazepam and cigarette smoking on the contingent negative variation in man. *Electroencephalography and Clinical Neurophysiology,* 1974, **37,** 59–71.

Ashton, H., Watson, D. W., & Sadler, J. Puffing frequency and nicotine intake in cigarette smokers. *British Medical Journal,* 1970, 679–681.

Auerbach, S. M. Trait–state anxiety and adjustment to surgery. *Journal of Consulting and Clinical Psychology,* 1973, **40,** 264–271.

Averill, J. R. Personal control over aversive stimuli and its relationship to stress. *Psychological Bulletin,* 1973, **80,** 286–303. (a)

Averill, J. R. The dis-position of psychological dispositions. *Journal of Experimental Research in Personality,* 1973, **6,** 275–282. (b)

Averill, J. R., Olbrich, E., & Lazarus, R. S. Personality correlates of differential responsiveness to direct and vicarious threat: A failure to replicate previous findings. *Journal of Personality and Social Psychology,* 1972, **21,** 25–29.

Azrin, N. H., Naster, B. J., & Jones, R. Reciprocity counseling. *Behavior Research and Therapy,* 1973, **11,** 365–382.

Bailey, K. D. Cluster analysis. In D. R. Heise (Ed.), *Sociological methodology.* San Francisco: Jossey-Bass, 1975.

Bales, P. F. *Interaction process analysis.* Cambridge, Mass.: Addison-Wesley, 1951.

Bandura, A. *Principles of behavior modification.* New York: Holt, Rinehart, & Winston, 1969.

Bandura, A. Analysis of modeling processes. In A. Bandura (Ed.), *Psychological modeling: Conflicting theories.* Chicago: Aldine-Atherton, 1971. (a)

Bandura, A. *Social learning theory.* Morristown, N.J.: General Learning Press, 1971 (b).

Bandura, A., Blanchard, E. B., & Ritter, B. Relative efficacy of desensitization and modeling approaches for inducing behavioral, affective, and attitudinal changes. *Journal of Personality and Social Psychology,* 1969, **13,** 173–199.

Bandura, A., & McDonald, F. J. The influence of social reinforcement and the behavior of models in shaping children's moral judgments. *Journal of Abnormal and Social Psychology,* 1963, **67,** 274–281.

Bandura, A., & Walters, R. H. *Social learning and personality development.* New York: Holt, Rinehart & Winston, 1963.

Bannister, D., & Salmon, P. Schizophrenic thought disorder: Specific or diffuse? *British Journal of Medical Psychology,* 1966, **39,** 215–219.

Barker, R. G. Explorations in ecological psychology. *American Psychologist,* 1965, **20,** 1–14.

Barker, R. G. *Ecological psychology.* Stanford: Stanford University Press, 1968.

Barratt, E. S. Anxiety and impulsiveness. In C. D. Spielberger (Ed.), *Anxiety. Current trends in theory and research.* New York: Academic Press, 1972.

Barrett-Lennard, G. T. Dimensions of therapist response as causal factors in therapeutic change. *Psychological Monographs,* 1962, **76**(43), Whole No. 562.

Bateson, G. *Steps to an ecology of mind.* New York: Ballentine Books, 1972.

Bateson, G., & Jackson, D. D. Some varieties of pathogenic organization. In D. McK. Rioch & E. A. Weinstein (Eds.), *Disorders of communication.* Baltimore, Md.: Williams & Williams, 1964.

Bell, R. Q. Contributions of human infants to caregiving and social interaction. In M. Lewis & L. Rosenblum (Eds.), *The effect of the infant in its caregiver.* New York: John Wiley, 1974.

Bem, D. J. Constructing cross-situational consistencies in behavior: Some thoughts on Alker's critique of Mischel. *Journal of Personality,* 1972, **40**, 17–26.

Bem, D., & Allen, A. On predicting some of the people some of the time: the search for cross-situational consistencies in behavior. *Psychological Review,* 1974, **81**, 506–520.

Benedict, R. *The Chrysanthemum and the sword.* Boston: Houghton-Mifflin, 1946.

Benzecri, J. P. *L'analyse des données.* Paris: Dunod, 1973.

Berkowitz, L. Some aspects of observed aggression. *Journal of Personality and Social Psychology,* 1965, **2**, 359–369.

Berkowitz, L. Words and symbols as stimuli to aggressive responses. In J. F. Knutson (Ed.), *Control of aggression: Implications from basic research.* Chicago: Aldine-Atherton, 1973.

Berkowitz, L. Some determinants of impulsive aggression: Role of mediated associations with reinforcements for aggression. *Psychological Review,* 1974, **81**, 165–176.

Berkowitz, L., & Alioto, J. T. The meaning of an observed event as a determinant of its aggressive consequences. *Journal of Personality and Social Psychology,* 1973, **28**, 206–217.

Berkowitz, L., & LePage, A. Weapons as aggressive-eliciting stimuli. *Journal of Personality and Social Psychology,* 1967, **7**, 202–207.

Berkowitz, L., Lepinski, J. P., & Angulo, E. J. Awareness of own anger level and subsequent aggression. *Journal of Personality and Social Psychology,* 1969, **11**, 293–300.

Berkowitz, L., & Turner, C. W. Perceived anger level, instigating agent, and aggression. In H. London & R. E. Nisbett (Eds.), *Thought and feeling: Cognitive alteration of feeling states.* Chicago: Aldine-Atherton, 1973.

Berlyne, D. E. Novelty and curiosity as determinants of exploratory behavior. *British Journal of Psychology,* 1950, **41**, 68–80.

Berlyne, D. E. A theory of human curiosity. *British Journal of Psychology,* 1954, **45**, 180–191.

Berlyne, D. E. *Structure and direction of thinking.* New York: John Wiley, 1965.

Berne, E. *Games people play.* New York: Grove Press, 1964.

Bieri, J., Atkins, A. L., Briar, S., Leaman, R. L., Miller, H., & Tripodi, T. *Clinical and Social judgment: the Discrimination of Behavioral Information.* New York: John Wiley, 1966.

Birdwhistell, R. *Kinesics and context.* Philadelphia, Pa.: University of Pennsylvania Press, London: Allen Lane, the Penguin Press, 1970.

Blalock, H. M. Jr. Simultaneous equations techniques. In H. M. Blalock (Ed.), *Causal models in the social sciences.* Chicago: Aldine-Atherton, 1971.

Block, J. *The Q-sort method in personality assessment and psychiatric research.* Springfield, Ill.: Charles C Thomas, 1961.

Block, J. *The challenge of response sets.* New York: Appleton-Century-Crofts, 1965.

Block, J. Personality measurement. *International Encyclopedia of the Social Sciences,* Vol. 12. New York: Macmillan, 1968. (b)

Block, J. Some reasons for the apparent inconsistency of personality. *Psychological Bulletin,* 1968, **70**, 210–212. (a)

Block, J. *Lives through time.* Berkeley, California: Bancroft Books, 1971.

Block, J., & Bailey, D. *Q-sort item analysis of a number of MMPI scales.* Technical Memorandum OERL-TM-55-7. Officer Education Research Laboratory, Maxwell Air Force Base, Montgomery, Alabama, May 1955.

Block, J., & Gough, H. G. *An application of the Q-sort technique to the California Psychological Inventory.* Technical Memorandum OERL-TM-55-8. Officer Education Research Laboratory, Maxwell, Air Force Base, Montgomery, Alabama, May 1955.

Block, J., & Petersen, P. *Q-sort item analysis of a number of strong Vocational Interest Inventory Scales.* Technical Memorandum OERL-TM-55-9. Officer Education Research Laboratory. Maxwell Air Force Base, Montgomery, Alabama, May 1955.

Block, J. H. Conceptions of sex roles. *American Psychologist,* 1973, **28,** 512–526.

Block, J. H., & Martin, B. Predicting the behavior of children under frustration. *Journal of Abnormal and Social Psychology,* 1955, **51,** 281–285.

Blurton-Jones, N. G. (Ed.) *Ethological studies of child behavior.* Cambridge, England: Cambridge University Press, 1972.

Blurton-Jones, N. G. Ethology and early socialization. In M. P. M. Richards (Ed.), *The integration of a child into a social world.* Cambridge, England: Cambridge University Press, 1974.

Bons, P. M., & Fiedler, F. E. Change in organizational leadership and the behavior of relationship- and task-motivated leaders. Administrative *Science Quarterly,* September 1976.

Boszormenyi-Nagy, I. A theory of relationships: Experience and transaction. In I. Boszormenyi-Nagy & J. L. Framo (Eds.), *Intensive family therapy: Theoretical and practical aspects.* New York: Harper and Row, 1965.

Bowen, M. Family therapy and family group therapy. In H. I. Kaplan & B. J. Sadock (Eds.), *Comprehensive group psychotherapy.* New York: Williams & Wilkins, 1971.

Bowers, K. S. Situationism in psychology: An analysis and critique. *Psychological Review,* 1973, **80,** 307–336.

Bowers, K. S. The psychology of subtle control: an attributional analysis of behavioral persistence. *Canadian Journal of Behavioral Science,* 1975, **7,** 78–95.

Bowers, K. S. *Hypnosis for the seriously curious.* Monterey, California: Brooks-Cole, 1976.

Bowlby, J. *Attachment and loss.* Vol. I. *Attachment.* London: Hogarth Press, 1969.

Bowlby, J. *Attachment and loss.* Vol. II. *Separation, anxiety and anger.* London: Hogarth Press, 1973.

Brody, N. *Personality.* New York: Academic Press, 1972.

Brouchon, N. Les mouvements expressifs et la personnalité. *L'année psychologique,* 1973, **73,** 311–337.

Bruner, J. S. Going beyond the information given. In H. Gruber *et al.* (Eds.), *Contemporary approaches to cognition.* Cambridge, Mass.: Harvard University Press, 1957.

Bruner, J. S. The organization of early skilled action. In M. P. M. Richards (Ed.), *The integration of a child into a social world.* Cambridge, England: Cambridge University Press, 1974.

Brunswik, E. The conceptual framework of psychology. International Encyclopedia of Unified Science, Vol. 1, No. 10. Chicago: University of Chicago Press, 1950.

Brunswik, E. Representative design and probabilistic theory in functional psychology. *Psychological Review,* 1955, **62,** 193–217.

Brunswik, E. *Perception and the representative design of psychological experiments.* Berkeley: University of California Press, 1956.

Bryant, B., & Trower, P. Social difficulty in a student population. *British Journal of Educational Psychology,* 1974, **44,** 13–21.

Burwen, L. S., & Campbell, D. T. The generality of attitudes toward authority and nonauthority figures. *Journal of Abnormal and Social Psychology,* 1957, **54,** 24–31.

Buss, A. H., Booker, A., & Buss, E. Firing a weapon and aggression. *Journal of Personality and Social Psychology,* 1972, **22,** 296–302.

Butterfield, H. *The origins of modern science.* New York: Free Press, 1957.

Campbell, D. T. Social attitudes and other acquired behavioral dispositions. In S. Koch (Ed.), *Psychology: A study of a science.* Vol. 6. New York: McGraw-Hill, 1963.

Campbell, J., & Chun, K. T. Inter-inventory predictability and content overlap of the 16 PF and the CPI. *Applied Psychological Measurement,* 1976, **1,** in press.

Campbell, D. T., & Fiske, D. W. Convergent and discriminant validation by the multitrait-multimethod matrix. *Psychological Bulletin*, 1959, **56**, 81–105.

Cantor, N., & Mischel, W. Traits as prototypes: effects on recognition memory. *Journal of Personality and Social Psychology*, 1977, in press.

Carlson, R. Where is the person in personality research? *Psychological Bulletin*, 1971, **75**, 203–219.

Carlson, R. Personality. *Annual Review of Psychology*, 1975, **26**, 393–414.

Carment, D. W., Miles, C. S., & Cervin, V. B. Persuasiveness and persuasability as related to intelligence and extraversion. *British Journal of Social and Clinical Psychology*, 1965, **4**, 1–7.

Carson, R. L. *Interaction concepts of personality.* Chicago: Aldine-Atherton, 1969.

Cartwright, D. S. Trait and other sources of variance in the S–R Inventory of Anxiousness. *Journal of Personality and Social Psychology*, 1975, **32**, 408–414.

Cary, M. S. Nonverbal openings to conversation. Paper presented at 45th Annual Convention of the Eastern Psychological Association, April 8, 1974.

Cattell, R. B. *Personality and motivation structure and measurement.* Yonkers-on-Hudson, N.Y.: World Book Company, 1957.

Cattell, R. B. *The Scientific Analysis of Personality.* Chicago: Aldine-Atherton, 1965.

Cattell, R. B. *Handbook of multivariate experimental psychology.* Chicago: Rand McNally, 1966.

Cattell, R. B. *Personality and mood by questionnaire.* San Francisco: Jossey-Bass, 1973.

Cattell, R. B., & Scheier, I. H. *The meaning and measurement of neuroticism and anxiety.* Ronald Press, New York, 1961.

Chein, I. *The science of behavior and the image of man.* London: Tavistock, 1972.

Chemers, M. M. Cultural training as a means of improving situational favorableness. *Human Relations*, 1969, **22**, 531–546.

Chemers, M. M., & Skrzypek, G. J. An experimental test of the contingency model of leadership effectiveness. *Journal of Personality and Social Psychology*, 1972, **24**, 172–177.

Chomsky, H. *Syntactic structures.* S' Gravenhage, Netherlands: Mouton, 1957.

Chown, S. Rigidity: A flexible concept. *Psychological Bulletin*, 1959, **56**, 195–223.

Clarke, D. The use and recognition of sequential structure in dialogue. *British Journal of Social and Clinical Psychology*, 1975, **14**, 333–339.

Clevenger, T., Motley, M., & Carlile, L. Changes in heart rate during classroom public speaking. Unpublished manuscript, University of Texas, 1967.

Cohen, J. The statistical power of abnormal-social psychological research: A review. *Journal of Abnormal and Social Psychology*, 1962, **65**, 145–153.

Cohen, J. *Statistical power analysis for the behavioral sciences.* New York: Academic Press, 1969.

Cohen, R. *Patterns of personality judgment.* New York: Academic Press, 1973.

Coie, J. An evaluation of the cross-situational stability of children's curiosity. *Journal of Personality*, 1974, **42**, 93–116.

Collett, P. On training Englishmen in the non-verbal behavior of Arabs: an experiment in intercultural communication. *International Journal of Psychology*, 1971, **6**, 209–215.

Cook, M. *Interpersonal perception.* Harmondsworth, Middlesex: Penguin, 1971.

Craik, K. H. Personality unvanquished. *Contemporary Psychology*, 1969, **14**, 147–148.

Cronbach, L. J. Processes affecting scores on "understanding of others" and "assumed similarity." *Psychological Bulletin*, 1955, **52**, 177–193.

Cronbach, L. J. Assessment of individual differences. *Annual Review of Psychology*, 1956, **7**, 173–196.

Cronbach, L. J. The two disciplines of scientific psychology. *American Psychologist*, 1957, **12**, 671–684.

Cronbach, L. J. Beyond the two disciplines of scientific psychology. *American Psychologist,* 1975, **30**, 116–127.

Cronbach, L. J., Gleser, G. C., Nanda, H., & Rajaratnam, N. *The dependability of behavioral measurements: Theory of generalizability for scores and profiles.* New York: John Wiley, 1972.

Cronbach, L. J., & Meehl, P. E. Construct validation in psychological tests. *Psychological Bulletin,* 1955, **52**, 281–302.

Cronbach, L. J., & Snow, R. E. *Aptitudes and instructional methods.* New York: Irvington, in press.

Crowne, D. P., & Marlowe, D. J. *The approval motive.* New York: John Wiley, 1964.

Csikszentmihalyi, M., & Getzels, J. W. Discovery-oriented behavior and the originality of creative products: A study of artists. *Journal of Personality and Social Psychology,* 1971, **19**, 47–52.

Dahl, H. A quantitative study of a psychoanalysis. In R. R. Holt & E. Peterfruend (Eds.), *Psychoanalysis and contemporary science.* Vol. 1. New York: Macmillan, 1972.

D'Andrade, R. G. Cognitive structures and judgment. Paper presented for T.O.B. R. E. Research Workshop on Cognitive organization and psychological processes. Huntington Beach, Calif., August 16–21, 1970.

D'Andrade, R. G. Memory and the assessment of behavior. Unpublished manuscript, University of California at San Diego, Department of Anthropology, 1973.

Davis, D. R. *Pilot error.* London: Her Majesty's Stationery Office, 1948.

Davison, G. B., & Valins, S. Maintainance of self-attributed and drugattributed behavior change. *Journal of Personality and Social Psychology,* 1969, **11**, 25–33.

Davison, G., & Wilson, G. T. Processes of fear-reduction in systematic desensitization: Cognitive and social reinforcement factors in humans. *Behavior Therapy,* 1973, **4**, 1–21.

Davitz, J. R. *The communication of emotional meaning.* New York: McGraw-Hill, 1964.

de Bonis, M. Etude de l'anxiété par la méthode des questionnaires. II. Travaux expérimentaux. *Revue de Psychologie Appliquée,* 1973, **23**, 105–131.

de Bonis, M. Content analysis of 37 anxiety inventories and rating scales. In P. Pichot (Ed.), *Psychological measurement in psychopharmacology: Modern problems in pharmacopsychiatry,* Vol. 7. Basel: Kargel, 1974. (a)

de Bonis, M. Evaluations subjectives et résponses psychologiques dans une situation de stress. *L'année Psychologique,* 1974, **74**, 473–486. (b)

de Bonis, M. Verbal versus somatic modes of response in experimental stressful situations and sex differences in anxiety-trait. Paper presented at the Symposium on Interactional Psychology, Stockholm, Sweden, June 1975.

de Charms, R. *Personal Causation.* New York: Academic Press, 1968.

Deci, E. L. *Intrinsic motivation.* New York: Plenum, 1975.

Dittmann, A. T., & Raush, H. L. The psychoanalytic theory of conflict: Structure and methodology. *Psychological Review,* 1954, **61**, 386–400.

Dollard, J., & Miller, N. E. *Personality and psychotherapy.* New York: McGraw-Hill, 1950.

Duncan, S. Some signals and rules for taking speaking turns in conversations. *Journal of Personality and Social Psychology,* 1972, **23**, 283–292.

Duncan, S. On the structure of speaker-auditor interaction during speaking turns. *Language in Society,* 1974, **2**, 161–180.

Duncan, S., & Fiske, D. W. Face-to-face interaction: Research, methods, and theory. Hillsdale, N.J.: Lawrence Erlbaum Associates, 1976.

Duncan, S., & Niederehe, G. On signaling that it is your turn to speak. *Journal of Experimental Social Psychology,* 1974, **10**, 234–257.

Eaves, L., & Eysenck, H. The nature of extraversion: A genetical analysis. *Journal of Personality and Social Psychology,* 1975, **32**, 102–112.

Eddy, G. E., & Sinnett, R. E. Behavior setting utilization by emotionally disturbed college students. *Journal of Consulting and Clinical Psychology,* 1973, **40,** 210–216.

Ekehammar, B. *Sex differences in self reported anxiety for different situations and modes of responses.* Report from the Psychological Laboratories, the University of Stockholm, 1972, No. 363.

Ekehammar, B., & Magnusson, D. A method to study stressful situations. *Journal of Personality and Social Psychology,* 1973, **27,** 176–179.

Ekehammar, B., Magnusson, D., & Ricklander, L. An interactionist approach to the study of anxiety. *Scandinavian Journal of Psychology,* 1974, **15,** 4–14.

Ekehammar, B., Schalling, D., & Magnusson, D. Dimensions of stressful situations: A comparison between a response analytical and a stimulus analytical approach. *Multivariate Behavioral Research,* 1975, **10,** 155–164.

Ekman, P., & Friesen, W. V. The repertoire of nonverbal behavior: categories, origins, usage, and coding. *Semiotica,* 1969, **3,** 49–98.

Ekman, P., Friesen, W. V., & Ellsworth, P. *Emotion in the human face.* New York: Pergamon Press, 1972.

Elliott, D. S., & Voss, H. L. *Delinquency and dropout.* Lexington, Mass.: D. C. Heath, 1974.

Ellsworth, R. B., Foster, L., Childers, B., Gilberg, A., & Kroeker, D. Hospital and community adjustment as perceived by psychiatric patients, their families, and staff. *Journal of Consulting and Clinical Psychology.* Monograph Supplement, Vol. 32, No. 5, 1968, 1–41.

Ellsworth, R., & Maroney, R. Characteristics of psychiatric wards and their effects on patient's adjustment. *Journal of Consulting and Clinical Psychology,* 1972, **39,** 436–447.

Endler, N. S. Estimating variance components from mean squares from random and mixed effects analysis of variance models. *Perceptual and Motor Skills,* 1966, **22,** 559–570.

Endler, N. S. The person versus the situation – a pseudo issue? A response to Alker. *Journal of Personality,* 1973, **41,** 287–303.

Endler, N. S. A person–situation interaction model for anxiety. In C. D. Spielberger & J. G. Sarason (Eds.), *Stress and anxiety.* Vol. 1. Washington, D.C.: Hemisphere Publ., 1975. (a)

Endler, N. S. The case for person-situation interactions. *Canadian Psychological Review,* 1975, **16,** 12–21. (b)

Endler, N. S. The role of person by situation interactions in personality theory. In F. Weizmann & I. C. Uzgiris (Eds.), *The structuring of experience.* New York: Plenum Press, 1976.

Endler, N. S., & Hunt, J. McV. Sources of behavioral variance as measured by the S-R Inventory of Anxiousness. *Psychological Bulletin,* 1966, **65,** 336–346.

Endler, N. S., & Hunt, J. McV. S–R Inventories of hostility and comparisons of the proportions of variance from persons, responses, and situations for hostility and anxiousness. *Journal of Personality and Social Psychology,* 1968, **9,** 309–315.

Endler, N. S., & Hunt, J. McV. Generalizability of contributions from sources of variance in the S–R Inventories of Anxiousness. *Journal of Personality,* 1969, **37,** 1–24.

Endler, N. S., Hunt, J. McV., & Rosenstein, A. J. An S–R Inventory of Anxiousness. *Psychological Monographs,* **76**(17), 1962.

Endler, N. S., & Magnusson, D. *Interactionism, trait psychology, psychodynamics and situationism.* Report from the Psychological Laboratories, the University of Stockholm, 1974, No. 418.

Endler, N. S., & Magnusson, D. *The interactional model of anxiety: An empirical test in an examination situation.* Reports, Department of Psychology, York University, No. 16, 1975.

Endler, N. S., & Magnusson, D. *Interactional psychology and personality.* Washington, D.C.: Hemisphere Publ., 1976.

Endler, N. S., & Magnusson, D. Toward an international psychology of personality. *Psychological Bulletin*, 1976, **83**, 56–974.

Endler, N. S., & Okada, M. A. multidimensional measure of trait anxiety: the S–R inventory of General Trait Anxiousness. *Journal of Consulting and Clinical Psychology*, 1975, **43**, 319–329.

Enke, W. *Die Psychomotorik der Konstitutionstypen*. Leipzig: Barth, 1930.

Epstein, S. The nature of anxiety with emphasis upon its relationship to expectancy. In C. D. Spielberger (Ed.), *Anxiety. Current trends in theory and research*. Vol. II. New York: Academic Press, 1972.

Exline, B. V. Explorations in the process of person perception: visual interaction in relation to competition, sex and need for affiliation. *Journal of Personality*, 1963, **31**, 1–20.

Exline, B. V., & Messick, D. The effects of dependency and social reinforcement upon visual behaviour during an interview. *British Journal of Social and Clinical Psychology*, 1967, **6**, 256–266.

Eysenck, H. J. *The structure of human personality*. London: Methuen, 1952.

Eysenck, H. J. *The biological basis of personality*. Springfield, Ill.: Charles C Thomas, 1967.

Eysenck, H. J. The measurement of emotion: psychological parameters and methods. In L. Levi (Ed.), *Emotions. Their parameters and measurement*. New York: Raven Press, 1975.

Eysenck, H. J., & Eysenck, S. B. G. *Eysenck personality inventory*. San Diego: Educational and Industrial Service, 1964.

Eysenck, H. J., & Eysenck, S. B. G. *Personality structure and measurement*. San Diego: Knapp, 1967.

Fairweather, G. W. *Methods in experimental social innovation*. New York: John Wiley, 1967.

Fairweather, C. W., Sanders, D. H., Cressler, D. L., & Maynard, H. *Community life for the mentally ill*. Chicago: Aldine-Atherton, 1969.

Feather, B., & Rhoads, J. Psychodynamic behavior therapy: I. Theory and rationale. *Archives of General Psychiatry*, 1972, **26**, 496–502. (a)

Feather, B., & Rhoads, J. Psychodynamic behavior in therapy. II. Clinical aspects. *Archives of General Psychiatry*, 1972, **26**, 503–511. (b)

Feldstein, S. Temporal patterns of dialogue. In A. W. Siegman & B. Pope (Eds.), *Studies in dyadic interaction*. Oxford: Pergamon Press, 1972.

Ferster, G. G. Transition from animal laboratory to clinic. *Psychological Records*, 1967, **17**, 145–150.

Feshbach, S. Reality and fantasy in filmed violence. In J. P. Murray, E. A. Rubinstein, & G. A. Comstock (Eds.), *Television and social behavior*. Vol. II. Washington, D.C.: U.S. Government Printing Office, 1972.

Festinger, L., & Carlsmith, J. M. Cognitive consequences of forced compliance. *Journal of Abnormal and Social Psychology*, 1959, **58**, 203–210.

Fiedler, F. E. A contingency model of leadership effectiveness. In L. Berkowitz (Ed.), *Advances in experimental social psychology*. New York: Academic Press, 1964.

Fiedler, F. E. *A theory of leadership effectiveness*. New York: McGraw-Hill, 1967.

Fiedler, F. E. Leadership experience and leader performance — Another hypothesis shot to hell. *Organizational Behavior and Human Performance*, 1970, **5**, 1–14.

Fiedler, F. E. Validation and extension of the contingency model of leadership effectiveness: A review of empirical findings. *Psychological Bulletin*, 1971, **76**, 128–148.

Fiedler, F. E. Personality, motivation systems, and behavior of high and low LPC leaders. *Human Relations*, 1972, **25**, 391–412.

Fiedler, F. E., Chemers, M. M., & Mahar, L. *Improving leadership effectiveness: The leader match concept*. New York: Wiley, 1976.

Fiedler, F. E., Mitchell, T., & Triandis, H. The Cultural Assimilator: an approach to cross-cultural training. *Journal of Applied Psychology*, 1971, **55**, 95–102.

Fishbane, M. Ideology and marriage. Unpublished masters thesis, University of Massachusetts, Amherst, 1974.

Fishbein, M., & Ajzen, I. Attitudes towards objects as predictors of single and multiple behavioral criteria. *Psychological Review,* 1974, **81,** 59–74.

Fiske, D. W. The inherent variability of behavior. In D. Fiske & S. Maddi (Eds.), *Functioning of varied experience.* Homewood, Ill.: Dorsey Press, 1961.

Fiske, D. W. *Measuring the concepts of personality.* Chicago: Aldine-Atherton, 1971.

Fiske, D. W. Can a personality construct be validated empirically? *Psychological Bulletin,* 1973, **80,** 89–92.

Fiske, D. W. The limits for the convential science of personality. *Journal of Personality,* 1974, **42,** 1–11.

Fiske, D. W. Methodological issues in research on psychotherapist. In A. S. Gurman & A. M. Razin (Eds.), *The therapist's contribution to effective psychotherapy: An empirical assessment.* Elmsford, N.Y.: Pergamon Press, in press.

Fiske, D. W., Cartwright, D. S., & Kirtner, W. L. Are psychotherapeutic changes predictable? *Journal of Abnormal and Social Psychology,* 1964, **69,** 418–426.

Fiske, D. W., & Rice, L. Intra-individual response variability. *Psychological Bulletin,* 1955, **52,** 217–250.

Forgas, J. P. The perception of social episodes: Categorical and dimensional representations in two different social mileus. *Journal of Personality and Social Psychology,* 1976, **34,** 199–209.

Fraczek, A. Informational role of situation as a determinant of aggressive behavior. Paper presented at International Conference on Determinants and Origins of Aggressive Behavior, Monte Carlo, 1973.

Fraczek, A., & Macaulay, J. R. Some personality factors in reaction to aggressive stimuli. *Journal of Personality,* 1971, **39,** 163–177.

Frankenhaeuser, M., Myrsten, A. -L., Post, B., & Johansson, G. Behavioral and psychological effects of cigarette smoking in a monotonous situation. *Psychopharmacologia,* 1971, **22,** 1–7.

Frederiksen, N. Toward a taxonomy of situations. *American Psychologist,* 1972, **27,** 114–123.

Frederiksen, N., Jensen, O., Beaton, A. (With a contribution by B. Bloxom) *Prediction of organizational behavior.* Elmsford, N.J.: Pergamon Press, 1972.

Frijda, N. H. Mimik und Pantomimik. In R. Kirchhoff (Ed.), *Handbuch der Psychologie. 5. Bd. Ausdruckspsychologie.* Göttingen: Hogrefe, 1965.

Frith, C. D. Smoking behavior and its relation to the smoker's immediate experience. *British Journal of Social and Clinical Psychology,* 1971, **10,** 73–78.

Frodi, A. The effects of experiences to aggression-eliciting and aggression-inhibiting stimuli and subsequent aggression. *Göteborg Psychological Report,* 1973, **3,** Whole No. 8.

Gadlin, H. Private lives and public order: A critical view of the history of intimate relations in the United States. Paper presented at Conference on Close Relationships, Amherst, Massachusetts, 1974.

Gaito, J. Expected mean squares in analysis of variance techniques. *Psychological Reports,* 1960, **7,** 3–10.

Galle, O. R., Gove, W. R., & McPherson, J. M. Population density and pathology: What are the relations for man? *Science,* 1972, **176,** 23–30.

Garfinkel, H. Trust and stable actions. In O. J. Harvey (Ed.), *Motivation and social interaction.* New York: Ronald Press, 1963.

Geen, R. G., & O'Neal, E. C. Activation of cue-elicited aggression by general arousal. *Journal of Personality and Social Psychology,* 1969, **11,** 289–292.

Geen, R. G., & Stonner, D. Effects of aggressiveness habit strength on behavior in the presence of aggression-related stimuli. *Journal of Personality and Social Psychology,* 1971, **17,** 149–153.

Geer, J. H. The development of a scale to measure fear. *Behaviour Research and Therapy,* 1965, **3**, 45–53.

Geer, J. H., Davison, G. C., & Gatchel, R. I. Reduction of stress in humans through nonveridical perceived control of aversive stimulation. *Journal of Personality and Social Psychology,* 1970, **16**, 731–738.

Getzels, J. W. Creative thinking, problem-solving and instruction. In E. R. Hilgard (Ed.), *Theories of learning and instruction.* (63rd Yearbook of the National Society for the Study of Education.) Part 1. Chicago: University of Chicago Press, 1964.

Ghiselin, M. T. *The triumph of the Darwinian method.* Berkeley, California: University of California Press, 1969.

Gibson, E. J. *Principles of perceptual learning and development.* New York: Appleton-Century-Crofts, 1969.

Gibson, J. J. The concept of the stimulus in psychology. *American Psychologist,* 1960, **15**, 694–703.

Gil, D. G. *Violence against children.* Cambridge, Mass.: Harvard University Press, 1970.

Gilmor, T. M., & Minton, H. L. Internal versus external attribution of task performance as a function of locus of control, initial confidence and success–failure outcome. *Journal of Personality,* 1974, **42**, 159–174.

Glass, D. C., & Singer, J. E. *Urban stress: Experiments on noise and social stressors.* New York: Academic Press, 1972.

Gleser, G. C., Cronbach, L. J., & Rajaratnam, N. Generalizability for scores influenced by multiple sources of variance. *Psychometrica,* 1965, **30**, 395–418.

Glick, I. D., & Haley, J. *Family therapy and research: An annotated bibliography.* New York: Grune & Stratton, 1971.

Goffman, E. *Relations in public.* London: Penguin, 1971.

Goldberg, L. R. Simple models or simple processes. Some research on clinical judgments. *American Psychologist,* 1968, **23**, 483–496.

Goldberg, L. R. The proliferation of personality scales and inventories: A historical analysis. In P. McReynolds (Ed.), *Advances in psychological assessment.* Vol. 2. Palo Alto, California: Science and Behavior Books, 1971.

Goldfried, M. R. Systematic desensitization as training in self-control. *Journal of Consulting and Clinical Psychology,* 1971, **37**, 228–234.

Goldfried, M. R., & Kent, K. N. Traditional versus behavioral personality assessment: A comparison of methodological and theoretical assumptions. *Psychological Bulletin,* 1972, **77**, 409–420.

Golding, S. L. Flies in the ointment: Methodological problems in the analysis of the percentage of variance due to persons and situations. *Psychological Bulletin,* 1975, **82**, 278–288. (a)

Golding, S. L. Individual differences in the construal of interpersonal interactions. Paper presented at the Symposium on Interactional Psychology, Stockholm, Sweden, 1975. (b)

Golding, S. L. Towards a more adequate theory of personality: Psychological organizing principles. Paper presented at Conference on Strategies for Personality Research, University of Chicago, Chicago, Illinois, 1975. (c)

Golding, S. L. Method variance, inadequate constructs, or things that go bump in the night? *Multivariate Behavioral Research,* 1976, in press.

Golding, S. L., & Knudson, R. Multivariable-multimethod convergence in the domain of interpersonal behavior. *Multivariate Behavioral Research,* 1975, **10**, 425–448.

Goldstein, K., & Scheerer, M. Abstract and concrete behavior: An experimental study with special tests. *Psychological Monographs,* 1941, **53**, 1–31.

Goldstein, M. J., Judd, L. L., Rodnick, E. H., Alkire, A. A., & Gould, E. A method for studying social influence and coping patterns within families of disturbed adolescents. *Journal of Nervous and Mental Disease,* 1968, **147**, 233–251.

Gormly, J., & Edelberg, W. Validity in personality trait attribution. *American Psychologist,* 1974, **29**, 189–193.

Gough, H. G. *Manual for the California Psychological Inventory.* Palo Alto, California: Consulting Psychologists' Press, 1957. (Rev. ed., 1964.)

Gough, H. G. Academic achievement in high school as predicted from the California Psychological Inventory. *Journal of Educational Psychology,* 1964, **55**, 174–180.

Gouch, H. G. College attendance among high aptitude students as predicted from the California Psychological Inventory. *Journal of Counseling Psychology,* 1968, **15**, 174–180.

Gough, H. G. Personality assessment in the study of population. In J. T. Fawcett (Ed.), *Psychological perspectives in population.* New York: Basic Books, 1973.

Gray, J. A. Causal theories of personality and how to test them. in J. R. Royce (Ed.), *Multivariate analysis and psychological theory.* New York: Academic Press, 1973.

Greenstein, F. *Personality and politics,* Chicago: Markham, 1969.

Griffitt, W., & Veitch, R. Hot and crowded: Influences of population density and temperature on interpersonal affective behavior. *Journal of Personality and Social Psychology,* 1971, **17**, 92–98.

Hake, H. W. Form discrimination and the invariance of form. In L. Uhr (Ed.), *Pattern recognition.* New York: John Wiley, 1966.

Haley, J. *Strategies of psychotherapy.* New York: Grune & Stratton, 1963.

Hall, W. B., & Mac Kinnon, D. Personality inventory correlates of creativity among architects. *Journal of Applied Psychology,* 1963, **53**, 322–326.

Hammond, K. R. (Ed.), *The psychology of Egon Brunswik.* New York: Holt, Rinehart & Winston, 1966.

Haney, C., Banks, C., & Zimbardo, P. Interpersonal dynamics in a simulated prison. *International Journal of Criminology and Penology,* 1973, **1**, 69–97.

Hare, R. D. Anxiety, stress, and psychopathy. In I. G. Sarason & C. D. Spielberger (Eds.), *Stress and anxiety,* Vol. 2. Washington, D.C.: Hemisphere Publ., 1975.

Harlow, H. F. The nature of love. *American Psychologist,* 1958, **13**, 673–685.

Harré, R., & Secord, P. F. *The explanation of social behavior.* Totowa, New Jersey: Littlefield, 1973.

Harris, T. A. *I'm OK – You're OK: A practical guide to transactional analysis.* New York: Harper & Row, 1967.

Harrison, R. Personal tempo and the relationships of voluntary and maximal rates of movement. *Journal of Genetic Psychology,* 1941, **24**, 343–379.

Hartshorne, H., & May, M. A. *Studies in the nature of character.* Vol. 1. *Studies in deceit.* New York: Macmillan, 1928.

Hays, W. L. *Statistics for psychologists.* New York: Holt, Rinehart, & Winston, 1963.

Hays, W. L., & Winkler, R. L. *Statistics: Probability, inference, and decision.* New York: Holt, Rinehart & Winston, 1971.

Heckhausen, H. *Hoffnung und Furcht in der Leistungsmotivation.* Meisenheim am Glan: Verlag Anton Hain, 1963.

Heckhausen, H. Fear of failure as a self-reinforcing motive system. In I. G. Sarason & C. Spielberger (Eds.), *Stress and anxiety.* Vol. II. Washington, D.C.: Hemisphere Publ., 1975.

Heider, F. *The psychology of interpersonal relations.* New York: Wiley, 1958.

Heise, D. R. *Sociological methodology.* San Francisco: Jossey-Bass, 1975.

Herndon, K. M., & Glass, D. The coronary-prone behavior pattern and learned helplessness in children. Unpublished manuscript, Department of Psychology, The University of Texas at Austin, 1975.

Hess, E. H. *Imprinting.* Princeton, N. J.: Van Nostrand, 1973.

Hinde, R. A. *Animal behaviour.* (2nd ed.) London and New York: McGraw-Hill, 1970.

Hinde, R. A. *Biological bases of human social behavior.* New York: McGraw-Hill, 1974.

Hiroto, D. S., & Seligman, E. P. Generality of learned helplessness in man. *Journal of Personality and Social Psychology*, 1975, **31**, 311–327.

Hodges, W. F. Effects of ego threat of pain on state-anxiety. *Journal of Personality and Social Psychology*, 1968, **8**, 364–372.

Hodges, W. F., & Felling, J. P. Types of stressful situations and their relation to trait anxiety and sex. *Journal of Consulting and Clinical Psychology*, 1970, **34**, 333–337.

Hodges, W. F., & Spielberger, C. D. The effects of threat of shock on heart rate for subjects who differ in manifest anxiety and fear of shock. *Psychophysiology*, 1966, **2**, 287–294.

Hoffman, L. Deviation-amplifying process in natural groups. In J. Haley (Ed.), *Changing families: A family therapy reader*. New York: Grune & Stratton, 1971.

Hollander, E. P., & Julian, J. W. Contemporary trends in the analysis of leadership processes. *Psychological Bulletin*, 1969, **71**, 387–397.

Holmes, D. S., & Houston, K. B. Effectiveness of situation redefinition and affective isolation in coping with stress. *Journal of Personality and Social Psychology*, 1974, **29**, 212–218.

Holt, R. R. Clinical judgment as a disciplined inquiry. *Journal of Nervous and Mental Disease*, 1961, **133**, 369–382.

Holt, R. R. Yet another look at clinical and statistical prediction: Or is clinical psychology worthwhile? *American Psychologist*, 1970, **25**, 337–349.

Holton, G. *Thematic origins of scientific thought*. Cambridge, Mass.: Harvard University Press, 1973.

Holzkamp, K. Zur Geschichte und Systematik der Ausdruckstheorien. In R. Kirchhoff (Ed.), *Handbuch der Psychologie. 5. Bd. Ausdruckspsychologie*. Göttingen: Hogrefe, 1965.

Holzman, P. S., Proctor, L. R., Levy, D. L., Yasillo, M. J., Meltzer, H. Y., & Hurt, S. W. Eye-tracking dysfunctions in schizophrenic patients and their relatives. *Archives of General Psychiatry*. 1974, **31**, 143–151.

Homans, G. C. *Social behavior: Its elementary forms*. New York: Harcourt, Brace and World, 1961.

Howell, F. C. *Early man*. New York: Time–Life, 1970.

Hultberger, M. Rökvanor i relation till personlighetsvariabler och situationsvariabler [Smoking habits in relation to personality and situations]. Unpublished thesis, University of Stockholm, 1974.

Insel, P. M., & Moss, R. H. Psychological environments: Expanding the scope of human ecology. *American Psychologist*, 1974, **29**, 179–188.

Jackson, D. N. *Personality research from manual*. Goshen, N.Y.: Research Psychologists Press, 1967.

Jaensch, E. R. *Studien zur Psychologie menschlicher Typen*. Leipzig: Barth, 1930.

Jaffe, J., & Feldstein, S. *Rhythms of dialogue*. New York: Academic Press, 1970.

Janssens, L., & Nuttin, J. Frequency perception of individual and group successes as a function of competition, coaction and isolation. *Journal of Personality and Social Psychology*, 1977 (in press).

Jarvik, M. E. The role of nicotine in the smoking habit. In W. A. Hunt (Ed.), *Learning mechanisms and smoking*. Chicago: Aldine-Atherton, 1970.

Jenkins, J. J. Remember that old theory of memory? Well, forget it. *American Psychologist*, 1974, **29**, 785–795.

Johnston, S. M., & Bolstad, O. D. Methodological issues and naturalistic observation: some problems and solutions for field research. In L. A. Hamerlynk, L. C. Handy & E. J. Mash (Eds.), *Behavior change: Methodology, concepts and practice*. Champaign, Ill.: Research Press, 1973.

Jones, E. E., & Davis, K. E. From acts to dispositions: The attribution process in person perception. In L. Berkowitz (Ed.), *Advances in experimental social psychology.* Vol. 2. New York: Academic Press, 1965.

Jones, E. E., & Gerard, H. B. *Foundations of social psychology.* New York: John Wiley, 1967.

Jones, E. E., Kanouse, D. E., Kelley, H. H., Nisbett, R. E., Valins, S., & Weiner, B. *Attribution: Perceiving the causes of behavior.* Morristown, N.J.: General Learning Press, 1972.

Jones, E. E., & Nisbett, R. E. *The actor and the observer: Divergent perceptions of the causes of behavior.* Morristown, N.J.: General Learning Press, 1971.

Jordan, P. A real predicament. *Science,* 1972, **175,** 977–978.

Kaartinen, A. Drawings of girls and boys as indicators of the differentiation of sex roles in school age. Reports from the Department of Psychology, University of Jyväskylä, 1960, No. 27.

Kagan, J. Reflection-Impulsivity: the generality and dynamics of conceptual tempo. *Journal of Abnormal Psychology,* 1966, **71,** 17–24.

Kagan, J., Rosman, B. L., Day, D., Albert, J., & Phillips, W. Information processing in the child: Significance of analytic and reflective attitudes. Psychological Monographs, 1964, 78(1, Whole No. 578).

Kanfer, F. H., & Phillips, J. S. *Learning foundations of behavior therapy.* New York: John Wiley, 1970.

Kanter, R. M., Jaffe, D., & Weisberg, D. K. Coupling, parenting, and the presence of others: Intimate relationships in communal households. Paper presented at American Psychological Association Annual Meeting, New Orleans, 1974.

Kaplan, A. *The conduct of inquiry.* San Francisco: Chandler, 1964.

Katkin, E. S. Relationship between manifest anxiety and two indices of autonomic response to stress. *Journal of Personality and Social Psychology,* 1965, **2,** 324–333.

Kazdin, A. E., & Bootzin, R. R. The token economy: An evaluative review. *Journal of Applied Behavioral Analysis,* 1972, **5,** 343–372.

Kelley, H. The process of causal attribution. *American Psychologist,* 1973, **28,** 107–128.

Kelly, G. A. *The psychology of personal constructs.* New York: Norton, 1955.

Kendon, A., & Ferber, A. A description of some human greetings. In R. P. Michael & J. H. Crook (Eds.), *Comparative ecology and behavior in primates.* London: Academic Press, 1973.

Kessen, W., Bronfenbrenner, U., Stevenson, H., Caldwell, B., Yarrow, M., & Maccoby, E. Children of China: Report of a visit. Symposium presented at the American Psychological Association Annual Convention, New Orleans, August 30, 1974.

Kipnis, D. *Character structure and impulsiveness.* New York: Academic Press, 1971.

Klages, L. *Ausdrucksbewegung und Gestaltungskraft.* Leipzig: Engelmann, 1913.

Klein, G. S. Cognitive control and motivation. In G. Lindzey (Ed.), *Assessment of human motives.* New York: Holt, Rinehart & Winston, 1958.

Klein, G. S. *Peremtory Ideation.* Psychological Issues, 18/19, New York: International Universities Press, 1967.

Klein, G. S., Barr, L., & Wolitzky, D. L. Personality. *Annual Review of Psychology,* 1967, **18,** 467–560.

Knudson, R., & Golding, S. Comparative validity of traditional versus S–R format inventories of interpersonal behavior. *Journal of Research in Personality,* 1974, 8, 111–127.

Koestler, A. *The act of creation.* New York: Dell, 1964.

Koffka, K. *Principles of Gestalt Psychology.* New York: Harcourt, 1935.

Kogan, N., & Wallach, M. A. *Risk Taking.* New York: Holt, Rinehart, & Winston, 1964.

Kohlberg, L. Development of moral character and moral ideology. In M. Hoffman & L. W. Hoffman (Eds.), *Review of child development research.* Vol. 1. New York: Russel Sage

Foundation, 1964.

Kohn, M. L., & Schooler, C. Occupational experience and psychological functioning: an assessment of reciprocal effects. *American Sociological Review*, 1973, **38**, 97–118.

Koltuv, B. Some characteristics of intrajudge trait intercorrelations. *Psychological Monographs*, 1962, **76** (33, Whole No. 552).

Konttinen, R. Relationships between graphic expansivity and extraversion as a function of anxiety and defensiveness. *Annales Academiae Scientiarum Fennicae*, 1968, B, 159.

Konttinen, R., & Karila, A. Intentional communication in the Tree Drawing Test. *Scandinavian Journal of Psychology*, 1969, **10**, 129–136.

Konttinen, R., & Olkinuora, E. Generality of graphic variables across drawing tasks. *Scandinavian Journal of Psychology*, 1968, **9**, 161–168.

Krasner, L., & Krasner, M. Token economies and other planned environments. In C. F. Thoresen (Ed.), *Behavior modification in education*. Chicago: Chicago University Press, 1973.

Krasner, L., & Ullman, L. P. *Behavior influence and personality: The social matrix of human action*. New York: Holt, Rinehart & Winston, 1973.

Krause, M. S. Use of social situations for research purposes. *American Psychologist*, 1970, **25**, 748–753.

Kretschmer, E. *Körperbau und Charakter*. 22. Aufl. Berlin: Springer-Verlag, 1951.

Kruglanski, A. W., Alon, S., & Lewis, T. Retrospective misattribution and task enjoyment. *Journal of Experimental Social Psychology*, 1972, **8**, 493–501.

Kuhn, T. S. *The structure of scientific revolutions*. Chicago: University of Chicago Press, 1962.

Kuhn, T. S. *The structure of scientific revolutions*. (2nd ed.) Chicago: University of Chicago Press, 1970.

Lacey, J. I. Somatic response patterning and stress: Some revisions of activation theory. In M. A. Appley & Trumbull (Eds.), *Psychological stress*. New York: Appleton-Century-Crofts, 1967.

Lader, M. H. The nature of anxiety. *British Journal of Psychiatry*, 1972, **121**, 481–491.

Lader, M. H., & Wing, L. *Psychological Measures, Sedative Drugs, and Morbid Anxiety*. London: Oxford University Press, 1966.

LaForge, R., & Suczek, R. The interpersonal dimension of personality: An interpersonal check list. *Journal of Personality*, 1955, **24**, 94–112.

Lakatos, I. Falsification and the methodology of scientific research programs. In I. Lakatos & A. Musgrave (Eds.), *Criticism and the growth of knowledge*. Cambridge, England: Cambridge University Press, 1970.

Lamb, D. H. The effects of public speaking on self-report, physiological, and behavioral measures of anxiety. Unpublished doctoral dissertation, Florida State University, Tallahassee, 1969.

Lamb, D. H. *Speech anxiety inventory: Preliminary test manual*. Normal, Ill.: Illinois State University, 1971.

Lamb, D. H. The effects of two stressors on state anxiety for students who differ in trait anxiety. *Journal of Research in Personality*, 1973, **7**, 116–126.

Larson, L. L., & Rowland, K. Leadership style, stress, and behavior in task performance. *Organizational Behavior and Human Performance*, 1973, **9**, 407–421.

Lawler, E. E., & Suttle, J. L. A. A causal correlation test of the need hierarchy concept. *Organizational Behavior and Human Performance*, 1972, **7**, 265–287.

Lawrence, J. E. S. Science and sentiment: Overview of research on crowding and human behaviour. *Psychological Bulletin*, 1974, **81**, 712–720.

Lay, C., Ziegler, M., Hershfield, L., & Miller, D. The perception of situational consistency in behavior: Assessing the actor–observer bias. *Canadian Journal of Behavioral Science*, 1974, **6**, 376–384.

Lazarus, A. A. Avoid the paradigm clash. *International Journal of Psychiatry*, 1973, **11**, 157–159.

Lazarus, R. S. *Psychological stress and the coping process.* New York: McGraw-Hill, 1966.

Lazarus, R. S. *Personality.* (2nd ed.) Englewood Cliffs. N. J.: Prentice-Hall, 1971.

Lazarus, R. S., & Alfert, E. The short-circuiting of threat by experimentally altering cognitive appraisal. *Journal of Abnormal and Social Psychology,* 1964, **69**, 195–205.

Leeper, R. W. A critical consideration of Egon Brunswik's probabilistic functionalism. In K. R. Hammond (Ed.), *The psychology of Egon Brunswik.* New York: Holt, Rinehart & Winston, 1966.

Lefcourt, H. M. Recent developments in the study of locus of control. In B. A. Maher (Ed.), *Progress in experimental personality research.* Vol. 6. New York: Academic Press, 1972.

Lefcourt, H. M. *Locus of control: Current trends in theory and research.* Hillsdale, N.J.: Lawrence Erlbaum Assoc., 1976.

Lefcourt, H. M., & Wine, J. Internal versus external control of reinforcement and the deployment of attention in experimental situations. *Canadian Journal of Behavioural Science,* 1969, **1**, 167–181.

Leitenberg, H. The use of single-case methodology. *Journal of Abnormal Psychology,* 1973, **82**, 87–101.

Leitenberg, H., Agras, W., Barlow, D., & Oliveau, D. Contribution of selective positive reinforcement and therapeutic instructions to systematic desensitization. *Journal of Abnormal Psychology,* 1969, **74**, 113–118.

Leon, B. Evidence for behavioral constancy. Manuscript submitted for publication, 1976.

Lepper, M. R., & Greene, D. Turning play into work: Effects of adult surveillance and extrinsic rewards on children's intrinsic motivation. *Journal of Personality and Social Psychology,* 1975, **31**, 479–486.

Levenson, E. A. *The fallacy of understanding: An inquiry into the changing structure of psychoanalysis.* New York: Basic Books, 1972.

Levin, J. Three-mode factor analysis. *Psychological Bulletin,* 1965, **64**, 442–452.

Levine, F. M., & Fasnacht, G. Token rewards may lead to token learning. *American Psychologist,* 1974, **29**, 816–820.

Lewin, K. *A dynamic theory of personality.* New York: McGraw-Hill, 1935.

Lewis, M. *Proposal to the Carnegie Corporation.* Fall, 1974.

Lewis, M., & Freedle, R. Mother–infant dyad: The cradle of meaning. In P. Pliner, L. Krames & T. Alloway (Eds.), *Communication and affect: Language and thought.* New York: Academic Press, 1973.

Lewis, M., & Rosenblum, L. A. *The effect of the infant on its caregiver.* New York: Wiley, 1974.

Leyens, J.-P., Cisneros, T., & Hossay, J.-F. Decentration as a means for reducing aggression after exposure to violent stimuli. Unpublished manuscript, 1975.

Leyens, J.-P., & Parke, R. D. Aggressive slides can induce a weapons effect. *European Journal of Social Psychology,* 1975, **5**, 229–236.

Liberman, R. Behavioral approaches to family and couple therapy. *American Journal of Orthopsychiatry,* 1970, **40**, 106–118.

Lindsay, P. H., & Norman, D. A. *Human information processing.* New York: Academic Press, 1972.

Lindsley, D. B. Emotion. In S. S. Stevens (Ed.), *Handbook of Experimental Psychology.* New York: Wiley, 1951.

Livesley, W. J., & Bromley, D. B. *Person perception in childhood and adolescence.* New York: John Wiley, 1973.

Loevinger, J. The meaning and measurement of ego development. *American Psychologist,* 1966, **21**, 195–206. (a)

Loevinger, J. Three principles for a psychoanalytic psychology. *Journal of Abnormal*

Psychology, 1966, **71**, 432–443. (b)

London, H., & Nisbett, R. E. (Eds.) *Thought and feeling: Cognitive alteration of feeling states.* Chicago: Aldine-Atherton, 1974.

London, H., Schubert, D. S., & Washburn, D. Increase of autonomic arousal by boredom. *Journal of Abnormal Psychology,* 1972, **80**, 29–36.

Lovaas, O. I., Freitag, G., Gold, V. J., & Karrorla, I. C. Experimental studies in childhood schizophrenia: I. Analysis of self-destructive behavior. *Journal of Experimental Child Psychology,* 1965, **2**, 67–84.

Luborsky, L., & Auerbach, A. The symptom-context method: Quantitative studies of symptom-formation in psychotherapy. *Journal of the American psychoanalytic Association,* 1969, **17**, 68–99.

Lykken, D. Multiple factor analysis and personality research. *Journal of Experimental Research in Personality,* 1971, **5**, 161–170.

Maccoby, E. E., Dowley, E. M., Hagen, J. W., & Degerman, R. Activity level and intellectual functioning in normal preschool children. *Child Development,* 1965, **36**, 761–770.

Magnusson, D. An analysis of situational dimensions. *Perceptual and Motor Skills,* 1971, **32**, 851–867.

Magnusson, D. *The person and the situation in the traditional measurement model.* Report from the Psychological Laboratories, the University of Stockholm, 1974, No. 426. (a)

Magnusson, D. The individual in the situation: Some studies on individual's perception of situations. *Studia Psychologica,* 1974, **16**, 124–131. (b)

Magnusson, D. *The individual and the situation in personality research.* Reports from the Department of Psychology, University of Stockholm, 1975. Suppl. 30.

Magnusson, D. The person and the situation in an interactional model of behavior. *Scandinavian Journal of Psychology,* 1976, **17**, 81–96. (a)

Magnusson, D. Consistency and coherence in personality: A discussion of lawfulness at different levels. Reports from the Psychological Department, the University of Stockholm, 1976, No. 472. (b)

Magnusson, D., Dunér, A., & Zetterblom, G. *Adjustment: A longitudinal study.* Stockholm: Almqvist & Wiksell, New York: Wiley, 1975.

Magnusson, D., & Ekehammar, B. An analysis of situational dimensions: A replication. *Multivariate Behavioral Research,* 1973, **8**, 331–339.

Magnusson, D., & Ekehammar, B. Anxiety profiles based on both situational and response factors. *Multivariate Behavioral Research,* 1975, **10**, 27–43. (a)

Magnusson, D., & Ekehammar, B. Perceptions of and reactions to stressful situations. *Journal of Personality and Social Psychology,* 1975, **31**, 1147–1154. (b)

Magnusson, D., Gerzén, M., & Nyman, B. The generality of behavioral data: I. Generalization from observation on one occasion. *Multivariate Behavioral Research,* 1968, **3**, 295–320.

Magnusson, D., & Heffler, B. The generality of behavioral data: III. Generalization potential as a function of the number of observation instances. *Multivariate Behavioral Research,* 1969, **4**, 29–42.

Magnusson, D., Heffler, B., & Nyman, B. The generality of behavior data: II. Replication of an experiment on generalization from observation on one occasion. *Multivariate Behavioral Research,* 1968, **3**, 415–422.

Mårdberg, B. A model for selection of classification in industrial pscyhology. *Reports from the Psychological Laboratories,* the University of Stockholm, 1973, Suppl. 19.

Marshack, A. *The roots of civilization.* New York: McGraw-Hill, 1972.

Martin, B. The assessment of anxiety by physiological behavioral measures. *Psychological Bulletin,* 1961, **58**, 234–255.

Martin, B., & Sroufe, L. A. Anxiety. In C. G. Costello (Ed.), *Symptoms of psychopathology.* New York: John Wiley, 1970.

Martinez-Urrutia, A. Anxiety and pain in surgical patients. *Journal of Consulting and Clinical Psychology*, 1975, **43**, 437–442.

Matarazzo, J. D., & Wiens, A. N. *The interview.* Chicago: Aldine-Atherton, 1972.

McGrew, W. C. *An ethological study of children's behavior.* New York and London: Academic Press, 1972.

McGuire, W. J. Personality and susceptibility to social influence. In E. F. Borgatta & W. W. Lambert (Eds.), *Handbook of personality theory and research.* Chicago: Rand McNally, 1968.

McGuire, W. J. The yin and yang of the progress in social psychology: Seven Koan. *Journal of Personality and Social Psychology*, 1973, **26**, 446–456.

Mead, G. H. *Mind, self and society.* Chicago and London: Chicago University Press, 1934.

Meehl, P. E. Some methodological reflections on the difficulties of psychoanalytic research. In M. Mayman (Ed.), Psychoanalytic research: Three approaches to the experimental study of subliminal processes. *Psychological Issues*, 1973, **8**, 104–117.

Medley, D. M., & Mitzel, H. E. Measuring classroom behavior by systematic observation. In N. L. Gage (Ed.), *Handbook of research on teaching: A project of the American Educational Research Association.* Chicago: Rand McNally, 1963.

Megargee, E. I. *The California Psychological Inventory Handbook.* San Francisco: Jossey-Bass, 1972.

Mehrabian, A., & Russell, J. A. *An approach to environmental psychology.* Cambridge, Mass.: MIT Press, 1974.

Mellstrom, M. Jr. General versus specific trait measures in the prediction of social anxiety, test anxiety and rat fear. Unpublished Doctoral dissertation, University of Delaware, May, 1976.

Mellstrom M. Jr., Cicala, G. A., & Zuckerman, M. General versus specific trait anxiety measures in the prediction of fear of snakes, heights, and darkness. *Journal of Consulting and Clinical Psychology*, 1976, **44**, 83–91.

Mellstrom M. Jr., Zuckerman, M., & Cicala, G. A. Anxiety: General versus specific trait in the prediction of snake fear. *Psychological Reports*, 1974, **35**, 317–318.

Meltzer, L., Hayes, D. T., & Schillenberg, C. Consistency of vocal behavior in dicussion. Paper presented at a meeting of the American Psychological Association, 1967.

Meuwese, W. A. T., & Fiedler, F. E. Leadership and group creativity under varying conditions of stress. Urbana, Ill., Group Effectiveness Research Laboratory, University of Illinois, 1965 (mimeograph).

Milgram, S. Behavioral study of obedience. *Journal of Abnormal and Social Psychology*, 1963, **67**, 371–378.

Miller, D., & Norman, S. Actor–observer differences in perceptions of effective control. *Journal of Personality and Social Psychology*, 1975, **31**, 503–515.

Miller, G. A. The magical number seven, plus or minus two: Some limits on our capacity for processing information. *Psychological Review*, 1956, **63**, 81–97.

Miller, G. A., Galanter, E., & Pribram, K. H. *Plans and structure of behavior.* New York: Holt, Rinehart & Winston, 1960.

Miller, N., & Campbell, D. T. Recency and primacy in persuasion as a function of timing of speeches and measurements. *Journal of Abnormal and Social Psychology*, 1959,**59**, 1–9.

Minton, H. L. Power as a personality constructs. *Progress in Experimental Personality Research*, 1967, **4**, 229–267.

Minuchin, S. *Families and family therapy.* Cambridge, Mass.: Harvard University Press, 1974.

Mischel, T. Piaget: Cognitive conflict and the motivation of thought. In T. Mischel (Ed.), *Cognitive development and epistemology.* New York: Academic Press, 1971.

Mischel, W. Preference for delayed reinforcement and social responsibility. *Journal of Abnormal and Social Psychology*, 1961, **63**, 116–124.

Mischel, W. *Personality and assessment.* New York: John Wiley, 1968.

Mischel, W. Continuity and change in personality. *American Psychologist,* 1969, **24**, 1012–1018.

Mischel, W. *Introduction to personality.* New York: Holt, Rinehart & Winston, 1971. (2nd ed., 1976.)

Mischel, W. Direct versus indirect personality assessment: Evidence and implications. *Journal of Consulting and Clinical Psychology,* 1972, **38**, 319–324.

Mischel, W. Toward a cognitive social learning reconceptualization of personality. *Psychological Review,* 1973, **80**, 252–283. (a)

Mischel, W. On the empirical dilemmas of psychodynamic approaches: Issues and alternatives. *Journal of Abnormal Psychology,* 1973, **82**, 335–344. (b)

Mischel, W. Processes in delay of gratification. In L. Berkowitz (Ed.), *Advances in experimental social psychology.* Vol. 7. New York: Academic Press, 1974.

Mischel, W., Ebbesen, E. B., & Zeiss, A. R. Selective attention to the self: Situational and dispositional determinants. *Journal of Personality and Social Psychology,* 1973, **27**, 129–142.

Mischel, W., Ebbesen, E. B., & Zeiss, A. M. Determinants of selective memory and the self. *Journal of Consulting and Clinical Psychology,* 1976, **44**, 92–103.

Mischel, W., Jeffery, K. M., & Patterson, C. J. The layman's use of trait and behavioral information to predict behavior. *Journal of Research in Personality,* 1974, 8, 231–242.

Mischel, W., & Moore, B. Effects of attention to symbolically – presented rewards upon self-control. *Journal of Personality and Social Psychology,* 1973, **28**, 172–179.

Mischel, W., & Staub, E. Effects of expectancy on working and waiting for larger rewards. *Journal of Personality and Social Psychology,* 1965, **2**, 625–633.

Mischel, W., Zeiss, R., & Zeiss, A. Internal–external control and persistence: Validation and implications of the Stanford Preschool Internal–External Scale. *Journal of Personality and Social Psychology,* 1974, **29**, 265–278.

Mishima, J. *Introduction to the morphology of human behavior: The experimental study of the mental tempo.* Waseda University: Tokyo Publ., 1965.

Molin, C., Schalling, D., & Edman, G. Psychological studies of patients with mandibular pain dysfunction syndrome. *Swedish Dental Journal,* 1973, **66**, 1–11.

Montalvo, B., & Haley, J. In defense of child therapy. *Family Process,* 1973, **12**, 227–244.

Moore, S. G. Displaced aggression in young children. *Journal of Abnormal and Social Psychology,* 1964, **68**, 200–204.

Moos, R. H. Situational analysis of a therapeutic community milieu. *Journal of Abnormal Psychology,* 1968, **73**, 49–61.

Moos, R. H. Sources of variance in responses to questionnaires and in behavior. *Journal of Abnormal Psychology,* 1969, **74**, 405–412.

Moos, R. H. Conceptualizations of human environment. *American Psychologist,* 1973, **28**, 652–665.

Moos, R. H. Systems for the assessment and classification of human environments. In R. H. Moos & P. M. Insel (Eds.), *Issues in social ecology.* Palo Alto: National Press Books, 1974.

Moos, R. H., & Insel, P. M. *Issues in social ecology.* Palo Alto: National Press Books, 1974.

Munsinger, H., & Kessen, W. Uncertainty, structure and preference. *Psychological Monographs,* 1964, **78**(9, Whole No. 586).

Murphy, G. *Personality: A biosocial approach to origins and structure.* New York: Harper, 1947.

Murray, H. A. *Explorations in Personality.* New York: Oxford University Press, 1938.

Murray, H. A. Preparations for the Scaffold of a Comprehensive System. In S. Koch (Ed.) *Psychology: A Study of a Science,* Vol. 3, Formulations of the person and the social context, 1959, pp. 7–54.

Myrsten, A.-L., Andersson, K., Frankenhaeuser, M., & Mårdh, A. Immediate effects of cigarette smoking as related to different smoking habits. *Perceptual and Motor Skills,* 1975, **40,** 515–523.

Naditch, M. P., & DeMaio, T. Putting the value back into expectancy X value theory. Unpublished manuscript, Department of Psychology, Cornell University, 1974.

Nebeker, D. M. Situational favorability & environmental uncertainty: An integrative study. *Administrative Science Quarterly,* 1975, **20,** 281–294.

Nebylitsyn, V. D., & Gray, J. A. (Eds.). *Biological bases of individual behavior.* New York: Academic Press, 1972.

Neisser, U. *Cognitive psychology.* New York: Appleton-Century-Crofts, 1967.

Neisser, U. Review of visual information processing. *Science,* 1974, **183,** 402–403.

Nelsen, E. A., Grinder, R. F., & Mutterer, M. L. Sources of variance in behavioral measures of honesty in temptation situations: Methodological analyses. *Developmental Psychology,* 1969, **1,** 265–279.

Nisbett, R. E., & Gordon, A. Self-esteem and susceptibility to social influence. *Journal of Personality and Social Psychology,* 1967, **5,** 268–276.

Nuttin, J. La structure Moi-Monde. In J. Nuttin (Ed.), *La structure de la personnalité, Chapter 8.* Paris: Presses universitaires de France, 1965.

Nuttin, J. Elaboration d'une nouvelle approche expérimentale en matière de perception de la personnalité. Bulletin de Psychologie, (Paris), 1969, **22,** nr. spécial, 671–675.

Nuttin, J. Das Verhalten des Menschen: Der Mensch in seiner Erscheinungswelt. In H. Gadamer & P. Vogler (Eds.), *Psychologische Anthropologie.* Stuttgart: Thieme Verlag, 1973.

Nuttin, J., & Abreu, M. V. Perception de la fréquence de réussites personnelles et de succès partagés *Année Psychologique,* 1977 (in press).

Nuttin, J., & Greenwald, A. G. *Reward and punishment in human learning. Elements of behavior therapy.* New York and London: Academic Press, 1968.

Olson, D. H., & Rabunsky, C. Validity of four measures of family power. *Journal of Marriage and the Family,* 1972, **34,** 224–234.

Olweus, D. *Prediction of aggression. On the basis of a projective test.* Stockholm: Skandinaviska Testförlaget, 1969.

Olweus, D. Personality and aggression. In J. K. Cole & D. D. Jensen (Eds.), *Nebraska symposium on motivation, 1972.* Lincoln: University of Nebraska Press, 1973. (a)

Olweus, D. *Aggression in the Schools.* Washington: Hemisphere Publishing Company, in press.

Olweus, D. Personality factors and aggression with special reference to violence within the peer group. In J. de Wit & W. W. Hartup (Eds.), *Determinants and origins of aggressive behavior.* The Hague: Mouton Press, 1974.

Olweus, D. "Modern" interactionism in personality psychology and the analysis of variance components approach. A critical examination. Paper presented at the Symposium on Interactional Psychology, Stockholm, Sweden, June 1975. (a)

Olweus, D. *Development of a multi-faceted aggression inventory for boys.* Reports from the Institute of Psychology, University of Bergen, Norway, 1975, No. 6. (b)

Osgood, C. E. Speculation on the structure of interpersonal intuition. *Behavioral Science,* 1970, **15,** 237–254.

Overmeier, J. B., & Seligman, M. E. P. Effects of inescapable shock upon subsequent escape and avoidance responding. *Journal of Comparative and Physiological Psychology,* 1967, **63,** 28–33.

Overton, W. F. On the assumptive base of the nature–nurture controversy: Additive versus interactive conceptions. *Human Development,* 1973, **16,** 74–89.

Overton, W. F., & Reese, H. W. Models of development: Methodological implications. In J. R. Nesselroade & H. W. Reese (Eds.), *Life Span Developmental Psychology: Methodological Issues*. New York: Academic Press, 1973.

Page, M., & Scheidt, R. The elusive weapons effect: Demand awareness, evaluation and slightly sophisticated subjects. *Journal of Personality and Social Psychology*, 1971, **20**, 304–318.

Palmer, T. B. An overview of matching in the Community Treatment Project. Paper presented at the Western Psychological Association Convention, San Diego, California, 1968.

Patkai, P. *Relations between catecholamine release and psychological functions*. Reports from the Psychological Laboratories, University of Stockholm, 1970, Suppl. 2. (Dissertation summary.)

Patterson, G. R. Reprogramming the families of aggressive boys. In C. E. Thoresen (Ed.), *Behavior modification in education*. Chicago: Chicago University Press, 1973.

Patterson, G. R. A basis for identifying stimuli which control behaviors in natural settings. *Child Development*, 1974, **45**, 900–911.

Patterson, G. R., & Cobb, J. A. Stimulus control for classes of noxious behaviors. In J. F. Knutson (Ed.), *The control of aggression: Implications from basic research*. Chicago: Aldine-Atherton, 1971. (a)

Patterson, G. R., & Cobb, J. A. A dyadic analysis of "aggressive" behaviors. In J. P. Hill (Ed.), *Minnesota symposium on child psychology*. Vol. 5. Minneapolis: University of Minnesota Press, 1971. (b)

Patterson, G. R., & Reid, J. B. Reciprocity and coercion: Two facets of social systems. In C. Neuringer & J. L. Michael (Eds.), *Behavior modification in clinical psychology*. New York: Appleton-Century-Crofts, 1970.

Pavlov, I. P. *Dvadtsatiletnii opit obiektivnovo izutchenia visshei nervnoi deiatelnosti*. (7th ed.) Moscow: Medgizdat, 1951.

Pepitone, A. Aggression – A matter of stimulus and reinforcement control. *Contemporary Psychology*, 1974, **11**, 769–771.

Pervin, L. A. Performance and satisfaction as a function of individual–environment fit. *Psychological Bulletin*, 1968, **69**, 56–68.

Peterson, D. R. Scope and generality of verbally defined personality factors. *Psychological Review*, 1965, **72**, 48–89.

Peterson, D. R. *The clinical study of social behavior*. New York: Appleton-Century-Crofts, 1968.

Pettersson, U., & Sköld, M. Självskattad upplevelse av obehag i olika typer av beskrivna situationer i relation till personlighetsdrag. (Self-rated unpleasantness in different types of situations as related to personality). Unpublished thesis, University of Stockholm, 1972.

Piaget, J. *La représentation du monde chez l'enfact*. Paris: Alcan, 1926.

Piaget, J. *The moral judgment of the child*. New York: Free Press, 1948. (First published in French, 1932.)

Piaget, J. *Biology and knowledge: An essay on the relations between organic regulations and cognitive processes*. Chicago: University of Chicago Press, 1971.

Pitkänen, L., & Turunen, A. Psychomotor reactions of aggressive and non-aggressive extravert children. *Scandinavian Journal of Psychology*, 1974, **15**, 314–319.

Plutchik, R. A structure model of emotions and personality. Paper presented at the American Psychological Association Meeting in New Orleans, August 30, 1974.

Polanyi, M. *Personal knowledge: Towards a post-critical philosophy*. New York: Harper Torchbook, 1964.

Pölkki, P., & Takala, M. *The effect of participation in a group task on person perception*. Reports from the Department of Psychology, University of Jyväskylä, 1975, No. 171.

Popper, K. R. *The logic of scientific discovery*. New York: Basic Books, 1959.

Posner, M. I., & Keele, S. W. On the genesis of abstract ideas. *Journal of Experimental Psychology*, 1968, 77, 353–363.

Postman, L., & Tolman, E. C. Brunswik's probabilistic functionalism In S. Koch (Ed.), *Psychology: A study of a science*. Vol. 1. New York: McGraw-Hill, 1959.

Powers, W. T. *Behavior: The control of perception*. Chicago: Aldine-Atherton, 1973. (a)

Powers, W. T. Feedback: Beyond behaviorism. *Science*, 1973, 179, 251–256. (b)

Prévost, C. M. *La psycho-philosophie de Pierre Janet*. Pairs: Payot, 1973.

Pribram, K. A review of theory in physiological psychology. *Voprosi, Psicholigii*, 1961, No. 2. (In Russian.)

Price, R. H. The taxonomic classification of behavior and situations and the problem of behavior–environment congruence. *Human Relations*, 1974, 27, 567–585.

Price, R. H., & Bouffard, D. L. Behavioral appropriateness and situational constraint as dimensions of social behavior. *Journal of Personality and Social Psychology*, 1974, 30, 579–586.

Propp, V. *Morphology of the folktale*. 1928 (Engl. transl. Bloomington: Indiana University Press, 1958.)

Proshansky, H. M., Ittelson, W. H., & Rivlis, L. S. (Eds.). *Environmental psychology: Man and his physical setting*. New York: Holt, Rinehart & Winston, 1970.

Raush, H. L. Interaction sequences. *Journal of Personality and Social Psychology*, 1965, 2, 487–499.

Raush, H. L. Naturalistic method and the clinical approach. In E. P. Willems & H. L. Raush (Eds.), *Naturalistic viewpoints in psychological research*. New York: Holt, Rinehart & Winston, 1969.

Raush, H. L. Process and change – A Markov model for interaction. *Family Process*, 1972, 11, 275–298.

Raush, H. L. Discussion presented at Conference on Close Relationships, Amherst, Massachusetts, 1974.

Raush, H. L., Barry, W. A., Hertel, R. K., & Swain, M. A. *Communication, conflict and marriage: Explorations in the theory and study of intimate relationships*. San Francisco: Jossey–Bass, 1974.

Raush, H. L., Dittmann, A. T., & Taylor, T. J. The interpersonal behavior of children in residential treatment. *Journal of Abnormal and Social Psychology*, 1959, 58, 9–26. (a)

Raush, H. L., Dittman, A. T., & Taylor, T. J. Person, setting and change in social interaction. *Human Relations*, 1959, 12, 361–378 (b)

Raush, H. L., Farbman, I., & Llewellyn, L. G. Person, setting and change in social interaction: II. A normal control study. *Human Relations*, 1960, 13, 305–333.

Raush, H. L., & Sweet, B. The preadolescent ego: Some observations of normal children. *Psychiatry*, 1961, 24, 122–132.

Regnier, A. *La crise du language scientifique*. Paris: Antropos, 1974.

Reid, D. W. Changing perspectives in I–E theory: A cognitive social learning approach and its application to poverty research. Unpublished manuscript, Department of Psychology, York University, Toronto, 1975.

Reid, D. W., & Ware, E. E. Multidimensionality of internal–external control: Implications for past and future research. *Canadian Journal of Behavioural Sciences*, 1973, 5, 264–270.

Reid, D. W., & Ware, E. E. Multidimensionality of internal versus external control: Addition of a third dimension and nondistinction of self versus others. *Canadian Journal of Behavioural Sciences*, 1974, 6, 131–142.

Richardson, M. W. Multidimensional psychophysics. *Psychological Bulletin*, 1938, 55, 659–660. (Abstract)

Rimoldi, H. J. A. Personal tempo. *Journal of Abnormal and Social Psychology*, 1951, 46, 283–303.

Robinson, J. P., & Shaver, P. R. *Measures of social attitudes.* Ann Arbor: Survey Research Center, 1970.

Romanczyk, R. G., Kent, R. W., Diament, C., & O'Leary, K. D. Measuring the reliability of observational data: A reactive process. *Journal of Applied Behavioral Analysis,* 1973, **6,** 175–186.

Rosén, A.-S. Personality traits as related to socialization: A test of three factor model for some personality scales. *Multivariate Behavioral Research,* 1976, **11,** 47–62.

Rosén, A.-S., & Schalling, D. On the validity of the California Psychological Inventory Socialization Scale: A multivariate approach. *Journal of Consulting and Clinical Psychology,* 1974, **42,** 757–765.

Rosenberg, S., & Sedlak, A. Structural representations of implicit personality theory. *Advances in Experimental Social Psychology,* 1972, **6,** 235–297.

Ross, M. Salience of reward and intrinsic motivation. *Journal of Personality and Social Psychology,* 1975, **32,** 245–254.

Rotter, J. B. *Social learning and clinical psychology.* Englewood Cliffs, N.J.: Prentice-Hall, 1954.

Rotter, J. B. The role of the psychological situation in determining the direction of human behavior. In M. R. Jones (Ed.), *Nebraska symposium on motivation.* Lincoln: University of Nebraska Press, 1955.

Rotter, J. B. Generalized expectancies for internal versus external control of reinforcement. *Psychological Monographs,* 1966, **80,** (Whole No. 609).

Rotter, J. B. Beliefs, social attitudes, and behavior: A social learning analysis. In J. B. Rotter, J. E. Chance, & E. J. Phares (Eds.), *Applications of a social learning theory of personality.* New York: Holt, Rinehart & Winston, 1972.

Rotter, J. B. Some problems and mis-conceptions related to the construct of internal control of reinforcement. *Journal of Consulting and Clinical Psychology,* 1975, **43,** 56–67.

Routtenberg, A. The two-arousal hypothesis: Reticular formation and limbic system. *Psychological Review.* 1968, **75,** 51–80.

Rozeboom, W. W. Disposition revisited. *Philosophy of Science,* 1973, **40,** 59–74.

Ryle, G. *The concept of mind.* New York: Barnes & Noble, 1949.

Sadoka, J. M. Factor analysis of Oss situational tests. *Journal of Abnormal and Social Psychology,* 1952, **47,** 843–852.

Sales, S. M. Threat as a factor, an authoritarianism: An analysis of archival data. *Journal of Personality and Social Psychology,* 1973, **28,** 44–57.

Sample, J. A., & Wilson, T. R. Leader behavior, group productivity, and rating of least preferred co-worker. *Journal of Personality and Social Psychology,* 1965, **1,** 266–270.

Sarason, I. G. Experimental approaches to test anxiety: Attention and the uses of information. In C. D. Spielberger (Ed.), *Anxiety: Current trends in theory and research.* Vol. 2. New York: Academic Press, 1972.

Sarason, I. G. Anxiety and self-preoccupation. In I. G. Sarason & C. D. Spielberger (Eds.), *Stress and anxiety.* Vol. 2. Washington, D.C.: Hemisphere Publ., 1975. (b)

Sarason, I. G. Test anxiety, attention and the general problem of anxiety. In C. D. Spielberger & J. G. Sarason (Eds.), *Stress and anxiety.* Vol. 1. New York: Hemisphere Publ., 1975. (a)

Sarason, I. G. *Abnormal psychology.* (2nd ed.) Englewood Cliffs, N.J.: Prentice-Hall, 1976.

Sarason, I. G., & Ganzer, V. J. Modeling and group discussion in the rehabilitation of delinquents. *Journal of Counseling Psychology,* 1973, **20,** 442–449.

Sarason, I. G., & Smith, R. E. Personality. *Annual Review of Psychology,* 1971, **22,** 393–446.

Sarason, I. G., Smith, R. E., & Diener, E. Personality research: components of variance attributable to the person and the situation. *Journal of Personality and Social Psychology,* 1975, **32**(2), 199–204.

Sarason, S. B. *The psychological sense of community – Prospects for a community psychology.* San Francisco: Jossey-Bass, 1974.

Sarason, S. B., Davidson, K., Lighthall, F., Waite, R., & Ruebush, B. *Anxiety in elementary school children.* New York: John Wiley, 1960.

Schachter, S. The interaction of cognitive and physiological determinants of emotional state. In L. Berkowitz (Ed.), *Advances in experimental social psychology.* Vol. 1. New York: Academic Press, 1964.

Schachter, S. Some extraordinary facts about obese humans and rats. *American Psychologist,* 1971, **26**, 129–144.

Schachter, S. Nesbitt's paradox. In W. L. Dunn (Ed.), *Smoking behavior: Motives and incentives.* New York: Holt, Rinehart & Winston, 1973.

Schachter, S. Paper presented in Stockholm, 1975.

Schachter, S., & Rodin, J. *Obese humans and rats.* Hillsdale, N.J.: Lawrence Earlbaum Assoc., 1974.

Schafer, R. Internalization: Process or fantasy? *Psychoanalytic Study of the Child,* 1972, **27**, 411–436.

Schafer, R. *Action: Its place in psychoanalytic interpretation and theory. The Annual of Psychoanalysis.* Vol. 1. New York: Quadrangle, 1973.

Schalling, D. *Contributions to the validation of some personality concepts.* Reports from the Psychological Laboratories, the University of Stockholm, Suppl. 1, 1970.

Schalling, D. Tolerance for experimentally induced pain as related to personality. *Scandinavian Journal of Psychology,* 1971, **12**, 271–281.

Schalling, D. Types of anxiety and types of stressors as related to personality. In. I. G. Sarason & C. D. Spielberger (Eds.), *Stress and anxiety,* Vol. 1. New York: Hemisphere Publ., 1975. (a)

Schalling, D. Psychopathic behavior: Personality and neuropsychology. Paper given at the Advanced Study Institute, Les Arcs, 1975. (b)

Schalling, D. Components of extraversion. Unpublished manuscript, 1975. (c)

Schalling, D. Anxiety, pain and coping. In I. G. Sarason & C. D. Spielberg (Eds.), *Stress and anxiety,* Vol. 3. Washington, D. C.: Hemisphere Publ., 1976.

Schalling, D., Cronholm, B., & Åsberg, M. Components of state and trait anxiety as related to personality and arousal. In L. Levi (Ed.), *Emotions. Their parameters and measurement.* New York: Raven Press, 1975.

Schalling, D., & Holmberg, M. *Extraversion in criminals and the "dual nature" of extraversion. Comments based on results obtained by inventories.* Reports from the Psychological Laboratories, The University of Stockholm, 1970, No. 306.

Schalling, D., & Levander, S. Ratings of anxiety-proneness and responses to electrical pain stimulation. *Scandinavian Journal of Psychology.* 1974, **5**, 1–9.

Schalling, D., Levander, S. E., & Wredenmark, G. Semantic generalizations as reflecting cortical functions in extravert and introvert subjects. Manuscript, 1975.

Schalling, D., Rissler, A., & Edman, G. Pain tolerance, personality, and autonomic measures. Reports from the Psychological Laboratories, The University of Stockholm, 1970, No. 304.

Schalling, D., Tobisson, B., Åsberg, M., & Cronholm, B. Trait anxiety components – Their measurement and construct validity. Manuscript, 1975.

Scheffler, I. *Science and subjectivity.* Indianapolis: Bobbs-Merrill, 1967.

Schneider, D. J. Implicit personality theory: A review. *Psychological Bulletin,* 1973, **79**, 294–309.

Scott, W. A. Varieties of cognitive integration. *Journal of Personality and Social Psychology,* 1974, **30**, 563–578.

Secord, P. F., & Backman, C. W. Personality theory and the problem of stability and change in individual behavior: An interpersonal approach. *Psychological Review,* 1961, **68**, 21–32.

Seligman, M. E. P., Maier, S. F., & Solomon, R. L. Unpredictable and uncontrollable aversive events. In F. R. Brush (Ed.), *Aversive conditioning and learning.* New York: Academic Press, 1971.

Sells, S. B. Dimensions of stimulus situations which account for behavior variances. In S. B. Sells (Ed.), *Stimulus determinants of behavior.* New York: Ronald Press, 1963. (a)

Sells, S. B. An interactionist looks at the environment. *American Psychologist,* 1963, **18**, 696–702. (b)

Sells, S. B. A multivariate model of personality. In J. R. Royce (Ed.), *Contributions of multivariate analysis and psychological theory.* London: Academic Press, 1973.

Shapere, D. The structure of scientific revolutions. *Philosophical Reviews* 1964, **73**, 383–394.

Shapiro, D. *Neurotic Styles.* Basic Books, 1965.

Shaw, R. E., & Wilson, B. E. Generative conceptual knowledge: How we know what we know. Unpublished manuscript. Center for Advanced Study in the Behavioral Sciences, 1974.

Shen, E. The place of individual differences in experimentation. In Q. McNemar & M. A. Merril (Eds.), *Studies in personality.* New York: McGraw-Hill, 1942.

Sherif, M., & Sherif, C. W. *An outline of social psychology.* New York: Harper & Brothers, 1956.

Sherif, M., & Sherif, C. W. Varieties of social stimulus situations. In S. B. Sells (Ed.), *Stimulus determinants of behavior.* New York: Ronald Press, 1963.

Sherrod, D. R. Crowding, perceived control, and behavioural after effects. *Journal of Applied Social Psychology,* 1974, **4**, 171–186.

Shiflett, S. C. The contingency model of leadership effectiveness: Some implications of its statistical and methodological properties. *Behavioral Science,* 1973, **18**, 429–440.

Shipman, V. C. *Disadvantaged children and their first school experiences: Structure and development of cognitive competencies and styles prior to school entry.* Princeton, N.J.: Educational Testing Service, 1971.

Shotter, J. The development of personal powers. In M. P. M. Richards (Ed.), *The integration of a child into a social world.* Cambridge, England: Cambridge University Press, 1974.

Shweder, R. A. Is a culture a situation? Unpublished manuscript, Harvard University, Department of Social Relations, 1971.

Shweder, R. A. How relevant is an individual differences theory of personality? *Journal of Personality,* 1975, **43**, 455–484.

Signell, K. A. Cognitive complexity in person perception and nation perception: A developmental approach. *Journal of Personality,* 1966, **34**, 517–537.

Silverman, L. An experimental technique for the study of unconscious conflict. *British Journal of Medical Psychology,* 1971, **44**, 17–25.

Silverman, L. Drive stimulation and psychopathology: On the conditions under which drive related external events trigger pathological reactions. In R. Holt (Ed.), *Psychoanalysis and contemporary science.* Vol. 2. New York: Macmillan, 1972.

Skinner, B. F. *Contingencies of reinforcement: A theoretical analysis.* New York: Appleton-Century-Crofts, 1969.

Skinner, B. F. About behaviorism. New York: Alfred A. Knopf, 1974.

Smith, G. M. Personality and smoking: A review of the empirical literature. In Hunt, W. A. (Ed.), *Learning mechanisms in smoking.* Chicago: Aldine-Atherton, 1970.

Sokal, R. R. Classification: Purposes, principles, progress, prospects. *Science,* 1974, **185,** 1115–1123.

Sokolov, E. N. Veroiatnostnaia model vospriatia. *Voprosi Psichologii* (USSR), 1960, No. 2.

Sommer, R. *Personal space.* Englewood Cliffs, N.J.: Prentice-Hall, 1969.

Speck, R. V., & Attneave, C. L. *Family networks.* New York: Vintage, 1974.

Spence, K. W. Types of constructs in psychology. In M. Marx (Ed.), *Theories in contemporary psychology.* New York: Macmillan, 1963.

Spielberger, C. D. Theory and research on anxiety. In C. D. Spielberger (Ed.), *Anxiety and behavior.* New York: Academic Press, 1966.

Spielberger, C. D. Anxiety as an emotional state. In C. D. Spielberger (Ed.), *Anxiety: Current trends in theory and research.* Vol. 1. New York: Academic Press, 1972. (a)

Spielberger, C. D. Conceptual and methodological issues in research on anxiety. In C. D. Spielberger (Ed.), *Anxiety: Current trends in theory and research.* Vol. 2. New York: Academic Press, 1972. (b)

Spielberger, C. D., Anton, W., & Bedell, J. The nature and treatment of test anxiety. In M. Zuckerman & C. D. Spielberger (Eds.), *Emotions and anxiety: New concepts in methods and applications.* New York: Lawrence Erlbaum Assoc., 1976.

Spielberger, C. D., Gorsuch, R. L., & Lushene, R. L. *Manual for the State–Trait Anxiety Inventory.* Palo Alto: Consulting Psychologists Press, 1970.

Spielberger, C. D., O'Neil, H. F., & Hansen, D. N. Anxiety, drive theory, and computer-assisted learning. In B. A. Maher (Ed.), *Progress in experimental personality research.* Vol. 6. New York: Academic Press, 1972.

Spielberger, C. D., Southard, L. D., & Hodges, W. F. Effects of awareness and threat of shock on verbal conditioning. *Journal of Experimental Psychology,* 1966, **72,** 434–438.

Staats, A. W., & Staats, C. K. *Complex human behavior.* New York: Holt, Rinehart & Winston, 1963.

Stagner, R. Traits are relevant: Theoretical analysis and empirical evidence. In N. S. Endler & D. Magnusson (Eds.), *Interactional psychology and personality.* Washington, D.C.: Hemisphere Publishing Corporation (J. Wiley), 1976.

Stephenson, W. *The study of behavior.* Chicago: University of Chicago Press, 1953.

Stern, G. G. *People in context: Measuring person–environment congruence in education and industry.* New York: John Wiley, 1970.

Stern, G. G., Stein, M. I., & Bloom, B. S. *Methods in personality assessment.* Glencoe, Ill.: Free Press, 1956.

Stevens, D. A., Stover, C. E., & Backus, J. T. The hyperkinetic child: effect of incentives on the speed of rapid tapping. *Journal of Consulting and Clinical Psychology,* 1970, **34,** 56–59.

Stogdill, R. *Handbook of Leadership.* New York: The Free Press, 1974.

Storms, M. D., & Nisbett, R. E. Insomnia and the attribution process. *Journal of Personality and Social Psychology,* 1970, **2,** 319–328.

Straus, M. *Family measurement techniques.* Minneapolis, Minn.: University of Minnesota Press, 1969.

Strauss, E. Couples in love. Unpublished doctoral dissertation. University of Massachusetts, Amherst, 1974.

Strodtbeck, F. T. Husband-Wife interaction over revealed differences. *American Sociological Review,* 1951, **16,** 468–473.

Strupp, H. On the basic ingredients of psychotherapy. *Journal of Consulting and Clinical Psychology,* 1973, **41,** 1–8.

Stuart, R. B. Operant-interpersonal treatment for marital discord. *Journal of Consulting and Clinical Psychology,* 1969, **33,** 675–682.

Stuart, R. B. *Marital pre-counseling inventory: Counselors guide.* Champaign, Ill.: Research Press, 1973.

Sullivan, H. S. *The interpersonal theory of psychiatry.* New York: Norton, 1953.

Swensen, C. H., Jr. *Introduction to interpersonal relations.* Glenview, Ill.: Scott, Foresman, 1973.

Tagiuri, R. *Movement as a cue in person perception.* In H. P. David & J. C. Brengelmann (Eds.), *Perspectives in personality research.* New York: Springer Verlag, 1960.

Takala, M. Studies in psychomotor personality tests I. *Annales Academiae Scientiarum Fennicae,* 1953, **B81,** 2. (Reprinted edition in *Research approaches to movement and personality.* New York: Arno Press, 1972.)

Takala, M. Psychomotor expression and personality study. I. Some theoretical and methodological considerations. *Scandinavian Journal of Psychology,* 1963, **4,** 149–160.

Takala, M. *The communication of personal styles.* Reports from the Department of Psychology, University of Jyväskylä, 1972, No. 128.

Takala, M. *First impressions and person perception: The predictability of peer ratings from the behavior of the "actors" in short encounters.* Reports from the Department of Psychology, University of Jyväskylä, 1973, No. 133.

Takala, M. *Consistencies of psychomotor styles in interpersonal tasks.* Reports from the Department of Psychology, University of Jyväskylä, 1974, No. 162. (a)

Takala, M. *Redundancy of information about individual style characteristics transmitted by verbal and non-verbal channels.* Reports from the Department of Psychology, University of Jyväskylä, 1974, No. 161. (b)

Takala, M. Consistencies of psychomotor styles in interpersonal tasks. *Scandinavian Journal of Psychology,* 1975, **16,** 193–202.

Takala, M., & Partanen, N. Psychomotor expression and personality study. III. The problem of personal tempo. *Scandinavian Journal of Psychology,* 1964, **5,** 161–170.

Takala, M., & Pölkki, P. *Channel of information and first impressions of personality.* Reports from the Department of Psychology, University of Jyväskylä, 1974, No. 170.

Takala, M., & Rantanen, A. Psychomotor expression and personality study. II. Generality of expressive variables. *Scandinavian Journal of Psychology,* 1964, **5,** 71–79.

Talmadge, M. Expressive graphic movements and their relationship to temperamental factors. *Psychological Monographs,* 1958, **72,** (Whole No. 469).

Tan, A. L. Contentment and change in a Phillipine setting. Unpublished doctoral dissertation, Cornell University, Ithaca, N.Y., 1974.

Taylor, J. A. A personality scale of manifest anxiety. *Journal of Abnormal and Social Psychology,* 1953, **48,** 285–290.

Tharp, R. G. Dimensions of marriage roles. *Marriage and Family Living,* 1963, **25,** 389–404.

Thibaut, J. W., & Kelley, H. H. *The social psychology of groups.* New York: Wiley, 1959.

Thoresen, C., & Mahoney, M. *Behavioral self-control.* New York: Holt, Rinehart & Winston, 1974.

Thornton, J. W., & Jacobs, P. D. Learned helplessness in human subjects. *Journal of Experimental Psychology,* 1971, **87,** 367–372.

Tilquin, A. *Le behaviorisme.* Paris: Vrin, 1950.

Tinbergen, N. *The study of instinct.* Oxford: Clarendon Press, 1951.

Toch, H. *Violent men: An inquiry into the psychology of violence.* Chicago: Aldine-Atherton, 1969.

Tolman, E. C. *Purposive behavior in animals and men.* Berkeley and Los Angeles: University of California Press, 1932.

Tomkins, S. *Affects, imagery, and consciousness.* New York: Springer Publ., 1962.

Tucker, T., & Messick, S. An individual differences model for multidimensional scaling. *Psychometrica,* 1963, **28,** 333–367.

Turner, C. W., & Goldsmith, D. Effects of toy guns and airplanes on children's anti-social free play behavior. *Journal of Experimental Child Psychology,* 1976, in press.

Turner, C. W., Layton, J. F., Fenn, M. R., & Simons, L. S. An investigation of behavior in an aggressive carnival game. Manuscript in preparation, 1976.

Turner, C. W., & Simons, L. S. Effects of subject sophistication and evaluation apprehension on aggressive responses to weapons. *Journal of Personality and Social Psychology,* 1974, **30,** 341–348.

Tversky, A., & Kahneman, D. Belief in the law of small numbers. *Psychological Bulletin,* 1971, **76,** 105–110.

Tyler, L. *The psychology of human differences* (3rd ed.). New York: Appleton-Century-Crofts, 1967.

Ulrich, R. E., Hutchinson, R. R., & Azrin, N. H. Pain-elicited aggression. *Psychological Record,* 1965, **15,** 111–126.

Underwood, B. J. *Psychological research.* New York: Appleton-Century-Crofts, 1957.

Valins, S. Cognitive effects of false heart-rate feedback. *Journal of Personality and Social Psychology,* 1966, **4,** 400–408.

Vernon, P. E. *Personality assessment.* London: Methuen, 1964.

von Uexküll, J. *Streifzüge durch die Umwelten von Tieren und Menschen.* Berlin: Springer Verlag, 1934.

Vreven, R., & Nuttin, J. Frequency perceptions of successes as a function of results previously obtained by others and by oneself. University of Leuven. Psychological Reports, No. 12, 1976.

Wachtel, P. L. Conceptions of broad and narrow attention. *Psychological Bulletin,* 1967, **68,** 417–429.

Wachtel, P. L. Psychology, metapsychology, and psychoanalysis. *Journal of Abnormal Psychology,* 1969, **74,** 651–660.

Wachtel, P. L. Field dependence and psychological differentiation: Reexamination. *Perceptual and Motor Skills,* 1972, **35,** 179–189. (a)

Wachtel, P. L. Cognitive style and style of adaptation. *Perceptual and Motor Skills,* 1972, **35,** 779–785. (b)

Wachtel, P. L. Psychodynamics, behavior therapy, and the implicable experimenter: An inquiry into the consistency of personality. *Journal of Abnormal Psychology,* 1973, **82,** 324–334. (a)

Wachtel, P. L. On fact, hunch, and stereotype: A reply to Mischel. *Journal of Abnormal Psychology,* 1973, **82,** 537–540. (b)

Wachtel, P. L. *Psychoanalysis and behavior therapy: Toward an integration.* New York: Basic Books, 1977.

Wallach, M. A., & Gahm, R. C. Personality functions of graphic construction and expansiveness. *Journal of Personality,* 1960, **28,** 73–88.

Wallach, M. A., & Leggett, M. I. Testing the hypothesis that a person will be consistent: Stylistic consistency vs. situational specificity in size of children's drawing. *Journal of Personality,* 1972, **40,** 309–330.

Waller, D. Studier av rökmotivation. (Studies of smoking motivation). Unpublished thesis. University of Stockholm, 1975.

Wallon, H. *Les origines du caractère chez l'enfant.* Paris: Boivin, 1934.

Wallon, H. *Del'acte à la pensée.* Paris: Flammarion, 1942.

Watzlawick, P., Beavin, J. H., & Jackson, D. D. *Pragmatics of human communication – A study of interactional patterns, pathologies, and paradoxes.* New York: Norton, 1967.

Watzlawick, P., Weakland, J. & Fisch, R. *Change – Principles of program formation and problem resolution.* New York: Norton, 1974.

Weiner, B., Frieze, I., Kukla, A., Reed, L., Rest, S., & Rosenbaum, R. M. *Perceiving the causes of success and failure.* New York: General Learning Press, 1971.

Weiss, J. M., Glazer, H. I., Pohorecky, L. A. Neurotransmitters and helplessness: A chemical bridge to depression? *Psychology Today,* 1974, **8**, 58–62.

Weiss, R. L., Hops, A., & Patterson, G. R. A social learning approach to reducing rates of marital conflict. In R. Stuart, R. Liberman, & S. Wilder (Eds.), *Advances in behavior therapy.* New York: Academic Press, 1973.

Weitzman, B. Behavior therapy and psychotherapy. *Psychological Review,* 1967, **74**, 300–317.

Weizenbaum, J. Contextual understanding by computers. *Communication of the A.C.M.,* 1967, **10**, 474–480.

Werner, H. *Comparative psychology of mental development.* New York: International University Press, 1948.

Wheelis, A. *How people change.* New York: Harper & Row, 1973.

Wiggins, J. S. In defense of traits. Invited paper at the Ninth Annual Symposium on the Use of MMPI, Los Angeles, February 28, 1974.

Wilkins, W. Desensitization: Social and cognitive factors underlying the effectiveness of Wolpe's procedure. *Psychological Bulletin,* 1971, **76**, 311–317.

Willems, E. P., & Raush, H. L. *Naturalistic viewpoints in psychological research.* New York: Holt, Rinehart & Winston, 1969.

Williams, R. L., & Moffat, G. H. Escapable/inescapable pretraining and subsequent avoidance performance in human subjects. *Bulletin of the Psychonomic Society,* 1974, **4**, 144–146.

Wilson, G. T., & Davison, G. Processes of fear reduction in systematic desensitization: Animal studies. *Psychological Bulletin,* 1971, **76**, 1–14.

Wilson, T. P. Conceptions of interaction and forms of sociological explanation. *Sociological Review,* 1973, **35**, 697–710.

Witkin, H. A., Dyk, R. B., Faterson, H. F., Goodenough, D. R., & Karp, S. A. *Psychological differentiation.* New York: John Wiley, 1962.

Wolf, R. The measurement of environment. In A. Anastasi (Ed.), *Testing problems in perspective.* Washington, D.C.: American Council on Education, 1966.

Wolitzky, D. L., & Wachtel, P. L. Personality and perception. In B. Wolman (Ed.), *Handbook of general psychology.* Englewood Cliffs, N.J.: Prentice-Hall, 1973.

Wolpe, J. *Psychotherapy by reciprocal inhibition.* Stanford: Stanford University Press, 1958.

Young, F. W. Scaling replicated conditional rank-order data. In D. R. Heise (Ed.), *Sociological methodology.* San Francisco: Jossey-Bass, 1975.

Zajonc, R. Social facilitation. *Science,* 1965, **149**, 269–274.

Zeigarnik, B. *Über das Behalten von erledigten und unterledigten Handlungen. Psychologische Forschung,* 1927, No. 9.

Zlotowicz, M. *Les peurs enfantines.* Paris: Presses Universitaires de France, 1974.

Zlutnick, S., & Altman, I. Crowding and human behaviour. In J. F. Wohlwill & D. H. Carson (Eds.), *Environment and the social sciences: Perspectives and applications.* Washington, D.C.: American Psychological Association, 1972.

Zuckerman, M. The development of an Affect Adjective Check List for the measurement of anxiety. *Journal of Consulting Psychology,* 1960, **24**, 457–462.

Zuckerman, M. General vs. specific traits as predictors of self-reported states and behavior in real situations. Paper presented at the Symposium on Interactional Psychology, Stockholm, Sweden, June, 1975.

Zuckerman, M. General and situation-specific traits and states: New approaches to assessment of anxiety and other constructs. In M. Zuckerman & C. D. Spielberger (Eds.),

Emotions and anxiety: New concepts, methods and applications. Hillsdale, N.J.: Lawrence Erlbaum Associates, 1976.

Zuckerman, M., & Lubin, B. *Manual for the Multiple Affect Adjective Check List.* San Diego, Calif.: Educational and Industrial Testing Service, 1965.

Zuckerman, M., & Lubin, B. *Bibliography for the Multiple Affect Adjective Check List.* San Diego, Calif.: Educational and Industrial Testing Service, 1968.

Zuckerman, M., Persky, H., & Link, K. Relation of mood and hypnotizability: An illustration of the importance of the state versus trait distinction. *Journal of Consulting Psychology,* 1967, **31,** 464–470.

Author Index

Subject Index